GENERAL PSYCHOLOGY SERIES EDITORS

Arnold P. Goldstein, Syracuse University
Leonard Krasner, Stanford University & SUNY at Stony Brook

HUMAN BEHAVIOR IN GLOBAL PERSPECTIVE

(VOL. 160)

Titles of Related Interest

Bochner CULTURES IN CONTACT: Studies in Cross-Cultural Interaction
Brislin CROSS-CULTURAL ENCOUNTERS: Face-to-Face Interaction
Ramirez PSYCHOTHERAPY AND COUNSELING WITH
MINORITIES: A Cognitive Cross-Cultural Approach

Related Journals

INTERNATIONAL JOURNAL OF INTERCULTURAL RELATIONS
WOMEN'S STUDIES INTERNATIONAL FORUM

HUMAN BEHAVIOR IN GLOBAL PERSPECTIVE

An Introduction to Cross-Cultural Psychology

MARSHALL H. SEGALL
Syracuse University, United States

PIERRE R. DASEN
Université de Genève, Switzerland

JOHN W. BERRY
Queen's University, Kingston, Canada

YPE H. POORTINGA
Tilburg University, The Netherlands

ALLYN AND BACON
Boston London Toronto Sydney Tokyo Singapore

Copyright © 1990 by Allyn and Bacon
A Division of Simon & Schuster, Inc.
160 Gould Street
Needham Heights, MA 02194

Printed in the United States of America

10 9 8 7 6 5 4   96 95

ISBN 0-205-14478-0

Library of Congress Cataloging in Publication Data

Human behavior in global perspective : an introduction to cross
  -cultural psychology / Marshall H. Segall . . . [et al.].
      p.   cm. --
  Includes bibliographical references.

  1. Ethnopsychology. 2. Human behavior. 3. Culture. 4. Social
psychology. I. Segall, Marshall H. II. Series.
GN502.H86   1990
302--dc20   89-28710
                                                           CIP

Contents

Foreword

Inevitably, no matter who we are, we are confronted with other persons. Some we meet; they are kinfolk, friends, acquaintances, peers, and adversaries. Others we do not meet; they may be inside or outside our area, or they live in lands we have visited or will never visit. We try to understand them because we know too well that they affect our welfare and our happiness, and perhaps a little less obviously, we affect theirs.

We employ the most varied means to try to understand these other persons. We experience them directly and we guide ourselves by the experience, sweet or bitter as it may be. We read about them in the press and in books, particularly in treatises purporting to portray their history and ours. We think we receive valid impressions about them in the mass media and through the arts they offer us. Somehow, if we are to remain reasonably sane, we must be able to make sense of these impressions and carry on.

You would not be reading these words if, unlike many individuals, you did not choose also to fortify yourself with another source of information: the systematic study of human thought, values, and behavior. Immediately, however, it is patently clear that there is no single scholarly or scientific discipline you can consult; rather, there are scores of disciplines ranging from the chemistry and neurophysiology of the brain to literary criticism and theology. Embedded in most but not all of these disciplines is the challenging problem of this book, cross-cultural psychology.

The four authors of this volume, who reside in different countries, implicitly and explicitly indicate and demonstrate the value of the cross-cultural psychology they expound. Somewhat humbly I will try to summarize their message concisely. I feel timidly qualified to assume that task, possibly because of my diverse but necessarily limited experiences in lands as different as Uganda and Cyprus or South Africa and the South Tyrol in northern Italy. I have plunged into the daily life of those societies and have reported my impressions and findings in challenging print. I have tried to practice, in short, what I am now saying.

Of course, perhaps you are thinking, in some instances we need not study peoples in foreign or exotic lands to comprehend how they react under some circumstances. Wherever the individual lives — in your country; close to the equator or one of the poles; in the first, second, third, or umpteenth world — he will sneeze when the nerve endings in his nose are irritated. But, in fact, will he sneeze? Will he try to inhibit this reflex action? What will he say, what will bystanders say, when he does sneeze? What will they think of him if he fails to turn away and sneezes in their faces? Do they and he consider sneezing an omen and, if so, is it a good or bad omen? Enough of sneezing, which has served only to alert us to the cultural — the cross-cultural — elements that can pervade even an elementary action.

It is too easy for you and for me to project on other persons our own explanations concerning human activities. We require a rounded view of individuals that psychology, among other disciplines, seeks to provide. But psychologists as we know them too often have tended perforce to select persons who are conveniently at hand to be subjects in their experiments or informants in their empirical work. May or can we generalize about all peoples on the basis of studies in Europe or North America where only English, French, German, Italian, Russian, or Spanish is spoken?

Cross-cultural psychology seeks to broaden our vision and deepen our insights. Viewing the tremendously varied beliefs of other persons helps us to avoid two sinful errors. We become less likely to project ourselves upon them (egocentrism) or to imagine smugly and incorrectly that men, women, and children think and act like our neighbors, peers, and fellow countrymen (ethnocentrism). The theories and research reported in this book impressively offer evidence concerning the fallacy resulting from those sins.

There are other advantages to grasping cross-cultural psychology that the authors, sometimes calmly, sometimes heatedly, suggest and document. You learn about yourself when you discover (or rediscover) that your way of thinking and behaving is not universal and hence may be less than perfect.

You are challenged to become more tolerant of cultures different from your own, and as a result, you may even adopt something new from them that can improve your own existence and render it more exciting or satisfactory. To know that there is almost always a cultural element in human activity is a necessary first step, yet to appreciate this state of affairs thoroughly demands continual reflection. Politely and sometimes impolitely you are being addressed by the evidence in these pages: Come, come, look beyond that self of yours and way beyond your own history and the history of your society. You may be unable to jump out of your own shell, but the authors are assisting you at least to peer outside of it. At the very least, when you meet strangers or other cultural groups or when you travel afar, you will commit fewer blunders; you and those so-called foreigners will be able to communicate with one another more easily, particularly if they know your language or if you patiently learn theirs — which you should certainly try to do — and if both of you anticipate the nuances in every language and the perils of translation.

Professional psychologists and other social scientists also benefit from cross-cultural psychology. They realize that inescapably their studies have cultural limitations. They observe that cross-cultural psychology has acquired a solid array of studies that meet scholarly standards; well established scientific methods have been employed, frequently under difficult circumstances that are avoidable in the comfortable, easily available confines of their own society. They value the honest and necessary admission, again and again, that almost all cross-cultural knowledge is tentative, as tentative, in fact, as knowledge always is and should be. They are not surprised to discover that frequently cross-cultural psychologists are at loggerheads with each other as they advocate their hypotheses and that they use jargon and neologisms that nevertheless serve the useful function of calling attention to phenomena that may otherwise be slighted or overlooked.

It must be noted that a significant but not always salient message pervades this impressive presentation of cross-cultural data and theories. Yes, indeed, there is cultural diversity, and the diversity can be subtle or unsubtle, difficult or easy to detect. Beneath the diversity that produces transcultural misunderstandings ranging from innocent faux pas to ghastly wars, however, there is a unifying fact that can and must transcend the variability: Whoever and wherever we are, we are human, and we possess similar strivings from birth to death. On occasion all of us sneeze, and more compelling, we also struggle with, are perplexed by, and overflow with the conviction that we share common attributes diversely.

Leonard W. Doob

Sterling Professor of Psychology *Emeritus*
Associate Director, Southern Africa Research Program
Yale University
New Haven, Connecticut, USA
August 29, 1989

Preface

Slightly over a decade ago, only a few cross-cultural psychology courses existed in North America and Europe. Psychology was thriving in universities there, and it seemed to many psychologists that they were getting along well enough without cross-cultural courses. Elsewhere in the world, if instruction in psychology existed, it consisted mostly of material that described the behavior of North Americans and Europeans. Psychology as taught in the 1970s left something to be desired everywhere.

A handful of psychologists felt strongly that cross-cultural psychology belonged in the undergraduate psychology curriculum in Europe and North America and that such courses could with good effect replace the Euro/American-centered courses that predominated elsewhere. But teaching materials for such courses were practically nonexistent. A need had to be met.

One response was a relatively brief text entitled *Cross-Cultural Psychology: Human Behavior in Global Perspective*, written by one of us (Segall) and published in 1979 in the United States. Its goal, expressed in its preface, was "to demonstrate to undergraduate students—beginners and advanced psychology majors alike—that human behavior is both delightfully varied and satisfyingly orderly. That is, human behavior *can* be studied in a systematic, scientific fashion, but, to do justice to this subject, attention must be paid to diverse ecological and cultural settings in which human beings live."

The present book, more than a revision of the 1979 book, is descended in a straight line from it. The other three authors of the present book (Dasen, Berry, and Poortinga), who subscribed then to the views expressed in that preface (and still do), found the earlier book useful in their own teaching of cross-cultural psychology. All four of us discovered in our classrooms (in the United States, Canada, Switzerland, France, and the Netherlands), however, that there was much more to be said about cross-cultural psychology than was covered in the slim 1979 volume. Each of us also had some particular material in mind that seemed to deserve inclusion in a "next" cross-cultural psychology textbook. Indeed, each of us, separately and in varying combinations, during the past decade, contemplated writing it!

When, from time to time, we would find ourselves together at cross-cultural psychology meetings, we would talk about the books that might be written. Then, at one such meeting (in Mexico, in 1984) we decided to join forces and produce *this* book. We began to plan it and soon discovered that it required two books.

This, the first, is an introduction to cross-cultural psychology. It can be used, we believe, in courses designed for students who have had no prior introduction to psychology. We expect that the book will be used that way in many parts of the world where it will serve new students of psychology better as an introduction to psychology than most books designed as general psychology texts.

This book can also be used effectively by students who have had some prior training in psychology. We expect that the book will be used in North America and in Europe mostly in courses that follow general psychology and social psychology. In such cases, a course built around this book will extend the students' awareness of behavioral phenomena and challenge what students have previously been taught about psychological theory; this, because we cover material that students will probably not have encountered in their prior courses in psychology. When they add this material to what they already know, they are likely to feel a need to reassess and reinterpret what they know about human behavior. Instructors are likely to discover that by using this book they will have set the stage for some lively, engaging discussions with their students. In our own teaching with working drafts, we have found this to be the case.

In Europe and North America, the parochialism that long characterized undergraduate teaching in most disciplines, including psychology, is now giving way to a more global perspective—a treatment of fundamental human concerns that acknowledges the increasing interdependence of the various regions of the world. In other parts of the world, where universities are newer and curricula still being developed, materials that pertain to local circumstances are needed for comparison and contrast with information regarding former colonial metropoles and other erstwhile "centers of power." From now on, educated persons everywhere need to cultivate a sense of their fellows everywhere—who we all are, what moves us, and how we cope, both similarly and differently, with the problems we face. There is a crucial role for psychology in this increasing effort to globalize knowledge and understanding.

For psychology to live up to the demands of this role, it must be a cross-cultural psychology that is informed by the insights of several neighboring disciplines, preeminent among them anthropology. The four of us owe a debt to anthropology for pointing out to us the need to do research in societies other than our own. All of us have done psychological fieldwork. So have many other psychologists, and it is the work of those who have occasionally behaved like anthropologists, for whom "the field" is their laboratory, that is featured in this book. Accordingly, the book might well be used in anthropology courses, for its contents will enrich traditional anthropological analyses by providing psychological data to be interpreted in varying ecocultural contexts.

Our other book, to be published by Cambridge University Press, and referred to frequently in this one, deals with several topics not covered here. It also focuses more on how cross-cultural research and applications are done. Thus, it is intended primarily for more advanced students and, especially, students who might be considering careers in or related to cross-cultural psychology. We expect, therefore, that our other book might be used *after* this one wherever the curriculum contains a two-course sequence in cross-cultural psychology.

Both books, however, can stand alone. This one contains more than enough material for a semester-long course. We cover several basic psychological domains, including perception, cognition, and human development, and a number of issues of continuing concern to social psychologists, including matters relating to sex and gender, aggression, and intergroup relations. We deal also with cultural change and various implications of the "modernization" that is occurring in most parts of the world. Educational implications of cross-cultural research constitute a recurring theme. We deal also with a number of theoretical approaches and we touch on some methodological concerns, some of them unique to cross-cultural psychology.

As coauthors, we collectively stand behind the whole book but let it be known that our sometimes diverse perspectives, grounded in our own cultures (but probably influenced also by our stubborn natures), produced numerous debates and discussions about what to say, how to say it, who should write it, and how much to keep or discard. Disputes were settled by striving for consensus; no one of us had veto power.

Logistically, the writing of this book was a case study in high-tech word processing (despite the fact that one of us remains wedded to paper and pencil). Our computers were linked by electronic mail, and drafts flowed many times both ways across the Atlantic. We also met from time to time, either in Syracuse, Kingston, Fribourg, or Geneva, to carry on our debates and discussions. The nerve center for the enterprise was Syracuse, where Segall put it all together, with much fine help from Kimberly Chang, a cross-cultural psychologist who took time out from her own graduate studies to be an active, albeit "silent" partner in this enterprise.

The four of us acknowledge her help, plus that of Sally Bennett Segall, Rachel Kelly, Tom Prutisto, Laura Marnell, and Carole Wenthen in Syracuse; Audrey Bailey in Kingston; Catherine Dasen in Geneva; and Rea

Bergmans in Tilburg. We thank also the editors and staff at Pergamon Press for believing in us and for deciding to publish a book in cross-cultural psychology while the number of courses in this exciting, vibrant, and growing field was still not large enough to guarantee large sales.

Marshall Segall
Pierre Dasen
John Berry
Ype Poortinga

Part I
A PROLEGOMENON

This book is an introduction to cross-cultural psychology, defined as the scientific study of the ways in which social and cultural forces shape human behavior. In Part I, which contains Chapters 1 through 4, we try to demonstrate that human behavior must be viewed in the sociocultural context in which it occurs if we are truly to understand it.

What we often call "human nature" is not only a reflection of human biological potential but also a product of culture and of its two classes of formative experience — socialization and enculturation. Together, these account for both the uniformities and the diversities in the behavior of human beings.

Chapter 1 makes clear that we are a biological and sociocultural species. This statement highlights our most striking biological characteristic, namely, that through an evolutionary process, *Homo sapiens* emerged as a symbol-using, self-conscious creature. We are linked over time and space with all other members of the species, including those who preceded and will follow us in time, and to our contemporaries, with most of whom direct contact is impossible. The emergence of language (in its full-blown form, a uniquely human phenomenon) facilitates these links and has made possible all the behavior that is distinctly human.

We will provide in Chapter 1 a conceptual framework that will be used throughout this book. It offers a way of studying human behavior in its "ecocultural" context. The first chapter also provides a way of understanding the concept of culture.

In Chapter 2, a foray into Freudian psychology will give us one compelling reason for doing cross-cultural psychology, and a historical review will reveal how much (and how little) attention to culture has characterized Western, academic, scientific psychological research. (We resist the temptation to employ an acronym for Western, academic, scientific psychology and shall refer to it, instead, as "mainstream" psychology.)

The historical review in Chapter 2 underscores the potential value of the ecocultural framework that we use throughout this book in our effort to understand human behavior. In Chapter 3, we will see that to realize the potential of a cross-cultural research approach, some complex methodological hurdles must be overcome.

A single example of a cross-cultural research project will constitute all of

Chapter 4. It will describe in detail a study that examined cultural differences in visual perception. This final chapter in Part I will serve to illustrate why human behavior should be studied in cultural context, to underscore the importance of the ecocultural framework, to link us once again with the history of scientific psychology, and, we believe, to reveal something intriguing — even surprising — about human behavior.

Chapter 1

The Sociocultural Nature of Human Beings

BEHAVIOR AND CULTURE

Human behavior must be viewed in the sociocultural context in which it occurs if we are truly to understand it. Distinctly human behavior is fundamentally social, involving (a) relationships with other people, (b) their behavior, and (c) various products of their behavior. All of these are social stimuli, since they involve other people. But other species are also social animals. Human beings are cultural as well as social.

Some Dimensions of Culture: A Preliminary Definition

Those social stimuli that are the products of the behavior of other people essentially constitute culture. Briefly, we employ culture — as did Herskovits (1948) — to mean "the man-made part of the environment." When we suggest that some behavior is shaped by culture, this will be shorthand for "this behavior is influenced by certain products of the behavior of other persons." These products can be material objects, ideas, or institutions. They are ubiquitous; it is rare (perhaps even impossible) for any human being ever to behave without responding to some aspect of culture.

Among the cultural products to which you might be reacting right now is a room. It has a particular shape that reflects someone's architectural ideas and carpentry skills. If you are in Paris, London, Nairobi, or any other city, the room is most likely rectangular. (There are places in the world however, where the probability of your being in a rectangular room is very low. There are noncarpentered environments, about which more will be said later in this

5

book.) As you read this chapter, you might also be in a semireclining position, in part because some time ago someone built objects called chairs. Thus, your behavior at this moment is partly shaped by that invention. (Again, however, there are places where the probability of your being in that position would be much lower. So would your position! There are, after all, societies without chairs.)

Some societies lack "classrooms;" others have them. The fact that in some societies students gather in classrooms, facing teachers, reflects another kind of sociocultural product, an institution. Some of our most important human creations are institutional, such as — in many societies — a formal educational system. It may have material aspects, including school buildings, and ideational ones, like the notion that school occupies a specific place and time or the idea that individuals should be evaluated and certified. The institution of education also provides behavioral expectations for all who participate — a series of "roles" to be played. These include privileges that apply to "teachers" and responsibilities that "students" have to shoulder, and vice versa. These, too, are products of the behavior of other people.

Much of our lives as human beings, then, involves responding to social stimuli. This is social behavior, and it is culturally influenced.

The Social and Cultural Context

As the foregoing suggests, human behavior takes place in a social and cultural context that varies widely from place to place. This variation occurs along certain dimensions that are signified by social science terminology that we use in cross-cultural psychology. A brief review of these terms follows.

Positions and Roles. The term *position* indicates where a person is in social space. One can occupy the position of daughter, mother, sister (in kin space); of employee, supervisor, and part-time music teacher (in occupational space); member, treasurer, and president-elect (in club space); citizen, party member, and candidate (in political space), and so on. One person can occupy all of these positions in a lifetime, often simultaneously. Every person has several such positions.

Role is the behavior that is prescribed, or expected, because one occupies a particular position. As relatives, workers, club members, and so on, our behavior in each case is guided by the role expectations held by others.

Norms and Social Control. Role expectations can take on a compelling, even obligatory, character, virtually controlling our behavior. *Norms* are the widely shared standards of conduct that control (within limits) the behavior of group members. Norms vary in the degree to which they influence behavior; thus, folkways (e.g., stir your tea with a spoon, not your thumb) are merely conventional practices, while mores (avoid making sexual advances to a sibling) are considered to be obligatory for the maintenance of social order, and formal laws not only forbid or make certain behaviors obligatory but have sanctions attached to them. Most often these norms are phrased negatively, in the form of proscriptions (e.g., "Thou shalt not . . . ," "It is illegal to . . . "). Proscriptions in the realm of mores are sometimes termed taboos, a word that originated in Pacific Island cultures and has become widely used by both social scientists and laypersons.

Social control is the enforcement of all norms, including folkways, mores, and laws. Socially acceptable behavior can be inculcated through socialization and enculturation (concepts discussed later in this chapter), whereby requisite behavior is acquired through social learning, resulting in most persons' wanting to behave in ways they are expected to behave. When socialization and enculturation fall short, further means of social control are available, embodied in enforcement agencies such as police, courts, the military, and in some societies, councils of elders and ecclesiastical authorities.

Social Structure. Societies vary in how they are structured or organized. The structure of a society is relevant to forms of social control employed in it. One dimension of structure concerns the degree of stratification of a society, which refers to possible forms of vertical hierarchies, wherein some persons are considered to be "higher" than others (and thus have power to control the behavior of others who are "lower"). Class and caste are examples of units of stratification. Some societies are more stratified than others.

All societies have one or another form of family structure. In cultural anthropology, there are four major areas of research dealing with issues of marriage, family, and kinship. These are, respectively, family type, residence pattern, descent rules, and kinship terminology. For students not familiar with these kinds of anthropological concerns, it would be useful to consult an introductory anthropology text (e.g., Ember & Ember, 1985). A brief discussion of these four areas of concern appears in Box 1-1.

All aspects of social structure, including some not discussed here, such as societal divisions of an economic kind, have important consequences for the behavior of individuals, since who we are, how we are related to people, and what stratum we find ourselves in (in other words, the status we have ascribed to us or which we achieve), contributes to the amount of social influence we can exert on others or find applied by others to us.

Finally, social structures vary in cultural complexity; in some societies, few status distinctions are made, whereas in others there are many. Murdock (1967) distinguishes such variation in a two-variable system: (1) the number

Box 1-1 Basic Anthropological Dimensions of Variation in Societies

1. *Family type* can vary from monogomy (one husband–one wife) to polygyny (one husband–several wives) to polyandry (one wife–several husbands). These variations do not appear to be randomly distributed, but are consistently related to some other factors; one of these factors is the economic base of a society, where monogamous unions (resulting in independent nuclear families) are more likely to exist in hunting and gathering societies (and in large-scale industrialized societies) whereas polygamous unions (including both polygyny and polyandry) are associated with extended families and are more common in agricultural societies.

2. *Residence patterns* refer to the localities where newlyweds establish their homes. Patrilocal residence, where sons reside with or near their fathers after marriage and daughters go with their husbands, is characteristic of about two thirds of all societies. Other residence patterns include matrilocal (the couple resides with or near the wife's mother, a form that is found in about 15 percent of societies), bilocal, where either of the two previous residence patterns are possible, and avunculocal, where the couple goes to live with or near the husband's maternal uncle.

3. *Rules of Descent* refers to ways in which persons in a society trace their ancestry. The variations are fourfold: In patrilineal descent (by far the most common), one traces one's origin to the father's side of the family; in matrilineal, to the mother's side; in bilateral, to both sides; and in ambilineal, to one or the other, resulting in descent groups in a society showing both male and female genealogical links.

4. *Kinship terminology* consists of the ways that people refer to the categories of family relationships. A number of different systems have been discovered in various societies by anthropologists, and these are usually named after one of the cultural groups employing them (viz., Omaha, Crow, Iroquois, Hawaiian, Eskimo, and Sudanese), which conveys little of their actual nature to the anthropologically uninitiated. The systems vary primarily in that kin that are lumped together in one system are separated in another, with a single term covering more cases in some systems than in others (e.g., "uncle" may refer to mother's brother, father's brother, mother's sister's husband, and father's sister's husband in some societies but not in others.)

of political levels above the local community (e.g., regional, provincial, national) and (2) presence/absence of class distinctions.

How should we think about the differences that characterize human groups? A basic perspective from which this book is written is that of cultural relativism (Herskovits, 1948), a view of the world in which the characteristic behaviors and the varying cultural contexts of human groups are described but not evaluated. They are not considered better or worse, or more or less civilized. Rather, every cultural system is seen as a solution to the problem of living that is workable in the particular conditions in which it evolved.[1]

These, then, are some basic notions about the social and cultural context in which all human behavior is shaped and displayed. That our behavior has this contextual characteristic is largely a reflection of the fact that we are a species endowed with language.

The Role of Language

The unique qualities of human behavior are due to language, which makes "culture" possible. Language underlies the uniqueness of human social behavior because language has permitted the appearance of human culture. Without language, there would be no culture.

The unique relationship involving human behavior, language, and culture is all the more striking in the light of research on communication and intergenerational transmission of learned behaviors in certain primates. What this research underscores (see Box 1-2) is the rudimentary nature of those processes in such close relatives of the human being as the chimpanzee.

The Use of Tools

Another hallmark of the human species is the manufacture and use of tools. Despite recent evidence of tool using among some other primates (consider the interesting example described in Box 1-3), their abilities in this respect are very rudimentary in comparison with those of humans. Only humans have the linguistic skills and the tool-using capacities that together have produced a cultural animal. Many other species are social animals; only humans are cultural ones as well.

How this linguistically endowed, tool-using animal — the human being — has created and continues to create cultures is a fit and critically important object for study. So is the manner in which culture, in turn, molds the human individual. Cross-cultural psychology concerns itself with both of these overarching questions.

To the cross-cultural psychologist, cultures are seen both as products of past human behavior and as shapers of future human behavior. We have produced social environments that continually serve to bring about continuities and changes in life-styles over time and uniformities and diversities in

---

[1]The cultural relativist position is a necessary antidote to a prevailing tendency of persons everywhere to evaluate their own culture (and by extension, themselves) as superior to others. This tendency, known as ethnocentrism, is something everyone of us is likely to display in our own behavior and thinking (as we shall see in Chapter 14). What a book like this can do for us, then, is both instruct us about a cultural relativist perspective and liberate us from our ethnocentrisms.

Box 1-2 Do Apes Have True Language?

Demonstrations of the ability of apes to communicate symbolically (e.g., Gardner & Gardner, 1975; Premack, 1976; Terrace, 1979) may appear to challenge the assertion that language is a uniquely human accomplishment. Many of these demonstrations have been described as efforts to teach language to apes and, as summarized by Risteau and Robbins (1982), some of these attempts appear to have succeeded. Particularly impressive have been findings that apes could use strings of two or more symbols, signifying a sentence-like utterance, such as "Mary give Sarah apple" (Premack, 1976). Considerable controversy surrounds the interpretation of the results of these efforts, however.

In fact, Terrace and colleagues (Terrace, 1979; Terrace, Petitto, Sanders & Bever, 1979) who carefully analyzed some 20,000 combinations of two or more signs made by a young male ape named Nim, convincingly argued that Nim's behavior displayed no real grammatical competence and that his "sentences" were nothing more than imitative responses elicited by his teacher's urging. They were more like the chaining behavior of a pigeon in a Skinner box than real sentences (and no one has yet suggested that pigeons have linguistic competence).

Terrace (1985) has more recently argued that the search for linguistic competence in nonhuman animals erred by emphasizing sentence generation as its hallmark. He suggested focusing instead on the ability to refer to objects with names (or "naming") as an equally important and perhaps more fundamental skill. There is no doubt that humans do this; from early in life, children refer to objects with verbal signs that are their names, not only to obtain them but to call others' attention to them. To date, no one has satisfactorily demonstrated referential behavior in an ape in the absence of a specific reinforcer.

Terrace, however, noted that Savage-Rumbaugh, Sevcik, Rumbaugh, and Rupert (1985) trained a two-and-a-half-year-old chimpanzee named Kanzi to use some arbitrary symbols apparently without step-by-step drills. Although Terrace was impressed by this, he worried that not all the specific reinforcers had been absent from that study and doubted that Kanzi's motivation was simply the transmission of information from a speaker to a listener (Terrace, 1985, p. 1025). We know that humans have this motivation; we have no evidence that other animals do. If naming is the sine qua non of true language, then we can still assert that language is a unique feature of humans.

---

life-styles over space. How human beings modify culture and how our cultures modify us is what cross-cultural psychology is all about. To all who would understand human behavior, to those who would predict it, and certainly to those who would seek consciously to modify it, knowledge of the network of interrelationships between culture and behavior is essential.

Box 1-3 Do Chimps Really Use Tools?

In the summer of 1960, animal behaviorist Jane Goodall, then secretary to the well-known paleontologist Dr. Louis B. Leakey, went to live in the Gombe Stream Reserve in Tanzania to study the life and habits of wild chimpanzees. During the 15 years that she lived there, she observed that chimpanzees are highly intelligent and social creatures whose behavioral repertoire includes many acts that are strikingly similar to behaviors displayed by humans.

One of Goodall's most exciting discoveries was that Gombe Stream chimpanzees use objects in their natural environment, such as sticks and leaves, as tools to assist them in such everyday activities as retrieving food and water. Goodall observed that not only do chimpanzees use sticks and grass stems to "fish" for termites or ants in their earthen mounds but they would often modify these objects—for example, stripping leaves from a stick or trimming edges off a grass stem—in an effort to make them into more useful tools (Goodall, 1971). Another example of this primitive form of tool making was the chewing of leaves to make them more absorbent and then putting them in hard-to-reach places to soak up rain water for drinking. Goodall also observed chimpanzees using leaves for other purposes, such as wiping blood, feces, or mud from their bodies.

The significance of these findings lies in the fact that prior to Goodall's work in the Gombe Stream, most scientists agreed that the ability to make and use tools was the one characteristic (aside from language) that separated humans from animals. Goodall's results challenged some scientists to reexamine their fundamental definition of man, whereas others seriously questioned what Goodall's observations really meant.

More recently, researchers studying a community of wild chimpanzees living in the tropical rain forest of Tai National Park, Ivory Coast, observed chimps selectively choosing either tree branches or stones and transporting these "tools" to specific locations to crack nuts (Boesch & Boesch, 1984). Researchers discovered that the chimps' choice of tool was highly dependent on the hardness of the nutshell that they intended to crack, with chimps nearly always using tree branches for cracking the softer Coula nutshell and employing heavier granite stones to crack the harder Panda nut.

Furthermore, the search and transport pattern of the chimps appeared to Boesch and Boesch to reflect an underlying strategy—chimps seemed to take into account both the weight of the tool and the distance to the nut-cracking site in order to maximize the rate of food acquisition. For Coula nuts, whose trees are abundant, the chimps employed a "least-distance strategy," transporting light branches over short distances to nut-cracking sites that were in close proximity. For Panda nuts, whose trees are relatively scarce and widely scattered throughout the forest, chimps still tried to minimize distances but were willing to carry heavy stones over longer distances to find the nearest Panda tree. In making all of these decisions, the chimps demonstrated evidence that they remembered the sites of both trees and tools and adapted their behavior so as to conserve distance and energy and optimize food acquisition.

In this introductory section on behavior and culture we have come close to a discussion of human nature. It is well to discuss it now explicitly.

The Centrality of Learning

Human beings acquire habits throughout life, continuously modifying behavior in response to environmental influences. This is the essence of the human potential.[2]

Human behavior can best be understood as the product of learning, particularly learning that results from experiences with other people or with ideas, institutions, or other products of the behavior of other people. In short, we are largely what we are because of culturally based learning.

Agreement from Social Psychology. One of the pioneers of social psychology in the United States, Floyd Allport, once defined the discipline as "a part of the psychology of the individual, whose behavior it studies in relation to that sector of his environment comprised by his fellows" (1924, p. 4). Some years later, Keller and Schoenfeld (1950) defined social psychology as the part of general psychology that deals with social stimuli. These two conceptions of social psychology cover a lot of ground. Indeed, very little in your environment at this moment, or at any other moment, is composed of nonsocial stimuli.

Right now, the room you are perhaps in was designed, built, and furnished by others. You are probably clothed in garments of human design and production, which you chose to wear in response to certain social pressures, however nonconformist you believe yourself to be.

Consider also an electric source of light energy reaching the light-sensitive receptors of your eye. This light per se is clearly a nonsocial stimulus. But your response to it would probably include recognizing its characteristic color. In other words, you would name it and, in a limited sense, "detect" its meaning. The meaning is not inherent in the physical stimulus itself, of course. In fact, your attribution of meaning to the stimulus is a response to the behavior of others. "Others," in this case, are those members of your linguistic community who, ages ago, divided the visual spectrum and desig-

---

[2]Early treatments of the habit concept in psychology are to be found in the works of the philosopher-psychologist John Dewey (1896), who helped found the discipline near the turn of the twentieth century. George Herbert Mead (1934) theorized that the individual, from the very beginning of life, becomes aware of others' responses and that these provide the basis of the individual's own evolving self-concept. Thus, we tend to view ourselves as whatever others seem to believe us to be. Mead saw even so personal a thing as a self-concept to be a product of social learning. In accord with this view, psychologists came to recognize the importance of social learning in human life. A major theme of American behaviorism from Watson (1925) onward was that behavior takes the particular forms it does because the behaving organism has learned to behave the way it does.

nated its various parts with labels such as red, fuchsia, and scarlet (cultural similarities and differences in color perception and naming will be one of the subjects covered in Chapter 6).

Another way of describing human beings is to recognize that they are both culture's creators and culture's creations. As the creation of culture, each person is the product of the allied processes of socialization and enculturation.

Human Nature

A hallmark of human beings is our capacity to learn from others. In the language of social-learning theory that is used by many psychologists, we are responsive to socioculturally mediated reinforcements. Reinforcements are those events that occur after you have made a response and that either strengthen or weaken it. Socioculturally mediated reinforcements are those dispensed by other people.

Consider for a moment a classroom, with 30 or so persons in the room, one of whom does most of the talking. How does it happen that the others spend so much time listening? As a social-learning theorist would see it, the typical student had a history of reinforcement for numerous behavior patterns or role expectations relating to school. These behaviors reflect customs. They are the product of social learning—the end result of experience in a particular culture, in which students learned to behave like students. Of course, if the example we had chosen here were that of a Quranic school, the students probably would have been talking aloud, simultaneously reciting different parts of the Quran while the teacher listened silently.

It is the nature of human beings to learn, and not only in school. What is to be learned, and how, is everywhere influenced mightily by social and cultural forces. The details of these learning processes will become clear later. For now, we merely contrast it with a centuries-old, rather tenacious, and misleading concept: human nature.

Pseudo Explanation for Human Behavior

Human nature—taken to mean a set of universally shared, unlearned tendencies, or instincts—used to be evoked to "explain" any human behavior that was considered noteworthy. Among the Greek philosophers, Aristotle attributed the very existence of societies to human beings' natural instinct to affiliate. Note that this notion reduces to "humans affiliate because they have an instinct to affiliate." In a similar vein centuries later, Adam Smith (1759) pointed to altruism as an intrinsic human quality. He explained our observed propensity to cooperate (sometimes) with our fellows: "How selfish soever man may be supposed, there are evidently some principles *in*

Box 1-4 A Classic Critique of Instinct Theories

A still adequate critique of instinct theorizing was provided by the experimental psychologist Beach (1955). In it, he considered why it is that "the instinct concept has survived in almost complete absence of empirical validation" (p. 401). The concept's roots lie in ancient philosophy and theology. Given the Western theologian's idea of a life after death—an idea that required the postulation of a human soul and that led to a classification system in which humans were set apart from animals—the concept of instinct had to be invented. The concept was first applied only to animal behavior and was considered its key, just as rational thought was the key to human behavior. If animals had no rationality, then only instinct could explain their behavior, which bore so many superficial similarities to human behavior. By attributing instinct to animals and rationality to human beings, the theologian was able to establish humans' unique link with the supernatural. To keep people apart from animals, the behavior of the latter alone was attributed to their natural instincts.

With the advent of Darwinian insights in biology, the traditional human/animal dichotomy was destroyed. The oft-detected similarities in the behavior of animals and humans were no longer dismissed as merely superficial. Rationality, at least interpreted as a capacity to learn and to adapt, was shown to be shared by humans and other animals. While correctly pointing to humanlike phenomena at many levels of animal behavior, the early post-Darwinians also pointed to human behavioral roots in animal behavior and then, as a final step, uncritically adopted the instinct notion to explain, in wholesale fashion, great chunks of human behavior.

This error was never more obvious than in McDougall's textbook, in which literally dozens of instincts were invented. It was perhaps inevitable that the generation of psychologists who came after McDougall reacted violently against the doctrine of instinct. In the 1920s and 1930s it became fashionable in American psychology to take the position that no behavior as actually performed by any animal could be instinctive. This reaction was, according to Beach (1955), a relatively ineffective polemic. It was not based on empirical findings. In denying a role to unlearned patterns of behavior, this line of argument not only may have been incorrect; it also inadvertently perpetuated an unfortunate distinction between heredity and learning and fed fuel to arguments in which "nature" and "nurture" were treated as competing explanations for behavior. In Beach's words, "The implication that all behavior must be determined by learning or by heredity, neither of which is more than partially understood, is entirely unjustified. . . . The final form of any response is affected by a multiplicity of variables, only two of which are genetical and experiential factors" (1955, p. 405). Beach went on to predict that the concept of instinct would gradually disappear from scientific, if not from popular, attempts to explain human behavior. In this particular respect, Beach was perhaps too optimistic.

his nature which interest him in the fortunes of others, and render their happiness necessary to him" (p. 1; italics ours).

Speculation about the nature of humans characterized early philosophical psychology. Laypersons still invoke human nature to explain particular actions. The tendency for people to desire intensely that which is tabooed is a favorite popular example of "human nature." But a desire to please authority figures has also been attributed to that same nature. Clearly, if a concept explains everything, it in fact explains nothing.

Instinct Theories

In some psychological theorizing, a human-nature argument, albeit relatively sophisticated, can also be found. Even as late as the 1980s, sociobiological arguments (e.g., Wilson & Herrnstein, 1985) continued a train of thought that has a long history in psychology. McDougall, in his pioneering social-psychology textbook (1908) argued that instincts—like curiosity, self-assertion, submission, food seeking, mating, acquisitiveness, flight, repulsion, and parental feeling—are the basis of human behavior.

Later writers both added to and subtracted from McDougall's list, offering their own inventories in its place. Instinct theorists have more recently claimed the territorial imperative (Ardrey, 1966) and aggression (Lorenz, 1963) to be unlearned. In such claims the formula is all too simple: Detect a behavioral tendency that appears to be universal, name it, invent an instinct for it, and consider the behavior explained.

The first difficulty with this is its logical circularity. To use this formula is to commit the nominal fallacy; the phenomenon is named, and its name is taken as its explanation. Ponder, for example, the empty statement that a bird flies because it has a flying instinct. It is no less empty to claim that mothers protect their children because they have a maternal instinct or that humans create societies because they have an affiliation instinct.

The second difficulty is that the human behaviors that have so often been attributed to instincts are seldom characteristic of the whole species, although the instinct doctrine virtually demands it. Every mother who abandons her children is an embarrassment to the instinct theorist. So is every pacifist a challenge to those who contend that all people instinctively rise to the defense of their homeland. To explain such "exceptions," of course, the instinct theorist need only invent new instincts. Not surprisingly, instinct theorists did just that, thereby compounding their original error. (See Box 1-4).

Sociobiology's Perspective

Modern biologists concerned with human behavior have revived interest in genetically based behavioral potentials. Primatologists, especially, have called attention to numerous similarities between the behaviors of various monkeys and apes and those of humans, similarities that are consistent with the view that much of human behavior is rooted in evolutionary developments over millennia. Much of the behavior that has been studied by modern students of sociobiology (see, e.g., Wilson, 1975) is basic social behavior, such as courtship and mating, child rearing, and dominance and submission interactions. Some controversy surrounds sociobiology, especially when its findings are applied to very complex social issues. An example is the question of causes of behavioral differences between human males and females, which we will discuss in a later chapter. And, even in more cautious applications of some of its findings, sociobiology seems to have resurrected the old, discredited instinct doctrine. It need not. Sociobiology, at its best, underscores the continuity of development of biologically related creatures while recognizing that no human behavior can be attributed solely to biological predispositions. Human behavior is surely affected by learning, which itself is a biologically rooted capacity.

As the distinguished student of primate behavior S. L. Washburn put it:

> I would be the first to agree that the full understanding of the behavior patterns of any species must include biology. But the more that learning is involved, the less there will be of any simple relation between basic biology and behavior. The laws of genetics are not the laws of learning. As a result of intelligence and speech, human beings provide the extreme example of highly varied behavior that is learned and executed by the same fundamental biology. Biology determines the basic need for food, but not the innumerable ways in which this need may be met.
>
> Out of the present controversy, which, on a positive level, has stimulated renewed interest in human and animal behavior, a new interdisciplinary biologically and socially based behavioral science may emerge. But in applying biological thinking we must take care not to ignore history, sociology, and comparative studies. For if we do, we will be condemned to repeat the scientific errors of the past. (Washburn, 1978, p. 75)

One of those errors was an 18th- and 19th-century idea about social evolution, a putative process from savagery through barbarism and so on until civilization was attained. (European thinkers developed the notion of social evolution; they saw European societies, their own if not all of them, as personifying civilization.[3])

Even up to the present, there is confusion about biological evolution and social evolution, both in contemporary writings in sociobiology and in social science responses to it. Some social scientists, while arguing the primacy

---

[3]As we shall see in a brief review in the next chapter of historical trends in psychological thought, 19th-century expeditions to non-Western lands were partly motivated by a search for peoples believed to represent an earlier level of social evolution. Related ideas are found in Chapter 5.

of culture in shaping human social behavior, have tended to treat human evolution as a fundamentally different process from that of animal evolution.

A Sophisticated View of Human Evolution

A balanced view has been presented by Boyd and Richerson (1985) who, while acknowledging that humans are cultural organisms, account for human evolution in an essentially Darwinian manner. In their view, which we share, human evolution involves both genetic transmission and cultural transmission. These two processes are different in certain important respects, but they have parallel features.

Cultural transmission, a uniquely human process involving intergenerational learning (via teaching and imitation), has features that distinguish it from biological transmission. For example, in cultural transmission, individuals are influenced by persons other than their biological parents, while in biological transmission, only parents may be the source of influence. Thus, humans, and only humans, have "cultural parents" (for example, members of extended families, teachers, priests, and other influential persons). Moreover, cultural evolution (unlike biological evolution) is not restricted to intergenerational influences. Ideas are transmitted within generations, too, so that it is even possible for older individuals to model their behavior after younger ones. Another difference between genetic and cultural evolution is that individuals are already somewhat shaped when they come under cultural influences, the effects of which will be conditioned by the state of the organism at the time the influence is applied.

On the other hand, the two processes are in some ways analogous. Both proceed in interaction with environmental contingencies; both biological and cultural evolution involve changes that become either established or lost depending on how adaptive they are (or how well they "fit" the environment in which they first occurred).

This position is similar to that of Campbell (1965, 1975) who argued that cultural evolution, like biological evolution, proceeds in a nonprescient manner (not predetermined, nor looking ahead to favorable outcomes) involving random variation and natural (environmental) selection. A related view is that of Skinner (1974), who describes cultural change as a process involving selection by consequences. These insights set apart the positions of Boyd and Richerson, Campbell, and Skinner from that of most sociobiologists, who don't deem it necessary to be concerned with the details of cultural transmission.

We believe the Boyd and Richerson dual-inheritance theory to be a more fruitful approach to the study of human behavior. By using it here, we hope to indicate that the nature versus nurture (or genetics versus culture) controversy to be an inappropriate conceptualization of the relationship between biological and cultural forces. While they may have different outcomes, and involve different processes as Boyd and Richerson have shown, they are parallel rather than competing forces.

A BALANCED APPROACH: AN ECOCULTURAL FRAMEWORK

Biological inheritance by itself explains little about human behavior. We agree that behavior is in part a function of a multitude of inherited potentialities; we stress that all human behavior is shaped by experience. All behavior, then, is a product of a complex interaction involving genetic and experiential factors, with both present and past experience weighted heavily in its ultimate determination.

Our thinking on the relationship of ecology, culture, genetics, experience, and human behavior is illustrated in a conceptual framework presented in Figure 1-1. This framework links ecological and sociopolitical contexts with various psychological characteristics, and also contains intervening process variables wherein both biological and cultural influences are transmitted from the context to the individual. Most, if not all, of the questions posed in cross-cultural psychology may be subsumed by Figure 1-1, and it will be instructive to return to it frequently and apply it to the topics in each chapter of this book.

The conceptual framework, which incorporates the diverse kinds of research done in cross-cultural psychology, was designed and modified by Berry (1971a, 1975, 1976a, 1986). The framework contains variables at the levels of populations and individuals. It includes background variables, process variables, and psychological outcomes. The background variables include two kinds of contexts, ecological and sociopolitical.

The basic premise is that ecological forces are the prime movers and shapers of culture and behavior. Ecological variables constrain, pressure, and nurture cultural forms, which in turn shape behavior.

Ecological Context Variables

These include climatic and other natural factors—such as water supply, soil conditions, temperature, and terrain—that combine to influence, among other things, any society's food-production system. By ecology, then, we mean any combination of natural conditions that affects food-production techniques, which are clearly fundamental to the functioning of society.

Underlying this emphasis on ecological factors is the assumption that, over a long period, basic strategies whereby a society feeds its members are

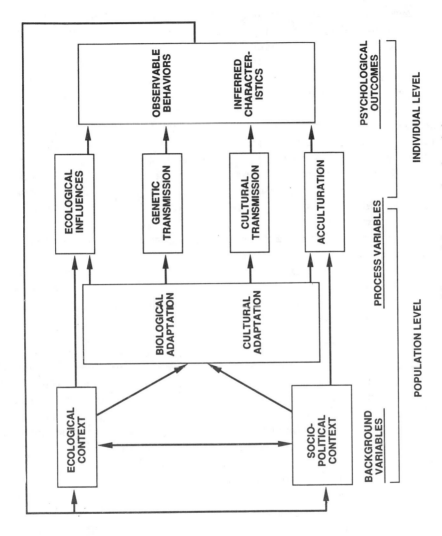

FIGURE 1-1. A conceptual framework for cross-cultural psychology

influenced by natural forces. A decision to feed primarily on meat from large animals depends on their availability, which in turn depends on climate, water supply, type of ground cover, and the like. Herding as a way of producing food depends on the availability of conditions favorable to animal husbandry. Fishing demands that one live near water.

A convenient way of categorizing different food-production systems is by degree of food accumulation. At the low extreme are societies that pursue hunting and gathering as a primary feeding technique. Food is not stored for later consumption but is merely out there to be sought when needed. It is sometimes abundant and sometimes in short supply, but it is seldom accumulated. Societies at the high extreme include those that employ agriculture, accumulating food by producing, storing, and planting seeds. Such societies, particularly if they also raise animals, typically store much of their food for later needs. Animal-husbandry societies are very high in food accumulation, investing resources in meat on the hoof that may not be needed for months.

There are well-replicated anthropological observations indicating that a society's degree of food accumulation is correlated with certain of its other characteristics. For example, high-food-accumulating societies, as well as technologically developed societies, tend to be sedentary and relatively dense in population. Low-food-accumulating societies tend to be composed of less dense, often migratory populations.

Adaptive Variables

Included in the diagram as "process variables," these include both cultural adaptation and biological adaptation that are, in turn, sociocultural and organismic characteristics of populations. Cultural adaptations include all inventions that are adaptive to the pressures of ecology. Another way of referring to such inventions, of course, is simply to call them "culture," since culture consists of all human institutions that in the long run help populations survive in a given ecological niche. These include social and economic systems, kinship systems, and socialization emphases. In any particular environment there are forces that make it likely that certain socialization practices are emphasized more than others, that certain kinship systems are organized rather than others, and so forth.

Without going into great detail here one can see how that seems plausible. If, for example, ecological forces influence food accumulation, which in turn is related to the probability of a society's being migatory or sedentary, that in turn will probably lead to a cultural invention that is compatible with being either sedentary or migratory. A migratory society is likely to have a different kinship system from one that is sedentary. A sociocultural variable such as kinship is thus an "adaptive" or process variable.

The second subcategory of adaptive variables, biological adaptation, includes any response a population makes over many generations that is basically genetic or physiological. Such extremely long-term evolutionary changes are responsive to the press of ecology. Thus, genetic differences across subpopulations of the human race are treated in this framework as biological adaptations to ecological pressure. These differences may show up, for example, as differential susceptibilities to certain diseases. These organismic differences do not reflect only genetic predispositions, of course. Health and nutritional status may also vary across populations because of cultural differences in diet and hygiene. But whatever their cause, they are differences in organismic status that reflect varying adaptations to ecological conditions.

These two subcategories of adaptive variables, biological and cultural, may also interact with one another. For example, cultural taboos regarding foods may reflect a society's experience in ages past with negative consequences of a food, consequences that may have had a genetic basis. Thus, there are ethnic groups in Africa that suffer an organic inability to digest milk. These groups also have a culturally sanctioned aversion to milk. Their diet is less than adequate in protein. Their nutritional status is probably a product of both sociocultural and organismic variables, in some complex interaction. However it came about, the complex of dietary practices and prevailing physical condition of a population is a part of that population's adaptation to its environment. Its adaptation is both cultural and biological.

Psychological Outcome Variables

These individual-level variables include all measurable aspects of individual behavior that can be shown to be linked to ecological or adaptive variables or to both. And since in psychological research one often is concerned with presumed-to-exist characteristics (like personality traits, values, motives, abilities, and the like) which are inferred from observed behavior, such characteristics are also included in the model.

This framework is thus a conceptual system in which ecocultural forces are viewed as influencing human behavior, either directly or through the intervening adaptive variables, both cultural and biological. But the direction of relationship is not exclusively from ecology through culture to behavior. Obviously, individual behavior can also influence culture. Indeed, individual behavior can even influence ecology. People do go out and cut down the forest or divert water or use up natural resources. The framework, then, is a feedback system, or a network of relationships. Its ultimate usefulness lies in its calling attention to the possible relationships to look for among any combination of ecological, adaptive, and psychological variables. This is what we mean when we say that the framework has "heuristic value."

The ecocultural framework clearly includes biological factors, since there are, among other things, hormonally influenced behaviors and reflexive responses at the human level. These reflexes are mediated by lower centers of the human nervous system in a relatively simple way. A distinguishing feature of a reflex is stereotypy, or sameness. At the human level, reflexes account for a small proportion of our behavior, most of which involves the highest brain centers, notably the cortex. The result is that most human responses lack the characteristic stereotypy of a reflex. For example, sexual behavior, which surely involves reflexive reactions in mouse and human alike, becomes almost bewilderingly convoluted among human beings, whose cortical functions incessantly interact with their glandular secretions.

Human mating behavior can hardly be described as reflexive. Partner preferences are a key feature of human sexual behavior. The bases of these preferences differ widely within societies, across societies, and over time. Our sexual behavior is affected by many rules, standards, values, and laws, with all of these controlling factors in a continuous process of change. One leading student of human sexuality, the sociologist Ira Reiss, whose work will be discussed more fully in Chapter 11, defined sexuality as "erotic and genital responses produced by the cultural scripts of a society" (Reiss, 1986, p. 37). To assert that human sexual behavior is determined by hormones or reflexes is to ignore a more complex reality.

Clearly, then, we need an answer to the question of the nature of human beings that is very different from that provided by the instinct theorists. And that, in part, is why we have cross-cultural psychology.

What then is human nature? Our nature is both sociocultural and biological. Like other animals, we are first of all biological creatures. We have certain vital needs. Before anything else, our behavior must tend to enhance our survivability; it must be functional in the sense that it answers our survival needs. But these survival needs are few in number. The essential ones include oxygen, water, food, stimulation, rest, elimination of waste products, and, for a time, some kind of sexual outlet. Our behavioral repertory for fulfilling these needs includes reflexes, which are simple, unlearned, inevitable reactions to specific stimuli, such as sneezing when irritated by dust or pollen. Mostly, however, our needs are met by more complex behaviors.

In fulfillment of these needs and in pursuit of a far more numerous set of unessential, but equally compelling, goals, we exercise our acquired skills and habits. Our sociocultural nature reflects a highly developed capacity to benefit from the lessons of experience, our own and our culture mates'. No other animal has this capacity to the same extent. No other animal has created whole systems of education. No other animal learns as much. As a result, we display many forms of behavior that are uniquely human, many of which are part of what we call culture.

SOCIALIZATION AND ENCULTURATION

From birth onward, all human beings learn to accommodate their behavior to that of others. This is an implication of the statement that human beings are social animals. What every person becomes is determined by both biological and social factors, coacting in a complex fashion. In this section, we emphasize the latter.

Like other primates, we are subject to socialization. Much of our socialization involves formal education, which is a distinctly human institution. Human beings alone are also subject to enculturation. Even the most fundamental appreciation of the whys of human behavior demands that these processes be understood.

Socialization

Child (1954) defined socialization as "the whole process by which an individual, born with behavioral potentialities of enormously wide range, is led to develop actual behavior which is confined within a much narrower range—the range of what is customary and acceptable for him according to the standards of his group" (p. 655).

This definition has the virtue of reminding us that all human beings are capable of a far greater repertory of behaviors than any single person ever exhibits. Each of us, because of the accident of birth, begins life in a particular social context, within which we learn to make certain responses and not others. The most dramatic illustration of this is our linguistic behavior. That one speaks one language rather than another, even though all languages are possible, aptly demonstrates this fact (cf. Bril, 1987). Less obviously, socialization also effectively narrows the range of responses each of us habitually makes in many other behavioral domains. The conditions under which we express emotions, and the ways in which we suppress them, are determined by socialization. (But see Chapter 8 for some possibly universal tendencies to interpret emotions from facial expressions.) Our reactions to authority figures, and their reactions to us, reflect the customs of the society into which we happened to be born. Many, if not all, of the behavioral differences that for centuries were attributed to "temperament," such as British coolness and Latin abandon, are attributable to the differential reinforcement of certain responses and the effective elimination of others.

While we are active creatures, able to choose within broad limits those with whom we come into contact, the probability of our behaving in certain ways is affected by them, at least by those who relate to us as socialization agents. Anyone who possesses power relative to us can socialize us. Most often socialization agents include parents, teachers, and other elders, who are more knowledgeable in the ways of their society. Under certain circumstances, however, even age peers can effect socialization. Whoever can present or withhold reinforcement can socialize.

Whenever interaction results in the shaping or selection of socially approved behavior, socialization is occurring. Typically, it involves rewarding approved behavior and punishing unwanted behavior. Equally important, although less obvious, is the nonreinforcement of unwanted behavior. This, too, serves to lessen the probability of future occurrences of socially disapproved responses.

The process of socialization often involves conflict between the individual and socialization agents, as sometimes occurs between pupils and teachers. Not only are some responses likely to be punished, some may be blocked by the behavior of others in very subtle, but effective, ways. For example, socialization agents may withhold opportunities to behave in certain ways except at a time and place they consider appropriate. The socialization of feeding behavior during infancy involves this mechanism to a very great extent.

All socialization involves efforts by others to control behavior. Socialization, then, consists primarily of deliberate tutelage, with doses of reward and punishment, applied in an effort to produce "acceptable" behavior.

If socialization were not enough to have the impact Child's definition foresees (the narrowing down of behavioral realities as compared with each person's behavioral potential), we have the additional process of enculturation. It is less direct, but no less effective, than socialization.

Enculturation

Much of what we learn is learned without direct, deliberate teaching. We all learn particular ideas, concepts, and values, simply because of the differential availability in different places of what is to be learned — for example, what is music and what is noise. What we identify as music depends primarily on what is there, previously labeled as music, to be learned. Similarly, in every society a high percentage of the people would agree on what is worth fighting for, and not because there is a course in the curriculum on "supreme causes." Instead, such values are widely transmitted, both directly and indirectly, and are learned very well because they are hardly ever questioned. It is this kind of learning that we call "enculturation." First employed by Herskovits (1948, pp. 39–42; 1955, pp. 326–329), enculturation refers to all of the learning that occurs in human life because of what is available to be learned.

Much of what every person learns about the ways of his or her society is learned without interpersonal conflict. When a child struggles with an older sibling, socialization is probably occurring, but what is struggled over and how the struggle is carried on probably reflect enculturation. What the child learns is worth struggling for must be part of the cultural content of his or her society. How the child expresses a desire for it will be determined by prevalent attitudes toward the expression of desire. The child will learn these as much by emulating others as by being taught deliberately. In the latter case, socialization is at work; in the former, the more subtle process of enculturation. Whenever we learn by observation (cf., Bandura, 1971), any part of the content of our society—content that has been culturally shaped and limited during preceding generations—enculturation is occurring.

Although effects of enculturation are obvious to the social scientist, enculturated individuals are usually unaware of how much of what they do reflects the process. People are not likely to be aware of what was unavailable in the society to be learned. This leads to the apparent paradox that persons who are most thoroughly enculturated are often the least aware of their culture's role in molding them.

Much of our learning involves both socialization and enculturation. Learning a language, for example, involves both. There is a certain amount of direct teaching of the language, as in grammar courses in elementary school. But a lot of the learning of language occurs (apparently) spontaneously, by children who must assume that there is only one language to be learned.

Both processes, socialization and enculturation, result in behavioral similarities within societies and behavioral differences across societies. Both processes involve learning from other people how to behave. In the case of socialization, the learning involves teaching. In the case of enculturation, teaching is not necessary for the learning to take place.

Since the term "enculturation" very neatly denotes the engagement of persons in their culture, the term also serves well as a generic label for all human learning, encompassing socialization as well.

In any case, the key to understanding the nature of human behavior is that human beings are the learners par excellence of the animal kingdom. And, since most of what is learned is contained in culture, we may take as the beginning point of our exploration of human behavior the premise that it is meaningful only when examined in sociocultural context.

THE CONCEPT OF CULTURE AS A BEHAVIORAL DETERMINANT

We have stressed that human behavior occurs in a sociocultural context. We must now consider the nature of culture.

Culture is the key concept of anthropology. Like many key concepts (for example, energy in physics or group in sociology) culture is variously and often ambiguously defined, yet it is used as if its meaning were clear. While definitions of culture abound (several useful ones appear in Box 1-5) they commonly point to some essential features of culture.

Culture, by almost any definition, includes the products of the behavior of others, especially others who preceded us. It connotes a set of social stimuli that to a very great extent have existence prior to us. Put very simply, culture is already there for all of us as we begin life. It contains values that will be expressed and a language in which to express them. It contains a way of life that will be followed by most of us, who through most of our lifetimes will unquestioningly assume that there is no better.

Following Moore and Lewis (1952) (see Box 1-5), we note that culture also

---

Box 1-5 A Few Definitions of Culture

According to Ember and Ember (1985), culture encompasses the learned behaviors, beliefs, and attitudes that are characteristic of a particular society or population. They also defined it as "the shared customs of a society" (p. 166).

For one anthropologist of an earlier generation, White (1947), culture denotes all the symbolic behavior, especially language, that makes possible the transmission of wisdom, in the form of techniques for coping with the environment, from generation to generation. As White saw it, culture is continuous, cumulative, and progressive.

Moore and Lewis (1952) culled from diverse anthropological writings what they considered to be the essence of the concept. It is first of all an abstraction, in the sense that it is merely a convenient label for a very large category of phenomena. It designates knowledge, skills, and information that are learned. Further, it is social knowledge, in the sense that it is taught to and learned by many individuals and is thus shared. Since it tends to persist over generations, it is more or less adaptive. Finally, it tends to be integrated; that is to say, its contents tend to be mutually reinforcing.

Given these characteristics of culture, it becomes possible to define it simply as the totality of whatever all persons learn from all other persons. Anything one person learns from another, then, is an element of culture, and it is recognized as such to the extent that it is adaptive and persistent over generations.

Camilleri (1985) offered a definition of culture that highlights some of its oft-cited features: (a) It includes the totality of learned meanings, which are widely shared and persist over time; and (b) it induces the sharing of attitudes, social representations, and values, and leads to shared behavior patterns that reflect these values.

Barnlund and Araki (1985) offered a behavioristic definition, namely, "Cultures have no existence except as they are manifest in the behavior of the people who constitute them. A culture is only an abstraction based on the communalities displayed in the behavior of a given community of people" (p. 9).

For still other definitions of culture, see Chapters 1 and 2 in Berry et al. (in press) and Bril and Lehalle (1988).

includes language, music, and art forms. It includes preferences, appetites, and aversions. It includes rules, norms, and standards. It includes hopes and fears, beliefs and attitudes, convictions and doubts, at least to the extent that such are shared, inculcated, and transmitted from people to people. To be considered a part of culture, anything, material or symbolic, need only be of human origin. Recall that Herskovits (1948, p. 17) defined culture as the man-made part of the environment.

If anthropologists had not invented culture, then psychologists probably would have. The concept enables the psychologist to account for the fact that social stimuli do not impinge on an individual with equal probability in different places at different times. Some social stimuli are more probable than others. Children in Europe are unlikely to greet a parent by prostrating themselves and kissing his feet. A Ganda householder in his East African grass-thatched house is not likely to be confronted with a bowl of cornflakes for breakfast. Because of cultural diffusion (see Chapter 13), all of these events, could, in fact, occur, if not today, tomorrow. Nevertheless, as this is being written, these events have differential probability of occurring in various parts of the world.

These last thoughts imply that culture and society are roughly coterminous. Because every society has a culture, behavior patterns tend to be different from society to society. But society is one thing, and culture another. Culture includes "learned meanings" (Rohner, 1984) and is a label for all the many different features that vary from society to society and that constitute the independent variables (Segall, 1984) that psychologists must use in their research on human behavior (see also Segall, 1986).

As Munroe and Munroe (1980) pointed out, "culture" is composed of numerous separable (but often correlated) factors, including subsistence patterns; social and political institutions; languages; rules governing interpersonal relations; divisions of labor by sex, age, or ethnicity; population density; dwelling styles; and more, and even more. Although the concept of culture may be an abstraction, as Barnlund and Araki (1985) asserted, it includes many real influences on human behavior, and by employing the concept, we are able to categorize and explain many important differences in human behavior that in the past were erroneously attributed to ill-defined biological differences.

SUMMARY OF OUR
CROSS-CULTURAL PERSPECTIVE

In this introduction to the scientific study of human behavior, we have learned that our subject matter can be understood only when viewed in its sociocultural context. Human behavior, we have found, is nearly always influenced by social stimuli. And many of those social stimuli constitute what we call culture. To understand how we each become what we are, we must take account of the fact that our biological heritage interacts with our experiences, mediated largely through the processes of socialization and enculturation. Thus, a study of human behavior that ignores culture does so at great risk. Accordingly, we will begin the next chapter with a demonstration of the riskiness of ignoring the sociocultural context of human behavior.

THE SCOPE OF THIS BOOK

Before we embark on this introduction to cross-cultural psychology, we should note the book's intent and limitations. We intend to range rather widely over this rapidly developing field, to discuss its history and methodology, and to consider cultural influences on basic psychological processes like cognition and perception, the development and change of cognitive and affective behaviors, attitudes and values, sex, aggression, intercultural contact and culture change, and intergroup relations. Still, coverage will be incomplete. Although we will review many studies from diverse sources, we can only sample from the many hundreds that are available. The sample we have chosen to present in the chapters that follow is composed of those studies that, for a variety of reasons, struck these four cross-cultural psychologists—two North Americans and two Europeans—as representative and most useful for undergraduate courses in psychology, education, and anthropology and in other domains in which understanding human behavior is the primary goal.

What is included adds up to a substantial body of material, but what is left out might fill another textbook. Readers of this book should understand that from it they will have learned *about* cross-cultural psychology and not necessarily how to do it. That is the purpose of a related book entitled *Cross-Cultural Psychology* (Berry, Poortinga, Segall & Dasen, in press), to which we will occasionally call your attention.

There are some topics keenly pursued by cross-cultural psychologists that are scarcely mentioned in the present book. Chief among them is psychopathology. Much of the literature on the many forms that psychopathology takes in various cultures has been produced by specialists within the applied field known as transcultural psychiatry. That their work has been given little attention in this book reflects not a judgment as to its intrinsic merit but a decision to limit the book to the study of "normal" behavior. The scholars we cite are predominantly social scientists—psychologists, anthropologists, sociologists, and, to a lesser extent, economists and political scientists— rather than scientists in the clinical, medical disciplines. But even an introductory student of cross-cultural psychology may wish to consult the transcultural psychiatric literature in order to round out his or her introductory knowledge of cultural influences on behavior.[4]

Armed with the introduction to the field that this book aims to provide, the student should be prepared to move on to more sophisticated sources, such as Berry et al. (in press) and the six-volume *Handbook of Cross-Cultural Psychology* prepared under the general editorship of Triandis (Triandis et al., 1980). Another more detailed source is the single-volume *Handbook of Cross-Cultural Human Development*, produced by a team of anthropologists and psychologists (Munroe, Munroe & Whiting, 1981), which repeatedly demonstrates that the laws governing human development are most likely to be discovered through systematic testing of hypotheses both within and across cultures.

Readers will note that the information contained herein comes primarily from professional publications, books, monographs, and, most often, scholarly journals. The latter appear periodically; thus the science of cross-cultural psychology is ever expanding. Even as this book is being written, it becomes out of date, in the sense that every empirically oriented text cannot contain findings published after going to press itself. So, the serious student should consult recent issues of these journals. The journals that are central to the field include *Journal of Cross-Cultural Psychology*, *International Journal of Psychology*, *International Journal of Intercultural Relations*, *Ethos*, and *Behavioral Science Review*. A main-stream psychology journal that encourages the publication of cross-cultural research is *Journal of Social Psychology*, and increasingly, cross-cultural studies can be found in other main-stream journals as well. And, with the publication of a book edited by Bond (1988), mainstream psychology may increasingly be responsive to research that emphasizes cultural factors.

Knowing, then, that there is much more to cross-cultural psychology than can be covered in this introductory text, let us begin to learn about this rewarding approach to the study of human behavior. In the next chapter we will learn why this global approach, albeit late in coming, has attracted so much attention in recent years.

---

[4]Cross-cultural researchers have shown that both "normal" and "abnormal" behaviors are differently perceived, defined, explained, and treated in different societies. At the same time, despite such differences, there are some provocative similarities, particularly with respect to features of psychotherapy, whether provided by traditional healers or Western-trained psychiatrists. See Triandis and Draguns (1980) for a thorough treatment of psychopathology in cross-cultural perspective.

Chapter 2

The Global Perspective in Psychology: A Brief History

THE NEED FOR A GLOBAL PERSPECTIVE

For too long, the study of human psychology was dominated by Western (and primarily U.S.) psychologists. As noted by Berry, Irvine, and Hunt (1988), "The vast majority of psychological research and practice has been developed and now takes place in the industrialized world; this includes primarily Europe and North America but also those other parts of the world settled from, or influenced by, these societies. Usually excluded are the vast populations of Africa and Asia, as well as those in Oceania and South America" (p. 1). Although psychology is part of the curriculum in universities all over the world, for most of its century-long history, the majority of teachers and students of psychology resided in universities in the United States and Europe. Most research on human behavior was done in the United States, and most of the publications, journal articles, and books that report this research were produced there. Even as psychology spread to "Third-World" countries, such as India, where its history has been richly described by Sinha (1986), the research done there tended to be replications of experiments originally performed in Western laboratories to test Western theories.

This is a matter of serious concern. The concern stems not from the fact of U.S. or Western domination per se; it would be as serious if any other nation or region of the world enjoyed a similar near monopoly. The problem is the culture-bound nature of the discipline. There is a very real danger that psychologists, by limiting their attention to the behaviors of individuals in a single society (however complex that society might be), may lose sight altogether of culture itself. The scientist, no less than the most unsophisticated layperson who knows only his or her own society, becomes prey to ethnocentric judgments. Behaviors that may in fact be heavily influenced by cultural forces may appear to the culture-bound psychologist to be manifestations of "human nature."

A Dream Exercise

Imagine that you are a clinical psychologist whose professional role is to help people who are troubled by their own behavior. Into your office comes a 12-year-old boy, who, at your request, relates a dream he recalls as profoundly disturbing. In it, he and his father were traveling together on a bus toward the science and technology museum, where both the boy and his father anticipated wandering through the exhibits of machinery. Suddenly, the bus swerved on the wet pavement and crashed headlong into a tractor-trailer. Amid grinding metal and shattering glass, the passengers were helplessly tossed about into the flesh-tearing projections of the wreckage. As the twisted hulk came finally to rest, the boy, miraculously unharmed, searched about frantically for his father. Groping his way over mangled bodies, the boy finally came upon his father's body, sprawled and bloodied, his legs crushed, his eyes staring at the boy in a piercing, accusing gaze of death.

His dream told, the boy breaks into sobs and tells you how painful it is even to talk about the dream, how saddening it is to contemplate the loss of his beloved father.

Freud's Interpretation

What can be made of all this? Sigmund Freud pursued an interesting path of interpretation when, in late 19th-century Vienna, he treated psychologically disturbed, upper-middle-class patients. His interpretation is paraphrased in Box 2-1.

As Box 2-1 reveals in some detail, Freud reasoned that the boy's dream is best understood as an expression of his unresolved Oedipus complex. The dream is understandable as a revelation of the dreamer's suppressed hatred for his simultaneously beloved father, with the hatred based on sexual jealousy of the father as mother's lover.

Freud's explanation seems plausible and persuasive. There are only a few assumptions in the argument, and it does hold together well. Certainly, several generations of psychologists and other intelligent and educated persons have found Freud's line of argument very acceptable. Some people are so profoundly persuaded by it that they even speak of Freud's *discovery* of the Oedipus complex, rather than describing it as an *invention*, which of course it is.

By calling the Oedipus complex a discovery, one implies that it was there

Box 2-1 Freud's Interpretation of Filial Ambivalence

Confronted with a dream report similar to the one in which an adolescent boy told of terrible things happening to his beloved father, Freud would probably have reasoned roughly as follows:

1. A dream is a wish-fulfilling mechanism. We all have wishes and desires that are difficult to confront openly. We suppress them, forcing them to reside in our unconscious. But they reveal themselves to us in indirect ways, including dreams, since our defenses are relaxed when we are asleep.
2. If the boy's dream revealed a subconscious wish, that wish must have been for his father to be obliterated, since the father's death was the critical incident in the dream and the source of greatest discomfort to the boy as he related the dream.
3. In the dream, or at least in its telling, there were numerous reminders that the boy loved his father. This suggests that the boy felt a strong need to assert that love, either because he actually loved his father less than he thought he should or hated him while simultaneously loving him. Since it was the boy's own dream in which this terrible thing happened to his beloved father, the boy must feel ambivalent toward him, loving and hating him at the same time.
4. A boy's love for his father probably needs no ingenious effort at explanation. On the other hand, why the boy might feel hostile toward his father is a harder question. It must have something to do with the boy's perception of his father's behavior. But what? Boys' fathers in late 19th-century Viennese upper-middle-class society did many things. As a sociologist or social psychologist might say, boys' fathers in that setting performed many different roles. One role that might be particularly salient to young boys, thought Freud, is the father's role as lover of the boy's mother. A big jump in the argument? Perhaps, but not altogether unreasonable. After all, . . .
5. Boys tend to feel strong and diffuse sexual urges as they approach manhood. As a result, they might well be exceedingly concerned with sexual matters. The boy's father is a significant male model who clearly has adult prerogatives, including—and especially—sexual ones. The boy might well, therefore, emulate his father and wish to be in his shoes, even in his bed. But . . .
6. The sex object in his father's bed is the boy's own mother! She is, properly, the sexual partner of the father, not of the boy. The boy seems to desire his own mother as a sex object. (After all, she was the first and most significant female in his life and was, from the start, warm, loving, and nurturant.) His desire for her necessarily leads to the felt need to be rid of his father, in order that the father be displaced by the boy as mother's lover. Besides . . .
7. Western literature contains stories like the powerful play about Oedipus, who killed his father and married his mother. That such stories are retold and reacted to by generation after generation of audiences suggests that the mother-son-father triangle constitutes a timeless and universal set of feelings, such that . . .
8. All males probably go through a psychosexual development that involves falling in love with their mother and developing jealousy toward their father, with the emergence of a hostile wish to destroy and displace him. This developmental process might appropriately be labeled, given the well-known Greek play, the Oedipus complex.

for Freud to stumble onto. It should, however, be clear to you that Freud created the Oedipus complex as an explanatory concept. The problem we must now deal with is why Freud invented the concept he did.

Might Freud not have come up with a different explanation because he did the psychologizing solely within the confines of a single cultural setting? Did it matter that the data he considered were limited to individuals and events characteristic of 19th-century Viennese society? Let's see how that might very well be so.

A Different Dreamer

What would you say if you were now confronted with an adolescent boy who reported a dream in which his uncle, with whom he was hunting, stumbled on his spear and was disemboweled? Does the theory that Freud developed fit such a dream? Or does this dream force you to search for an alternative theory that would fit both dreams and that would account for hostility toward a father in one case and hostility toward an uncle in the other?

Malinowski's Contribution

One such theory can be derived from some interesting observations that were part of an eminent anthropologist's fieldwork in the 1920s. Malinowski (1927) had read Freud's interpretation of male adolescents' ambivalence toward their fathers. Armed with that knowledge, Malinowski observed adolescent boys in the Trobriand Islands in Papua New Guinea, where disciplining of boys is the responsibility of the boys' maternal uncles (mothers' brothers). (This is a cultural feature of societies known to anthropology as avuncular, so-called because of the importance of uncles in the kinship and socialization systems.) In the Trobriand Islands, Malinowski would have expected no instance of nightmares in which fathers suffered but rather ones in which misfortunes befell uncles. The second dream could well have been dreamed by a Trobriand Island boy, according to Malinowski's view of the concerns such boys would have. You must have noted that the second dream was similar to the first one, except that in the Trobriand-like dream the accident victim is the dreamer's uncle. What can be made of this second dream? One could go through the first three steps of the original Freudian argument without a hitch. Thus, it could be argued that (1) the dream reveals a suppressed wish (2) to be rid of the uncle, so (3) the boy must feel hostile toward his uncle. But then one would have to wonder why a boy might feel hostile toward his uncle. Not being the boy's mother's lover, the uncle could not possibly be the object of the boy's sexual jealousy. So one would here have to depart from the earlier theory.

The clue may be found in the fact that the Trobriand Island society is an avuncular society (note that this word has the same root as uncle), a society in which boys' fathers are mothers' lovers but boys' uncles are the boys' disciplinarians. Could it be that adolescent boys anywhere wish terrible things would happen to their *disciplinarians*, who are fathers in many societies and uncles in fewer?

The revised argument would then be that both dreamers were reacting to whoever plays the adult male role of disciplinarian. We would end up with an efficient, four-step argument (compared with the much longer original one) that fits the dreams from both societies. Our new theory, in summary, would be that (1) the dreams reveal a suppressed desire (2) to be rid of a powerful, male, adult figure (3) toward whom the dreamer feels hostile, (4) because the male adult has the power to enforce his will on the dreamer, to administer sanctions, and otherwise to control his behavior.

This revised theory, which is very parsimonious (a characteristic of a theory that handles multiple facts and makes few assumptions), accounts for both dreams. It fits two sets of facts, two different dream reports that originated in two different cultures.

The Underlying Principle

This brings us to the essential point of the exercise, which is a principle about the strategy of research, not a substantive point about the meaning of dreams. In other words, we are not primarily interested here in learning how to understand dreams. We are interested in the process by which psychologists try to comprehend the meaning of any behavior, including dream reports.

To illuminate that process and uncover the principle about research strategy that we are seeking, let us consider what Freud did when he invented the Oedipus complex. Recall that the critical problem for Freud was to explain a Viennese boy's hostility toward his father. In seeking an explanation for that, Freud focused on the fact that (most) boys' fathers were (often) the boys' mothers' lovers. But it was also true that in that same setting, as well as in some others, fathers were their sons' disciplinarians. (Indeed, there is some reason to speculate that Viennese fathers tended to be more diligent in the role of disciplinarian than in that of mother's lover.) In any event, for our present purposes the essential fact is that, in Vienna, both roles were performed by the same person, the boy's father. A technical way of stating this fact is to say that the two roles were confounded, or inextricably linked.

Freud chose to ignore one of these confounded roles—that of disciplinarian—and he chose to focus on the other—that of mother's lover. Had Freud chosen instead to focus on the disciplinary role of the father, he probably would have come up with our second explanation of adolescents' suppressed hostility. But even if he had, ambiguity would still have prevailed. Let us see why.

Suppose Freud had suggested that adolescent boys hate their fathers because their fathers punish them. Couldn't we then have challenged Freud and said, for example, "Now, wait a minute. You've overlooked the far more interesting possibility that fathers, because of their sexual relationship to their wives, are the objects of their sons' sexual jealousy"?

Of course we could have said that, but we still would have been missing the most critical point. As long as we had available only the Viennese dream reports, collected in a single culture in which the two roles were confounded, there would really be no empirical (grounded-in-fact) way of choosing between the two explanations.

The Unconfounding Function. The importance of data like Malinowski's, then, is that they permit an "unconfounding" of what was confounded in the single-culture data. In the Trobriand Islands the two roles that compete for our attention are performed by two different persons, either of whom could be the leading figure in a nightmare. So, if Trobriand boys have nightmares about their fathers, we would have good reason to retain the sexual jealousy theory. But if Trobriand boys have nightmares about their uncles, the sexual jealousy theory is challenged; technically, it is no longer tenable. Likewise, the tenability of the resentment-of-discipline theory is strengthened. The value of having the Trobriand Island data lies in their permitting us to choose between the two competing explanations. It is a choice neither we nor Freud could have made on the basis of the Viennese data alone.

You should understand that the point of all this was not to criticize Freud for having made the wrong choice. We are not, in fact, sure that he did. Rather, it was to show how he lacked the necessary data even to make a choice. Even if Freud happened to make the right choice, as many people continue to believe, or the wrong one, as the preceding exercise implied, Freud asserted a putative universal on the basis of culture-specific data.

The principle that you should now have grasped is that it is sometimes necessary to collect data in more than one culture in order to disentangle certain facts that are intertwined in a single culture. We may label this principle the unconfounding function of cross-cultural data. Because some events that might be influencing the behavior we seek to explain co-vary in a particular society, we have to collect data in other societies in order to separate those events and thereby determine which of them matter.

The exercise you have just performed and the principle that has been derived from it are based on the teachings of the psychological methodologist, Donald T. Campbell (1961). In Box 2-2 you may read his argument, as revised in 1972 with Raoul Naroll, an anthropological methodologist.

Oedipus Revisited

This argument by Campbell and Naroll is put in doubt by Spiro's statement that Malinowski's reports of dreams of uncles' deaths contained no data on frequencies of occurrence (Spiro, 1982, p. 29) and were probably very rare. Spiro (1982) added new fuel to this long-simmering controversy by

---

Box 2-2 Dad: Mother's Lover or Boy's Disciplinarian?

Freud validly observed that boys in late Habsburgian Vienna had hostile feelings toward their fathers. Two possible explanations offered themselves—the hostility could be due to the father's role as the disciplinarian, or to the father's role of the mother's lover. . . . Freud chose to emphasize the role of the mother's lover. However, working only with his patient population there was no adequate basis for making the choice. The two rival explanations were experimentally confounded, for among the parents of Freud's patients the disciplinarian of little boys was usually the mother's lover. (Remember that in Freud's day it was the morality of one's parents more often than their immorality that drove one to choose the analyst's couch over other couches, so that Freud got a biased sample.) Malinowski (1927) studied a society in which these two parental roles were experimentally disentangled, in which the disciplinarian of young boys and the mother's lover were not one-and-the-same person. And in this society, the boys' hostility was addressed to the disciplinarian, not to the mother's lover. (Campbell & Naroll, 1972)*

---

*From "The Mutual Methodological Relevance of Anthropology and Psychology" by D. T. Campbell and R. Naroll. In F. L. K. Hsu (Ed.), *Psychological Anthropology* (rev. ed.) (p. 437), Cambridge, MA: Schenkman. Copyright 1972 by Schenkman Publishing Co.

reanalyzing Malinowski's data, forcing us to ask once again whether the Oedipus complex is universal as Freud alleged, or culturally specific.

Spiro's conclusions were that love for the mother and hatred of the father were, contrary to Malinowski's assertions, stronger in the Trobriand Islands than in the West. Spiro argued that many of the data employed by Malinowski to argue against an Oedipus complex in the Trobriands were not relevant to it (this because Malinowski misunderstood the Oedipus complex) and that the data he offered as evidence for an alternative complex were meager and subject to a contrary interpretation.

Also relevant is Spiro's argument, based on Malinowski's own claim that brother-sister incestuous feelings prevailed in the Trobriands, that a mother's brother would be perceived by her son as a rival for her affection, so that even if the uncle were a target of hostility, that would be Oedipus-like in its underlying dynamics. Finally, Spiro also presented evidence that the father was actually "the prime target of the boy's hostility in the Trobriands" (Spiro, 1982, p. 145).[1]

---

[1] The cross-cultural study of the Oedipus complex has inspired much discussion. For further reading, see, for example, Ortigues and Ortigues (1966) and Kline (1977). A good summary and discussion is provided by Erny (1981).

Whereas Campbell and Naroll (and we) stressed the possibility that adolescent hostility toward relevant adult males is grounded in resentment of authority rather than sexual jealousy, Spiro properly argued that both motives can operate together. But he confidently asserted that the latter exists everywhere, since "it is the biological mother who is the child's central (if not exclusive) early mothering figure, and the biological father his most salient rival for her love in all known societies" (Spiro, 1982, p. 174).

Spiro's argument is scholarly and compelling and forces us to reemphasize that Malinowski's comparison of Vienna and the Trobriands was not enough to constitute a definitive test of competing theories. As early as 1961, as we see in Box 2-3, Campbell warned that such a comparison could not reveal the process underlying male adolescent hostility.

Nevertheless, the methodological point made by Campbell and Naroll — namely, that hypotheses generated in a single culture need to be tested cross-culturally, with such tests potentially providing an unconfounding of relevant variables — remains valid.

It should be clear that we are not saying that research done in only one society necessarily results in errors of explanation. Generalizations derived from any single case may, of course, hold true for all cases. But, given the cultural complexities of human life and the importance of culture as a behavioral determinant, it obviously behooves psychologists to test the cross-cultural generality of their principles before considering them established. It is obvious, then, that the scientific study of human behavior requires that we employ a cross-cultural perspective.

Box 2-3 Too Many Rival Explanations

Between Trobriand and Vienna there are many dimensions of differences that could constitute potential rival explanations and that we have no means of ruling out. For comparisons of this pair, the ceteris paribus (other things being equal) requirement becomes untenable. But data collection need not stop here. Both the avunculate and the European arrangement are so widely distributed over the world that if testing Oedipal theories were our purpose, we could select a dozen matched pairs of tribes from widely varying culture areas, each pair differing with regard to which male educates and disciplines the boy, but as similar as possible in other respects. Assuming that collections of dreams from boys showed the expected differences between each pair, then the more such pairs we had, the fewer tenable rival hypotheses would be available and, thus, the more certain would be our confirmation (Campbell, 1961, pp. 344–345).

Internationalizing Psychology

This requirement has become even more pressing as psychology, both as a scientific discipline and as a helping profession, spreads into other societies, many of which face serious problems of social and economic development to which it may be tempting to apply psychological theories, concepts, and measuring instruments. A special issue of the *International Journal of Psychology* (Sinha & Holtzman, 1984) was devoted to a discussion of the potentially damaging impact of Western psychology in China (Ching, 1984), Turkey (Kagitcibasi, 1984), the Philippines (Lagmay, 1984), several Arab nations (Melikian, 1984), Venezuela (Salazar, 1984), and Africa (Serpell, 1984). In all these settings, according to these writers (all psychologists who live and work in them), social science and its applications need to be relevant to particular national interests, and it is doubtful that Western psychology is well suited to address them.

The possible inappropriatenesss of Western psychology is particularly apparent when one considers its most common form of application, clinical psychology, which is grounded primarily in the famous work of Freud, who, as we have seen, was not very sensitive to cultural concerns. Aside from the errors that plague its underlying theories, there exist some culturally related values that may make its practice less effective outside the United States and Europe than within.

For example, viewed from the perspective of Eastern (Hong Kong Chinese) culture, clinical psychology is seen by Ho (1985) as rooted in ideological biases that reflect Western individualism. The writer, a clinical psychologist and trainer of clinical psychologists in the University of Hong Kong, has explored values that prevail both in the East and the West and considered their implications for mental health and clinical psychology in both settings. As regards the West, Ho noted that the individualism that is expressed in the Judeo-Christian tradition "affirms the uniqueness, autonomy, freedom, and intrinsic worth of the individual" (1985, p. 1215) but that consequently Westerners tend to view those persons who fail to achieve self-reliance with contempt and rejection. "If salvation is a matter of individual responsibility, then it is up to the individual to make the efforts necessary for change" (1985, p. 1216). The individual per se is the object of the treatment, not the individual in the community. Hence, Ho argued, the community mental health movement in the West has been impeded while private practice thrives.

By contrast, in the East, collectivism, which encourages enhancement of the well-being of the group, leads to various kinds of support systems that may be mobilized to help people who are in difficulty. But since so many clinical psychologists in the East have been, according to Ho, "captivated by the values of Western individualism" (1985, p. 1217), there has been little use of these support systems by professionally trained clinical psychologists.

Ho's cross-cultural perspective allowed him to recognize that clinical psychology is not merely an abstract body of knowledge and techniques but a historiocultural phenomenon. His analysis also uncovered the promising notion that awareness of the different social contexts in which clinicians work could lead them to reconceptualize their practices, exploiting diverse values (such as Eastern collectivism and Western individualism) in creative ways, thereby improving the practice of clinical psychology both in the East and West.

Ho clearly believes that there is a need for this kind of examination of clinical psychology in the United States, "a society that has more clinical psychologists (and other mental health professionals) than the rest of the world combined . . . [but] . . . appears to be nowhere close to solving its mental health problems" (1985, p. 1215). As regards other settings, Ho would have mental health professionals make serious efforts to preserve those social institutions rooted in the culture that contribute to genuine healing and not merely "rely on the artificiality of creating new ones" (Ho, 1985, p. 1217).

We have seen several reasons why psychology, both as a science and as a profession, needs to be internationalized. If we turn now to the history of psychology, we will discover that this need was unrecognized by many psychologists for a long time.

CROSS-CULTURAL CONCERNS IN THE HISTORY OF WESTERN PSYCHOLOGY

Herman Ebbinghaus, one of the founders of experimental psychology, was quoted by Boring in his classic *A History of Experimental Psychology* (1929) as having said that "psychology has a long past, but only a short history" (p. vii). Cross-cultural psychology has as long a past, but an even shorter history.

From classical Greek scholars onward, philosophers, political theorists, novelists, playwrights, and poets treated topics that in one form or another are today part of the scientific study of human behavior. Still, the discipline of anthropology didn't begin until the end of the 19th century, and a formal psychology concerned with social influences on human development started even later, about 1910. And it wasn't until the 1960s that cross-cultural psychology, as a discipline, was born. Psychology included little concern for culture until quite recently. To understand why, we must trace psychology's prehistory, its 19th-century roots in Europe, and its rapid growth as a predominantly laboratory science in North America during the first half of the 20th century. And we must note some relevant developments in sociology and anthropology, since these disciplines contribute significantly to cross-cultural psychology.

The Prehistory of Psychology

Humanity, society, culture, and their evolution were all subjects of interest before any of the disciplines of psychology, sociology, or anthropology were founded. In Europe in the 18th century, there was much concern with social development from "savagery" to "civilization," that could be studied, according to the intellectuals of the day, by examining "primitive" peoples. As the 19th century was about to dawn, French scholars (including philosophers, naturalists, and even physicians concerned with mental illness) founded the Société des Observateurs de l'Homme. This and comparable scholarly organizations attended to, and had influence on, expeditions launched from Europe to pursue not only commercial and political goals but "scientific" ones as well. One expedition to Tasmania early in the 19th century included measuring physical strength in a sample of 85 "natives" by one of the explorers, inspired to do so by a French philosopher, Degerando, a founder of the Société. According to Jahoda, this was "probably the first cross-cultural study employing psychological instrumentation" (1982, p. 11). But, as we are about to see, a long time was to pass before psychology became cross-cultural again. While some developments in Europe during the 19th century pointed toward a culturally concerned psychology, others led away.

19th-Century European Developments

German Roots

If the scientific study of social influences on human behavioral development is a 20th-century phenomenon, its roots lie in the 19th century. These roots were nourished mostly in Germany, largely because of the intellectual atmosphere generated there by such works as J. F. Herbart's influential *Lehrbuch zur Psychologie* (1816). Herbart's ideas reveal that a concern for culture as a behavioral determinant was present in psychology from its beginning. He argued that psychology must free itself from metaphysics and embrace the methods of science. If it is to explain our mental life, it must recognize the importance of experience. Further, psychology must recognize that experience is shaped by the temper of the Volksgeist, which can be revealed to the psychologist only through ethnography, the systematic description of ethnic groups. In ethnographic work will be found the forces that shape human psychology.

Herbart's call was answered by the launching in 1860 of a scholarly journal, *Zeitschrift fur Volkerpsychologie und Sprachwissenschaft*, which was devoted to the study of "national psychology" with an emphasis on language and other customs and institutions. In spite of residual mysticism, metaphysics, and even racism in the works of most 19th-century students of human behavior, there were some anthropologists in Germany calling for empirical research on the "mentality of primitive peoples." Whatever the reasons for their interest in this topic, it gave impetus to the development of a cross-cultural psychology.

Even Wundt, who in 1879 had founded the first psychology laboratory, displayed an active and incredibly productive interest in cross-cultural research. Best known for his experimental analyses of sensation and perception, Wundt was also the author of the ten-volume *Volkerpsychologie* (1900–1920). In that work he discussed topics such as language, myth, and custom. It is perhaps ironic that Wundt, known as the father of experimental psychology, launched his ambitious folk-psychology project after becoming convinced, according to Jahoda (1982), that the study of individual consciousness in the laboratory had very definite limitations. In fact, as early as 1862, Wundt made his first published plea that psychology attend to the social influences on human behavior as described by anthropology. This initial call for a *Volkerpsychologie*, according to Murray (1983), appeared in Wundt's *Beitrage*, the introduction to which appears in English in Shipley (1961). It is also noteworthy that Malinowski, the anthropologist whose work in the Trobriands on adolescent hostility was reviewed above, was a postgraduate student of Wundt.[2]

French Offshoots

At about the same time, in France, there were other developments that influenced psychology, but these did not emphasize cultural forces. That culture was not a major concern of the 19th-century French sociologists may go a long way toward explaining why most American and American-influenced psychologists during the first half of the 20th century paid scant attention to cultural variables.

French developments depended largely on interest in the phenomenon of suggestion, the object of much research in French medical circles during the 19th century. This research served as a stimulus for early 20th-century social psychological research, concerned as it was with the behavior of some persons as a stimulus for the behavior of others. Its medical implications, particularly with regard to hypnotism as a therapeutic technique, were enormous. Among those young physicians influenced by this medicopsychological research was Freud. And later, Freudian theory, allegedly a universally applicable model of human development, influenced many psychologists over several generations. It also had an impact on French social theorists

---

[2]An interesting survey of recent psychological research by German-speaking psychologists who attend to cultural variables has been provided by Trommsdorff (1987).

such as Le Bon (1896) and Tarde (1903), whose emphasis on irrational imitation and crowd behavior led the first few generations of social psychologists to study social influence processes such as conformity and attitude change, processes that seemed most amenable to study in laboratory settings. Thus, one of the indirect influences of French social science was to send social psychologists into the laboratory, from which few were to emerge.

If the trend deriving from German folk psychology emphasized intercultural differences, the trend deriving from French sociology emphasized intracultural similarities. Together, these two trends could have added up to a cross-cultural psychology. With few exceptions, however, psychology during the first half of the 20th century followed the French lead. Many of Tarde's ideas were repeated rather uncritically by Ross in his social psychology textbook (1908), and several generations of sociologists perpetuated them.

Another influence stemmed from Emile Durkheim (1897), who, although conversant with other cultures, was mostly concerned with the influence of forces within a society and their deleterious effects on individual behavior—for example, suicide. So, social and developmental psychology in their early years focused mostly on intracultural studies, leaving the study of culture to the anthropologists. But some late 19th-century intellectual developments in Britain were to keep alive the notion that anthropology and psychology needed each other.[3]

Early Cross-Cultural Concerns in Britain

As in Germany, the psychology of "primitive" peoples was a concern in Britain. As early as 1879, John Stuart Mill proposed a science of "ethnology" that would study both the individual mind and the relationship between the individual and his or her environment. Also in Britain, toward the end of the 19th century, Tyler studied social institutions in a comparative way, thus laying the groundwork for anthropology. Tyler also provided one of the first definitions of the concept of culture: "That complex whole which includes knowledge, belief, art, morals, law, custom, and any other capabilities and habits acquired by man as a member of society" (Tyler, 1871/1958). But Mill's and Tyler's influence was mainly on anthropology.

At the turn of the century, several British psychologists and anthropologists together launched programs of research in which some of the best quantitative techniques of the new experimental psychology were applied in studies of non-Western peoples. A classic example is the Cambridge Expedition to the Torres Straits (between Australia and Papua New Guinea), which included research by Rivers on sensation and perception in the Pacific

---

[3]See Mauviel (1984) for more details on French intellectual traditions; those pertaining to human competence are summarized in Chapter 4 of this book.

(1901), a topic he pursued later in India (Rivers, 1905). We will return to this work in Chapter 6.

Early 20th-Century Trends in the United States

Sociology

In the United States near the turn of the century, interest in cross-cultural psychology was exemplified best in the work of William Graham Sumner, a sociologist at Yale University. Perhaps his most significant contribution was to go beyond the German concept of *Volksgeist*, which was based on the assumption that the characteristic traits of a people are biologically transmitted. Sumner (1906) argued that folkways are habits of the individual and customs of the society that arise from efforts to satisfy needs. They become regulative for succeeding generations and take on the character of a social force. We will deal with some of Sumner's ideas in Chapter 14.

Anthropology

Another major development in the United States in the early years of the 20th century was the introduction into anthropology by Boas of psychological concerns that were picked up by many of his students, including Kroeber, Benedict, and Mead, all of whom contributed to the culture and personality approach, about which more will be said later. But few psychologists attended to this work and hardly ever without criticism.

Psychology

During the first half of the 20th century, psychology developed both as a social science and a behavioral science. Because that development occurred mostly in U.S. universities, its distinguishing features reflected the dominant values of science in the United States: empiricism, quantification, and wherever possible, experimentation. To uphold these values, it was obviously necessary for social and developmental psychologists to focus on problems that could be treated rigorously, and this meant in practice dealing with relatively molecular issues. The social psychologists, influenced, as we have seen, by French ideas concerning social influence processes, worked mostly on problems amenable to controlled experimentation.

The products of their efforts were extremely valuable ones. Among them were numerous important advances in methodology, such as techniques for the precise measurement of individual attitudes. Research also yielded knowledge about some very basic social processes, such as how attitudes are affected by the expressed judgments of others. Moving beyond the laboratory, some described how child-rearing practices shape human development. These rigorous psychologists achieved numerous theoretical insights, some contributed by sociologists, such as the concepts of status, role, and reference group. All of these developments greatly enhanced our understanding of human behavior. In the pursuit of these values, however, the majority of psychologists looked only inside their own society. Only a few displayed an active interest in culture.

One important research center that did was the Institute of Human Relations at Yale University. There, during the 1930s and 1940s, an interdisciplinary group of anthropologists, sociologists, and psychologists concerned themselves with the study of human behavior in the broadest of terms. At the same time, the Yale group maintained a standard of scientific rigor that was unsurpassed anywhere. The dominant theoretical emphasis at Yale during those exciting years was a neobehavioristic learning theory, empirically grounded in laboratory experimentation and mathematically sophisticated. This theory was exemplified by the work of Hull (1943), the most famous learning theorist of his time. The major goal of the Yale group was to apply this rigorous stimulus/response learning theory to the study of complex social behavior. While they looked to the psychologist for principles of how an organism interacts with its environment, they looked to the anthropologist for information about the nature of that environment. Only by integrating the two could the social scientist explain human behavior. This was their faith, and their research mirrored it.

A most significant development at Yale during this period was the establishment of the Human Relations Area Files, a compilation of ethnographic reports arranged in such a manner that quantitative, cross-cultural testing of hypotheses became a real possibility. This kind of research has come to be called "hologeistic." Hologeistic research involves macrolevel studies of large samples of societies in an effort to search for general laws that apply to all of humankind. A classic example of such work was the study by Whiting and Child (1953) of child-rearing practices in many different societies and their concomitant effects on adult personality. A thorough account of their study may be found in Berry et al. (in press).

The concern for relations between culture and personality, as exemplified by Whiting and Child's work and that of others at Yale in the 1940s, was also shown by a few other groups, composed mostly of anthropologists and psychologists, many of whom found inspiration at first in the theoretical contributions of Freud and later in the more behavioristic psychology of the Yale variety. Anthropologists who participated in this movement included Malinowski, Mead, Benedict, Sapir, Du Bois, Kardiner, Linton, and Kluckhohn.

Textbooks in social or developmental psychology that stressed cultural determinants were rare during the first half of the century. And with very few exceptions, they were produced by social scientists who were not primarily identified as psychologists. A most important textbook, which appeared toward the end of this period, was by Kluckhohn and Murray (1953). It was built around a simple premise: "Every man is in certain respects like all other men, like some other men, like no other man" (p. 53). With these words Kluckhohn and Murray expressed the need for a multidisciplinary approach to the study of human behavior that would encompass anthropology, sociology, and psychology.

One of the few textbooks by a psychologist to stress anthropological content was that of Klineberg (1940). His text summarized well what little was known at the time about human behavior in diverse cultural settings and viewed even that knowledge with a healthy skepticism. Klineberg's examples drawn from ethnography underlined the diversity of human behavior patterns and forced the student to question the validity of existing principles of behavior that purported to be universal. Perhaps the book's most important contribution was its challenge to prevalent ideas of biological determinism, particularly those of a racist variety.

These, then, were the major efforts that can be described as cross-cultural psychology during that half century of rapid growth in psychology. We have tried to make clear that a cross-cultural emphasis was *not* the dominant trend of this period. At the same time there were those who obviously believed that a human psychology that ignored culture and an anthropology that ignored individual behavior were both incomplete.

CURRENT DEVELOPMENTS IN CROSS-CULTURAL PSYCHOLOGY

In the decades following World War II, cross-cultural psychology grew, much as an adolescent grows, in spurts. By the 1980s, cross-cultural psychology had come of age.

The postwar decades were marked by the decline of colonialism, the birth of many new nations, and competition between political and social ideologies for the attention of the populations of the less developed new nations. As a consequence, opportunities became available for psychologists in unprecedented numbers to break loose from their laboratories and board jet planes headed for (sometimes literally) greener pastures. Also contributing to the rapid growth of cross-cultural research were enhanced funding for psychological research, by public and private agencies alike, and the growing numbers of young psychologists with foreign experience as military personnel, Peace Corps volunteers, or exchange students. Faster means of transportation were also a factor.

Once a rather exotic subspeciality, cross-cultural psychology became an established, thriving intellectual enterprise peopled by hundreds of scholars from many parts of the world. Some of the many theories and facts generated by cross-cultural psychologists during the remarkably prolific era of the

1960s and 1970s were compiled and organized by a team of scholars and made available in a six-volume work entitled *Handbook of Cross-Cultural Psychology* (Triandis et al., 1980). It is a landmark in the young history of the field. Its coverage is encyclopedic; whole volumes cover methodology, basic psychological processes, developmental psychology, social psychology, and psychopathology and, taken as a whole, this handbook shows the field of cross-cultural psychology to be rich in questions worth asking, in efforts to devise workable ways of answering them, and in motivation to extract understanding from a dazzling array of facts about an awesome variety of human behaviors.

Another scholarly team composed of anthropologists and psychologists (Munroe, Munroe & Whiting, 1981) produced *The Handbook of Cross-Cultural Human Development*, which reviews the burgeoning literature on cultural differences in child development. Twenty-six chapters contained in a single volume provide impressive evidence that there are indeed scientific laws governing human development and that it is through systematic testing of hypotheses within and across cultures that these laws are most likely to be discovered.

As these two handbooks make apparent, it is no longer necessary to preach the need for a global perspective in psychology. Psychologists in various cultures are now aware of the discipline's culture-boundedness and the inappropriateness of many psychological theories and findings when applied to particular societies. See, for example, Moscovici (1972), Faucheux (1976), and especially Berry (1983), who warned that some of the content of psychology produced in the United States is "so culture-bound and so culture-blind that it should not be employed . . . in cultures outside the United States, not even in Canada." Happily, however, more and more psychological research is being done cross-culturally, as we shall see in chapters to come. Our present problem is not how to encourage its doing but ensuring that it is done well. That is the issue to which we will turn in the next chapter. Before we do, however, let us recall the ecocultural framework introduced in Chapter 1.

The Heuristic Value
of the Ecocultural Framework

Figure 1-1 provided a comprehensive framework for the research designs of cross-cultural psychology. The framework suggests the kinds of connections our research ought to seek.

An adaptive class of variables that could be singled out for research is cultural transmission, which includes, of course, enculturation and socialization, the techniques by which the older generation conveys its norms and standards to the young. Embedding the concept of socialization in the ecocultural model reminds us to expect certain relationships among, say, population density, socialization practices, and individual personality. The framework suggests that socialization practices tend to be designed to produce those behaviors that are maximally adaptive, that lead to enhanced survival under whatever ecological conditions prevail.

The basic feature of this heuristic device—this framework that suggests relationships to be sought and tested—is its stress on Darwinian functionality. It assumes that human behavior is ultimately adaptive, that people tend to behave in ways that enhance their survival. In each ecological setting, behaviors evolve that produce institutions, life-styles, and shared beliefs and values that in turn influence the way children are reared. These socialization methods produce succeeding generations who behave in more or less adaptive ways.

As a heuristic device this framework can lead cross-cultural psychologists to search for connections between specific ecological variables and specific cultural variables. Or we might seek out relationships involving other combinations of ecological, adaptive, and individual-development variables.

Here is a concrete example. Research might be designed to test the hypothesis that variations in family structure (nuclear family versus extended family, for example) relate to the degree of food accumulation (see Nimkoff & Middleton, 1960). As it turns out, nuclear families (husband, wife, and their children) tend to be found more often both in nomadic hunting-gathering and in industrial societies, whereas extended families tend to be found in sedentary, agricultural societies.

Or, research might focus on ecology and socialization techniques (see, for example, Barry, Child & Bacon, 1959). As we shall see in considerable detail later in this book, economic systems are related to the degree to which populations stress obedience and compliance among their children. Or, differences in perceptual processes across different cultures might be suggested on the basis of certain natural and human features of the environment in which people happen to be raised (see, for example, Segall, Campbell & Herskovits, 1966, which is discussed in detail in Chapter 4). Or, cognitive style (the manner in which persons characteristically approach analytic problems) might be predicted to vary either with socialization practices or with degrees of food accumulation or both (Witkin & Berry, 1975), discussed in detail in Berry et al. (in press).

Any study, then, that collects individual behavioral data and seeks to relate it to ecological and sociocultural variables is a study in cross-cultural psychology that can be incorporated into the ecocultural framework. All such studies, assuming that they are well done, tell us something about the way in which nature, culture, and behavior interrelate.

Actually doing research that relates behavior confidently to ecological and sociocultural variables is harder than saying one ought to or will do it. The methodological problems inherent in cross-cultural psychological research are formidable ones. It is to some of these problems that we turn in the next chapter.

Chapter 3

How Cross-Cultural Psychology Is Done

In the preceding chapter we saw how a global perspective entered psychology somewhat belatedly. In this chapter we will survey the kinds of questions addressed in cross-cultural research. Then we will consider some of the difficulties of doing behavioral research cross-culturally and, finally, some solutions to them.

CROSS-CULTURAL PSYCHOLOGY'S SCOPE: QUESTIONS IT ASKS

Cross-cultural psychologists try to determine how sociocultural variables influence human behavior. To do so, they sometimes focus on behavioral differences across cultures and sometimes on universal patterns of behavior. But the ultimate goal is always to discover how culture and individual behavior relate.

It is helpful to have an overall framework of ideas about possible relationships, such as the ecocultural one that we introduced in Chapter 1. First, however, we shall discuss a precursor to contemporary cross-cultural psychology, an anthropological approach to the study of psychological issues: the culture-and-personality school that was created by anthropologists when hardly any psychologists bothered to attend to culture.

The Culture-and-Personality School

For several decades, beginning in the 1930s, much anthropological research was guided by a formulation that asserted axiomatically that culture and personality are interrelated. Influenced by a Freudian emphasis on early experience as a primary determinant of adult personality, anthropologists in this school of thought viewed culture as a set of conditions determining early experience and hence as a major shaper of personality. For example, Kardiner (1945) and Linton (1945a) suggested that different societies develop different basic personality types. Their argument, as summarized by Linton in his foreword to the 1945 volume by Kardiner, is presented in Box 3-1.

According to the Kardiner and Linton formulation, because of socialization pressures, certain communalities in individual development are produced within a society. This is not to say that everybody has the same

---

Box 3-1 Basic Personality: A View From Early Anthropology

The concept of basic personality types requires four postulates:

1. Individuals' early experiences exert a lasting effect on their personalities, especially on the development of basic values.
2. Similar experiences tend to produce similar personality configurations in the individuals who are subjected to them.
3. The techniques that the members of any society employ in child rearing are culturally patterned and tend to be similar, although never identical, for various families within the society.
4. The culturally patterned techniques for the care and rearing of children differ from one society to another.

According to Linton (1945b), it follows from these postulates that:

1. The members of any given society have many elements of early experience in common.
2. As a result of this they have many elements of personality in common.
3. Since the early experience of individuals differs from one society to another, the personality norms for various societies also differ.
4. Every society has a basic personality type.

The fourth step should cause you to feel a little uneasy. What in fact did Linton mean by *basic personality type?*

> The basic personality type for any society is that personality configuration which is shared by the bulk of the society's members as the result of the early experiences which they have in common. It does not correspond to the total personality of the individual but rather to the "projective systems" or the value-attitude systems which are basic to the individual personality configuration. Thus, the same basic personality type may be reflected in many different forms of behavior, and may enter into many different total personality configurations. (Linton, 1945b, pp. vii–viii)

personality; each total personality differs from every other total personality. But somehow at the core of each something is shared — some basic values and attitudes — that they called the *projective system*. This was thought to be indirectly observable by means of projective tests. Developed initially in clinical settings for use by psychiatrists and psychologists as diagnostic devices in treating neurotic and psychotic individuals, projective tests (e.g., the Rorschach or TAT) attracted the attention of anthropologists partly because the instruments seemed to lack culturally specific content and were presumably applicable in any cultural setting.

They were also linked conceptually with psychoanalysis, which in many respects constituted a novel and attractive way of understanding behavior. That psychoanalytic theory purported to be a universally applicable system for understanding human development also made it seem useful to students of non-Western cultures.

It is perhaps not surprising that the themes and related techniques of clinical psychology (especially the allegedly penetrating projective tests) attracted anthropologists and contributed to the emergence of a culture-and-personality school of thought.

From Freudian theory, many field workers were led to look for relations between child-rearing practices and certain aspects of adult personality. Many studies spawned by this expectation yielded interesting empirical findings. But clinical psychology had some effects on anthropology that were not so salutary. (These will be discussed shortly.)

Nonetheless, like more modern conceptual frameworks (including the eco-cultural framework we employ in this volume), the culture-and-personality approach carried the implication that there is a mutual relationship between social systems and personalities. As one anthropologist (Spiro, 1961) put it, a social system creates "the personality needs which, in turn, are satisfied by and motivate the operation of the social system" (p. 121). (This formulation was derived, as Spiro noted, from the Kardiner model discussed above.) In other words, culture somehow induces people to want to behave in ways that sustain the culture. Every society has developed cultural norms and the devices by which its members come to conform with these norms. Much of that conformity is manifest willingly by individuals because they have internalized motives and role expectations that are compatible with the norms. To behave otherwise would be to court not only externally administered negative sanctions but also self-administered anxiety, a frequent cost of nonconformity.

As a general conception of the manner in which culture and personality interrelate, this point of view is hard to fault. The research that is stimulated, however, had some deficiencies.

Shortcomings in Early Culture-and-Personality Research

A major difficulty with the culture-and-personality school was its relative disregard of individual differences within societies. Researchers set out to find core personalities, those personality characteristics that "had to be" shown by all members of a given society. A. F. C. Wallace (1961) criticized this tendency to conceive of societies as culturally homogeneous and to expect individuals in them to share a uniform nuclear character. Wallace reminded us that there is much diversity not only across cultures but also within them. To him, diversity is the natural order of things and is not pathogenic, or nonfunctional, as some of the culture-and-personality theorists seemed to imply.

As Wallace saw it, the "core personalities" produced by this research tradition were either abstractions gleaned from descriptions of individual personalities — with nonshared characteristics simply ignored — or, worse, deductions from cultural descriptions. Many studies thus resulted in "discoveries" of core personality traits that were logical imperatives but not empirical facts.

Another difficulty was the heavy dependence of culture-and-personality research on projective techniques. Numerous studies of national character and modal personality employed the Rorschach test and so ended up describing people in clinical terms. A typical work is Cora DuBois's *The People of Alor* (1944). This study included the analysis (by a Swiss expert on the Rorschach test) of about 50 Rorschach protocols collected from the Alorese, an Indonesian-island group. "Findings" led the author to describe the core personality as characterized by fearfulness, suspicion, distrust, egocentricity, greed, shallowness of personal relations, and lack of emotional responsiveness but, surprisingly, perhaps, in light of the foregoing, as having "no evidence of neurotic conflict." In Lewis's study of Tepoztlan, Mexico (1951), a chapter by Abel and Calabresi was based on an analysis of about 100 Rorschach protocols leading to the assertion that the typical person in the community could be characterized as unfriendly, rigid, and unlikely (or unable) to engage in fantasy.

On the Misuse of Inkblots. Lindzey (1961, especially Chapter 6) reviewed many studies that employed Rorschach tests cross-culturally. He concluded that they contained so many methodological faults that their findings simply could not be evaluated. Box 3-2 contains Lindzey's succinctly summarized criticisms.

For reasons like those presented by Lindzey, the use of projective tests in cross-cultural research diminished, and the search for modal personality ceased. Still, the notion that there are traits shared by members of a society and that these traits are compatible with the society's values is tenable. It merely expresses an expectation of finding functional relationships among elements of culture and aspects of behavior. It is embodied in the ecocultural framework that we employ in this book. But despite the heuristic value of the concept, culture-and-personality research of the early variety was not productive.

The ecocultural framework suggests that we ought to examine all aspects of human behavior and try to discover how and to what degree any is influenced

---

**Box 3-2 Difficulties in Using Projective Techniques
in Culture and Personality Research**

Although projective techniques are useful for many purposes in psychology, problems abound in the way they were used in culture-and-personality research.

1 The technique imposes the language of pathology; thus modal personalities that emerge from a scoring of Rorschach protocols almost necessarily appear more or less sick.
2. The data are difficult to quantify and treat statistically. The studies seldom specified the nature of the sampling procedures used, so that whatever description emerged was of an unknown degree of applicability to the population in question.
3. By searching for supposedly "deep-seated, underlying personality traits," whatever they may be, the culture-personality researchers usually ignored overt behaviors.
4. The use of projective techniques in the culture in which they were devised— the Euro-American regions of the world—is difficult enough. Their use requires the detection of subtle linguistic cues; the objectivity of their scoring procedures is dubious; and responses may reflect structural variables, such as recent experiences, attitudes toward test taking elicited by the behavior of the tester, and so on. Every one of these problems is simply exacerbated when such instruments are employed in a culture that is foreign to the investigator.*

---

*Adapted from *Projective Techniques and Cross-Cultural Research* by G. Lindzey, 1961, New York: Appleton-Century-Crofts. Copyright 1961, by Appleton-Century-Crofts, a division of Prentice-Hall, Inc. Used with permission of the author.

"emic/etic" distinction. The distinction also refers to problems inherent in the by the ecological and cultural contexts in which it occurs. And that is what contemporary cross-cultural psychologists, for the most part, are doing.

METHODOLOGY IN CROSS-CULTURAL RESEARCH: SOME PROBLEMS AND SOME SOLUTIONS

Designing a study of human behavior to produce unambiguous findings is not easy. It is difficult even when the study is done in the investigator's own society, where the psychologist knows the language, is knowledgeable about prevailing attitudes, is using measuring instruments of known reliability, and is able to detect subtle cues in the behavior of the subjects. Psychologists who work only in their own societies acknowledge that, despite these advantages, their research always carries the risk of invalidity. Imagine, then, the problems confronting cross-cultural psychologists.

First, they may not know the language and will probably be unable to read subtle cues familiar to insiders. In addition, theories, concepts, methods, and instruments developed in one society may not be applicable to the behaviors of individuals in any other society.

Three methodological worries especially acute in cross-cultural research concern measurement problems, sampling problems, and administrative problems. Each of these categories raises several interesting issues.

Measurement Problems

What to Measure

The primary measurement problem in cross-cultural research is, simply, *what* to measure. That this is a problem may not at first be obvious (which, incidentally, compounds the problem.).

Suppose you begin with an interest in aggressive behavior among adolescents in diverse cultures. Don't you and your colleagues on this project simply go to various cultures and observe adolescent aggression? Of course, but what kinds of behaviors are valid indexes of agression? Aggression, after all, is only a name that we give to a class of behaviors, and even in our own societies we are often not sure which kinds of behaviors should be counted as aggression.

When psychologists leave their own culture, they may be confronted with behaviors that would be interpreted one way in their own society but quite differently in another. Thus, in a cross-cultural study it might be inappropriate to study the same behaviors in two or more different societies. We might, in fact, have to study different behaviors in order to study the same psychological phenomenon. These behaviors would be functionally equivalent (Goldschmidt, 1966).

Although often overlooked in the search for cross-cultural differences, there are universal aspects of human behavior. Surely at some level of abstraction we are all alike, all human. In the early 20th century this was called the "psychic unity of mankind." Although aggressive behavior varies in form from place to place, some form of aggression occurs in all societies. Aggression is a cultural universal (Lonner, 1980); how it is expressed may be culturally specific.

This distinction between culture-specific and universal behaviors is one version of what has come to be known in cross-cultural psychology as the cross-cultural use of instruments developed in a single culture. (See Box 3-3 for more details on this terminology.)

We can say, for example, that if there is a universal behavior, like aggression at a high level of abstraction, that behavior is an "etic." We would refer to a specific variety of aggressive behavior, one that might be peculiar to a given society, as an "emic." We are here suggesting that there are two different levels of analysis in the study of human behavior—emic or etic. Whether a researcher chooses to focus on cultural differences or cultural similarities will often determine what behavior is examined. The emic approach, which is typical of much ethnographic anthropological research, emphasizes the uni-

---

Box 3-3 Emics and Etics, Imposed and Derived

Emic and *etic* are terms originally employed by the anthropologist Pike (1954). These neologisms reflect concepts long used in linguistics to indicate the differences between phonemics (the study of sounds whose meaning-bearing roles are *unique* to a particular language) and phonetics (the study of *universal* sounds used in human language, their particular meanings aside.) Later (1967), Pike made it clear that emic and etic should be thought of as designating two different viewpoints for the study of behavior—"the etic viewpoint [which] studies behavior as from outside of a particular system, and as an essential initial approach to an alien system" and "the emic viewpoint [which] results from studying behavior as from inside the system."

Both viewpoints, or approaches, are part of cross-cultural psychology. The so-called emic/etic distinction has, nevertheless, troubled cross-cultural psychologists (some of whom wonder if it is a distinction that has any real implications for how research is actually done). Several efforts have been made to clarify this distinction and its implications for research. Berry (1969) began such an effort by agreeing with Pike (1967) that research must begin somehow, and that almost always this means that step one involves an instrument or observation technique necessarily rooted in the researcher's own culture (hence, an emic for that culture) used as if it were an etic (brought in from outside, assumed to be valid in the alien culture and, hence, also assumed to be valid for comparison purposes). Berry called such an instrument an *imposed etic*. Obviously, great risk attends the use of an imposed etic, since there would be no way of knowing whether it made any sense to use it in any culture other than its culture of origin.

Then, Berry advocated that the researcher working in the alien culture strive (through participant observation and other ethnographic methods) to grasp local points of view in an effort to attain emic knowledge. Bringing together the investigator's own emic, and the alien culture emic, and seeking the features that they have in common, the investigator might then emerge with what we can now call a *derived etic*.

This process is graphically illustrated in Figure 3-1.

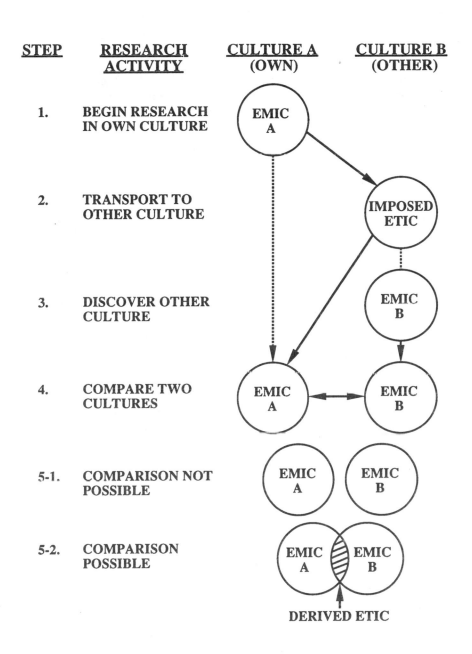

STEP	RESEARCH ACTIVITY	CULTURE A (OWN)	CULTURE B (OTHER)
1.	BEGIN RESEARCH IN OWN CULTURE	EMIC A	
2.	TRANSPORT TO OTHER CULTURE		IMPOSED ETIC
3.	DISCOVER OTHER CULTURE		EMIC B
4.	COMPARE TWO CULTURES	EMIC A	EMIC B
5-1.	COMPARISON NOT POSSIBLE	EMIC A	EMIC B
5-2.	COMPARISON POSSIBLE	EMIC A	EMIC B

DERIVED ETIC

FIGURE 3-1. Steps in operationalizing emics and etics

queness of every culture by focusing on culture-specific phenomena such as the behaviors, norms, values, customs, and traditions, of a particular society. Cross-cultural psychologists, on the other hand, are more likely to use an etic approach, seeking to identify universal behavioral phenomena.

There are dangers inherent in the etic approach, as we saw in Box 3-3. Since cultures differ widely in the ways in which they express (for example) friendship, researchers seeking generalizations might still have to measure different behaviors in the various societies in which friendship was being studied. Because the researchers are, themselves, strongly rooted in and influenced by their own cultural backgrounds, there is the danger that they may be reflecting their own cultural biases when they select the behavior to observe. An investigator might erroneously choose a behavior that could only be considered an act of friendship in the investigator's own society, thereby employing an "imposed etic" (Berry, 1969).

In general, the danger of a researcher imposing his or her own cultural classification system on the behaviors of another cultural group is greater in the etic approach than in the emic approach. This is because emic researchers typically use methods such as participant observation, employment of local people to serve as informed observers, and local test construction in an attempt to tap a culture's own indigenous system of classification or what has also been termed "subjective culture" (Triandis, 1972). A researcher who seeks etics, however, may enter another society armed with theory-testing instruments that may be inappropriate for application in another culture.

While some researchers argue that the emic/etic distinction is simply not a useful conceptual tool (Jahoda, 1977, 1983), still others recommend a number of alternative strategies for dealing with the problem of imposed etics. Most of these strategies (e.g., Berry, 1969; Triandis, 1978; Hui & Triandis, 1985) suggest, as we did in Box 3-3, that a combined emic-etic approach be used.

Other strategies for dealing with the imposed etic problem have been tried. For an account of an alternative approach to uncovering cultural universals, one that begins with a theory of human behavior that has its origins in the East, see Box 3-4.

How to Measure

Closely related to the problem of deciding *what* to measure is the problem of *how* to measure it. Consider a classic study by Gordon (1923), who was interested in a group of very poor people who eked out a livelihood on boats that plied the canals of England. The canal-boat children only irregularly attended school.

Their life-style generated disdain on the part of members of the more affluent core culture. The canal-boat people were considered lazy and stupid, and their failure to behave like middle-class English was attributed to a basic lack of intelligence. That is a common reaction of the dominant people

Box 3-4 Chinese Values and the Search for Psychological Universals

A major hazard of research in cross-cultural psychology is the problem of the "imposed etic"—the importation or exportation of a theory of human behavior which has been developed in one culture (typically the U.S.) to be tested in another cultural context where its application may be inappropriate. In the search for cross-cultural universals, one must take into consideration the possibility that the meanings and behaviors which are associated with a psychological variable in one culture may be quite different in another, and therefore a "good" theory of human behavior must be broad enough to account for the full range of cultural variation on any given variable. More importantly, the instruments which have been developed to test this theory must be designed in such a way that comparable measures of the same variables are taken in each culture included in the sample.

Above, in Box 3-3, we presented one method for reaching a circumstance in which cross-cultural comparisons may be made. In a related fashion, an international network of cross-cultural researchers known as The Chinese Culture Connection (1987) suggests a method of uncovering cultural universals which takes as its unique starting point an emic theory of human behavior which has its roots in an Eastern culture, China. This is a unique approach because, unfortunately, most psychological theories of human behavior and most of the instruments which have been developed to test those theories have grown out of distinctly Western cultural belief systems. Given the 4,000 year recorded history of Chinese civilization and its pervasive cultural influence on all of East Asia, China provides a useful and logical place to begin the search for cultural universals.

This approach also differs from others in its emphasis on cultural diversity as a means of getting at universals. It proposes beginning simultaneously with two distinctly different emic views of human behavior (one Eastern and one Western), deliberately developing tests which have a strong cultural bias. After testing each theory in a wide variety of cultural settings, the resultant test scores for those cultural groups which are common to more than one sample are compared. If, despite the strong emic biases inherent in this method, those scores correlate, then that would strongly suggest the existence of some sort of cultural universal.

This method, called "teasing etics out of emics", was employed in a cross-cultural study of human values comparing results from a Chinese Value Survey (CVS) with results from Hofstede's (1980) international survey of Western work-related values. The Chinese survey was deliberately ethnocentric in its construction, selecting for its 40 test items only those values deemed relevant and pertinent to Chinese culture. Chinese Culture Connection colleagues in 22 countries administered the CVS, in the appropriate local language, to homogeneous bodies of students who were fairly comparable in terms of the academic standards of their institutions. Data was analyzed at the cultural level and a factor analysis yielded four factors (values loading $> .55$) operating within this data, subsequently named CVS I (Integration), CVS II (Confucian Work Dynamism), CVS III (Human-Heartedness), and CVS IV (Moral Discipline). Each of the 22 cultural groups was then ranked according to where they fell on scales for each of these four factors (The Culture Connection, 1987).

(continued)

Box 3-4 *Continued*

Countries which were common to both studies (N = 20) were then compared, revealing correlations among the CVS factors and Hofstede's four dimensions of Power Distance (PD), Uncertainty Avoidance (UA), Individualism
(IDV), and Masculinity (MAS). Specifically, a significant cross-study correlation
was found between Hofstede's PD and IDV (which together correlate negatively) and CVS I and CVS IV. A significant correlation was also found between
Hofstede's MAS and CVS III. Finally, CVS II was found to be unrelated to any of
Hofstede's dimensions.

How did the Chinese Culture Connection interpret these findings? First,
they argue that the fact that Power Distance, Individualism, Integration, and
Moral Discipline all cluster together in a second-order factor analysis strongly
suggests that these four dimensions all tap into a single complex universal
construct. Since the dimensions which make up this universal are all concerned with the dichotomy between self-seeking behavior and the maintenance of group harmony, they propose that this construct be named "collectivism."

A second universal emerged from the strong positive correlation between
the dimensions of Masculinity and Human-Heartedness. Common to both is
the opposition between "masculine" or "task-centered" considerations and a
"feminine," "human-hearted" view. Eastern countries fall decidedly more on
the "feminine" end of the dimension.

Finally, a construct emerged from this study which has a distinctly "Oriental
flavor." Confucian Work Dynamism was the only Chinese value which did not
correlate with any of Hofstede's Western work values. It seems to be an emic
value which is peculiar to Eastern cultures, with Taiwan, Hong Kong, Japan,
South Korea, and Singapore falling at the top end of this dimension. Furthermore, a high positive correlation (r = .70) was found between this construct and
growth in Gross National Product, offering strong support for the "post-Confu-
cian Hypothesis" which attributes the amazing economic growth and development of modern Oriental cultures to their strong heritage of Confucian social
philosophy. The emergence of this emic, which Hofstede's survey was unable
to tap, also points up the importance of developing indigenous theories and
instruments in non-Western cultures in order to get at those unique ways of
being that the foreign eye many miss altogether.

---

in a society to anyone who, for whatever reason, is not achieving what the
society's myths say everyone could achieve.

Gordon doubted that the canal-boat people's behavior reflected inherent
deficiency in intelligence. So he set out to measure the intelligence of the
canal-boat children. Binet's IQ test had recently been translated into English. Using it, Gordon found an appallingly low average score equivalent to an
IQ of 60. Even more interesting, he found a decline of IQ with age. The older
the children, the "less intelligent" they appeared to be. Gordon was intrigued
by this second finding because it said to him that the children were subject to

negative influences on their intellectual performance that accumulated with age. He concluded, then, that the children's test performances were more a reflection of the cultural conditions to which their canal-boat environment subjected them than a measure of their potential intellectual abilities.

Given what we know about the diverse determinants of performance on an IQ test, Gordon deserves praise for being so right so early in the history of psychological testing. His results force us to consider the possibility that the test wasn't even measuring intellectual performance of the canal-boat children. Perhaps it was measuring their patience and willingness to answer what might have seemed very silly questions put to them by a somewhat bizarre stranger. Or maybe the test was a measure of the familiarity they had with the content of a culture other than their own, a familiarity that would also decline with increasing immersion in their own subculture.

Just because a test is called an intelligence test does not guarantee that it is measuring intelligence. The point has been made, perhaps best, by Robert LeVine (1970): "Standard intelligence tests measure [only] the current capacity of individuals to participate effectively in Western schools" (p. 581). That much, IQ tests do measure; whether they measure anything else is very dubious. Most psychologists accept this limitation on what an IQ test does. An IQ score is simply a shorthand expression for an individual's level of performance relative to other individuals on a sample of tasks chosen because the tasks predict school performance well. Why they do is another matter.

If we recall the history of IQ tests, we appreciate that they were originally meant to do only that. Binet constructed his test in response to a request from the board of education of Paris, which felt that the city could not afford to send everybody to school. The board members wanted to be able to detect in advance the children who were likely to fail. They asked for a test that would find those children who were unlikely to succeed in the Paris school system. That's all the IQ test was designed to do. Despite the fact that people generally believe that IQ tests measure some internal quality called intelligence, an IQ test is only a scholastic aptitude test.

That point is well known and widely accepted, at least by psychologists. But the second point — that an IQ test applied in a culture other than the one in which it was developed may not even measure scholastic aptitude — needs also to be understood.

It is hardly a new discovery that IQ tests are biased against those whose cultural background differs from that of the test's original normative sample. In 1927 the anthropologist Melville Herskovits commented:

> Environmental background, cultural as well as natural, plays a tremendous part in whatever manifestations of innate intelligence an individual may give us through . . . standardized tests. . . . Thus it has been found that the American Indians usually rate somewhat lower in psychological tests than whites, and that this holds true when the tests are of a nonlanguage variety, where the

use of words is reduced to a minimum. But the consideration of the fact that the tests ordinarily used have been constructed by persons of a background different from that of the subjects is usually overlooked; and were there to be presented, for consideration as to what is wrong with a given picture, a six-clawed bear rather than a net-less tennis court, one wonders whether the city-dwelling white might not be at a loss rather than the Indians. (p. 3)

Over the decades since Herskovits warned that intergroup differences in intelligence test scores might tell more about the tests than about the groups, attempts have been made to produce "culture-free" or "culture-fair" IQ tests, but none of these has been successful. Clearly, culturally mediated experience always interacts with test content to influence test performance.

DeVos and Hippler (1969), who reviewed many cross-cultural studies, have made it clear that the once so-called culture-free tests are unavoidably biased in favor of urban, advantaged, Western peoples. As educational and economic conditions anywhere come to resemble those characteristic of the West, test scores reach Western norms. Husén (1967) showed this to have happened in Japan and Biesheuvel (1949), McFie (1961), Price-Williams (1961), and Vernon (1965, 1967) in Africa.

Evidence of IQ tests' cultural bias in the United States was reviewed by Klineberg (1954, pp. 263–269). These early studies showed for Northern urban blacks born in Southern rural settings a positive correlation between length of time in the North and IQ scores. Clearly, the more exposure to the kind of culture in which the tests were first developed, the better the performance on the tests.

In a discussion of the culture-boundedness of tests (Frijda & Jahoda, 1966), a distinction was drawn between *culture-free* and *culture-fair*. The culture-free label would be applied to an instrument that actually measures some inherent quality of human capacity equally well in all cultures. Obviously, there can be no such test.

A culture-fair test could be a set of items that are equally unfamiliar to all possible persons in all possible cultures, so everyone would have the same possibility of passing the items. This is, as Brislin, Lonner, and Thorndike (1973, p. 109) put it, a virtual impossibility. Or, a culture-fair test could consist of multiple sets of items, modified for use in each culture to ensure that each version of the test would contain the same amount of familiarity. These would be emic tests, and members of each culture would have about the same probability of being able to deal with one version of it.

Culture-fair tests are possible in theory. In practice, they are difficult to construct. And it is virtually impossible, once they have been constructed, to assess their degree of culture fairness.

The root of all measurement problems in cross-cultural research is the possibility that the same behaviors may have different meanings across cultures or that the same processes may have different overt manifestations. As a result, the "same" test might be "different" when applied in different cultures. Therefore, the effort to devise culture-fair testing procedures will probably never be completely successful. The degree to which we are measuring the same thing in more than one culture, whether we are using the same or different test items, must always worry us.

In the long run, of course, we will acquire confidence that we are measuring truly comparable phenomena if we accumulate evidence that they relate to other variables in a predictable, understandable fashion. But, until such evidence has been accumulated, we cannot be sure of the comparability of what we are measuring when we apply a test, any test, in more than one culture.

One more point about this measurement problem: Its importance varies somewhat, depending on the purpose for which performance scores in any test are accumulated and the interpretation made of those scores. This point has been made by Vernon (1965, 1967), who himself used various aptitude tests with samples of students in East Africa and the Caribbean. When we are not disposed to interpret performance differences as manifestations of inherent qualities of personality, the problem is less severe.

When we intend merely to assess the current capacity of individuals to perform some task and don't care at all what that current capacity reflects, our difficulties are lessened. An example is the use of an aptitude test to select workers who will require the least amount of training to perform a task. In this case the problem of culture fairness almost disappears. Even here we might not get a valid assessment if the testing procedure itself somehow inhibits the persons being tested from displaying their current skills. So, cross-cultural psychologists need to be constantly vigilant with respect to measurement.

Sampling Problems

Sampling problems abound in cross-cultural psychology (as noted by Frijda & Jahoda, 1966; Campbell, 1961; Naroll, 1970a,b; Brislin, Lonner & Thorndike, 1973; and Lonner & Berry, 1986). Of course, sampling is always a problem in psychological research. We have to worry about the representativeness of a sample, to what population the findings can be generalized. Whenever we compare samples, as we so often do in cross-cultural research, we have to worry also about their comparability.

Obtaining Comparable Samples

There is a seeming paradox here. Whenever we do a cross-cultural study we presumably want to work with samples that are different from each other. Yet we want them to be comparable. How can they be both comparable and different at the same time? The point is, of course, that we want differences in some respects, for example, the dietary practices of two or more cultures, and communalities in other respects, for example, years of formal education, so we can investigate the hypothesized effect of some difference on people who are *otherwise* comparable.

Say we have a hypothesis about the long-term consequences of a protein-deficient diet on problem-solving ability. We might want to test this hypothesis by comparing cultural groups whose childhood diet is rich in animal protein with groups where children are fed only low-protein vegetables. We would try to compare groups that have had roughly equal amounts and kinds of schooling, because formal schooling provides some training in problem-solving skills.

Unfortunately, when we move from culture to culture, we find that age and years of schooling are highly correlated in some places but not in others. In other words, whereas in Culture A persons who are, say, in their sixth year of schooling are likely to be within a year or two of 12 years of age, in Culture B they might represent a much wider range of ages and probably be higher in average age. Certainly, if Culture B were in a traditional, less-developed, non-Western society, persons with six years of schooling would be older, would range widely about the average age, and would be relatively rare persons within their own societies. They would probably be richer, disproportionately male, and so on. So, when we hold one variable constant, we are almost inevitably confronted with variations along some unknown number of other variables.

The aspect of the sampling problem that we have just discussed—the virtual impossibility of obtaining samples from more than one society that are truly comparable—is the major reason that Campbell has warned (first in 1961 and again in 1972, with Raoul Naroll) that all studies that consist solely of single-pair comparisons are uninterpretable. The example Campbell used was Malinowski's material on Trobriand Island dreams compared with Freud's material on Viennese dreams. As we saw in Chapter 2, this comparison demonstrated the need for cross-cultural testing of hypotheses spawned in a single culture. It should be recalled, however, that Campbell asserted that such a comparison would *not* reveal the process underlying male adolescent hostility, because between merely two societies there are many differences that could constitute potential rival explanations. But recall also that Campbell pointed out that data collection need not be limited to a single pair of societies (Campbell, 1961, pp. 344–345).

Clearly, then, our sampling objective in any cross-cultural study must be to obtain a large number of societies (certainly more than two) that may be different in some respects (or we wouldn't be interested in them) but similar enough in other respects that they can be meaningfully compared. The objective is, of course, easier to state than to achieve. But it is always worth knowing what our objective is, if only to know how much any study falls short of achieving it.

Finding A Representative Sample

Another sampling problem is accessibility. Much intracultural psychological research, especially the vast majority of psychological experiments conducted in laboratories, employs student subjects who are invited, expected, and induced to volunteer. They are a kind of captive audience. As a result, accessibility is a minimal problem in such research (although representativeness may be a major one).

In cross-cultural studies, locating, reaching, and inducing persons to participate is difficult, time consuming, and expensive. Consequently, there may well be subtle pressures on the investigator to recruit relatively accessible subjects. These are likely to be persons on the beaten track (quite literally). They are likely to have had relatively high degrees of previous contact with outside cultures. They may be of above-average wealth and education and have linguistic skills or other characteristics that make them unrepresentative of the population they are (erroneously) taken to represent.

Moreover, it seems exceedingly plausible to argue that the more inaccessible a population is, the more likely a sample drawn from it will be unrepresentative. This is because the greater the difficulties are, the more the investigator will be willing to settle for people with whom he or she can most conveniently interact. Thus, a cross-cultural study done in societies that vary in accessibility may reduce to a study in which the samples are differentially representative.

The accessibility problem in cross-cultural sampling has an interesting parallel in traditional ethnographic research. Sometimes an anthropologist employs a member of a society as an "informant" about the customs and institutions of that society. Anthropologists need as an informant someone with whom they can communicate. And persons likely to apply for such a job are in some ways — linguistically, educationally, or otherwise — different from most in their own society. Informants, if members of the elite, would have a specialized atypical knowledge about the society.

As a result, what the anthropologist learns from the informant about the society may be true enough, but it may not be the most *generally* true set of facts that the anthropologist hoped to be acquiring. Thus, what is ultimately "known" about the culture — as in the records of the Human Relations Area Files, for example — would have been doubly filtered, through a foreign observer and an unrepresentative insider.

Although we have by no means exhausted the types of sampling problems confronting cross-cultural research, enough has been said to make clear that it matters not only what we study and how we study it but also whom we study.

We have seen that measurement problems and sampling problems present cross-cultural research with large hurdles to overcome. And there is still a third category of methodological problems that are particularly acute in cross-cultural research. These we will call administrative problems, and it is to some of these that we now turn.

Administrative Problems

Administrative problems refer to threats to the validity of a study that derive from the interaction between investigators and those whose behavior they are investigating. Obviously, people in other societies will be very different from the investigator in many respects. (That is why, after all, they are being studied.) Some intriguing methodological problems emerge from these differences.

For instance, there are likely to be serious impediments to communication, so serious that the subjects may misinterpret the task they are supposed to perform or the investigator may misinterpret the performance. There may be certain misperceptions by the subjects of the investigator's role and status, and these misperceptions may affect their performance in any variety of unknown ways. The subjects may be frightened, awed, cowed, or otherwise placed in some state of mind that will affect their motivation to perform. They may say or do whatever they think they have to in order to please, placate, or get away from someone they perceive as a tax collector, census enumerator, or policeman.

Once again, if these difficulties are more prevalent in some societies than in others included in a single study, there will be the problem of differential meaningfulness of the behaviors observed in the societies. In some, the behaviors may be typical of what occurs when subjects are relaxed. In others, the behavior may be that which occurs when people are frightened out of their wits. Needless to say, comparability will have been threatened.

Minimizing Miscommunication

Suppose, as is so often the case in cross-cultural research, that respondents in one society perform the task one way and respondents in another society do it a different way. This is another way of saying that they give different responses and earn different scores. We would like to be sure that this difference across groups represents a "real" difference. But what if the two (or more) groups merely understood the tasks differently and were, in effect, performing different tasks?

Campbell (1964) dealt with this general problem by linking it to a concrete instance of a cross-cultural study of visual perception (Segall, Campbell & Herskovits, 1966), which we will discuss in detail in Chapter 4. For our present purposes it suffices to know that the study yielded striking differences among a large number of societies in the degree to which they seemed susceptible to a number of optical illusions. That is, whereas in one society subjects tended on average to indicate that two lines appeared equal when one line was actually 8 percent longer, in some other society subjects tended to indicate equality of length when one line was 15 percent longer. For theoretical reasons, such a difference in performance would be interpreted as evidence that these two groups were actually seeing things differently. But how can we tell when we are communicating well enough to know that people are indeed seeing things differently?

In dramatic fashion, Campbell (1964) elucidated the problem:

> Suppose that we parachuted an anthropologist and a test booklet into a totally isolated New Guinea tribe and that the anthropologist had first to learn the language without the help of an interpreter. The process of language learning would then become a part of the operations which we would have to detail. It would become obvious that no person ever learns another's language perfectly; that the existence of "interpreters" should not be taken for granted; that here is a problematic situation in which the cues and presumptions of communication need to be specified. It turns out that the anthropologist's main cue for achieved communication is similarity between the response of the other to a stimulus and the response which he himself would make. Disagreement turns out to be a sign of communication failure. How then can disagreement on an optical illusion test item be taken instead as a difference in perceiving the world? (p. 317)

In the case of the Segall, Campbell, and Herskovits (1966) study, the problem was confronted in a variety of ways, but we will present only one here. This involved the use of four preliminary (or "comprehension check") stimuli. They were all prepared in such a way that if the respondent did not respond exactly as the anthropologist would have, it could only be assumed that misunderstanding of the task was involved. For example, one such item was composed of a *very* short black line and a *very* long red line. The question asked was, "Which line is longer, the red or the black one?" If (as almost never happened) someone were to have said "black," we would not have concluded that to that person the black line appeared longer. Rather, we would have concluded that he had misunderstood one or a combination of the words "line," "longer," "black," or "red" or something else about what he was being asked to do.

Yet for the real test items, of course, we were prepared to interpret whatever responses we received at face value. The key to understanding this is to recognize that our preliminary items required comparisons of such extremely exaggerated line differences that anyone would find it incredible to interpret an incorrect response as indicating anything other than a failure of communication. Once it is shown that communication is not failing on the preliminary items, the assumption of achieved communication may then be confidently carried over to the test items.

Because nearly all persons everywhere had behaved alike on the preliminary items, we could treat instances in which they did behave differently on the test items as genuinely interesting and not merely artifacts of miscommunication. That the various groups in the study behaved similarly enough in certain respects made it possible to treat the differences that did show up as meaningful differences. As Campbell (1964) has put it, the preventive steps taken by Segall, Campbell, and Herskovits illustrate one important general principle:

> Discrepancy can be noted and interpreted only against the background of an overwhelming proportion of nondiscrepant fit, agreement, or pattern repetition. This principle is found in operation in knowledge processes as varied as binocular vision and astronomy. Again and again in science, the equivocal interpretations are available: separate entity vs. same entity changed, moved, or perceived from a different perspective. And in all such instances where the second interpretation occurs, it is made possible by the overwhelming bulk of stable nonchanging background. Consider the reidentification of a single planet on successive nights, plus the inference that the planet migrates in an eccentric backtracking manner. Had Jupiter been the only star in the sky, this might never have been documented, certainly not by a nomadic people. Had all the stars been planets, it would also have gone unascertained. Had the oscillations in the locations of the fixed stars been so great as to subtend several degrees of visual angle, the backtracking would not have been observed. It was the recurrent "fixedness" of 99.9 percent of the stars which made the wanderings of the few planets interpretable as such. (p. 327)

Applying this principle to cross-cultural research, then, the dictum is obvious. Design the research in such a way that you ensure finding identical behaviors as well as different ones, for differences alone can only be ambiguous. A difference is interpretable only when embedded in a context of sameness.

We have seen enough in this chapter to understand, in a rather abstract fashion, how cross-cultural research ought to be done. We have not, of course, discussed all the methodological issues that confront cross-cultural psychologists in the detail that those issues require. Fortunately, such discussions are accessible (see, for example, Chapter 7 in Berry et al., in press). We now, however, have an appreciation for problems of comparability and are ready to look at some research and begin to learn about some of the substantive issues that our methodological sophistication helps us to appreciate. We begin, in the next chapter as promised, with the study of optical illusions.

Chapter 4

Perception of Visual Illusions:
A Case Study in the
Methodology of
Cross-Cultural Psychology

INTRODUCTION:
WHY STUDY PERCEPTION
CROSS-CULTURALLY?

We devote this chapter to a single research question—cultural influences on visual-illusion susceptibility. This issue spans much of the history of cross-cultural psychology, having been a focus of the circa 1900 Cambridge Expedition to the Torres Straits (recall the discussion in Chapter 2 of this first cross-cultural application of experimental psychology) and the object of a large cooperative cross-cultural project directed by Segall, Campbell & Herskovits some sixty years later. Looking more closely at this issue will enrich our sense of the history of cross-cultural psychology and, as noted at the end of the last chapter, illustrate some important methodological concerns. Furthermore, the issue is substantively an intriguing one, with some interesting theoretical implications for psychology.

Even to someone unsophisticated in psychology, it is obvious that certain aspects of a people's behavior are shaped to a marked degree by their social and cultural background. For example, beliefs, attitudes, values, and lifestyles differ in striking ways across social classes, ethnic groups, religions, and nations; these clear differences are taken for granted and hardly seem to require explanation. Nobody is surprised that capitalists and socialists differentially value multinational corporations or that various religious groups hold different standards regarding how much of a woman's body may be uncovered in public. Later in this book, beginning with Chapter 10, we shall examine such value-linked behaviors, learning, to nobody's surprise perhaps, that they differ markedly across cultures.

In contrast, it is not commonly thought that groups of human beings differ in such fundamental ways as in how they perceive space, size, distance, or color; it is widely assumed that these are basic psychological processes common to all. Thus, there seems little intuitive reason to expect that a sharp, distinct photograph of a woman's face would not immediately be recognized as such by any viewer, in any society. Nor would one expect systematic differences across cultural groups in the way they detect length differences in two straight lines. However much various viewers of the photograph might be expected to vary in their judgments of the photographed subject's attractiveness or intelligence, we would expect them to agree at least that they were looking at a human face. And however much error people might make when judging the relative lengths of two straight lines, the errors should not differ systematically across cultural groups.

However reasonable this expectation of underlying similarity in basic psychological processes might seem, cross-cultural psychologists question it. So have philosophers and other scholars through the ages. At least from the time of ancient Greek civilization, philosophers have questioned whether individual human organisms merely receive sense impressions or whether they might participate actively in their perceptions of external objects and events.

This suggests that any experience a person has is influenced by that person's previous experiences. To the extent that previous experiences are determined by the accident of birth at a particular time in a particular place, it becomes probable that the "same" event will be different events, even in very fundamental ways, to members of different cultural groups.

Not surprisingly, then, cross-cultural psychologists have wondered greatly about both differences and uniformities in the very basic cognitive behavior of human beings, including the ways they perceive the physical world. In this chapter we will concentrate on research that has revealed—and sought explanations for—some fundamental perceptual differences. These involve such basic perceptual activities that the mere fact that differences exist is striking. We will focus on what is perhaps the most basic of all: visual perception of the physical world.

Concentrating, as we are about to do, on a single issue in visual perception does not mean that other issues in this domain have been neglected by cross-cultural researchers. There are, for example, extensive bodies of work on pictorial depth perception and color perception. These are interesting issues in their own right and, incidentally, are not unrelated to the issue of illusion susceptibility. These other cross-cultural perception issues are discussed in Berry et al. (in press). But we will tell here only the story of cross-cultural research with optical illusions, after setting the stage with some epistemological concerns that have long been a part of Western philosophy. (Epistemology is the branch of philosophy concerned with knowledge. How do we know what the world is really like? is an epistemological question.)

Seeing Is Believing . . . or Is It?

The premise that the world is what it appears to be was challenged many centuries ago by Plato (circa 390 B.C.) in his famous parable of the cave (*Republic* 7). People are imprisoned in the cave, able to see only shadows and reflections of what transpires about them. Plato's point was that the prisoners will take these shadows for reality. If the prisoners are released and directly witness the objects and events that are casting the shadows, Plato said, the objects and events will appear less real than their reflections.

Subsequently, Locke in 1690 and Berkeley in 1713 extended Plato's suggestion that the world, rather than appearing to us as it is, appears to us in ways determined by our prior experience. These two philosophers employed a particularly compelling example: a single event generates two opposite impressions in the same observer at the same time! Box 4-1 provides a famous account of such a bizarre phenomenon (Berkeley's version, originally published in *Three Dialogues Between Hylas and Philonous* [1713, p. 18]).

In this dramatic experience, which, incidentally, can be repeated by anyone with three basins of water—one hot, one lukewarm, and one cool[1]— Berkeley demonstrates the way the state of the observer helps determine his or her observations. He and many other philosophers have thus warned us against "naïve realism." A psychological counterpart to that philosophical concept has been called *phenomenal absolutism* (Segall et al., 1966). This term calls attention to the widespread tendency of human beings to assume, naively, that the world is exactly as it appears. That tendency is probably reinforced by the phenomenal clarity, constancy, and thing-ness of the content of our perceptions. The notion of phenomenal absolutism suggests that, given the way the world is filtered through our sense organs, it appears solid and real and constant, . . . even when it isn't.

Perceptual constancy is an old research topic in psychology. The research shows that judgments about a varying stimulus are constant over a wide range of variation. For example, there have been many studies in size constancy. An experiment usually employs an object whose distance from a viewer is varied. The subject in such a study of this kind must judge the

---

[1]Place one hand in the hot water and the other hand in the cold water, keep them there for about three minutes, then plunge both into the lukewarm water. You will be impressed, even though you know what to expect.

Box 4-1 How Warm Is Hot; How Cool Is Cold?

Berkeley's seeming paradox is recounted as follows:

Philonous: Is it not an absurdity to think that the same thing should be at the same time both cold and warm?
Hylas: It is.
Philonous: Suppose now one of your hands was hot, the other cold, and that they are both at once put into the same vessel of water in an intermediate state: Will not the water seem cold to one hand, and warm to the other?
Hylas: It will.
Philonous: Ought we not therefore by your principles to conclude it is really both cold and warm at the same time? That is, according to your own concession, to believe an absurdity?
Hylas: I confess it seems so.

---

object's size. As it moves farther from the viewer, so that its image gets smaller on the retina of the eye, there is, within a certain range at least, a tendency to see the object as maintaining its size.

Nativism Versus Empiricism

There are two main schools of thought in research on perceptual constancy: *nativism* and *empiricism*. On the one hand, the nativists typically assert that perceptual constancy and other perceptual phenomena reveal the structural demands of the human nervous system. Nativists consider experience of minor import for perception.

The empiricists, on the other hand, say that the way the organism behaves when it is looking at something reveals a major role for experience. Empiricist psychologists suggest that human beings regularly interpret cues and are easily misled by prior experience to be phenomenal absolutists. Phenomenologically, the world seems to be perceived absolutely. But, the empiricists suggest, there is actually considerable relativity in our perceptions, the nature of any experience is relative to the state of the perceiver. Perception is not stimulus-determined. It is the product of experience in interaction with a stimulus. Box 4-2 presents an account of the nativism/empiricism controversy in psychology.

Brunswik's Empiricist Theory:
A Base for Cross-Cultural Research

There are many versions of empiricist theories, one of which was employed by Segall, Campbell, and Herskovits in a cross-cultural study begun in the late 1950s. The one they used is that of Egon Brunswik (1956). Most

---

Box 4-2 Nativism or Empiricism?

In a history of experimental psychology by Boring (1942), this controversy was described as one of the oldest in experimental psychology. During the 18th and 19th centuries, arguments flowed back and forth without being settled. The controversy continued into the present century, and there have been recent efforts to resolve it with research.

For example, consider the work of Gibson (1950), who took a nativist position. Gibson argued that the problem of how an organism perceives a three-dimensional world, even though that world is projected visually on a two-dimensional surface—the retina of the eye—is essentially no problem at all. What happens, according to Gibson, is that the retinal image contains all the information the organism needs for the brain to process the information automatically. Hence, individuals know immediately, intuitively, without really having to process that information, that they are living in a three-dimensional world. In Gibson's view, the brain (at least that part of the brain involved in visual perception) has built into it an innate ability to perceive that the world is three dimensional.

Empiricists, in contrast, say that the key to answering this question lies somewhere in an analysis of experience. In short, people somehow learn something from earlier experiences, and what they learn enables them to perceive a three-dimensional world.

---

of the European psychologists who studied in the first half of the 20th century, known collectively as Gestalt psychologists, were nativists. Brunswik was an exception. His point of view, *transactional functionalism*, asserted that perception involves functional transactions between the organism and the incoming sensory material. By functional, he meant adaptive, with most transactions contributing to the survival of the organism. Thus perception helps the person get around in the world and prevents nasty accidents, like walking into walls. To Brunswik the perceived properties of an object are the combined product of the object and the perceiver, whose past experience plays a very important part. Brunswik's theory is explained more fully in Box 4-3.

The position that Segall et al. (1966) took is essentially Brunswikian. They argued that individual perception of objects comes to us with such vivid clarity that it is hard to imagine that learning is involved. But, they said, it may be so. Furthermore, if perception *is* influenced by learning, then there may well be ecological and cultural differences in perception because people who grow up in different environments may learn to interpret cues differently. But we are getting a little ahead of the story. We must next consider optical illusions, those tricky drawings familiar to all students of psychology, such as the one shown in Figure 4-1.

Brunswik's transactional functionalism can be applied in an explanation

---

Box 4-3   A Chair Not to Take Sitting Down

In Brunswik's laboratory, subjects would look through a peephole and report what they saw. In a typical experiment, subjects would "see" a chair. Then Brunswik could say, in effect, "I've got you. What I have done is suspend some strings in an otherwise darkened room, hanging them from the ceiling and tying them up in such a way that they *look like* a chair. But they are not a chair. They are just a bunch of strings."

If you look at a photograph of a chair, it is really nothing more than shades of gray arranged in a particular pattern. And yet you "know" it is a chair. What Brunswik demonstrated was that we conclude that a certain pattern of visual stimulation is "something" because of our previous experiences with things like it. Clearly, Brunswik argued, it is functional to use whatever cues we have learned in the past to be connected with, say, chairness. If those cues reappear, we conclude that we are looking at a chair. That is functional because, in the vast majority of instances when those cues are present, we will indeed be looking at a chair. It is only on occasional instances that chair cues will emanate from something that is not a chair.

The important points in this Brunswikian argument are that (1) people will interpret cues as they have in the past, (2) it is functional to do so because they will usually be right, but (3) under certain circumstances the very same cues can be misleading. Whenever we look at something, we make an assumption about what we are looking at. These assumptions have been built up over the years on the basis of experience. The assumptions usually lead us to accurate perceptions, but they don't always have to. In Brunswik's view, all the cues that we look at are inherently ambiguous. The cues that tell us we are looking at a chair could come from something else that is not a chair at all.

---

of optical illusions. This simply requires a hypothesis that any illusion taps a process that is functional in general but misleading in the particular instance. What makes the process misleading is the ecological unrepresentativeness of the situation: it is unlike the general run of situations to which the process is functionally adaptive.

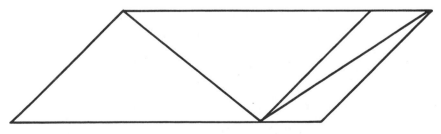

FIGURE 4-1. The Sander parallelogram illusion

Thus, optical illusions may be thought of as providing atypical settings offering misleading cues.

CULTURAL DIFFERENCES IN THE PERCEPTION OF OPTICAL ILLUSIONS

To involve culture requires a simple extension of this theory: *If human groups differ in their visual inference systems, it is because their environments differ.* It also seems reasonable to assume that neither by learning nor by genetic selection would populations have come to differ on these processes unless the ecological validities of the processes differed. (Note the compatibility of this logic with the ecocultural framework, which we introduced in Chapter 1.)

Three Empiricist Hypotheses

Starting from this position, Segall and his colleagues (1966) derived three specific hypotheses: (1) the carpentered world, (2) front-horizontal foreshortening, and (3) symbolizing three dimensions in two. We will discuss each briefly.

The Carpentered-World Hypothesis

This hypothesis applies to illusions like the Sander parallelogram, an example of which appeared in Figure 4-1. For this drawing, the well-established tendency (at least of Western or Westernized respondents) is to judge the left diagonal as longer than it really is. This bias is understandable as the result of a tendency to perceive a parallelogram drawn on a flat surface as a representation of a rectangular surface extended in space. Hence, the viewer judges the distance covered by the left diagonal as greater than the distance covered by the right diagonal.

This judgment reflects a habit of inference that has ecological validity in highly carpentered environments. Many societies provide environments replete with rectangular objects. These objects, when projected on the retina, are represented by nonrectangular images. The tendency to interpret obtuse and acute angles in retinal images as deriving from rectangular objects is likely to be so pervasively reinforced in carpentered settings that the tendency becomes automatic and unconscious relatively early in life. For those living where carpentered structures are a small portion of the visual environment, straight lines and precise right angles are a rarity. As a result, the influence habit of interpreting acute and obtuse angles as right angles extended in space would not be learned, at least not so well.

The application of this line of reasoning to the Müller-Lyer illusion shown in Figure 4-2 is somewhat more complicated.

We again assume that persons raised in a carpentered world would tend to perceive the Müller-Lyer figure as a representation of three-dimensional objects, extended in space. In this instance, the two main portions of the drawing represent two objects. For example, for the portion on the left, if the horizontal segment were perceived as the representation of, say, the edge of a box, it would be a *front edge*. For the portion on the right, if the horizontal segment were perceived as the edge of another box, it would be the *back edge* along the inside of the box. Hence, the left-hand horizontal would "have to be" shorter than the drawing makes it out to be, while the right-hand horizontal would "have to be" longer.

Front-Horizontal Foreshortening

Lines in the horizontal plane that extend away from an observer appear to be more foreshortened than lines that cross the viewer's line of vision. Picture a sidewalk one yard wide and marked off in squares one yard long (see Figure 4-3).

Consider first the square at your feet, then a square 50 yards away. In terms of retinal images (or extent on the surface of a photograph), whereas all dimensions of the square are reduced in the 50-yard case, the edges parallel to the line of regard are much more foreshortened.

Thus, as Woodworth (1938) observed, "A short vertical line in a drawing may represent a relatively long horizontal line extending away from the observer. The horizontal-vertical illusion can be explained by supposing the vertical to represent such a foreshortened horizontal line" (p. 645). Such an inference habit would have varying validity in varying environments. For people living on flat plains with open vistas, there would be great ecological validity in interpreting vertical lines on the retina as long lines extending into the distance. The opposite should pertain for canyon dwellers or rain-forest dwellers, for whom vistas are constricted and who should be less susceptible, therefore, to the horizontal/vertical illusion than plains dwellers are.

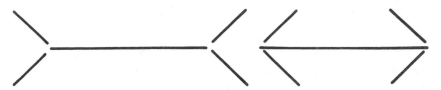

FIGURE 4-2. The Müller-Lyer illusion

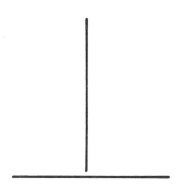

FIGURE 4-3. The horizontal-vertical illusion

Symbolizing Three Dimensions in Two

Another dominant ecological factor relevant to the line illusions is the pervasive role of symbols on paper in Western civilization. Although most of this symbolization is connected with the representation of language, it has also been used for an iconic representation of space, as in maps and figures of persons, animals, houses, and so on. An increasingly dominant portion of such drawings has involved representing three-dimensional spatial arrays on the two-dimensional surfaces of paper, canvas, or wall.

It is hard for many people today to realize that this tradition of representing three dimensions in two also has the character of an arbitrary convention, since it is now so widespread. Nonetheless, it is a convention and, as such, it contributes to illusion susceptibility. The more experience we have with pictures, the more susceptible we will be to certain optical illusions.

To summarize the theoretical argument:

1. So-called optical illusions may result because learned habits of inference are inappropriately applied.
2. In different physical and cultural environments, different habits of inference are likely to be acquired, reflecting differing ecological validities.
3. There is a learned tendency among people in carpentered environments to interpret nonrectangular figures as rectangular, to perceive the figures in perspective, and to interpret them as two-dimensional representations of three-dimensional objects. Such a tendency produces, or at least enhances, the Müller-Lyer illusion and the Sander parallelogram illusion. Since the tendency is assumed to have more ecological validity for peoples in carpentered environments, it is predicted that they will be more susceptible to these illusions than people who dwell in uncarpentered environments.

4. The horizontal/vertical illusion results from a tendency to counteract the foreshortening of lines extended into space away from a viewer. Since the tendency has more ecological validity for peoples living mostly outdoors in open, spacious environments, it is predicted that they will be more susceptible than Western peoples in urban environments. But some non-Western people should also be less susceptible to the illusions, for example, rain-forest or canyon dwellers.

5. Learning to interpret deficiencies in representational drawings and in photographs should enhance these illusions.

Initial Support for the Empiricist Theory

To test these ideas, stimulus materials based on geometric illusions were prepared for standardized administration under varying field conditions. Over a six-year period, anthropologists and psychologists administered these tests to 14 non-European samples of children and adults. The samples, most located in Africa, with one in the Philippines, ranged in size from 46 to 344. There were also three "European" groups: a sample ($N=44$) of South Africans of European descent in Johannesburg, a North American (U.S.) undergraduate sample ($N=30$), and a house-to-house sample ($N=208$) in Evanston, Illinois. In all, data were collected from 1,878 persons.

The stimulus materials consisted of many items, each one a variation of several straight-line illusions, including the Müller-Lyer, the Sander parallelogram, and two forms of the horizontal/vertical illusion. More details on the methods employed in the research are in Box 4-4.

Analysis of the choices made by people in the several samples provided evidence of substantial cross-cultural differences. The evidence constituted strong support for the empiricist hypothesis that the perception of space involves the acquisition of habits of perceptual inference.

On both the Müller-Lyer and Sander illusions the three "European" samples were more susceptible than non-European samples. On the two horizontal/vertical illusions, the European samples had relatively low scores, with many but not all of the non-European samples earning significantly larger mean scores. When the samples were ranked according to mean number of illusion responses, the rank orders varied across two classes of illusion. The Müller-Lyer and Sander parallelogram illusions composed one class; the two horizontal/vertical illusions, another. The overall pattern indicated not only cross-cultural differences in illusion susceptibility but also differences in both directions. This outcome had been anticipated by the findings of W. H. R. Rivers, a participant in the turn-of-the-century Cambridge expedition to the Torres Straits. (see Box 4-5.)

To illustrate their findings, Segall, Campbell, and Herskovits (1963, 1966) calculated the proportions of individuals in each sample choosing the typi-

---

Box 4-4 Administrative Details of the Illusion Research

For each illusion employed in the Segall et al. study, the discrepancy in length of the segments to be compared varied from item to item. As each stimulus was shown, the respondent's task was simply to indicate the longer of two linear segments. If a respondent chose the usually exaggerated segment, this was scored as "an illusion-supported response." Each respondent received such a score on each illusion; each sample received a "mean number of illusion-supported responses" score on each illusion. The higher the score, the greater the illusion susceptibility.

To minimize difficulties of communication, the linear segments to be compared were not connected to the other lines and were printed in different colors. Respondents could indicate choice by selecting one of two colors (saying "red" or "black") in response to the horizontal/vertical items and by indicating right or left for the other illusions. Another step taken to be sure that people in different samples understood the task was the administration of a short comprehension test requiring judgments similar to, but more obvious than, those demanded by the stimulus figures.

---

cally overestimated line segments. Graphs were constructed from these proportions, and points of subjective equality (or the average discrepancy at which two lines were seen as equal) were determined from these graphs. Figure 4-4 contains four sets of graphs that illustrate (1) the lesser susceptibility of the combined non-European samples to the Müller-Lyer and Sander illusions and (2) the greater susceptibility to the two horizontal/vertical illusions shown by one non-European sample group as compared with one European sample, and the lesser susceptibility of another non-European sample.

So, what we have seen so far is evidence for cross-cultural differences in susceptibility to optical illusions. These differences accorded well with a theory that attributes perceptual tendencies to ecologically valid inference habits.

That the data fit the theory does not mean, however, that the data rule out alternative theories. Nor can it be asserted that the data fit the theory perfectly. In the next sections we will consider an aspect of these data that does not fit the ecological theory very well, and then we will consider a plausible alternative theory.

Age Trends in the Illusion Data:
A Challenge to the Empiricists

One aspect of the Segall et al. cross-cultural findings that does not accord well with empiricist theorizing is the repeated tendency for illusion susceptibility to decline with age. This age decline was found for all illusions and in

---

Box 4-5 Illusion Findings in the Cambridge Expedition

Rivers collected quantitative data using two geometrical illusions (the Müller-Lyer figure and the horizontal/vertical figure) among several samples in the Torres Straits and in Southern India. For comparison purposes, data were also collected among English adults and children. Rivers (1901, 1905) reported that non-Western groups were *more* subject to the horizontal/vertical figure and *less* subject to the Müller-Lyer illusion than were English groups. Most provocative was the fact that differences between Western and non-Western people existed in both directions: the non-Western people were less subject to one illusion but more subject to another. Obviously, the failure to find differences consistent in direction eliminates any simple explanation of the existing differences. One of those explanations, prevalent during the 19th century, held that because "primitive" peoples are less well endowed intellectually than "civilized" people they should be more easily duped by illusions and therefore consistently more subject to them. The suggestion in River's data that for the Müller-Lyer illusion the "primitives" might actually be *less* subject to the illusions was embarrassing to any such hypothesis.

---

nearly every society. Decline in illusion susceptibility with increasing age is a widely replicated phenomenon. It was first reported by Binet (1895), and it was confirmed for several illusions by Stewart (1973) and Weaver (1974).

The empiricist line of thinking has to predict, for carpentered-world dwellers, at least, an increase in Müller-Lyer and Sander illusion susceptibility with age. In an effort to explain the failure of their own data to show any such increase — but, instead, a decline — with age, Segall and his associates suggested that the relevant learning that is assumed to produce susceptibility to illusions appears by early childhood (no later than age 6). They further suggested that following early childhood, analytic skills are acquired that permit individuals to counteract their tendencies to rectangularize nonorthogonal junctures. This "analytic-sophistication" hypothesis permitted retention of the empiricist theory.

Until recently, the hypothesis was purely "after the fact." But recent studies employing another illusion seem to clarify matters. The problem of age trends in illusion susceptibility is salient in some studies of the Ponzo illusion, a version of which appears in Figure 4-5.

The Ponzo is an illusion to which ecological factors, such as experience with railroad tracks and with many other perspective cues, are very plausibly thought to contribute. Indeed, that such cues *should* contribute is intuitively obvious. Not surprisingly, this suggestion has been made by many psychologists from the very early days of research on visual perception. See, for example, Wohlwill (1962) for a historically oriented discussion of some

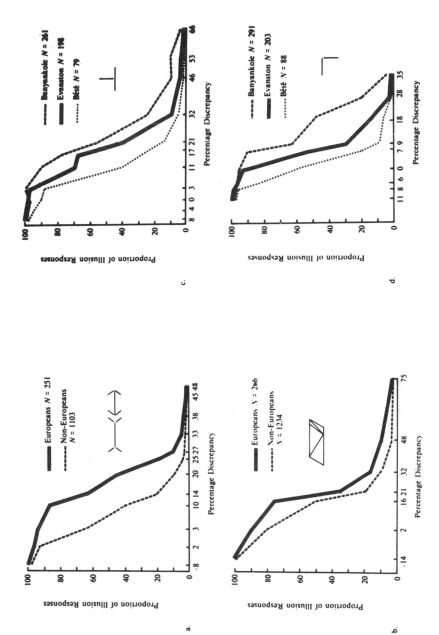

FIGURE 4-4. Proportion of illusion responses

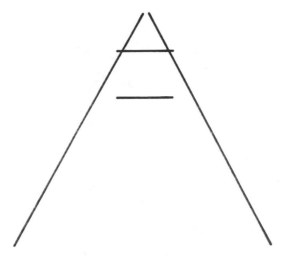

FIGURE 4-5. The Ponzo illusion

effects of perspective on pictorial perception and Gregory (1966) for a theory of "misplaced constancy," which explains illusions in much the same manner as does the ecological-cue-validity approach and which applies to the Ponzo illusion more obviously than to any other.

Cross-Environment Differences, Ignoring Age

Using various versions of this illusion, several investigators have, in fact, found differences across samples that had grown up in different environments (see, e.g., Leibowitz, Brislin, Perlmutter & Hennessey, 1969; Leibowitz & Pick, 1972; Brislin, 1974; Kilbride and Leibowitz, 1975; and Brislin & Keating, 1976). The last study, done in Hawaii, is described in some detail in Box 4-6.

Intra-environment Differences Across Stimulus Variations

In several earlier studies of two-dimensional versions of the Ponzo (see, for example, Leibowitz et al., 1969; Brislin, 1974), it was also shown that for young-adult subjects, the more depth cues included in the stimulus, the more potent the illusion. The version shown above in Figure 4-5, a line drawing, is sparse and abstract. It contains virtually the bare minimum of perspective cues. But they are compelling ones. Thus, the two converging lines could be interpreted as parallel lines extending into space away from the viewer. And the fact that one of the horizontal comparison lines is above the other could lead to the inference that it is farther away. According to the

---

Box 4-6 Perspective Inferences and the Ponzo Illusion

Brislin and Keating, in their Hawaiian research, arranged wooden boards to form a large Ponzo figure. The figure was displayed horizontally on the ground 13 meters (approximately 40 feet) from three sets of adult respondents, all of whom had recently arrived in Hawaii.

One group was from the mainland United States, another from the Philippines, and a third from various small islands in Micronesia, Melanesia, and Polynesia. The third group had grown up in environments that had very few constructed perspective cues. The other two groups (one Asian, and the other U.S.) were from environments rich in such cues. Hence, Brislin and Keating reasoned that, if the ecological hypothesis *did* explain the Ponzo illusion, the Philippine and mainland U.S. samples should *both* be more susceptible to it than the small-islands sample. This is what they found, confirming earlier cross-cultural results with two-dimensional versions of the illusion. They showed that ecologically valid inferences about perspective are apparently elicited by three-dimensional shapes in a natural environment, a phenomenon that heretofore had been assumed but not actually demonstrated.

---

ecological hypothesis, the illusion should be strongest for persons who have grown up in environments in which such depth cues are prevalent.

Consider now another version, in which the two horizontal lines are superimposed on a photograph of a field. On such a picture, contextual depth cues have been added. Consider still another, in which the comparison lines are placed against a photograph of a railroad track extending perpendicularly across a field, thereby adding additional contextual cues for depth. These latter two versions of the Ponzo figure are usually more potent than the abstract version, at least for adults in the United States, for example, American college students (Leibowitz et al., 1969).

What we have seen so far about the Ponzo illusion is all in accord with the kind of ecological, empiricist theorizing that has been stressed in this chapter. But, as already noted, the age trends that have been discovered in studies employing this illusion present a sticky problem.

Age Trends With the Ponzo Illusion: A Clarification

Some researchers employing one or another version of the Ponzo illusion have found increased susceptibility with age (which is what empiricists would expect). But some have found a decrease, some a decrease followed by an increase, and some no trend at all.

Confronted with these contradictory findings and taking note of the existence of different versions of the illusion as just described (abstract, "field," and "railroad track"), Wagner (1977) attempted to sort it all out in a study done in Morocco.

To allow age trends to reveal themselves, Wagner employed 384 boys in four different age groups (approximately 7, 11, 14, and 19 years of age). To study the possible effects of schooling, Wagner constructed half of his sample with school-going boys and the other half with boys who had never been schooled or had less than one year of schooling. To allow ecological conditions to influence illusion susceptibility, Wagner selected half of the sample in Marrakesh, an urban, "carpentered" environment, and the other half from a rural setting in the middle Atlas Mountains.

The several versions of the Ponzo illusion were administered to all the subjects, plus a "control" figure composed simply of two horizontal lines. Obviously a complex research design, Wagner's study yielded complex results. These will be described briefly and selectively, in the interest of comprehension.

For the abstract version of the Ponzo illusion, susceptibility decreased slightly, but consistently, with increasing age for all subjects, schooled or unschooled, urban or rural. Since this version is structurally simple, Wagner (1977, p. 172) suggests that it might be well to think of it as an example of what the Swiss developmental psychologist Jean Piaget (1969) has called a "primary," or Type 1, illusion. Piaget asserts that this kind of illusion decreases with age (or intellectual development) as children become increasingly able to make multiple glances that diminish the "Gestalt" of the compelling illusion.

Whether or not we accept the Piagetian theoretical idea, or even Piaget's terminology, this result of Wagner's (the decline with age in susceptibility to the abstract Ponzo) accords with an empiricist view mentioned earlier. This view holds that whatever produces the illusion in the first place (be it an innate disposition or an early-learned tendency) either decays from middle childhood through adolescence *or* is counteracted by other tendencies acquired as one matures, without necessary help from schooling or urban experience.

But for the two context-rich versions of the Ponzo illusion, the field and track pictures, susceptibility increased with increasing age. It increased more for urban dwellers than for rural dwellers, more for schooled than for unschooled boys, and most for boys who were both urban and school going. Moreover, although for all groups combined the abstract illusion was more potent on average than the two context-rich ones, the oldest schooled subjects were more susceptible to the two complex illusions than to the abstract one. Thus, the finding described in this paragraph provide evidence for the view that susceptibility to the more complex Ponzo figures grows as a product of increasing perceptual and cognitive activity of the kinds made more probable by living in an urban environment and going to school.

These findings seem quite compatible with an ecological, empiricist argument:

First, for two out of three versions of the Ponzo there is increasing susceptibility with increasing age, a finding that Segall et al. (1966) had sought in vain.

Second, these positive age trends, as Wagner has put it, seem to require "perceptual development that is not merely 'age-related' or maturational," because they depend on schooling and an urban environment.

Third, because the more context-rich figures are *in general* less potent illusions than the abstract version, it makes sense in light of the empiricist theory that the complex figures accrue potency, especially for subjects who have opportunities to acquire illusion-enhancing inference habits (older, urban, schooled boys). These relatively weak versions, obviously not yet "at ceiling" for younger boys, can reveal the effects of relevant inference habits as these habits are acquired by older boys. By the same token, the abstract version of the illusion is already so strong for 7-year-olds that age trends will either be flat or, as Wagner found, declining.

All in all, then, this well-designed study from Morocco goes a long way toward clarifying heretofore confusing age-trend data on the Ponzo illusion. Might a similar phenomenon apply to other illusions (for example, the Müller-Lyer figure and Sander parallelogram)? We simply don't know.

A Plausible Rival Hypothesis

Despite the support now available for the ecological theory, a physiological hypothesis must also be considered. Because several investigators had found decreasing illusion susceptibility with age, and since Pollack (1963) found that older subjects have greater difficulty detecting contours, he suggested that illusion susceptibility might be functionally related to contour-detection ability. Indeed, Pollack and Silvar (1967) showed a correlation between contour-detection ability and susceptibility to the Müller-Lyer illusion. The harder it was for subjects to detect contours, the less susceptible they were to the illusion.

The same two investigators (Silvar & Pollack, 1967) also showed that retinal pigmentation is correlated with contour-detection threshold. In other words, persons with denser retinal pigmentation (e.g., dark-skinned persons) have more difficulty detecting contours.

Another physiological/anatomic factor, corneal density, correlates with age and with exposure to sunlight. So Pollack has suggested that either this factor or retinal-pigmentation density, both of which might have varied

Box 4-7 Support for Pollack From Berry and Jahoda

Berry (1971a) administered the Müller-Lyer illusion to samples of Scottish, Sierra Leonean, Australian aboriginal, Eskimo, and New Guinean groups. Berry ordered his samples along two dimensions—carpenteredness and skin pigmentation—and then calculated the rank-order correlation of illusion susceptibility with each of those two dimensions. His calculations yielded correlation coefficients of .64 between susceptibility and carpenteredness and .82 between susceptibility and skin color. When Berry refined his reanalysis by calculating partial correlations—that is, the correlation of susceptibility and pigmentation with carpenteredness controlled, and vice versa—he obtained support for the view that skin pigmentation accounted for more of the cross-cultural variance in Müller-Lyer susceptibility than did carpenteredness.

The analytic technique employed by Berry may fairly be criticized as somewhat imprecise, with its numerical outcome dependent on the investigator's own ranking of the five societies with respect to carpenteredness and pigmentation. A change of position along either dimension for any two of the societies would have resulted in correlation coefficients of different magnitude. Nevertheless, Berry's 1971 paper showed that pigmentation could account for his cross-cultural differences in illusion susceptibility at least as well as, if not better than, degree of carpenteredness.

Data collected by Jahoda (1971) from Scottish and Malawian university students (24 in each society) also provided support for Pollack's line of argument. To understand the implications of Jahoda's study, we must consider how the color of stimuli relates to their visibility. It is in the shortwave region of the spectrum that density of retinal pigmentation is correlated with contour detectability. This was why, incidentally, Pollack and Silvar (1967) presented their Müller-Lyer stimulus under blue lighting. If Pollack were correct, Jahoda reasoned, it should matter whether or not a Müller-Lyer stimulus is presented in red or blue, but only for darkly pigmented subjects. Jahoda summarized this line of reasoning, modified it slightly, and then tested a very interesting cross-cultural prediction. Jahoda's argument went as follows:

> Scottish and African Ss ought to be equally susceptible when the lines are red, but Africans should experience a lesser illusion with blue lines. Such a formulation assumes that retinal pigmentation is the sole determinant of differential susceptibility; . . . such an assumption is probably too strong. Hence the hypothesis was cast in the following form: . . . African Ss will show a significantly greater susceptibility to a red Müller-Lyer illusion than to a blue one, while there will be no such difference for Scottish Ss. (Jahoda, 1971, p. 202)

That predicted difference was the only significant difference obtained by Jahoda. As such, it supports the pigmentation hypothesis of Pollack.

Later, however, Jahoda (1975) attempted to replicate his 1971 study but failed to obtain the same findings. This failure, of course, cast doubt on his 1971 findings.

across the samples employed in Segall and his colleagues' cross-cultural study, could account for what they took to be differences that were eco-cultural in origin. Noting that their non-Western samples were all non-Caucasian, Pollack suggested that race might be responsible for what Segall and his associates had accepted as cultural differences.

An early challenge to Pollack's physiological hypothesis was provided by Armstrong, Rubin, Stewart, and Kuntner (1970). They administered the Müller-Lyer and Sander illusions, along with the Ames Distorted Room, to 65 white and 65 black children (aged 5 to 19 years) in Evanston, Illinois. The investigators also assessed the retinal pigmentation of their subjects. The pigmentation scores correlated very highly with race, so race was employed as an independent variable, along with age and sex, in analyses of illusion susceptibility. For all three illusions, only age related to susceptibility.

That race showed no relationship to illusion susceptibility seriously challenged, at the least, the generalizability of Pollack and Silvar's (1967) finding. Their own particular experiment had employed an unusual variant of the Müller-Lyer illusion, presented under very special illumination conditions.

Some early support for the physiological hypothesis appeared in two studies described in Box 4-7.

Still, other efforts to test the Pollack position included a provocative attempt to link, theoretically, what is known about cross-cultural differences in color naming with parallel facts about illusion susceptibility (Bornstein, 1973). Bornstein suggested that people whose environment promotes the development of dense eye pigmentation, as is the case near the Equator or at high altitudes, would suffer from a relative inability to perceive blueness, and Bornstein (1973, p. 71) argued, like Pollack but in far less detail, that this differential pigmentation lies at the root of illusion-susceptibility differences.

A Challenge to the Rival Hypothesis

Struck by Bornstein's innovative attempt to integrate color-naming and geometric-illusion phenomena, Bolton, Michelson, Wilde, and Bolton (1975) undertook a well-designed study of illusion susceptibility with two groups of people living in the Central Andes of Peru. Both samples lived about 15 degrees south of the Equator, and they were equally carpentered. One sample, however, lived on a 13,000-foot-high plateau and the other at a much lower altitude of 4,500 feet. The two samples also differed in openness of vistas—great for the high-altitude sample and limited for those living at the lower altitude.

Bolton and his colleagues reasoned that Bornstein's pigmentation hypothesis would predict lower susceptibility to four different illusions (Müller-Lyer, Sander, and the two versions of the horizontal/vertical) for the high-altitude sample, since they are more exposed to sunlight. An ecological hypothesis, on the other hand, would predict intersample differences in the *opposite* direction, but *only* for the horizontal/vertical illusions, since the other illusions have nothing to do with openness of vistas.

The only significant differences obtained were for the two horizontal/vertical illusions. On these, the high-altitude dwellers, who "can see to distant horizons from 30 to more than 100 miles away" (Bolton et al., 1975, pp. 412–413), were more susceptible than the sample dwelling on forested hillsides 8,500 feet lower. Their data showed precisely what the empiricist hypothesis predicted.

This illusion study thus provided, as the authors stated, "additional confirmation for the hypothesis presented by Segall, Campbell, and Herskovits" (Bolton et al., 1975, p. 422) and, by implication, another challenge to the nativistic, pigmentation hypothesis of Pollack. Still another was provided by Stewart, in a study described in Box 4-8.

One More Study of Illusion Susceptibility

We will consider one more study that tests the "learned-habits-of-inference" position (Pollnac, 1977). In examining a report amusingly subtitled "Is the carpentered-world hypothesis seaworthy?" we discover that the author in fact tested not the carpentered-world hypothesis but its companion piece, the frontal-plane-foreshortening hypothesis. Employing a sample of 21 fishermen who work a very broad expanse of ocean along the Pacific coast of Costa Rica, Pollnac demonstrated that susceptibility to the inverted-T form of the horizontal/vertical illusion was significantly related to years of fishing experience and to degree of responsibility for navigation. The correlation between mere chronological age and susceptibility reduced to zero when it was controlled for by those two indexes of experience in making survival-crucial judgments of distance and size.

Thus, Pollnac demonstrated that variance in illusion susceptibility, within such a small sample occupying a single ecological niche, is very well accounted for by relevant experience. This is impressive support indeed for the ecological interpretation of visual illusions that we have so painstakingly examined in this chapter.

Conclusions Regarding Illusion Susceptibility

The several studies that have been reviewed in considerable detail in this section, beginning with the Segall et al. (1963, 1966) study and continuing with several others done by various investigators, mostly agree that there are systematic differences in illusion susceptibility across cultural groups and mostly support the empiricist line of interpretation, namely, that illusion

---

Box 4-8 Environment, Not Race, in Evanston and Zambia

Stewart (1973) correctly pointed out that Pollack's challenge to ecological theory underlines the need for a dual research strategy. First, one holds environmental carpenteredness constant while varying race. And second, one tests across environments while holding race constant. In short, race and environment have to be unconfounded in order to assess their possible contributions to illusion susceptibility. To test across race with environment held constant, she administered the Müller-Lyer and Sander illusions to 60 black and 60 white schoolchildren, ranging in age from 6 to 17 with the sexes equally represented and selected randomly from three schools in Evanston, Illinois. She found no significant difference in susceptibility between the two racial groups.

To test across environments with race constant, Stewart administered the same stimulus materials to Zambian school-aged children, again ranging in age from 6 to 17 and again with the sexes equally represented. In Zambia, however, the five levels sampled ranged widely from a group of unschooled Tonga children living in the very uncarpentered Zambezi Valley region to a group of middle-class children living in Zambia's cosmopolitan capital, Lusaka. A total of 432 Zambian subjects, all blacks, were tested. The major finding was that for both illusions susceptibility rose with increases in the degree of carpenteredness. Stewart's overall findings are summarized here in tabular form.

Mean Numbers of Illusion-Supported Responses

	Zambezi Valley unschooled	Lusaka middle cl	Evanston black	Evanston white
Müller-Lyer	4.63	5.81	6.10	6.10
Sander	4.24	5.33	5.59	5.40

Clearly, susceptibility to both illusions increased with increasing carpenteredness of environment, whereas race mattered not at all. Stewart's research failed to replicate Pollack's research, even though she varied race in the same geographical setting as Pollack had, the Chicago metropolitan area. Her study's support for the ecological hypothesis is quite strong, because she employed more than one illusion and got essentially the same findings with both. Moreover, she actually used a third instrument in Zambia—a miniature version of the Ames Distorted Room—and got similar results. Clearly, Stewart's research findings offer strong support for the empiricist point of view.

---

susceptibility is a reflection of acquired habits of inference, habits that are ecologically valid ones. The single most plausible alternative hypothesis — Pollack's (1963, 1970) pigmentation and contour detection theory — has not fared as well. Limited to the Müller-Lyer illusion, Pollack's hypothesis is, at best, no better able to account for cultural differences than is the empiricist hypothesis. And, as regards other illusions, the Pollack hypothesis is irrelevant. So, the empiricist hypothesis is as tenable today as it was at the outset of this research project, begun many years ago and inspired by that historic Cambridge Expedition to the Torres Straits.

Indeed, by the late 1980s, the issue of cultural differences in illusion susceptibility, and the reasons for those differences, had apparently become of historical interest only. We can find hardly any studies in the literature that were done later than the ones reviewed in this chapter. A thorough review, however, of "the evidence stimulated by [one of the] two dominant cross-cultural approaches to studying real and represented spaces: Segall, Campbell, and Herskovits' (1963, 1966) worldwide investigations" was prepared in the late 1980s by Deregowski (1989). Thus, although new empirical studies on illusion susceptibility are hard to find, the issue remains of interest.

CONCLUSION

After a quarter century of cross-cultural research on visual perception, it may be stated with confidence that people perceive in ways that are shaped by the inferences they have learned to make in order to function most effectively in the particular ecological settings in which they live. The research we have considered in this chapter confirms that we learn to perceive in the ways that we need to perceive. Thus, environment and culture shape our perceptual habits.

In the next section of this book, we will see whether a similar phenomenon exists with regard to some basic mechanisms of cognition. Might it also be the case that our culture provides guidelines for—and limits to—the way we think?

Part II
CULTURE AND COGNITION

The second part of this book (Chapters 5 to 9) deals with cultural influences on cognition and learning. When we use the term *cognition*, we are talking about the processes humans engage in when they gain and use knowledge about the world they live in, when they recognize, label and categorize, when they plan and analyze, when they consider probabilities, and when they solve problems — in short, all those activities we consider to be intellectual.

The study of cognitive activity is fundamental to psychology and to education. Students of the learning process, developmental psychologists, psychometricians, and educational researchers have all been concerned with aspects of cognition. Learning theorists have sought the general principles of the process of how knowledge and skills are acquired. Developmental psychologists have tried to delineate the growth of understanding that occurs as maturation and experience interact to produce changing views of the world. Psychometricians have developed techniques and instruments for measuring and describing both general and specific aptitudes. Education has been the prime area of application of psychological research along these lines. For the most part these psychological and educational specialists have worked in European and North American settings, but they have nevertheless had as their goal the discovery of panhuman generalizations about cognition.

Such generalizations cannot be achieved without cross-cultural research. The goals of cross-cultural cognitive psychology are twofold (Berry & Dasen, 1974):

1. To understand the range, the variability, the differences in cognitive processes as a function of cultural (including ecological and social) variables.
2. To understand the uniformities, the panhuman consistency in cognitive processes, so that valid generalizations may be made about human cognitive functioning.

Before we consider some issues in the cross-cultural study of cognition, we need to set the stage. Research, even though it may be "scientific" is never "neutral": it occurs in a specific historical and ideological context that gives it an implicit imprint. We therefore must return briefly to recent history to discover how some of the basic issues in the study of culture and cognition have arisen, if only to spot relics of the past that are often still hidden in paradigms of the present. There clearly are, even today, alternative views of human competence, and it is the purpose of Chapter 5 to consider these in some detail.

In Chapters 6 and 7, we will consider both universals and differences in the process of cognitive growth and development. To what extent do humans everywhere move through stages of intellectual growth? Do these stages follow in fixed order everywhere, and at the same rate? Or do they emerge in different orders and at different speeds in different social settings? That topic will lead us to study education as the generic term for cultural transmission, and in Chapter 6 we will examine in some detail various aspects of informal or so-called traditional education and the learning processes that are involved.

Cognitive processes are available to all intact human beings, but the contexts to which they are applied are culturally influenced. As we will see, information is processed by active minds employing rules that are based in culture. Some of the ways in which culture influences the use of cognitive processes will be the subject of Chapter 8. We will examine empirical research on categorization and sorting behavior, concept discovery and formation, memory, problem solving, and more complex behaviors such as the drawing of inferences about causal relationships. We shall also examine the effects of schooling and literacy on cognitive skills, a question that has given rise to extensive cross-cultural research. Finally, in Chapter 9, we shall examine how knowledge is acquired in everyday settings and how such "everyday cognition" differs from knowledge acquired in school.

We will see that culture indeed provides the context for, and much of the content of, these uniquely human activities. Despite almost a century of discussion and a few decades of empirical cross-cultural research, theories and expectations about cultural differences in cognition are still varied, just as in mainstream cognitive psychology there are different epistemological orientations, e.g., structuralism and empiricism. In an early review of cross-cultural cognitive-development research, Serpell (1976) noted that, correspondingly, some students of cognition postulate differences in very general and very basic intellectual processes, whereas others expect differences in specific skills only. There are also differences of opinion regarding the magnitude and the significance of cultural differences. Some take a quantitative, "matter-of-degree," position, sometimes accompanied by a retardation view; others have a qualitative, "different-in-kind" expectation (Berry & Dasen, 1974; Serpell, 1976). We shall attempt to simplify a very complex and controversial field of research; in-depth study of any one of the topics to be covered would reveal a much greater richness in both data and debate.

Chapter 5

Alternative Views on Human Competence

PROBLEMS STUDYING COMPETENCE CROSS-CULTURALLY

Europeans, from their earliest contacts with non-European societies, have felt a need to discover how non-Europeans think. They have long believed that "they, the primitives" don't think quite as rationally as "we, the civilized" do and that there is a form of thinking somehow adequately described as "primitive." To put it bluntly, many Westerners have thought that so-called primitive peoples are, simply, intellectually inferior.

Unfortunately, this is not just an accident of history that has finally been expurgated. Some still believe in a "great divide" between "civilized" and "primitive." Many more reveal their implicit ethnocentrism by positing their own social group (usually middle-class Western) as the standard against which others must measure up. Even recent research in psychology and education, some of it cross-cultural, contains latent ethnocentric biases. Sometimes ethnocentrism is almost inevitable, and some of it remains in this very chapter, if only because of the kind of questions that are asked here, questions that originate in European theorizing about cognition.

Ethnocentrism universally is a consequence of enculturation into a particular society, each of which values its own ways of being and behaving. A positive feature of ethnocentrism is a sense of belonging; its negative aspects are denigration and rejection of out-groups (Herskovits, 1948; Preiswerk & Perrot, 1975). Ethnocentrism is not unique to Europeans or Americans; it is pervasive worldwide, as we shall see in Chapter 14. Here, however, we are concerned with the particular kind whereby Europeans and Americans are considered intellectually superior to other groups.

Most recent, more sophisticated cross-cultural research underscores the invalidity of the "superior/inferior–us/them" world view by showing it plausible to expect that people in different cultural settings would vary in the way they learn to solve problems and in the patterns of skills they acquire. Now it is understood that cultures vary in the salience attached to certain skills, in the combination of basic cognitive processes that are called upon in any given context, or in the order in which specific skills are acquired (see, e.g., Cole & Scribner, 1974; Irvine & Berry, 1988).

Thus, while abandoning the ethnocentric expectation of gross differences in the level of cognitive activity, cross-cultural psychologists still expect performance differences and seek to understand how cognitive behavior in each setting is influenced by culturally shaped experiences. Thus, contemporary cross-cultural psychology does not deny the existence of cultural differences in cognition, but interprets them in the light of cultural relativism. This was not always so, as we see from some of the early history of research on culture and cognition.

The Legacy of Lévy-Bruhl

Early European research on the intellectual performance of non-European peoples was, as noted above, premised on inferiority and was conceived as a search for qualitative differences, usually interpreted as deficits. Although this ethnocentric premise dates back to the earliest contacts between Europe and non-Europe, we find its echoes up to the present.

Early in this century, the influential French scholar Lévy-Bruhl (1910, 1922, 1949) characteristically analyzed non-Western thought processes as "pre-logical."[1] As was common in those days, Lévy-Bruhl did not carry out any fieldwork himself, but relied mainly on the reports of travellers and missionaries. Lévy-Bruhl considered that prelogical thought was not alogical, or antilogical, or in fact (despite the prefix *pre* that seems to betray an evolutionary bias) a reflection of a stage prior to logical thought, but a totally different world view, its main characteristics being (1) the absence of a need to avoid contradiction, and (2) the law of participation.

To illustrate the first characteristic, the absence of a binary logic that does

---

[1]See Berry & Dasen (1974, pp. 2–12) for a short summary of early influences on the cross-cultural study of intellectual performance, Jahoda (1982) for a more thorough analysis, and Horton (1973) more especially on Lévy-Bruhl and Durkheim. For histories of anthropology, see Harris (1968) or Schulte-Tenckhoff (1985), and on the history of the concept of culture, Mauviel (1984).

not admit contradiction, Lévy-Bruhl used an anecdote gleaned from the report of a missionary. The story is that of a South American Indian, who dreams that his neighbor is stealing one of his pumpkins. The next morning he goes to inquire and finds that this particular neighbor had been in a town some 150 kilometers distant for the past few days. For the Indian, however, this is not a valid alibi, and when the neighbor returns, he goes to complain. According to Lévy-Bruhl, the Indian does not distinguish between dreaming and reality, he does not feel compelled to chose between incompatible alternatives.

For Lévy-Bruhl the law of participation refers to an alleged confusion between human beings and objects or animals. In totemic societies, for example, people identify with a particular animal as their common ancestor in mythical times, performing rituals believed to ensure the continual existence of that particular species, and sometimes saying they "are" the animal. For Lévy-Bruhl this meant that they lacked a clear sense of individual identity:

> Primitive mentality does not recognize an individual existence as such: individuals, human or otherwise, only exist inasmuch as they participate in their group and their ancestors. . . . To exist is to participate in a power, an essence, a mystical reality. (1910, pp. 250–251, our translation)

Many of Lévy-Bruhl's conclusions were based on the study of mystical or religious beliefs. This reflected the zeitgeist of French sociology of his day, influenced by Durkheim, that considered the existence of social facts (so-called collective representations) as independent from individuals. This problematic paradigm is still found in some social sciences.

Ignoring individual psychology, Lévy-Bruhl willingly inferred individual cognitive functions from collective representations. It is as if the logical thinking of European individuals was assessed solely by examining Christian doctrine (e.g., a child born to a virgin); might it, too, appear to be prelogical?

Lévy-Bruhl (1910, p. 10) stated that "primitives perceive nothing in the same way as we do" and attributed this to environmental causes: "The social milieu which surrounds them differs from ours, and precisely because it is different, the external world they perceive differs from that which we apprehend" (p. 10). Lévy-Bruhl also described "primitive" mental activity as less differentiated, not purely intellectual, with emotional and motor elements always involved.

In a later, posthumous work, Lévy-Bruhl (1949) reconsidered his positions to some extent, partly because he had come under severe attack from anthropologists with field experience, such as Boas and Malinowski. For example, he wrote, "I should have said: primitives perceive nothing exactly in the same way as we do" (p. 245). He also came to acknowledge situational variability. For example, he now admitted that the mystical orientation was not all pervasive, and that "primitive mentality, in everyday practical situations and in the technical domain, conforms to the laws of causality between phenomena observed sometimes with minute attention" (Lévy-Bruhl, 1949, p. 244, our translation).

He maintained, however, such thinking would become mystical, that is, prelogical, in case of an accident or some other unusual event such as sickness.[2]

19th-Century Cultural Evolution

After the publication of Darwin's *Origin of Species* (1859), the notion of unilinear cultural and social evolution was developed mainly by Tylor (1865), Spencer (1876), and Morgan (1877). It asserted that humanity had moved from savagery through barbarism to civilization via a series of stages, and that all social groups were subject to the same type of evolution, albeit at different speeds, with some societies being arrested at different levels along the way (See Box 5-1).

The theory of cultural evolution suited the colonial imperialism of the time, by "scientifically" justifying European conquest and domination. It also influenced Marxism to a large extent, especially in the writing of Engels. In the social sciences, its influence was widespread. Spencer (1875), for example, had explained the origins of religion as the progressive elaboration of animism, and Tylor (1871) and Frazer (1890) explained the magical thinking of "savages" as a kind of false science.

As noted by Jahoda (1982), Frazer's documentation was not always drawn from "primitive" peoples for, as he explained, the same confusion of ideas could be found among what he called "the ignorant classes" of Europe. "From this it is evident that Frazer was not a 'racialist,' but merely judged other people's modes of thinking by an implicit standard derived from the Victorian intelligentsia" (Jahoda, 1982, p. 170).

Much social science theory concerned with psychological growth, including developmental psychology and education, reflects this evolutionary bias. Theorists have tended to think of development, both individual and social, as a kind of linear unfolding process. Thus, the development from childhood through adulthood is sometimes viewed as analogous to a devel-

---

[2]Fully 50 years later the eminent British social anthropologist Evans-Pritchard (1971), although asserting that Lévy-Bruhl's conclusions about primitive mentality could no longer be accepted, still bowed in the direction of a qualitative difference. He asserted that "much of the thought of primitive people [sic] is difficult, if not impossible, for us to understand" (p. 283).

Box 5-1 The Stages of Cultural Evolution
According to Tylor and Morgan

In the second half of the nineteenth century, ethnologists such as Tylor (*Researches into the Early History of Mankind*, 1865), and especially Morgan (*Ancient Society*, 1877) gave a historical classification of societies according to their level of technical development. These are the "stages of cultural evolution" that all societies are supposed to have followed, some present-day societies having been "arrested" en route:

1. Lower status of savagery: Subsistence based on the gathering of fruit, berries, and seeds, eaten raw; appearance of language. No present-day society is at this stage.
2. Middle status of savagery: Use of fire to cook roots and fish in the embers; tools and hunting equipment made of wood and flaked stone. This stage is supposed to be represented by Australian Aborigines and most Polynesians.
3. Upper status of savagery: Invention of bow and arrow, basketry, and polished stone tools. Some West-coast American Indian groups are supposed to be at that stage.
4. Lower status of barbarism: Invention of pottery, some cultivation and sedentary settlements. Most North American Indians.
5. Middle status of barbarism: Beginning of irrigated agriculture and construction of houses with adobe bricks or stones. Most Indian groups in Central and South America would represent this stage in the New World, and pastoral societies based on the domestication of animals would represent it in the Old World.
6. Upper status of barbarism: Discovery of iron, agriculture with plow, and ideographic writing. It is to this stage that Homeric Greek tribes and Germanic tribes at the time of Caesar are said to have belonged.
7. Civilization appears with the invention of writing. (See text for a critical appraisal of this theory.)

opment from "primitive" society to "civilization." "Ontogeny recapitulates phylogeny" is the famous expression of this misconception. The validity of the analogy concerning human groups is extremely dubious, yet developmental psychologists (see, for example, Piaget, 1926, Werner, 1948, and Werner & Kaplan, 1956) occasionally assigned the "mental development" of non-Western peoples to a category that includes children and mental patients (see Hallowell, 1955). Similarly, G. Stanley Hall, perhaps the most famous early American educational psychologist, regarded nonwhites as the "children of the human race" (Muschinske, 1977, quoted in Jahoda, 1982, p. 187).

The cultural evolution notion "justified" the racist view that non-Western peoples suffer from arrested development. If this idea were not so recurrently fashionable and if it were not reasserted by otherwise competent and respected scholars, it could be dismissed as ludicrous. But it is, sadly, tenacious.

Our inability to understand people from a different culture tends to be facilely attributed to their qualitatively different, primitive way of thinking. Thus was the Lévy-Bruhlian model of qualitative difference joined to the evolutionary value system wherein one form of thought is judged as inferior/superior to another.

Lévy-Bruhl severely criticized the evolutionary views of Tylor and Frazer, however. To Lévy-Bruhl, postulating "a basic identity of the 'human mind,' absolutely identical in its logic in all times and all places" (Lévy-Bruhl, 1910, p. 7) was to imply that "the 'savages' have a mentality like children rather than adults" (p. 27). Lévy-Bruhl rejected this idea.

In fact, Lévy-Bruhl used the word "primitive" because it was convenient and current at the time but clearly stated that its usage as such was improper and only designated "the most simple societies that we know" (1910, p. 2). Perhaps Lévy-Bruhl himself did not necessarily attach a derogatory value to the terms pre-logical and primitive, but this was done by most of his readers.

Boas and the "Unity of Mankind"

The doctrine of the "psychic unity of mankind," first stated in modern anthropology by Boas (1911) and developed by his student Kroeber (1948), by Wallace (1961b), and Kluckhohn (1953) and others, dates back to the 18th-century Enlightenment, in particular to the writings of Helvetius, Volney, and Turgot (Harris, 1968; Mauviel, 1984), but had been displaced in the 19th century by cultural evolutionism.

The vast bulk of contemporary cross-cultural studies on intellectual performance, as we shall see in a later chapter, seems to confirm Boas's early generalizations and is congruent with what Kroeber and Herskovits (1948) lead us to expect. Scribner and Cole (1973), for example, reviewing a large amount of research including their own extensive field-work in Liberia, conclude that "all cultural groups thus far studied have demonstrated the capacity to remember, generalize, form concepts, operate with abstractions, and reason logically" (Scribner & Cole, 1973, p. 553). Or elsewhere: "Cultural differences in cognition reside more in the situations to which particular cognitive processes are applied than in the existence of a process in one cultural group and its absence in another" (Cole, Gay, Glick & Sharp, 1971, p. 233). In other words, cultural variation occurs in the readiness with which people engage in particular cognitive operations in a given context.

Lévy-Bruhlian Revival

Qualitative cultural differences in cognition, with or without an evolutionary component, are still posited by several "great-divide" theorists. In Table 5-1, we list several polar opposites that illustrate some great-divide distinctions.

Although the dichotomy in Table 5-1 is heuristically useful, it simplifies and exaggerates contrasts. The work of Lévi-Strauss, for example, is more complex than the contrasts set out in the table would make it appear. Greenfield's hypothesis of action-magic (in Piagetian conservation tasks) has never been replicated in other work; she has since taken a much more subtle position, not equating formal learning with Western and informal learning with non-Western (as we shall see in Chapter 7). The scheme developed by Bruner, however, defining schooling as "out-of-context" learning, and examining its consequences for cognition, is still being discussed and is congruent

Table 5-1. An Outline of the "Great Divide" Theories.

Theorist	Primitive	Civilized
	Non-Western	Western
Lévy-Bruhl, 1910	Prelogical	Logical
Lévi-Strauss, 1962	Bricoleur	Scientist
	Concrete	Abstract
	Signs	Concepts
	Myths, sorcery	Science
Greenfield, 1966; Furby, 1971	Action-Magic	Scientific thinking
Greenfield & Bruner, 1966	Context-bound learning	Out of context
Horton, 1967a,b	Closed	Open
Goody, 1968	Illiterate	Literate
	Pre-literate	
Goody, 1977	"Savage"	Domesticated
Luria, 1974 (Vygotsky)	Graphico-functional	Hypothetico-deductive
		Abstract
		Taxonomic
Scribner, 1979	Empiric	Theoretic
Mangan, 1978	Mythico-magical	Empirico-scientific
	Traditional	Transitional
	Field-dependent	Field-independent
	Contextual	Generalizable
Hallpike, 1979	Preoperational	Formal
	Concrete	
Denny, 1983	Inclusive	Selective
	Contextualizing	Isolating

with the historical-anthropological writings of Goody, and the sociohistorical school of Vygotsky and Luria (see Chapter 8).

What is exaggerated in Table 5-1 is the division of humanity; the terms civilized and primitive, having gone out of fashion, are replaced by Western and non-Western, literate and illiterate, and so on. An explicit instance of what is most objectionable in this is Hippler's (1980) assertion that "cultural evolution may have resulted in clearly more adequate meta-capacities" (p. 2) in Western society. He asks cross-cultural scholars "to recognize that such differences can be objectively hierarchical *in the light of human potential*" (p. 2, italics in text), their failure to do so is interpreted by Hippler as a result of "oedipal anxiety and a need to deny that one is symbolically taking the parental place" (p. 3). Mangan (1978) and Hallpike (1979) are more careful, and refute such ethnocentric value judgments, but they selectively use (and misuse) empirical cross-cultural data collected by others to prove their point. For example, Mangan (1978) erroneously equates "field-dependent" with non-Western; Hallpike (1979) selects data from Dasen's (1974) Piagetian research with Australian Aborigines to attribute incorrectly a preoperational level to this population.

Are There Racial Differences in Cognition?

In many multicultural societies, both qualitative and quantitative differences in cognitive competence are frequently attributed to genetic (racial) instead of cultural differences. This issue was hotly debated in relation to the so-called Jensen controversy on racial differences in IQ scores in the United States (Jensen, 1969), popularized in Britain by Eysenck (1971), and quickly taken up in France by the "Nouvelle droite," seeking a "scientific" justification for their racist politics (see, for example, the French translation of a South African book, published under the pseudonym Hebert, 1977).

Research on so-called racial differences in intelligence has a long and distressing history. Much of the writing and thinking about race and intelligence has been sloppy, irrational, politically motivated, and extremely costly in human terms. In multiracial societies where whites have been politically and economically dominant and blacks and other non-whites have long been targets of discrimination, some of the most pernicious and inhumane discriminatory acts have been "justified" on the basis of erroneous beliefs regarding the causes of so-called racial differences in intelligence.

In the United States, for example, as Gould (1981) has compellingly demonstrated, biological determinism permeated not only popular thought but some scientific thought as well, including that in the field of psychometrics, almost unchallenged up to World War II. Gould's history of this sad chapter in psychological thinking includes critical accounts of studies that allegedly revealed cross-racial differences in brain size, where the data were without doubt distorted by the biased expectations of the researchers. Gould also described programs of legally enforced sterilization operations performed without consent or even awareness on women who scored low on IQ tests. Gould's sober account of this program, legally mandated in at least one state in the United States as recently as 1972, illustrates dramatically — almost unbelievably — the extreme implications that can flow from the naive belief that intelligence is biologically determined and that test performance accurately reflects it.

Genetic explanations for intergroup differences in intellectual performance continue to be defended by Jensen (1978, 1980, 1981) and others, but the overwhelming weight of evidence disputes them. See, for example, Jacquard (1978), Flynn (1980), Taylor (1980), Blau (1981), Gould (1981), and Scarr (1981).

Reasons for rejecting the genetic explanations are many. Recounted in Segall (1976), they include the following:

1. However much genetic factors may contribute to intellectual performance of people *within* any group, between-group differences may still be entirely produced by nongenetic factors. The point that between-group and within-group IQ heritability estimates (a cornerstone of Jensen's famous arguments) are totally independent of each other was first made by Scarr-Salapatek through a compelling agricultural analogy:

    > Draw two random samples of seeds from the same genetically heterogeneous population. Plant one sample in uniformly good conditions, the other in uniformly poor conditions. The average height difference between the populations of plants will be entirely environmental although the individual differences . . . within each sample will be entirely genetic. (Scarr-Salapatek, 1971, p. 1286)[3]

2. IQ is probably more influenced by environmental factors among some groups than it is among others. In other words, the within-group heritability of IQ is not even the same for all groups.
3. The environmental factors that are known to depress IQ scores are far more prevalent for groups with lower average scores.
4. Negative biasing factors inherent in the tests themselves apply far more to the very groups who have been maligned as "racially inferior" than to those who score high and prefer to think of all scores as revealing inherent capacity.

---

[3]The analogy between plant height and human IQ scores is not perfect, but the point still holds, since any two heritability estimates (within and between) are completely independent of each other.

5. Recent research in genetics shows that interindividual variation in genes is much larger than intergroup variation.

Many of these ideas have already been anticipated in earlier chapters of this book. Thus, earlier we learned that cross-cultural psychologists are very wary of using standard IQ tests with populations other than those on which the tests were standardized. This caution reflects an awareness that the tests are biased against other populations.

In earlier discussions in this book, we also made it clear that no behavior is determined solely by culture nor is any behavior determined solely by biology. The two major classes of behavioral determinants always operate in such an interactive manner that they are difficult to separate. For intelligence, as for any other human characteristic, biological factors provide a broad range of potential and the outer limits or constraints of that potential, but experience has much room to operate within those limits.

And since, as Boyd & Richerson (1985) made very clear, the action of biological evolution (Darwinian selection) is very slow, there has been virtually no biological evolution to speak of since the beginnings of homo sapiens; on the other hand, the action of "cultural evolution"[4] is fast, so differences between groups are therefore likely to be more cultural than genetic in origin.

CULTURE-SPECIFIC DEFINITIONS
OF COMPETENCE

Any discussion about possible racial differences in cognition is based on the premise that human competence can be defined in the same way in different human groups, each of which is endowed with a different quantity of this hypothesized universal competence. A second necessary assumption in this paradigm is that this competence can be validly measured in these different groups. Is mental capacity or mental power, to use earlier terms for cognitive competence, or what we commonly call intelligence, a universal characteristic of the human species?

Earlier in the century, psychologists had no doubt that their intelligence tests were measuring an innate capacity, of which individuals and societies could have more or less. Porteus, for example, had developed a maze test that was supposed to measure intelligence; he first travelled throughout the Australian desert, comparing "mental tests with delinquents and Australian

---

[4]This was defined by Gould as "the inheritance of acquired characters. Whatever one generation learns, it can pass to the next by writing, instruction, inculcation, ritual, tradition, and a host of methods that humans have developed to assure continuity in culture" (1981, p. 325).

Aboriginal children" (Porteus, 1917), before extending his program of testing worldwide and attempting a hierarchical classification of societies according to their mental capacity (Porteus, 1937). Many other such uncritical attempts to use Western psychometric tools cross-culturally could be mentioned (for one, Maistriaux, 1955).

Biesheuvel (1943, 1959) provided an early critique of this approach, distinguishing between mental competence and performance, a distinction, in the words of Hebb (1949) between intelligence A (the genotype, that can only be inferred), and intelligence B (the phenotype, that can be observed). Biesheuvel attributed differences between groups to the differential stimulation of the environment:

> Differences between cultures and subcultures within a society may exist both in terms of g and in the terms of the "machines" or specific abilities through which g manifests itself. Cultures are not equally intellectually stimulating; their socio-economic conditions vary as do their habits of child rearing. They practice different pursuits and value different skills. . . . A multitude of circumstances, including differences in nutritional levels, complexity of material environment, parental outlook and education, and schooling facilities, affect intellectual growth. (Biesheuvel, 1959/1974, p. 223)

Biesheuvel (1959/1974) further examined the implications of such a view for the use of intelligence tests:

> Hence measures of intelligence, as indications of the power of mind, are strictly comparable only within homogeneous cultures. There is no possibility of comparing the ultimate intellectual capacity of different ethnic or cultural groups. . . . (p. 223)

Vernon (1955) introduced the notion of intelligence C, the fact that an IQ test can only be a sample of intelligence B. For cross-cultural comparisons, because of the differences in what is valued and practiced, this implies that a different sampling may be necessary for each culture, or to return to Biesheuvel's wording, "tests should strictly speaking be specially constructed and standardized for every distinct cultural group" (1959/1974, p. 223).

Further evidence for the noncomparability of psychometric tests came from the construct-validation of test batteries through factor analysis, a statistical technique through which the results of a large number of psychometric tests, usually obtained with fairly large samples, are examined on the basis of the complete matrix of correlations among the tests. Dimensions, or factors, emerge from the analysis: Those tests that measure a same psychological dimension are said to "load" on the same factor. These loadings are expressed as correlation coefficients. In one such study, MacArthur (1973) used 35 standard tests, among which were several forms of the well-known Raven's Progressive Matrices (PM), with Inuit adolescents in Canada and Nsenga Africans in Zambia. For the Inuit, a classical pattern of three first-order factors emerged: verbal-educational (v:ed), inductive reasoning with nonverbal stimuli (i), and spatial-mechanical (k:m). For the Nsenga sample, on the other hand, the same test battery yielded only two factors, i being grouped with v:ed. Thus, the same tests did not measure the same abilities in different cultural groups. McArthur's study demonstrates, as do many others, that the PM is not even a "culture-fair" test. And, it is now generally agreed that there is no such thing as a culture-free test.

A long time ago, Biesheuvel suggested that cognitive capacity may be the same in all human groups, but that in some circumstances, the environment does not allow individuals to develop to their full capacity: "Some depression of the mental power of Africans below its genetic potential can therefore be expected" (Biesheuvel, 1959/1974, p. 223). Implied is the idea of underprivileged circumstances that lead to some deficiency. A more radical view has it, as we shall see below, that cultural differences are not deficits against some common norm, but merely cultural differences. This implies that cognitive competence, or "intelligence," should be defined differently in each culture. As Wober (1969) phrased it, the question "How well can *they* do *our* tricks?" should be replaced by "How well can *they* do *their* tricks?" Advocates of this position of "radical cultural relativism" (Berry, 1972) have emerged in numbers over the last couple of decades: In addition to Wober and Berry, there is Serpell (1976) and Price-Williams (1975), and all those researchers who have studied so-called indigenous concepts of intelligence, a topic to which we now turn.

The Social Meaning of Intelligence

Dasen (1980, 1983) and Berry (1984) consider "universal general intelligence" only a hypothesis requiring empirical testing. Both also reject the view that intelligence consists only of unrelated specific aptitudes. They prefer to think of groups of cognitive functions, constituting "cognitive styles," that relate to certain ecocultural variables.

In this section, we will examine the "naive" or popular definitions of intelligence in different societies (which correspond to the parental ethno-theories of human development that will be discussed in the next chapter).

Bisilliat, Laya, Pierre & Pidoux (1967) did the first study of this kind among the Djerma-Sonhai in Niger in West Africa. They investigated the concept *lakkal*, a term that translates into English as intelligence but that signifies simultaneously discernment (understanding), know-how, and knowing how to live in accord with social norms. Lakkal is a gift of God, present at birth, but invisible before about age 7. In fact, parents do not use an age criterion; they say that lakkal should be there once the infant knows how to count to 10. If children don't have lakkal by then, they never will, although the medicine man can administer certain treatments to augment it. A child who has lakkal has a good understanding of many things, has a good memory, is obedient, and does rapidly or even spontaneously what is expected. The child displays respect toward elders and observes the "thou shalts" and the "thou shalt nots." Thus, this concept has at least two dimensions, one of them concerning aptitude and know-how, and the other, social competence.

Among the Baganda (in Uganda in East Africa), Wober (1974) studied a similar term, *obugezi*, which refers equally to wisdom and to social skills. To Baganda villagers, this term denotes slow, stable, cautious, and friendly, whereas to schoolchildren and urban-dwelling Baganda in the capital city, Kampala, it has connotations similar to those of the English term *intelligence*.

Mundy-Castle (1974), in a theoretical article, distinguished two dimensions of an African definition of intelligence—technological and social. In the Western world the first has been emphasized at the expense of the second, largely through the influence of writing. In Mundy-Castle's view, literacy allows an impersonal objectivity and the kind of analytic thinking that is the basis of technological development. This essentially Western dimension of intelligence involves the manipulation of objects and control of the environment. Social intelligence, on the other hand, involves "being" more than "having," and interpersonal relations more than relations with objects. It is a dimension of intelligence that involves "the art of the soul," to which traditional education in Africa attached primary importance.

Mundy-Castle insisted that in many places in Africa these two dimensions are integrated, with the technological subsumed by the social. For example, school-based knowledge would not be part of intelligence unless it could be put to practical use in the service of the social group more than for individual gain. Mundy-Castle & Okonji (1976) attributed the origin of this social intelligence to the socialization emphases present in some parts of Africa during early childhood, particularly in the way mothers directly interact with their babies. These interactions do not involve objects as intermediaries. If the connection between these socialization practices and parental ethnotheories is difficult to demonstrate, the social dimension of the African definition of intelligence is well confirmed by Serpell's (1977a, 1989) research among the Chewa of Zambia, by Putnam & Kilbride (1980) among the Songhai in Mali and the Samia in Kenya, and by Super (1983) among the Kipsigis in Kenya.

Is this social dimension specifically African, or does it exist as well in other societies? Several studies compared populations in the Far East and in Australia. Gill & Keats (1980) asked students in Malaysia and Australia to define the term intelligence (*kecerdasan*) and to designate the behaviors that are characteristic of persons who are more or less intelligent. On the whole, the data showed strong similarities across the two groups, but whereas the Australians specified reading, speaking, and writing as the three most important aptitudes, the Malays chose speaking and social and symbolic skills. Thus, here too, there is a suggestion of the importance of a social dimension in the concept of intelligence that the authors attribute to "the Islamic idea of integration of oneself into one's environment" (p. 241).

In a comparative study of Chinese and Australians, Keats (1982) asked informants to designate the characteristics of an intelligent person. Results showed that the two groups equally often mentioned having an enquiring mind, creativity, originality, problem-solving skills, and the possession of knowledge. The Chinese chose imitation, observation, carefulness, and precision of thought, however, whereas the Australians more often mentioned communication and linguistic skills. The personality traits associated with an intelligent person by the Chinese were perseverance, effort, determination, and social responsibility, whereas the Australians emphasized confidence, happiness, and effectiveness in social relations.

Klein, Freeman & Millet (1973) studied the Ladino in a rural environment in Guatemala, in the only Latin American study we know of how intelligence is understood. The Ladino term *listura* does not appear to have a social dimension. This term connotes vital, alert, resourceful, and gifted. The children who are *listo* have the ability to express themselves, have a good memory, are independent, and are physically very active.

The researchers asked young village women to judge the listura of children to whom the researchers had administered various psychological tests. They found, for a small sample of boys, statistically significant correlations between the judged listura and scores on both the Embedded Figures Test and short-term memory tests. Listura and verbal aptitude, however, were not correlated.

In the same Guatemalan community, for another sample of boys, Irwin, Klein, Engle, Yarbrough & Nerlove (1977) found that listura correlated significantly with Embedded Figures and with a vocabulary test, but not with short-term memory. For girls, the correlations with all the psychological tests were significant. Although there was less than perfect correspondence, it seems that the definition of listura refers primarily to whatever it is that Western intelligence tests measure.

Moreover, the estimations of listura also correlated with "natural indicators of cognitive development" based on spot-observations of daily activities. For example, there was a statistically significant correlation ($r = .51$) between listura evaluations for girls (but not for boys) and the number of tasks that the girls performed. It seems reasonable that parents give children more tasks if they think they're capable of doing them in a satisfactory way;

this measure thus reflects parental perception of the maturity of their children. At the same time, the execution of these tasks involves learning, which can influence the judgments of the adults on the one hand, and the test performances on the other. In any case, correlational studies do not reveal the *direction* of causality (which in this case may well be circular).

Nerlove, Roberts, Klein, Yarbrough & Habicht (1974) developed a number of indicators for use in the Ladino community. One such indicator, called "self-managed sequences," also showed a significant correlation with listura for girls only. This indicator involved all activities that allow the child to move about the village, including simple tasks carried out without parental control, more complex tasks carried out under adult supervision, rule games (games of strategy, e.g., card games), interactive role play, and constructing objects.

Serpell (1977a) commented that these indicators are not truly derived from local culture and do not reflect local values. He noted that the presence of foreign researchers may have influenced the expectations of the informants, thus affecting the derived definition of listura. A reciprocal validation between the three sets of measures (listura evaluations by the adults, natural indicators, and psychological tests) does not, according to Serpell, guarantee the emic character of this research.

In his own research, Serpell (1977b) employed tests constructed specifically for the Chewa of Zambia: imitating hand positions, copying a human figure with iron wire or with clay, a verbal comprehension test in Chi-Chewa, and a nonverbal psychometric test of general aptitude (the Queensland Test of McElwain & Kearney, 1970). There were no significant correlations between the results of these tests and adult evaluations of children's intelligence. Serpell concluded that these tests, because they consisted solely of cognitive aptitudes, did not measure what the Chewa themselves define as intelligence, e.g., cooperation and obedience.

In light of these results, we may hypothesize that there is no relationship between this African conception of intelligence and the results of Piagetian tests at the level of concrete operations. Dasen et al. (1985) set out to test this question by exploring the concept of *n'glouèlê* among the Baoulé in Cotê d' Ivoire. Like elsewhere in sub-Saharan Africa, this concept certainly has a social dimension to which the more technological or cognitive dimension is subordinate. Among the different components of this concept, the most frequently mentioned one is ô ti kpa, "a willingness to help." A child has more n'glouèlê if it voluntarily offers services and carries its share of both domestic and agricultural tasks. This is not a question simply of obeying when an adult demands a service; the child is much more ô ti kpa if it carries out the task well, spontaneously, and responsibly. For example, Baoulé adults describe a child who is ô ti kpa as "one who helps parents instead of playing with friends," "one who does the dishes and other chores without parents' telling him or her to do so," or as one who "when I leave my daughter with her brothers in the village, and when she notices that the children are hungry she prepares porridge for them, and picks up her baby sister and puts her on her back when she cries."

The importance of obligingness in this concept of intelligence — of a readiness to carry out tasks in the service of the family and the community — may even be pan-African. Super (1983) provided the following example given by a Kipsigis woman that could very well have emerged from the mouth of a Baoulé woman: "A girl who is *gnom* after eating sweeps the house because she knows it should be done. Then she washes the dishes, looks for vegetables, and takes good care of the baby." (p. 202) Other components of the definition of n'glouèlê are listed in Table 5-2.

Among the components that Dasen et al. (1985) consider "technological" is *I sa si n'glouèlê* (manual dexterity), which is translated literally as "the hands are intelligent." For the Baoulé, manual dexterity is not independent of the intellect, as sometimes seems to be the case in Western culture. *O si floua* (school-based intelligence) is a part of n'glouèlê only insofar as scholarly accomplishments are employed for the good of the group. On the whole, these facts confirm Mundy-Castle's (1974) hypothesis that different components of intelligence in Africa are integrated into a concept that includes both a social dimension and a subordinate technological dimension.

DEFICIENCY VERSUS DIFFERENCE INTERPRETATIONS OF INTELLIGENCE TEST SCORES

It is beyond dispute that large differences exist between cultural groups, and between socioeconomic groups within complex industrial cultures, in various aspects of achievement in skills that are highly valued by the dominant cultures or sub-cultures: success in school; in speaking the dominant language "correctly"; in competing for jobs; and in gaining social status, recognition, and political power. The proper interpretation of such differences in achievement is unclear. There are two alternative models that have implications for the search for causes, for the assessment of consequences, and for the strategies to be used (if any) for intervention. These two different world views can be labelled the "deficit" or "deficiency" model, and the "difference" model, or what McShane & Berry (1988) have described as D-models.

The first authors to seriously deal with the implications of the two ap-

Table 5-2. *N'glouèlè*: Its Components and Their Meanings.

O yo n'glouèlè forè	Who will have *intelligence*
	Social
— *O ti kpa*	Obligingness, responsibility, initiative, know-how, obedience, honesty
— *Agnyhiè*	Politeness, obedience, respect
— *O si hidjo*	To retell a story (or an event) with precision: verbal memory
	To speak in a socially appropriate way
	Adults: to speak well in public, to know how to use proverbs
— *Angundan*	To act like an adult.
	Reflection, responsibility, memory
	Adults: wisdom
	Technological
— *I gni ti klè klè*	Observation, attention, fast learning, memory
— *O si floua*	Literacy, school intelligence
— *I ti ti kpa*	Memory (especially for school)
	To be lucky, to bring luck
— *I sa si n'glouèlè*	Manual dexterity
	At school: writing and drawing

proaches for psychology and psycholinguistics were Cole and Bruner (1971), later followed by an excellent review and expansion by Howard and Scott (1981), and others (e.g., McShane, 1983).

The Deficit Interpretation

Here is how Cole and Bruner (1971/1974) aptly summarized the most prevalent view of the source of ethnic and social-class differences in intellectual performance, the "deficit hypothesis":

> It rests on the assumption that a community under conditions of poverty . . . is a disorganized community, and this disorganization expresses itself in various forms of deficit. One widely agreed-upon source of deficit is mothering; the child of poverty is assumed to lack adequate parental attention. Given the illegitimacy rate in the urban ghetto, the most conspicuous "deficit" is a missing father and, consequently, a missing father model. The mother is away at work or, in any case, less involved with raising her children than she should be by white middle-class standards. There is said to be less regularity, less mutuality in interaction with her. There are said to be specialized deficits in interaction as well — less guidance in goal seeking from the parents, less emphasis upon means and ends in maternal instruction, or less positive and more negative reinforcement.
>
> More particularly, the deficit hypothesis has been applied to the symbolic and linguistic environment of the growing child. His linguistic community as portrayed in the early work of Basil Bernstein (1961), for example, is characterized by a restricted code, dealing more in the stereotype of interaction than

in language that explains and elaborates upon social and material events. The games that are played by poor children and to which they are exposed are less strategy bound than those of more advantaged children; their homes are said to have a more confused noise background . . . and the certainty of the environment is sufficiently reduced so that children have difficulty in delaying reinforcement or in accepting verbal reinforcement instead of the real article. (pp. 876–877; pp. 231–232 in 1974 version)

The social science literature dealing with lower-class populations and minority ethnic groups, especially in the United States, contains many such descriptions. "They imply failure or inability to behave in an appropriate way and so imply social and personal deficits" (Howard & Scott, 1981, p. 113). There are a host of characteristics that seem to occur together, that are part of a system, a subculture, sometimes described as the "culture of poverty" (Lewis, 1966). "It would be helpful to think of the subcultures of poverty as the zero point on a continuum which leads to the working class and middle class" (Lewis, 1969, p. 190, quoted in Howard & Scott, 1981, p. 116). In other words, the culture of poverty is defined only in negative terms, as what is lacking of the middle-class features, as "cultural deprivation."

Just as "primitive mentality" served as a rationalization of colonial domination, the "culture of poverty" concept and the deficiency model serve to blame economic deprivation on the poor themselves. "The poor are less intelligent — otherwise they wouldn't be poor — and they transmit their inferior genes to their offspring" is not an uncommon opinion that links the deficit hypothesis to biological determinism.

Of course such a model also has implications for the choice of intervention policies: Since something is lacking, it has to be supplied from outside (like giving food to the malnourished), the deficits have to be compensated. The intervention model that matches the deficit hypothesis is therefore "early stimulation" and "compensatory education"; in the intellectual sphere, this usually means practice in middle-class standard language, practice in using abstractions, occasionally providing a setting that allows self-initiated discovery. As Howard and Scott (1981) have phrased it:

Perhaps the ultimate conclusion to which one is drawn is that the deficiency perspective, by labeling people as incompetent, tends to generate remedial structures that perpetuate powerlessness and dependence, thereby validating the initial judgments" (p. 147).

The Difference Interpretation

Now, what is the alternative? The difference model first of all criticizes the way in which social-science research with minority groups has been done, namely by starting with the "imposed etic" of the dominant group (McShane & Berry, 1988) and studying only those skills and values that are particular to the dominant subculture. Using a methodology (such as psychometric tests) that has been developed in and for the dominant subculture may be inappropriate and put minority groups at a disadvantage. Thus it is claimed by the opponents of the deficit model that differences in aptitudes have been artificially exaggerated, that they are artifacts of testing, that they are more superficial than real, that is, at the level of "performance" rather than at the level of "competence" (in one of the formulations we shall come to in a later chapter), or in "content" rather than in "process."

> The crux of the argument, when applied to the problem of "cultural deprivation," is that those groups ordinarily diagnosed as culturally deprived have the same underlying competence as those in the mainstream of the dominant culture, *the differences in performance being accounted for by the situations and contexts in which the competence is expressed.* (Cole & Bruner, 1971; p. 238 in 1974 version)

Another, slightly different alternative, is not to deny that true differences exist, but to interpret these in a non-evaluative fashion: Differences are just that, differences, and not deficits. This approach, however, also implies that the researcher looks for those skills and values that the subculture chooses for itself, that is, an emic approach as we defined it in the previous chapter, or a "substantive framework," in the words of Howard & Scott (1981). As an example of research taking this option, there is, among others, the work of Howard and Gallimore in Hawaii (e.g., Gallimore, 1981) who found that industriousness (e.g., school achievement) in Hawaiian-American children is linked to the expressed need to affiliate with a social group rather than to individual competitiveness and achievement, as it is in Anglo-Americans. Cole and Bruner (1971) mention the work of Labov (1970), who demonstrated that African-American ghetto language, if appropriately observed, displays the same grammatical competence as middle-class Standard English, but according to its own rules rather than as a deviation from the "norm."

The difference model also has its critics, who usually argue that whereas the model itself may be correct and although minority groups do have their own strengths, they are nevertheless confronted practically with a world in which only the behaviors valued by the dominant social group are rewarded by economic and status benefits; in practice, then, they have to learn the tricks, or else remain marginal (and poor), and remedial programs are needed to help them learn those tricks. For example, De Lacey and Poole (1979) conclude a volume on the Australian situation in the following way: "In the pragmatic bread-and-butter world, the reality has to be faced: It is the Anglo-Australian majority that is likely, naturally enough, to call the linguistic and cultural tune. Let us be realistic enough to acknowledge this and to plan, educationally and socially, accordingly" (p. 390).

A difference interpretation need not imply ignoring policies designed to secure a more equitable distribution of wealth, quite to the contrary. That the poor are poor or the minorities economically less successful is not questioned, but the reasons for this are in fact attributed to the social organization of the complex society and its political structure, rather than to any inherent incompetence. Programs based on the difference model will therefore acknowledge the need for structural social changes. Without them, little will be accomplished. Such policies include the transfer of specific cognitive skills needed to cope with the demands of the dominant social environment. The most important aspect of programs of this kind is that they attempt to build up the group's own strengths, autonomy, and cultural identity. Becoming more competent in its own culture allows the group to become more competent also in the dominant culture (Feuerstein, 1980).

This digression into the study of minority groups in complex societies may seem rather far from the concern of cross-cultural approaches to psychology and education, but this is not so. The study of so-called ethnic groups (minority subcultures, immigrants, refugees, and so on) is recognized as an integral part of this field of study (Berry, 1984). Second, it will become obvious in subsequent chapters that the issues raised here are basically the same whether we deal with subcultures in larger societies or with separate cultural entities, because the latter are usually at the periphery (the "Third" World) in relation to a dominant and acculturating center. In each particular case, the historical context of dominant-minority group relations has to be taken into account, a topic we shall cover in greater detail in Chapter 13 on acculturation and Chapter 14 on intercultural relations.

The results of studies on cultural differences in cognition are not neutral. They are not neutral, first, because the methodology that has produced them is not, and second, because they can be interpreted in different frameworks, some of which have been reviewed in this chapter. Social scientists who claim neutrality still implicitly have frames of interpretation, the influence of which may be treacherous by the very fact of remaining unstated.

SUMMARY AND CONCLUSIONS

What we have seen in this chapter is that the study of culture and cognition does not occur in a vacuum; it is related to historical trends in social science, each of which brings with it a particular frame of reference. We have claimed that it is important to be aware of these paradigms to understand better in what context the research findings have been obtained and can be interpreted. For this very reason, this chapter is placed before any specific cross-cultural research on cognition is reviewed.

Chapter 6

The Developmental Niche

WHY STUDY DEVELOPMENTAL PSYCHOLOGY CROSS-CULTURALLY

In this chapter and the one that follows, we selectively discuss child development from a cross-cultural perspective. Throughout the history of developmental psychology (a specialty of many university psychology departments and reported on in numerous learned societies and journals), many theories have been spawned, all rooted in Western industrial society (North America and Europe, including the Soviet Union) and thus, to a certain degree, ethnocentric. The theories purport to be universal, despite their being based on observations and experiments involving a very narrow range of samples, usually children of a middle-class sociocultural background, studied in nurseries and schools. As in all branches of psychology, it is necessary to distinguish between what is in fact characteristic of human development everywhere and what is unique to a given culture.

A cross-cultural approach to developmental psychology is relatively new, but it has already yielded several texts and reference works. The reader may wish to delve more deeply into these than we will do in this chapter.[1]

---

[1]Particularly recommended are handbooks by Triandis and Heron (1981); Munroe, Munroe, and Whiting (1981); Wagner and Stevenson (1982); a special issue of the *International Journal of Behavioral Development*, edited by Dasen and Jahoda (1986); the excellent introduction by Bril and Lehalle (1988); and the handbook by Cole and Cole (1989). There are some developmental psychology handbooks based on research carried out in specific cultural arenas that provide examples of developmental facts particular to their settings; among these are South East Asia (Suvannathat, Bhanthumnaven, Bhuapirom & Keats, 1985), India (Sinha, 1986; Saraswathi & Dutta, 1987), and Africa (Oppong, 1980; Ohuche & Otaala, 1981; Curran, 1984).

We will not cover topics relating to early childhood development, despite its importance to developmental psychology. Numerous cross-cultural studies of early childhood have been summarized and analyzed in detail by Bril and Lehalle (1988). Berry, Poortinga, Segall, and Dasen (in press) cover in turn phylogenetic, hologeistic, and psychological approaches to early childhood development. These studies show that in early childhood development, there is both universality in the hierarchical structuring of stages (of motor development, sensory-motor intelligence, and semiotic functioning) and, at the same time, many differences in the timing of development that are related to differing cultural values and to varying opportunities to perform certain behaviors. Certainly, what might be called the contents of behavior varies as a function of the availability of models. Which models are available, of course, varies markedly across cultures. This enculturation proceeds certainly throughout the course of child development, and as behavior becomes more and more culturally marked, it eventually comes to conform to the adult model.

In the next chapter, we will emphasize childhood and adolescence, paying very close attention to two developmental theories, those of Witkin and of Piaget. Here, we suggest an overall framework within which to study child development from a global perspective.

THE DEVELOPMENTAL NICHE

The developmental niche notion, proposed by Super and Harkness (1986; Harkness & Super, 1983), is a means for integrating findings from psychology and anthropology. Traditionally, developmental psychology tended to study the child out of sociocultural context, while cultural anthropology emphasized the context per se and the already socialized adult. The synthesis of these two approaches is to make the child in its context the unit of analysis.

The developmental niche has three components: (1) the physical and social contexts in which the child lives, (2) the culturally determined rearing and educational practices, and (3) the psychological characteristics of the parents.

B. Whiting (1980) has noted that culture influences child development primarily by serving as a "provider of settings;" that is, by furnishing the diverse contexts of daily life. For example, in some parts of Africa, children participate fully in the daily activities of the extended family, a setting where several different people are continuously involved with the infant. This is a very different setting from that of a young child who spends much of its first few years in a crib or a playpen. The social context, formed by the persons with whom the infant interacts, shapes social behavior, norms, and values.

By the same token, certain characteristics of the social context are also strongly influenced by institutions (e.g., school).

The customs and mores that surround child care and prevailing educational practices vary enormously across societies. For example, different baby-carrying techniques determine the type and amount of bodily contact with the mother and thus the habitual posture, both of which can influence motor development and perhaps even the personality of the child (cf. Berry, Poortinga, Segall & Dasen, in press; Bril & Lehalle, 1988).

Super and Harkness (1986) attach importance to the psychology of parents (or of other caretakers), including the beliefs and values held about the development of children. These may be called parental ethnotheories.[2] Undeniably, these ethnotheories influence child development, in particular by determining contexts and training practices (Goodnow & Knight, 1981; Zack & Bril, 1989). Ethnotheories thus are reactive with respect to the behavior they seek to explain. (But so are theories formulated by professional psychologists like Freud and Piaget, which, once entered into popular consciousness, influence the very development they purport to explain. Thus, even "scientific theories" of child development may be reactive.)

The developmental niche is a system in which the component parts interact and function in coordinated fashion. Moreover, it is an open system where each component is linked with other aspects of the more general environment. For example, the mode of carrying a baby is tied to the climate (Whiting, 1981), and socialization practices are influenced by such sociocultural factors as the degree of food accumulation.

Super and Harkness (1986) also suggested that the organism and the developmental niche adapt to one another. Thus, as the individual adapts to its surroundings, the niche also adapts to the individual. There is a kind of coevolution. Certain maturational changes in cognition and personality determine the expectations that adults have with respect to children of different ages. The developmental niche thus changes itself in the course of ontogenesis.

In the following sections, we will examine studies that deal with important aspects of the developmental niche. We will first review studies of everyday activities (in particular, games played and chores carried out in the service of the family group) that are among the features of the cultural context which shape development (Whiting, 1980). These provide both so-

---

[2]These might better be called "social representations" (Moscovici, 1984; Doise 1985; Mugny & Carugati, 1985), since they are not theories in the sense of a set of scientific laws. They are prevailing ideas about developmental steps, their determinants (whether innate or acquired, the role of the spiritual domain, etc.), and valued goals of child training (Goodnow, 1981a,b, 1985; Miller, 1988).

cial and intellectual learning opportunities and are thus part of *informal* education. This is a concept we will examine in some detail, contrasting it with formal education, or schooling.

Children's Everyday Activities

Cross-cultural psychologists have learned some intriguing facts about children by watching them in real-world settings.

Observational Techniques

Real-world observation and ethnographic description may be distorted by the observer's expectations.[3] Thus, it is well to develop precise and, if possible, quantitative measurement techniques. Bril (1983, 1984), for example, has studied the socialization process in detailed fashion by making precise, quantifiable observations. Using video recorders, which allowed computerized analyses of different bodily movements, Bril observed young Bambara girls in Mali learning the task of crushing millet. She demonstrated in an eloquent manner how the girls' gestures gradually come to resemble those of an adult model, with perfect conformity achieved by the age of 6 years.

Whiting and Whiting (1975) made systematic behavioral observations of children in six cultures: Gusii in Nyansongo, Kenya; Mixtec Indians in Juxtlahuaca, Mexico; the village of Tarong on the northwest coast of the Philippines; Taira in Okinawa (Japan); the Rajput caste in the village of Khalapur of the Uttar Pradesh in India; and Americans in Orchard Town, a surburban New England community in the United States. The technique that they employed, sometimes called continuous observation, required observers to familiarize themselves with and integrate themselves into the situation so as to become as unobtrusive as possible. Notes were made on children's behaviors and their interactions with the physical and social environment during a predetermined period of time. These observations were distributed across entire days (but included only a single observation per day and per child). In order to standardize the analyses, Whiting and Whiting used only the first five minutes of the observations. In this manner, the research team was able to study 24 children between the ages of 3 and 10 years in each cultural group, with a minimum of 15 continuous observations per child.

Another technique, developed by Munroe and Munroe (1971), is the method of spot observations. This also requires the observer to be familiar both with the children to be observed and their surroundings, and even better, to be a member of the same ethnic group. Children's behavior is

---

[3]See for example the controversy raised by the work of Freeman (1983), whose description of adolescence in Samoa contrasts markedly with that given earlier by Mead (1928).

sampled on a daily basis at different hours of the day. For each observation, the observer makes a written snapshot of the situation, noting where the child was located, who the child was with, what the child was doing, etc. The observer may also question the child in order to learn, for example, whether the activity observed was demanded of the child by someone else and, if so, by whom. But this intervention in the flow of activity is minimal, in contrast to continuous observation techniques where the intervention can modify the behavior being observed. Thus, spot observation is a less reactive type of measurement.[4]

In the Munroe and Munroe (1971) study, spot observations were made on a strict daily schedule and, in the case of school-going children, during nonschool hours.

Play Time and Work Time

Observational techniques have been successfully employed in the study of time allocation for work and play. Whiting and Whiting (1975) found that the relative proportions of these two kinds of activities varied across cultural groups. This difference was particularly striking between the Nyansongo children (Kenya), who devoted 41% of their time on average to work, and the American children (Orchard Town), who worked only 2% of the time. Munroe, Munroe, and Michelson (1983), in a spot-observation study of Kenyan, Peruvian, and American children (aged 3 to 10 years) and their mothers, outside of school hours, confirmed this: on the average, 5% work time for the Americans and 50% work time for the Kikuyu of Kenya.

The Whiting and Whiting (1975) study, while revealing important cultural differences, nevertheless had some weaknesses. For example, there were only sedentary groups practicing agriculture, herding, or industrial production included in this study. There were no nomadic hunters, among whom adults typically spend relatively little time dealing with subsistence tasks (Sahlins, 1972) and who consequently demand very little from their children (especially from their sons) until about 9 years of age. This, of course, does not prevent children from imitating adults in their games or from participating in tasks if they wish (Hamilton, 1981). Unfortunately, we have few quantitative observations for these kinds of populations. Draper (1976), in what we believe to be the only such study of nomadic hunters, found that !Kung San

---

[4]Reactivity of measurement is a concern in all science and, especially, social science. Whenever a measuring instrument is inserted, its mere presence may modify what is being measured. Obviously, the more reactive a measure is, the less valid is the observation. For a critical discussion of the spot-observation technique, see Rogoff (1978); for other observational techniques in natural settings see Longabaugh (1980), Bochner (1986), and Postic and de Ketele (1988).

children between the ages of 4 and 9 years devote only 3% of their time to work tasks.

Thus, the relation between cultural complexity and time devoted to work by children is an inverse U-shaped one. Work time, for adults as well as for children, increases with the intensification of human control over the environment, rising to a maximum in agricultural societies with dense populations, and then diminishes with industrialization (Munroe, Munroe & Michelson, 1983; also see Minge-Klevana, 1980).

Furthermore, the demands made of children change with age. Whiting and Whiting (1975) asked parents to report how old children ought to be before they might comfortably be asked to perform particular tasks. Combining parental responses with direct observations, Whiting and Whiting determined the minimum age at which more than half of the children performed various tasks. The findings are displayed in Table 6-1.

As these data show, certain societies not only expect more participation by children in chores, they require it at an earlier age. This was particularly striking for the Kenyan society, where all the tasks included were performed by 3- to 4-year-old children. In Juxtlahuaca (Mexico) and in Tarong (Philippines), 3- to 4-year-old children carry loads, do washing, and tend animals but don't work in the gardens until 7 to 10 years of age. In Khalapur (India) and in Taira (Japan), children don't participate at all in agricultural labor and don't begin to tend animals until the 7- to 10-year-old period. Children participate in food preparation as early as 3 to 4 years of age in Nyansongo (Kenya), Tarong, and Khalapur, from 7 to 10 in Juxtlahuaca, and not at all in Taira or in Orchard Town.

The spot-observation technique allows an even more precise quantification of the age changes in the time spent proportionally at work or play. In a study of children up to 9 years of age among the Kipsigis of Kenya, a Nilotic

Table 6-1. Task Assignments: Youngest Age at Which Over Half the Children of a Given Age Group Were Reported or Observed Performing a Given Chore or Task.*

Chore or task	Nyansongo	Juxtlahuaca	Tarong	Taira	Khalapur	Orchard Town
Carrying wood and water	3–4	3–4	3–4	7–10	5–6	–
Preparing food	3–4	7–10	3–4	–	3–4	–
Gardening	3–4	7–10	7–10	–	–	–
Cleaning	3–4	5–6	3–4	3–4	5–6	3–4
Taking care of animals	3–4	3–4	5–6	7–10	7–10	–
Number of tasks performed by 3- to 4-year-olds	5	2	3	1	1	1

*From Whiting and Whiting, 1975, p. 94. Adapted by permission.

population practicing animal husbandry and itinerant agriculture, Harkness and Super (1983) found a rapid increase from infancy through 6 years of age in the time devoted to carrying out tasks in the service of the family group. From 15% at 2 years, the increments are approximately 10% each year, reaching 60% between 6 and 9 years. In contrast, the time devoted to play diminishes regularly from 40% at 2 years to approximately 8% at 8 to 9 years. Similar studies have been conducted by Dasen (1988a), who made 1,662 spot observations on 54 5- to 16-year-old Kikuyu[5] children in Kenya. The observations were taken during school vacation times or during non-school-going hours. Dasen also made 1,410 similar observations in Cotê d'Ivoire in West Africa, involving 47 8- to 9-year-old Baoulé[6] children. Results are summarized in Table 6-2.

These data essentially replicate the findings of Harkness and Super (1983) for 5- to 7-year-old Kipsigis children; that is, about 50% of the time was devoted to work. But in contrast with Kipsigis children, Kikuyu chil-

Table 6-2. Percentage of Spot Observations for Which Kikuyu of Various Ages and Baoulé 8- to 9-Year-Olds Play or Do Work.

Age (Years)	Kikuyu				Baoulé
	5–7	8–9	10–11	12–16	8–9
Play:					
Boys	24	30	22	50	39
Girls	22	17	2	3	13
Work:					
Boys	45	48	70	50	42
Girls	50	60	70	80	70
Number of subjects:				Totals:	
Boys	8	7	7	6	28 23
Girls	8	6	5	7	26 24
					54 47
Number of spot observations:					
Boys	268	228	221	188	905 672
Girls	220	168	151	216	755 738
					1662 1410

---

[5]Kikuyu are a predominantly agricultural East African Bantu population who also do some herding.
[6]The Baoulé are an Akan group engaged in subsistence agriculture in the context of a tropical forest.

dren's work time continued to increase after age 7, reaching 80% for 12- to 16-year-old girls. From 10 years of age, Kikuyu girls devote no more than 3% of their daily time to play. Thus, among the Kikuyu, a very sharp sex difference exists in the amount of time children spend working or playing. We will have more to say about sex differences below.

One might expect that a child who spends half of the out-of-school time working for the good of the social group would acquire not only the necessary job know-how, but also an appropriate value system. In a multivariate analysis of observed social behavior of the children of six cultures, (Whiting & Whiting, 1975), a dimension that emerged ranged from "nurturant-responsible" to "dependent-dominant." Those children who did more work were closer to the "nurturant-responsible" end, often offered affection or assistance, and made altruistic suggestions. In contrast, those at the "dependent-dominant" end sought attention or assistance and tended to make selfish suggestions.

Munroe, Munroe, and Shimmin (1984) confirmed this in a study of 48 3- to 9-year-old children, employing the spot-observation method in four cultures: Logoli in Kenya, Newars in Nepal, Garifuna in Belize, and Samoans in the Pacific. The children more engaged in domestic and subsistence-related tasks, even when not engaged in work, made more altruistic suggestions, scolded the others, and demanded assistance from them, and the others often obeyed them. "The picture is one of businesslike, efficient, purposeful behavior: Working children engage in a pattern of interaction that itself seems work-like." (Munroe, Munroe & Shimmin, 1984, p. 375). Children, certainly girls, who are often engaged with younger children, extend the behaviors they employ with them to other social situations. They often offer assistance or affection to people generally.

Differences Between the Sexes

As Munroe, Shimmin, and Munroe (1984) noted, societies differ considerably in the degree to which they distinguish between the sexes. Those that make a stong distinction have a tendency to involve girls from a very young age in subsistence activities, domestic tasks, and child care, in fact, in all the tasks that are typically defined as feminine in the society in question (see Ember, 1973). Very young boys are also likely to be induced to carry out these "feminine" tasks, especially if there is no older sister in the family, but the distinction between the sexes becomes quite clearcut subsequently. In Dasen's (1988a) study in Côte d'Ivoire, 8- to 9-year-old girls performed typically feminine activities in 53% of the cases and masculine activities in only 4%; for the boys, typically masculine activities represented 25%, whereas feminine activities represented 16%. In Chapter 11, we will examine other sex differences in more detail.

Play

The importance of play as a context for learning and socialization is obvious. Preschool teaching in the West makes heavy use of it, but in many non-Western societies the value of play in formal schooling is contested because parents consider school a place to work and not to play (N'guessan, 1989). Under the pressure of social change, traditional games have a tendency to disappear and to be replaced by television and commercially manufactured toys. Many researchers, sometimes sponsored by institutions such as UNICEF and OMEP (the World Organization for Preschool Education), have inventoried traditional games in Third World countries and in industrialized nations (e.g., Béart, 1955; Durojaiye, 1977; Traoré, 1979; Nijhuis, 1981; Muralidharan, Khosla, Mian & Kaur, 1981; Baudet & Sarazanas, 1982; Grand, Puhl, Tagini, Simonin & Niederer, 1983; Ivic & Marjanovic, 1986) and with native peoples in industrialized countries (Larose, 1988).

Games

The ethnographic literature is rich in descriptions of games; thus the Human Relations Area Files (HRAF) can be used to study their world-wide distribution. An excellent summary of hologeistic studies of games may be found in Sutton-Smith and Roberts (1981), who distinguish between "games" and "play." The former in principle involve two parties (either individuals or groups) who compete with each other in accord with well-defined rules until a winner is declared. They further distinguish between three types of games: (1) games of physical skill (e.g., racing, dart throwing), (2) games of chance (outcome determined by a guess or random event, e.g., roulette), and (3) games of strategy (outcome determined by rational choices).

Games of skill are found in all societies. Games of chance, on the other hand, are frequent in societies where economic or social uncertainty prevails, in particular in nomadic hunter-gatherer societies. Chance games are usually absent or even forbidden in sedentary agricultural or animal husbandry societies, where socialization is more authoritarian. In these societies, games of strategy prevail that demand conformity to rules and planning, values that are certainly important in societies practicing agriculture or animal husbandry or both (Roberts & Barry, 1976).

Thus, there is a relationship between the type of subsistence economy and types of games, with each type reflecting a different value system. Chance games encourage becoming accustomed to risk, while knowing that everyone sooner or later will, in egalitarian fashion, win. Not only are chance games particularly frequent in societies that traditionally live by hunting and gathering, such games prevail even as these societies modernize, as in the

Australian Aborigines (see, for example, Davidson, 1979) and the Inuit (Glassford, 1970). According to Glassford, among the Inuit, complex games of chance are played more frequently by the young, whereas the adults prefer simpler games that require cooperation and skill.

Make-Believe

Making believe permits novelty, creativity, and flexibility. It allows reversals of some power contingencies and the reversal of social control. (It is for this reason that role playing is often used in psychotherapy.) Whereas in games only the winner is "first," in playing make-believe, all can pretend to win. All can become what they are not, as when children pretend to be parents. Consider also the normative function of make believe in enculturation. Children making believe imitate and learn adult roles; thus, make-believe facilitates the socialization of aggression, the learning of power tactics, and social interactions.

Whether make-believe serves primarily to encourage creativity or to maintain traditional values varies systematically across cultures (Sutton-Smith & Roberts, 1981). Unfortunately, we don't know of any detailed study of role playing in hunting-gathering societies. In other traditional societies, however, with little work-role diversification, total conformity to adult roles seems to be the rule. Dasen (1988a) observed that Baoulé girls play domestic scenes in which they imitate the work that they will, before long, perform in reality: preparing a meal or a medicinal treatment, taking care of a doll (if not already responsible for the care of a real infant), looking for water or washing clothes, in short, all the maternal roles. Meanwhile, the boys imitate the agricultural jobs of their fathers, mimic the ritual dances, and practice those nontraditional occupations that are accessible to them, such as truck driving.

Media-influenced social change has augmented the number of adult roles that it is possible to imitate. In industrialized societies, children tend to role-play numerous real roles (doctor, astronaut, cowboy, or Indian) or fictional ones (Superman, Goldorak, or Asterix)[7] that are highly unlikely to have any real correspondence with future adult activities. The learning of a large number of potential roles and learning to deal with unexpected novelty probably stimulates flexibility, an important characteristic in societies undergoing rapid change.

---

[7]Superman is a well-known comic-strip character who first appeared in *Action Comics* in 1939 and has been the star of several motion pictures. Goldorak is a hero in a Japanese television series. Asterix is a famous and well-travelled (albeit ethnocentric) hero in French comic books.

Toy Construction

Most societies (for example, in sub-Saharan Africa) provide children with relatively few commercial toys. In such cases, not surprisingly, children make toys themselves. For example, Africanist scholars have documented the toy cars made from iron wire (and, if not available, from natural materials) by young boys all over Africa. Lombard (1978) gave a detailed description of these constructions among the Baoulé: car models with easily recognizable trade names and steering devices that control moveable wheels; bicycles; and little carts with wheels made from tree nuts, spinning tops, and the like. (See Figure 6-1).

These constructions, even those that are largely copies of objects in the adult world, express a remarkable creativity. The process of making these toys teaches children how to plan work, to organize tools and materials, to make measurements, and to conceive of objects in three-dimensional space — to mention only the cognitive features of the activity. In technologically developed societies, the toy-making industry tends to mass-produce single-purpose objects. These prepare the child to become a consumer and encourage possession, enhancing the importance of "to have" as opposed to "to do." Even commercially prepared building kits are now highly specialized; instead of generic blocks or elements with which one can create almost

FIGURE 6-1. Bicycle constructed of wire by a Zambian boy

unlimited combinations, the toy store offers prefabricated fire engine, tank, or outer-space base kits, the elements of which can be assembled in one way only.

Even among the Baoulé, however, not everyone enjoys the potential creativity of toy making. It is the boys, from about 10 years of age and up (and sometimes with the help of younger peers), who make the toys. Making toys constitutes about 10% of the play activities of 8- to 9-year-old children (Dasen, 1988a), but already by this age, the difference between the sexes is sharp. In several African societies, toy making is an activity reserved for boys; boys are also more likely than girls to be asked to assist in repairing a roof or fixing a chair.

Serpell (1979) asked Zambian boys familiar with wire constructions and second-grade English schoolchildren to reproduce geometric forms using various materials. Using paper and pencil to reproduce the forms, the English children performed better than same-grade Zambians. When copying the models with iron wire, however, the Zambian children performed much better than the English. There were no differences between these groups when copying with clay or plasticine (materials familiar to both groups) or when miming representations using hand gestures. This experimental finding demonstrates the specificity of certain cognitive skills. Contrary to what happens during early infancy, when familiarity with content seems to be of little cognitive importance (Dasen, Inhelder, Lavallée & Retschitzki, 1978), older children do not automatically apply certain cognitive competencies to all contexts. This implies that poor performance on a particular task does not necessarily indicate the absence of the cognitive capacity that the task purports to measure. As will be illustrated in the next chapter, it is quite possible for a capacity to exist but to be difficult to express in particular contexts. We are touching here on a fundamental question, that of the cultural specificity of particular cognitive functions; we will return to it in the next chapter.

INFORMAL EDUCATION

In current parlance, *education* usually connotes schooling; we use the term generically to include informal learning as well. Throughout life, our behavior is almost continuously being shaped by "educational" influences that impinge on us in diffuse fashion, originating with the people who surround us. As we saw in Chapter 1, enculturation refers to all those influences (of which we are usually unaware) that reduce the range of likely behaviors to those that are culturally acceptable in each society. Socialization refers to the explicit selection of behaviors approved of by the society's members. These include all attempts to control another's behavior, whether in two-person interactions, in families, or in larger social groups, whatever the ages of the protagonists, even though the influence usually flows from older to younger persons. Socialization often proceeds informally in everyday situations, in response to momentary needs, and sometimes involves simply observation and imitation and other times active inculcation.[8]

Socialization often includes relatively structured learning situations, with instruction provided at prearranged times and places by persons who are specialists to some degree. Examples include initiation ceremonies and instruction provided in age-grades and secret societies.

On the dimension from formal to informal, Ahmed (1983) distinguished the following categories of education:

1. Formal education or schooling.
2. Nonformal, or out-of-school education, which includes all educational programs aimed at those left out of formal education (very young children, the discards of the school system, young people in post-primary education, nonliterates, etc.).
3. "Traditional" or "parallel" education, which might also be called informal education. In contrast with the first two, it is neither provided nor directed by government institutions.

Informal education characteristic of the Third World is sometimes called "precolonial education," even though it still occurs. We prefer "traditional education." Traditional education should not be confused with "traditional teaching," which refers to a Western type of schooling employing more or less archaic pedagogical methods. This kind of teaching, spread by European colonial conquests and fueled by the zeal of Christian missionaries, still predominates in a number of countries. It may be contrasted with "reformed teaching" or schooling that is informed by modern pedagogy (Désalmand, 1983, p. 39). There is an abundant literature on traditional education (Fortes, 1938, 1970; Kaye, 1962; Kenyatta, 1938; Knapen, 1970; Laye, 1963; Leis, 1972; Santerre & Mercier-Tremblay, 1982, to cite just a few) which we do not analyze here.

Traditional education, in contrast with traditional teaching, is in essence adapted to the local cultural system, which it tends to perpetuate. Désalmand (1983) summarized the major characteristics of traditional education (see Table 6-3). From Greenfield and Lave (1982) (an article to which we will return) we extract the material presented in Table 6-4. These two schemas contrast traditional education with traditional teaching. (Beware! The contrast is not as clean in reality as suggested in the Tables.)

---

[8]More studies of socialization have been done than we can report in detail here. See, for example, Goslin (1969), Kagitcibasi (1988), Sinha (1988), Camilleri (1989), and Clanet, (1989) for socialization research done in a variety of settings.

Table 6-3. Characteristics of Traditional Education and School-Based Teaching in Africa.*

Traditional Education	Traditional School Teaching
1. Education is provided *everywhere*.	Occurs in *specialized* place, distinguished from the environment by the construction and decoration of the school.
2. Education is provided *all the time*.	Occurs at a *specialized time*. Separation between school days and vacation and during each day between school hours and free time. In the life cycle, separation between schooling and active life.
3. Education is provided by *everyone*.	Provided by *specialized personnel*, whose status and behaviors are different from those of the learners.
4. Education is tied closely to *environment*.	Tends to be *cut off from real world* (despite efforts to avoid gap between school and community).
5. Education *directly addresses needs of society*.	*Falls short of society's needs*, underscoring the tragedy of the unschooled – those rejected by the system. Also, limited access to jobs for school leavers.
6. *Integration* with *productive* work is established early on.	Is *separated* completely from *production*, particularly in technical schools not attached to the economy.
7. Training insists on a *cooperative community spirit*.	Emphasizes *individual competition*.
8. Education is for *everybody*.	Fosters *elitism*. Even where 100% of school-aged population enters school, system works like a series of filters.

(continued)

Table 6-3. Continued

Traditional Education	Traditional School Teaching
9. Education has a *broad character*.	Accents the intellectual aspect, *neglecting physical and moral education*. Manual labor is discredited.
10. Society is oriented toward the *maintenance of an equilibrium*. In societies where the major preoccupation is to subsist, a tendency to block innovation.	Society is oriented toward the conquest and *transformation* of the world. Major preoccupation is progress, innovation and creativity encouraged in business; schools reflect this only very slowly.
11. Magic and *spiritual* phenomena play a fundamental role.	Primacy is given to the *scientific* ethos.
12. Religion and the *sacred* are present in all of life, and education often participates in the sacred.	A tendency toward *secularization* in society and particularly in the schools. Religion a separate domain.
13. *Parents* play an *important* role in the education of their children.	*Parents* remain pretty much *outside* the activities of the school, playing little part in teaching but some in shaping educational policy.
14. *Old age* is accorded *positive* value and elders play an important role pedagogically.	A *disparaging* image of old *age*.
15. Relations among participants are *personalized*.	Emphasizes *business-like* interactions, which partly explains the debasement of old age — the old person is not productive or profitable.
16. The education models are elaborated by the society itself and emanate from it. The *language of the people* is used.	The educational system is imported, imposed from outside. A *foreign tongue* is spoken.
17. Knowledge is transmitted *orally*.	Learning involves *both oral and written* activities, but the latter are privileged.

*From Désalmand, P. (1983). *Histoire de l'éducation en Côte d'Ivoire* [The history of education in Côte d'Ivoire]. Abidjan: Centre d'Edition et de Diffusion Africaines. pp. 33–35. Reprinted by permission.

From Désalmand, P. (1983). *Histoire de l'éducation en Côte d'Ivoire* [The history of education in Côte d'Ivoire]. Abidjan: Centre d'Edition et de Diffusion Africaines. pp. 33–35. Reprinted by permission.

Table 6-4. Some Idealized Characteristics of Informal and Formal Education.*

Informal Education	Formal Education
1. Embedded in daily life activities.	1. Set apart from the context of everyday life.
2. Learner is responsible for obtaining knowledge and skill.	2. Teacher is responsible for imparting knowledge and skill.
3. Personal; relatives are appropriate teachers.	3. Impersonal; teachers should not be relatives.
4. Little or no explicit pedagogy or curriculum.	4. Explicit pedagogy and curriculum.
5. Maintenance of continuity and tradition are valued.	5. Change and discontinuity are valued.
6. Learning by observation and imitation.	6. Learning by verbal interchange, questioning.
7. Teaching by demonstration.	7. Teaching by verbal presentation of general principles.
8. Motivated by social contribution of novices and their participation in adult sphere.	8. Less strong social motivation.

*From Greenfield and Lave, 1982, p. 183. Reprinted by permission.

In most situations, formal teaching and informal education coexist. Officials often seek to supplant informal education by schooling. Whereas in Western societies a role of the school is social and cultural reproduction, school-based education in non-Western societies is often an agent of social change. This still usually proceeds unidirectionally—toward a Western model—and is frequently called "modernization" or even "progress." These are notions to which we will return in Chapter 13, which deals with social change and acculturation.

The Transmission of Know-How

In instances where informal education transmits specific, economically useful knowledge, particularly knowledge tied to crafts and occupations, informal education can include a very structured, albeit implicit, pedagogy.

In a study of weaving apprenticeship among Zinacanteco girls in Mexico (Greenfield & Childs, 1977; Childs & Greenfield, 1980) and the tailoring profession in Liberia (Lave, 1977), master craftspersons formulated their verbal instructions in close correspondence with the productions of the students, constantly adapting to their needs. They organized the apprenticeship steps in order of ascending difficulty. Moreover, they employed scaffolding[9] to effect a progression within each step, allowing trial and error only in the beginning when there is no risk of real loss.

Informal education thus involves more than just observation and imitation. Verbal instruction on the part of the master is an integral part of the apprenticeship processes, at first in the form of orders and later including confrontations and questions. The pupils, by contrast, speak only a little and do not ask questions.[10]

Chamoux (1981, 1983, 1985, 1986) worked also in Mexico, but in a more ethnosociological research mode, studying apprenticeship of different technical skills, including weaving. Chamoux (1981) provided a typology of know-how ("savoirs-faire") and its transmission. The typology employs a distinction by Barel (1977) between "incorporated know-how" and "the mastery of algorithms." Incorporated know-how results from the personal, concrete experience of particular individuals or groups. For them, incorporated know-how is neither analyzable nor decomposable—it is merely understood.

> The worker knows precisely what to do but he doesn't completely know how he knows to do it that way. In other words, this "incorporated know-how" is not readily transmitted via teaching. It is only handed down through apprenticeship, or by the very conduct of the work itself. . . . When the "savoirs-faire" are analyzable and able to be broken down, the knowing (savoir) and the doing (faire) may be disconnected. The knowing would then be embedded in some non-human aid (or amplifier), like a book, a contract, a plan, a set of instructions, a rough draft, and the like. (Barel, 1977, cited by Chamoux, 1981, p. 74, our translation)

Both incorporated know-how and algorithmic knowledge exist in any society; for example, we can find technical domains in all societies that scarcely depend on algorithms, "as if there always existed a bit of incorporated know-how, albeit secret, in all human, technical activity" (Chamoux, 1981, p. 75).

Chamoux distinguished two kinds of incorporated know-how: general, which is transmitted to everyone (or to a whole subgroup, e.g., females,

---

[9]Scaffolding is a kind of effective control of the learning process by adults. This term, as well as other technical terms referring to learning processes, will be explicated in Chapter 9.

[10]The observations of Childs and Greenfield (1980) were made by video taping quasi-natural situations. Since the taping sessions had to be prearranged, the technique was somewhat intrusive, but it allowed very fine interaction analysis. We will return frequently to this study, which we consider a model of its genre.

when there is a division of labor by sex), and particular, transmitted only to certain individuals or groups who become specialists.[11]

This distinction is illustrated with examples from a rural Nahua community in Mexico. There, agriculture is "man's work," while cooking and weaving are "women's work." Nevertheless, Chamoux's observations revealed that women possess all the agricultural skills, although they normally don't use them. Similarly, the men know how to make tortillas (cornmeal pancakes) if circumstances require them to. In contrast, weaving is an exclusively female activity.

Chamoux (1981) further distinguished transmission of know-how by a master (either informal or established) from transmission through a process of gradual *immersion*[12], whereby the whole family or indeed the whole village assumes the role of teacher. In the latter case, there is no specific apprenticeship relationship. Immersion occurs when there is a common cultural fund of gestures and activities that can frequently be observed and experienced.

This classification gives rise to the following schema, which includes the four logically possible combinations of types of know-how and modes of transmission. Although one might expect general know-how to be always transmitted through immersion, in fact Chamoux provides examples of all four combinations in the daily life of the Nahuas (see Table 6-5).

Agricultural know-how is an example of general know-how, even if practiced only by Nahua men (except for the spreading of fertilizer, the sowing of plants, and harvesting). Chamoux attributed this to passive learning during the early childhood years. In agricultural and domestic domains, children of both sexes can observe different skills being practiced just so long as they live with their parents in the village. Over the years, through simple observation, the children acquire, more or less unconsciously, the gestures, the

---

[11]Chamoux reviewed the methodological problems inherent in empirical research on technical know-how. For incorporated know-how there could be competence without performance; in other words, one could know how but not do it. An outside observer can neither rely on the observation of practices alone (which might not reveal hidden competences) nor on discourse alone (which often denies the distinction between competence and performance). Instead, the observer must attend to the division of tasks and performances according to social distinctions, sex, or specializations, and to the technical competences that are not usually translated into actions. In fact, Chamoux insists on the fact that the technical know-how is inseparable from historical processes and social relationships. It is the latter that very much determine the transmission of know-how and hence its division between social groups, according to what Chamoux calls "the process of social appropriation."

[12]Chamoux used the French word *imprégnation*, meaning "to be permeated, to be saturated, to soak up"; this is a neat metaphor for the process of enculturation, as distinguished from socialization. We might also suggest that the child learns "by osmosis" as a consequence of "being immersed."

Table 6-5. Savoir-Faire Transmission Modes Among the Nahuas.

	Via immersion	*From a teacher*
General know-how	Agriculture	Plowing, hunting
	Carrying loads	Embroidery
Particular know-how	Butchering	Weaving
	Meat processing	Music

sequences, and the operational chains of behavior. What is observed is always a real activity, a productive one, and not some simulation or demonstration.

Nahua Informal Education and Ethnotheories

Chamoux (1986) explained that observing attentively is the most generally used learning method among the Nahuas. The only instructions provided to children by adults are to "watch carefully" and "concentrate." Rarely are verbal instructions employed. Adults intervene only if the learner clearly fails to resolve a difficulty on his or her own. Intervening is subordinate to other modes of transmission.

Trial-and-error learning is conspicuously absent. For example, even in learning to drive a car, "youngsters learn to drive cars by spying on the drivers of the cars in which they happen to be riding" (Chamoux, 1986, p. 230). There have been anecdotal reports that learning "strictly by observation" occurs frequently among Amerindians (Native Americans) and in Asia. This topic merits further study.

In informal Nahua education, there are no formal steps or grades, no initiation ceremonies or rites of passage. No particular time is set aside for teaching. Since learning can take place, in effect, any time and anywhere, it is embedded in a great diversity of activities. No adult activity is hidden from any age group or from either sex. Chamoux (1985, 1986) contrasts this with school-based teaching, which she likens to the behavior of a theatre company, "hiding its backstage, keeping its rehearsals closed, and thus maintaining its 'magic' and its power over its audience, the learners" (Chamoux, 1986, p. 215).

Among the Nahuas, pressure to learn is seldom applied. In childhood, the only chore is to carry burdens. Only during adolescence, when an "active" phase of apprenticeship begins and when it is time for a young person to become "responsible," does pressure to learn become obvious. Physical punishments may then be introduced, but they are used rarely. The usual negative sanction is laughter, but even this is not to mock the faulty learner but rather to ridicule the bizarre product. Most often, the only reward is verbal, such as a general call to all onlookers to admire the success. For the

Nahuas, learning depends on the will of the apprentice and not on that of the adult educator.

Apprenticeship always involves real materials and full-sized products. The mark of success resides in the utility of the product. A potential for simulation exists in a few toys, but Nahua society does not value play.

Much like Super and Harkness (1986), for whom the psychology of the caretakers, or "ethnotheories of development," are one of the facets of the developmental niche, Chamoux (1986) grants importance to "indigenous theories of education" that appear to structure the pedagogical modalities in a coherent fashion. Chamoux's rendering of the Nahua ethnotheory is summarized in Box 6-1.

There is an important difference between Chamoux's account and that of Childs and Greenfield (1980) on weaving among the Zincantecos. According to Chamoux, the role of the adult is minimal; learning happens through observation (first passive, then active), paying attention, and concentration. In Chamoux's accounts, we find none of the so-called scaffolding reported by Greenfield and her colleagues. This stems from the fact that they focused on specific adult-child interactions (weaving), whereas Chamoux used a more ethnographic, holistic description of a wide variety of apprenticeships.

Schooling or Apprenticeship by Experience: A Few Occupations in Europe

Cador (1982) relied on testimony by masters responsible for advanced apprentices, readings related to the history of peasantry, and on his knowledge of medical practice to contrast schooling and on-the-job training. He posits different cognitive functioning for each. The student (in school) learns to manipulate symbols and to derive general principles but lacks access to concrete things that might be directly apprehended. The apprentice, on the other hand, and the professional craftsperson work more by analogy, having learned "to read the facts." Their cognition always relates to practice, and they are capable of extracting abstract ideas from reality without resorting to language. Thus, there seems to be an immediate, global, nonverbalized know-how, highly adapted to unexpected situations and to the reality of concrete objects. School-based knowledge, on the other hand, provides the ability to reason theoretically, to be able to explain how something works, rather than to make it work.

Cador stated that a combination of the two modalities is necessary for the practice of medicine. In effect, a young doctor, about to begin a career, is almost obliged to relearn the profession. He attributes this to the extended period of study, the style of the examinations, and the increasingly high-tech

---

Box 6-1 The Parental Ethnotheory of the Nahuas in Mexico

In the Nahuas' ethnotheory, the soul is not present from birth but gradually develops later. An individual has "soul levels," one of which is inborn and connotes character or destiny, whereas others may be acquired through personal effort. The progressively acquired soul may also be lost, and it is the duty of the adults to conduct rites designed to ward off this possibility. Soul loss would be manifest in illness, or in a developmental retardation, which are never attributed to the child's constitution but rather to external perturbations. (This is also the case in Africa, where similar ideas shape coherent theories of psychopathology and of psychotherapy [Sow, 1977, 1978].)

> Entire portions of Nahua educational practices can be understood as deriving from this conception. The models of normal development are only guides to be sure that all goes well. Authoritarianism is an absurdity, since one can't influence stages. . . . Punishments cannot be contemplated except when the child has already acquired a good portion of his soul (or his conscience). In brief, education can neither modify nor correct the process of acquisition of the soul. It can only make sure that this process is not hindered, and conserve what has already been acquired. It can also draw to the attention of the young their own maturation and the models to be followed. In a certain manner, it is the individual, the learner himself, who can best influence his own learning. (Chamoux, 1986, p. 235)

---

nature of medicine. These features of medical education have increased the barriers between physicians and patients.

The French Marsh Sweepers

Delbos, a rural sociologist, and Jorion, an anthropologist, conducted research on the coastal populations of Brittany engaged in salt processing, shellfish raising, and coastal fishing. In their book "*La transmission des savoirs*" (1984) they reflect on how empirical knowledge is conveyed and related to scientific and school-based knowledge. (Although they don't use the term, they are in fact studying enculturation.)

In these activities where competence is acquired through experience, within the family structure, skill rather than knowledge is transmitted. Empirical knowledge is not so much explicitly transmitted as reorganized by each generation.

> A craft can be learned nowhere except through practice; but it can be learned through any reference to it in everyday life, even serendipitously, through a conversation about it or any other topic. One learns the skill in any order and at any time, because it, the craft, is life itself. Marsh sweepers say precisely that when they state "You are born there, so, . . . you know it." (Delbos & Jorion, 1984, p. 140)

Thus, empirical knowledge is transmitted as if it were an unquestionable truth. Again, we see that with no opportunity to view things from a different perspective, ethnocentrism results from enculturation.

> The world teaches one to live, although it is not possible to attribute to it a specific educational action. From the whole environment knowledge wells up which can be received: to know how to do, how to talk, how to live, all these are learned willy-nilly, discovered by oneself, but corrected if necessary. It's the very fact that these have been learned without having been taught that gives them the glow of evidence, and makes all other representations of the world impossible. "One doesn't do things like that" . . . Obviously, what we know is "knowledge" while others have mere "beliefs," and while our beliefs are evidence, those of others are mere prejudices. (Delbos & Jorion, p. 141)

Informal education among the marsh sweepers is described in more detail in Box 6-2.

Delbos & Jorion (1984) contrast practical knowledge (or procedural knowledge acquired on the job, which is necessarily specific) with school-based knowledge, which is claimed to be general and even scientific. The power of the latter

> is in its plasticity. It is transposable to a multiplicity of circumstances where it can be applied with equal ease. In fact, however, . . . things are not quite so simple. To the degree that school-based knowledge fails to be authentically theoretical and is often simply "propositional," it lacks plasticity and becomes tied to a specific context—the classroom—the only place where disjointed propositions have any legitimacy. Inversely, procedural knowledge, as a set of routine actions, is in fact transposable to other contexts. For as long as it constitutes an authentic experience of nature, of the material world, it is general and is easily transposed, through the process of analogy. (Delbos & Jorion, 1984, p. 15)

Thus, the old marsh sweepers think of school, as well as of training programs and institutionalized professional apprenticeship, as useless. In the Maritime Trade School, parents often preferred to send their children into the commercial section, where "at least they would learn something." They wouldn't learn to fish or how to care for a salt swamp but instead the ritualized language of law and economics, and how to understand banking and administrative systems, and other means for avoiding being labelled as country bumpkins. "A schooled person knows how to juggle the account books, how to speak well, how to present a case, and how to get the advantage in the competition for grants and government subsidies" (Delbos & Jorion, 1984, p. 37).

What schooling provides, then, is more symbol than content; it provides the insignias of power. Although schooling is far from useless, it doesn't provide practical knowledge, which it despises, nor does it provide scientific knowledge. "What school transmits authoritatively is not science, but a shared common-sense particular of a time in history and a culture . . . , versatile like science, but to the opposite of science, empirical in its constitu-

---

Box 6-2 Informal Education Among French Marsh Sweepers, According to Delbos and Jorion (1984)

In marsh sweeper families, who also do a little farming and animal raising, children accompany the mother in all her work and very quickly learn little jobs. In the swamps, they learn first to do little ancillary jobs that parents prefer not to do themselves because they take too much time; these include, for example, watching the rising tide and opening the flood gates. Then, little by little, the "ancillary" becomes the "complementary" for boys of about 10 years of age, thus allowing an increase in production. Little girls, however, don't participate in this. It is said, "It's too hard for her, and besides, it is not her place," except when an urgent helping hand is needed.

In the space of about five years, boys will practice successively all of the tasks that are performed in the swamps, reaching levels of expertise on each successive task, in an order determined by the elders. The latter claim to follow the order of increasing responsibility and to give children only those tasks that carry no risk; in practice, this principle is breached in two ways: Risky tasks are occasionally authorized and, besides, other tasks with no material consequences are sometimes discouraged. For example, in order to free up a man, a boy may be entrusted to harness two horses to pull more than a ton of salt, while at the same time, he is not allowed access to certain zones of the swamp except according to a progressive schedule, involving a symbolic hierarchy defined by concentric circles emanating from the exterior of the swamp toward the interior.

At no time do adults speak of teaching per se. Never does a father give an explanation. He only gives orders, asserts prohibitions, and exclaims dirty words.

The boy finds himself involved in adult activities and holds his own in them, without anyone explicitly explaining the rules of the game. The child must discover through approximations, following the simple principle that if he doesn't get scolded, all is well. The notion that one can learn simply by copying others is here not applicable because never is it demanded that the child do the same thing that adults do. Instead, the child must do other things and they must be done elsewhere. Mimicking would not work. Learning requires observation and differed imitation, without demonstration and without verbal instruction.

---

tion, for it is subject to the constraint of taking the world as it presents itself" (Delbos & Jorion, 1984, p. 204).

FORMAL ASPECTS OF TRADITIONAL EDUCATION

The term *formal education* usually means Western-style schooling. It is generally assumed that informal education predominates in nonindustrialized societies. As noted by Strauss (1984), this typology is as false as it is ethnocentric (in more than one respect). Not only does informal education occupy a significant role in industrialized societies, there are also some traditional forms of education that are completely formal. Wagner (1983) calls these training systems "indigenous education;" they are characteristically well integrated in the life of a community, rooted in its history and religion, and make use of culturally adaptive practices.

In Europe, up to the Renaissance, all education was religiously based; only recently did education become secular and mandatory. All over the world, school systems linked to religious traditions (e.g., Judaism [Roskies, 1979], Buddhism [Tambiah, 1968], Hinduism, Confucianism, and Islam) still exist. These parochial school systems have not been well studied and only recently has attention been brought back to them, as for example, in studies of Quranic schools (e.g., Santerre, 1973; Santerre & Mercier-Tremblay, 1982; Wagner & Lofti, 1980; Wagner, 1987). A brief description of Quranic education, based on Mellah (1979) is provided in Box 6-3.

When Mellah says that Quranic education is in decline, he is referring only to postprimary levels, where official, government schools, usually based on the Western model, are taking over. Today, Quranic schools tend to be preschools, or supplementary schools. In fact, worldwide, the number of children attending Quranic schools is actually increasing (Wagner, 1982).

Wagner (1988b) characterizes formal traditional education as follows:

1. The schools are organized to pursue religious and other values of the society.
2. Memorization and mastery of sacred texts, often written in foreign and nonspoken languages, are the principal objective of the education. Recitation without comprehension is perfectly acceptable, especially early on in the educational experience.
3. Teaching, particularly for older children, often occurs in a two-person setting involving master and apprentice.
4. The master's role extends beyond transmitting knowledge in the school to influencing the social life of the community as well.
5. The pupils are not grouped into classes by age. They progress through stages as a function of what they already know. There is no concept of academic failure.
6. Schoolmasters and pupils are most often males. This is particularly true in Islamic societies, where attendance by girls in Quranic schools is a recent phenomenon but one that is spreading (Wagner, 1985).

Quranic schooling is often condemned in government circles as an impediment to development. Rote memorization (without comprehension and without critical thinking) is often criticized by educators. Is this justified? In longitudinal research in Morroco, Wagner and Spratt (1987) found that children who had completed Quranic schooling before entering government schools performed better than children who had not had any preschooling.

Box 6-3 Quranic Schooling: An Institution Near Extinction?

(Our translation from the original, in French, by Fawzi Mellah, 1979.)

Each society produces the institutions that maintain and reproduce the norms, values, and behaviors on which it is (or is believed to be) founded. Thus, the societies that have been partly shaped by Islam have produced, among other institutions, a particular system of socialization: Quranic schooling.

What is Quranic Schooling?

Quranic schooling is often seen as a sort of catechism or religious training through which Muslim children are force-fed the Quran and led to absorb the precepts that this holy book contains. Such an image is simplistic. While Quranic schooling is based on the Quran, its function goes well beyond religious teaching. It is in fact an educational system that spans many years from preschool to university and is designed to cover the complete education of the young Muslim.

It is true that this schooling starts with the memorization of the Quran and of the values and rules it contains, but rather early on (after about the age of 4), the pupils are introduced to other subjects such as grammar, poetry, and history. Later, they are exposed to an exegesis of the Quran, theology, and law.

Who Is in Charge of Quranic Schools?

In his study of Quranic schooling among the Peuls of Cameroun, Santerre (1973) remarks that this educational system is neither strictly public nor private but community-based. Indeed, it is not the state that creates, organizes, and runs these schools, nor is it the private sector as such; it is really a Muslim community initiative at the level of a village or a neighborhood. The teacher or "master" who is in charge of a Quranic school is not as such elected or designated. He actually emerges from the group itself. His functions will therefore depend directly on the confidence and the credibility that he enjoys in the group. Thus, there is no fixed salary, no school fees, and no compulsory compensation for the services of the master. He may be paid a small sum of money given regularly by the parents or a few gifts such as food, clothing, or animals, or even some work done for him by the pupils.

How Does It Work?

Quranic schooling was not compulsory by law, but few families would dare to withhold their children from this institution. The social pressure was very strong. Furthermore, Islam values knowledge and instruction, and thus almost all young Muslims used to receive some Quranic education. The percentage of schooled people was very high in the Arab world and in Muslim Africa and Asia before colonial penetration.

There is no fixed age at which Quranic schooling begins. The pupils start by learning to read and write (usually in Arabic, the language of the Quran). They write on small wooden boards, first the alphabet and then verses of the Quran, starting with the shorter ones. Then they have to chant these verses aloud and

(continued)

Box 6-3 *Continued*

to memorize them. Elementary schooling is completed when the pupil has written and learned the totality of the Quran. A celebration is organized to mark the event. The number of years this may take depends on the capacities and skills of the pupils themselves. The master does not impose any particular pace for learning, no schedule, and no exams.

Then begins, for those who want to go on, a cycle of studies that is more elaborate and rich in subjects such as history, poetry, and exegesis of the Quran. In turn, this secondary schooling can lead to more advanced studies in institutions that are essentially universities; the most prestigious of these in the Arab world are the Al Azhar in Cairo, the Zitouna in Tunis, and Al-Qarawijin in Fez.

The three cycles of studies have two points in common. First, Quranic schooling is meant to be a global education that transmits faith and general knowledge rather than a system of instruction that produces specific skills. Second, orality and memorization play a most important part in the learning process.

Whither Quranic Schooling?

Everywhere in the Arab world, and in Muslim Africa and Asia, Quranic schooling is declining. The elementary level is still functioning as a place to learn the Quran, sometimes in parallel with official government schooling (either after school hours or during school holidays), or it serves as preschool. But official schooling, whether public or private, now dominates. "As soon as the young Muslim has set foot in an official school, he is virtually lost for Quranic schooling" said Santerre (1973), and this is true in all Muslim countries.

It is to the credit of this formal but traditional educational system that it provides an important pedagogical experience, a sound knowledge of the environment, and a constant reserve of potential masters, appraised and accepted by the group. At a time when the school systems that were imported from the West prove more and more their inability to meet the expectations of Muslim societies, we can think (or dream!) that national or foreign policy makers may have enough imagination and creativity to integrate this Muslim heritage into their search for appropriate educational systems. We remain convinced that despite its obvious weaknesses, Quranic schooling can still be useful . . . if only for the preservation of cultural identity.

Wagner (1988a) speaks of "appropriate education" (by analogy to appropriate technology), to suggest that traditional education has a definite contribution to make, given the needs of Third-World countries.

Several projects, using techniques derived from the psychological laboratory, have examined the impact of Quranic schooling on performance in memory tasks (e.g., Wagner, 1978a,b; Scribner & Cole, 1981). While great feats of memory might be expected from persons who have learned by heart the entire Quran, the results of these studies have, in the main, not found any striking prowess. Only one kind of memorizing — serial incremental recall, whereby one keeps adding an element to a repeated series of related elements — showed any heightened performance by children schooled in the Quranic tradition. The notion of a general memory capacity is made questionable by these results. This is an issue we will come back to in Chapter 8.

CONCLUSIONS

We have seen in this chapter a sample of studies that place child development in its cultural context. The studies all related to the concept of the developmental niche presented at the beginning of this chapter.

Instead of concentrating only on psychological development per se, cross-cultural developmental psychology takes into account the physical and social contexts in which this development takes place and the relevant socialization practices and parental ethnotheories. In this manner, a coherent picture of human development is beginning to emerge.

In the next chapter, we will consider some theories of child development and assess them in the light of this emerging picture.

Chapter 7

Theories of Human Development

The course of human development has long been of interest to psychological theorists. In this chapter, we will review in varying detail two theoretical approaches, both spawned in Western psychology, and we will consider how they have fared in the light of cross-cultural research.

WITKIN'S PSYCHOLOGICAL DIFFERENTIATION THEORY

A diverse set of facts relating to individual differences, sex differences, and cross-cultural differences in some fundamental behaviors makes sense when considered in the context of "psychological differentiation" theory.

A Brief Overview of the Theory

Witkin and colleagues (Witkin, Dyk, Faterson, Goodenough & Karp, 1962; Witkin, 1978; Witkin & Goodenough, 1981; Huteau, 1987) developed a theory with a strong developmental component, and it has inspired considerable cross-cultural research. We will not go into great detail here on the theory itself or the cross-cultural studies it has inspired. Interested readers may find summaries and critical discussions of the Witkin-related cross-cultural research in Witkin and Berry (1975); Berry (1976b, 1979, 1981); Berry et al. (1986); Serpell (1976); Okonji (1980); LCHC (1979); Huteau (1987); and Berry, Poortinga, Segall and Dasen (in press), where a thorough presentation may be found. We provide here a very brief introduction, one that nevertheless serves to illustrate how the theory fits the ecocultural framework featured in this book.

The theory of psychological differentiation derives from laboratory studies done in the late 1940s dealing with the perception of verticality. In these studies, Witkin noted rather marked individual variation: Some subjects seemed primarily to employ internal, bodily cues (proprioceptive or postural sensations), whereas others seemed to use mainly external references (visual cues) when judging the verticality of a stimulus. This kind of individual difference (internal vs. external) occurred systematically over a number of different experimental tasks, but especially in the "Rod and Frame" test (RFT), in which a tilted rod that is enclosed in a frame that itself is inclined by 28 degrees must be adjusted to a subjectively vertical orientation. Those subjects who could do this well, with minimal distraction from the surrounding frame, were called by Witkin "field independent" (FI), and those who reacted to and were apparently distracted by the frame he called "field dependent" (FD).

There is another test that has become almost the marker for the dimension of field dependence/independence (FDI). It is the Embedded Figures Test (EFT), in which the task is to locate and recognize a simple figure contained in a more complex one. On this test, some persons display considerable analytic skills (such as restructuring), while others seem to use a more global, impressionistic approach.

Subsequently, Witkin uncovered many relationships involving this essentially perceptual dimension and various personality features, body style, neurophysiological functions, and even psychopathology. This complex of findings inspired the concept *cognitive style*. With respect to certain social behaviors, field-dependent persons tend to display more sensitivity to contextual cues and seem to be more sensitive and empathic than field-independent persons. They, in contrast, tend to be more autonomous, self-oriented, even distant. Field-dependent persons tend more to select careers that provide human contact, as in social domains such as paramedical occupations, whereas field-independent persons are oriented more to the scientific and technical professions.

From its original formulation in 1962, psychological differentiation theory took on a strong developmental coloration. It was argued that in the course of individual development the personality moved from a scarcely differentiated state toward a more complex structure, composed of more interrelated and hence better integrated elements, with the personality becoming more clearly distinguished from the environment. But even if all individuals pass from a less differentiated state toward a more differentiated one, the individual differences that we have discussed above are nevertheless very important.

These individual differences, even though influenced by heredity, are rooted predominantly in socialization and other formative processes. Generally speaking, mothers of field-independent persons tend to encourage their children to be autonomous, whereas mothers of field-dependent children encourage dependence, conformity, and respect for social norms, and they tend to limit their children's outdoor activities. They discourage the assumption of responsibility and they discourage aggressive behavior. The mothers of field-dependent children tend also to be more authoritarian, strict, and punitive.

As we shall see in Chapter 11, there are sex differences in psychological differentiation. A grossly oversimplified summary of these differences is that from adolescence onward, males tend, on the average, to be more field-independent than females. In Witkin's theory, this tendency is explained as a consequence of differing socialization emphases for boys and girls.

The Ecocultural Antecedents of Psychological Differentiation

One can almost derive the origins of cross-cultural differences in field independence/dependence from what we know about the origins of individual differences, since we know, of course, that socialization emphases vary considerably between societies. Barry, Child, and Bacon (1959), for example, showed that nomadic hunting societies (low food accumulation) favor independence in their educational practices, whereas high food accumulating societies (e.g., sedentary agricultural and pastoral societies) emphasize respect for norms and mutual dependence.

Taking off from this distinction, and recalling the ecocultural framework illustrated in Figure 1·1, we can locate the population-level variables that are the cultural and ecological antecedents of intersocietal mean differences in field independence/dependence. That is what led Berry (e.g., 1966, 1976b) to make the following predictions, summarized in 1979:

> With respect to the ecological factors, it is possible to predict that those peoples who engage the physical environment through hunting and gathering activities will be called upon to develop restructuring skills to a high degree: Tracks, signs, odors, and sounds all need to be isolated from context in order to carry on this subsistence pattern. Furthermore, the nomadic settlement pattern associated with hunting and gathering requires a developed sense of space. . . . It is difficult to conceive of a successful hunter without the skills to find game and to return again to camp. In contrast, these skills are unlikely to be of similar value to agriculturalists. . . .
>
> Both the ecological and cultural factors to be found cross-culturally among subsistence-level peoples are predictive of greater FD among agriculturalists and great FI among hunters and gatherers. (Berry, 1979, pp. 125–126)

By first studying two well-contrasted societies, located at opposite ends of the food-accumulation dimension (Berry, 1966), then adding two societies that occupied intermediate positions (Berry, 1971b), and finally expanding the study to include 17 societies (Berry, 1976b), Berry was able to verify his predictions. For example, the correlation between performance on the EFT and the degree of food accumulation over 17 societies was .88. It should be noted that Berry's predictions involve both independence/dependence and spatial domain performances. These two, although often empirically linked, are theoretically distinct.

Van Leeuwen (1978) carefully reviewed 35 cross-cultural studies (from a set of more than 200) with a view toward understanding sex differences. She based her work on ideas derived from Berry's ecocultural model. Briefly, Van Leeuwen noted that the sex differences were very small, even nonexistent, in low food accumulating societies. (This is a finding that we will examine in greater detail in Chapter 11.) In low food accumulating societies, even though they, like all societies, have a division of labor by sex, role flexibility is great and women's work is more highly valued than in high food accumulating societies. In the latter, social conformity is both essential and more rigorously demanded of girls than of boys. In such societies, sex differences in field independence/dependence occur even before adolescence.

Another cross-cultural research question concerns the universality of cognitive style. How general are the relationships among different characteristics that earlier we saw exist in North American samples? Whereas some studies confirm the relationships (e.g., Witkin & Berry, 1975), others don't, and on the basis of this fact, some cross-cultural psychologists (e.g., Serpell, 1976, and Okonji, 1980) have taken a very critical position. Wober (1966, 1967) has gone so far as suggesting that in Africa there is a particular "sensotype," more proprioceptive than visual, but this notion is not confirmed empirically, even though correlations in Africa between the RFT and EFT are systematically weaker than would be predicted by the theory (cf., Berry et al., 1986).

In general, it may be stated that macrocultural studies (which compare societies in a global manner) have provided support for Witkin's theory in its principal aspects, whereas microcultural studies, which compare subgroups within societies, have produced more ambiguous findings. This suggests that psychological differentiation theory needs to be refined in order to apply it to diverse cultural contexts.

PIAGETIAN THEORY: CONCRETE
AND FORMAL OPERATIONS

The theory of Jean Piaget and the so-called Geneva school has had a significant impact on developmental psychology. The formal name of this theory, Genetic Epistemology, reflects its fundamental paradigm — the study of the genesis of scientific thinking. For Piaget, the essence of genetic epistemology resides in studying both the history of science and the development of the individual human being (Piaget & Garcia, 1983). According to this view, adult reasoning is intelligible only insofar as we succeed in retracing its development. The steps or "stages" of cognitive development necessarily unfold in a fixed order; at each stage, the "structures" of the preceding stage are incorporated or "reconstructed" in a process called "equilibration." This process simultaneously involves "assimilation" (the integration of new external elements) and "accommodation" (the adaptation of internal structures to external novelty). We cannot here provide a complete summary of this very complex and thorough theory. To acquire the basics in Piagetian theory, the reader may consult one of the many introductions that have been written, e.g., Flavell, 1963; Ginsburg and Opper, 1969; Droz and Rahmy, 1972; or the masters themselves: Piaget and Inhelder, 1966; Piaget, 1970.

The Stage of Concrete Operations

For the purposes of this chapter, it suffices to know that a child acquires, in a progressive manner, a reasoning system based on "concrete operations." Concrete operational reasoning allows the child logically to resolve concrete problems (problems that involve manipulating real objects). This new-found logic follows a particular mathematical model ("grouping") and is characterized by, among other things, the construction of invariants ("conservation") and by "reversibility" (the ability to invert an operation mentally). The development of concrete operational thought relates to many different kinds of concepts, including number, measurement, space, and time, to mention only a few. The development of concrete operational thought is studied by means of standardized experimental situations called "operational tasks" (see, for example, Laurendeau-Bendavid & Pinard, 1968; Inhelder, Sinclair & Bovet, 1974; Longeot, 1974; Pearson, 1980). These employ a "clinical" method involving semistructured, interactive dialogue with the subject. The conceptual domains that have been most thoroughly studied are conservation, elementary logic, and space. That these are indeed separate *domains* has been confirmed by factor analytic studies employing many different tasks (Dasen, 1984; Lautrey, de Ribaupierre & Rieben, 1986, in press; Shayer, Demetriou & Pervez, 1988). Within a single domain, the same structure may appear at different ages depending on the content to which it is applied. For example, the conservation of quantity is acquired before the conservation of weight, which appears before the conservation of volume. This is what Piagetians call "horizontal decalages,"[1] a term not to be confused with the successiveness of stages.

---

[1]One could translate the French word *décalage* as "discrepancy;" this translation distorts Piaget's meaning. So, it has become standard practice in English to employ the term "decalage."

The stage of concrete operations is followed by formal operations, so named because in theory they can be applied to any content whatsoever, even imaginary content. The structure of formal operational reasoning (which can be formalized by the mathematical theory of groups) permits hypothetico-deductive reasoning, scientific experimentation (viz., holding all but one factor constant), and the exhaustive examination of all possible combinations. Later on in this chapter, we will devote a whole section to a discussion of formal operational reasoning.

Cross-Cultural Testing

Since 1966, the year in which Piaget himself called for cross-cultural research in an article in the inaugural issue of the International Journal of Psychology, numerous studies have been conducted in different societies, inspired more or less accurately by Piagetian theory and using operational tasks. Early results of these cross-cultural studies were summarized and analyzed by Dasen (1972a); subsequently, many reviews on this topic have been published (See, for example, Ashton, 1975; Carlson, 1976; Lautrey & Rodriquez-Tome, 1976; Dasen & Heron, 1981; Price-Williams, 1981; LCHC, 1983). We can deal here only with the essential questions, and only superficially at that.

Whether or not the hierarchical succession of stages is culture-bound has often been treated as fundamental. In fact, it is a pseudoproblem. In effect, the hypothesis is untestable because it is essentially unfalsifiable. We must, therefore, reformulate the question, breaking it into three parts, as we will explain below.

But first, we must clarify the confusion between the succession of stages and the horizontal decalages. Some researchers thought they had challenged Piaget's theory by showing that the relative difficulty of different operational tasks varied across situations. For this reason, one finds in the literature long discussions inquiring whether a particular concept (for example, conservation of length) appears before or after another (for example, conservation of quantity). This question could have some interest for an educational psychologist, but it is surely not crucial to Piagetian theory. These are merely decalages.

Sometimes inversions in the order of learning have been shown to be nothing more than artifacts; for example, Dasen (1972b) was able to show that the inversion between the acquisition of conservation of weight and conservation of quantity among the Australian Aborigines, described by de Lemos (1966), was probably produced by the unvarying order of task presentation. In other cases, real differences have appeared, and we will return to some meaningful examples, but these are of interest only under two conditions: (1) A detailed ethnographic description must have led to a priori predictions of differences, since tentative post hoc explanations of cultural differences are always suspect. (2) The different decalages must be analyzed at the level of individuals through a hierarchical analysis[2] and not by averages or frequencies pertaining to the whole sample. Thus, Dasen (1974) could demonstrate the existence of numerous individual decalages using different conservation tasks among Australian children both of European and Aboriginal origin. Subsequently, the existence of different access routes to concrete operations has been confirmed by differential studies done in Switzerland itself, the society in which the theory was born, (de Ribaupierre, Rieben & Lautrey, 1985), and in neighboring France (Longeot, 1978).

Moreover, cultural differences in horizontal decalages appear not to be systematic; for example, Shayer, Demetriou and Pervez (1988), in a study involving large samples of children in Great Britain, Australia, Greece, and Pakistan, found that a battery of Piagetian tasks in the areas of conservation, elementary logic, and space reveal a similar factorial structure and present the same scale of relative difficulty in each of the societies studied.

Here, then, are the three reformulations of the original issue:

Universal Categorization Into Stages of Behaviors. Behaviors observed beyond the actual test responses, including the verbal explanations given by the children, contribute to the categorization by stages. Can this categorization be made in a reliable fashion in all cases and in all cultural contexts?

This question underscores immediately the serious methodological problems with which the researcher is confronted when she tries to transpose a test, whether psychometric or Piagetian, from one cultural context to another. As we first saw in Chapter 3, this is not simply a translation problem; it is possible that the experimental situation has different meanings for subjects in different societies. Does it have the meaning that the researcher intended it to have? Many discussions have dealt with cultural subtleties which, if not recognized and controlled, constitute a threat to validity. Moreover, many empirical studies have dealt with the importance of the language in which the questioning takes place, with results varying according to circumstances: better performance in English than in the maternal language (Kelly & Philp, 1975), just the opposite (Nyity, 1982), or even no influence of language (e.g., Keats, 1985). Familiarity with content (Price-Williams, 1961, 1962; Okonji, 1971) or even the skill with which the clinical method is applied (Kamara & Easley, 1977) have also been noted as potential methodological concerns. Too many researchers treat Piagetian tasks as if they were standardized psychometric tests, sometimes even re-

---

[2]Different techniques of hierarchical analysis exist, the best known being Gutman scaling. These analyses derive from the principle that if the development of behaviors follows a constant order, it must be possible to classify the observable behaviors (for example, test items) in a manner that reduces inversions to a minimum.

ducing the results to simple pass/fail scores (e.g., Irvine, 1983a). Another concern arises when Piagetian tasks are analyzed with parametric statistical methods that are inappropriate to the nominal or ordinal data[3] that result from Piagetian tasks. Furthermore, the importance of familiarity with the test situation is underscored by the fact that simply repeating a task at the end of a session can significantly change the obtained results; it is thus appropriate to systematically accompany the sequence of tests with training sessions (e.g., Dasen, Ngini & Lavallée, 1979).

Despite these important methodological difficulties, researchers in numerous societies and cultures have, on the whole, been able to employ Piagetian stage categorizations without much difficulty, at least for tasks at the level of concrete operations. Some exceptions exist, but no more often in cross-cultural studies than in single-culture studies. *Whenever people use concrete operational reasoning in a particular task, they display it similarly everywhere.*

The Existence of Culturally Unique Stages. Is it possible to have supplementary stages with respect to the sequence described by Piaget? A cautious response suggests itself. In effect, the finer the analysis, the better able we are to delineate more stages, without having to postulate so-called supplementary stages. A supplementary stage is therefore one that is needed only to account for results obtained in a certain culture, when that stage was not described by Piaget or other researchers in Western children.

The possibility of culturally unique stages was first suggested by Bovet (1974) in a study of conservation of liquids[4] among non-school-going Algerian children. At about 7 to 8 years of age, although they would say that the amounts to drink in the two containers (A and B′) were "the same," they could not explain why. Bovet showed, in fact, that they were not paying any attention to the dimensions of the receptacles and were simply persisting in giving their initial answer. After a training session, which directed their attention to the container dimensions, they gave classic *non*conservation

---

[3]"Nominal" and "ordinal" are terms that refer to the nature of the numbers employed in a set of scores. Nominal numbers indicate only that two things that bear different numbers are not the same. Ordinal numbers carry an additional meaning, viz., that the thing with a higher number is more than the other (for example, that stage 3 occurs after stage 2). Many mathematical operations, including those used in parametric statistical tests, assume a higher level of meaning of numbers. Parametric statistics are those procedures based on the normal distribution (means and standard deviation); they require measurements to occur on an equal-interval scale (such as a yardstick or a meter-stick, where an 8 is indeed 2 times 4).

[4]In the conservation of liquids task, two equal amounts of liquid are poured into two identical glasses, A and B. The initial equality in the "amount to drink" having been recognized by the subject, the contents of glass B are poured into a glass B′ of a different shape (longer and narrower, or broader, or several different containers), and the question is asked, "Is there the same amount in A and B′, or is there more to drink in one of the glasses"?

responses, as did the 9- to 10-year-olds without any prompting. This led Bovet to speak of "pseudoconservation," a supplementary stage preceding nonconservation that had never before been described. Probably, part of the results of Greenfield (1966) among the Wolof of Senegal and those of Dasen (1974) among the Australian Aborigines could also be explained this way, but this supplementary stage of pseudoconservation has never been formally replicated.

Saxe (1981, 1982) studied the construction of the concept of number among the Oksapmin of Papua New Guinea, who use a number system that employs the names of body parts (see Figure 7-1).

Saxe observed the same stages in the development of number skills that are known to prevail for European and American children. In particular, there is a stage where the child knows how to count the elements within each of two sets (for example, two groups of nine sweet potatoes each) but cannot use the results to make comparisons between the two. Depending on the spatial array of the potatoes, they may agree that although there are nine in each group, there are more on one side than on the other. Saxe also found this stage, which he called premediational, among the Oksapmin children, but at approximately 9 years of age as compared with 5 to 6 years for Euro-American children.

The Oksapmin number system presents a specific difficulty that is tied to the use of symmetrical parts of the body. Oksapmin children (even between 12 and 16 years of age) experience difficulty distinguishing between the cardinal values of two symmetrical parts (for example, they think that the

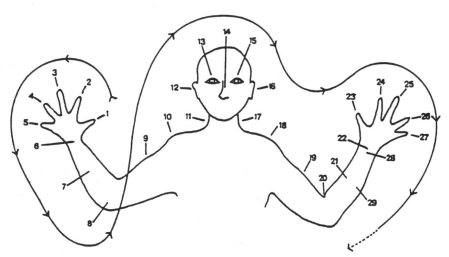

FIGURE 7-1. Body parts numbering system of the Oksapmin of Papua New Guinea. Reprinted with permission from Saxe, 1981a, p. 307. Copyright © The Society for Research in Child Development, Inc.

left eye and the right eye have the same value), even after they no longer have difficulty with asymmetrical parts. Later, they become capable of completely dissociating number from its bodily equivalent, at which time they are able to resolve hypothetical problems ("And what if one began to count by the left thumb?"), or, for purposes of addition, to call one part of the body by another part. There is, thus, for Oksapmin children, a supplementary step to get through that is tied to the peculiarities of their numerical system.

This, however, is the only convincing demonstration of a culturally specific sequence of development that we know of, and it constitutes only a minor amendment to what has convincingly been revealed as a universal succession of stages.

Rhythms of Development or "Temporal Decalages." Third, we ask, At what age are the different stages attained? Piaget (1966) considered this question of relatively little importance. He, in fact, expected to find differences on the order of one to two years as a consequence of variations in the degree of stimulation provided by various environments. Actually, cross-cultural studies have brought to light much larger differences, occasionally time-lags of five to six years. Some members of a given population may even appear to lack concrete operational reasoning for a particular concept altogether. This lack is reflected in so-called asymptotic developmental curves,[5] which level off at less than 100% operational responses, after the age at which all individuals in Western samples have acquired the particular concept.

The meaning of these asymptotes was examined by Dasen and his colleagues (Dasen, Lavallée & Retschitzki, 1979; Dasen, Ngini & Lavallée, 1979; Dasen, 1982) by means of techniques involving training. The researchers were able to show that various 12-year-old children (among the Inuit in Canada, Baoulé in Côte d'Ivoire, and Kikuyu in Kenya) who did not *spontaneously* use concrete operational reasoning in a given task, nonetheless did so following a brief learning sequence or when the task was presented a second time at the end of the testing sessions. The asymptote in the developmental curves is thus a performance phenomenon rather than one of competence. In other words, these adolescents obviously could use concrete operations if they were incited to do so but would not necessarily use them spontaneously.

Certain writers (for example, Kamara & Easley, 1977; Nyiti, 1982; Irvine, 1983a) believe that all cultural differences in concrete operational development are nothing more than performance phenomena, or even methodological artifacts. This point of view suits, on the one hand, orthodox Piaget-

---

[5]The usual way to represent data relevant to rate of development is to plot, as a function of age, the proportions of persons in the sample giving a concrete operational response. This yields a "developmental curve."

ians, who dislike seeing the universality of the theory put into question, and on the other, those who seek to deny cultural differences for ideological reasons or because they fear that these will be misinterpreted. According to Cole and Scribner (1977), for example, any use of a developmental theory necessarily leads to interpretations of differences in terms of "deficit" or "retardation" in relation to ethnocentric Western norms. They fear that the apparent absence of concrete operational reasoning for a particular concept can only cause a whole society to be labeled as being arrested at a preoperational stage of development. This would result in equating adults in those societies to Western children.

Such profound mistakes, with social evolutionary overtones, have in fact surfaced. An example may be found in a work by Hallpike (1979) entitled *The Foundations of Primitive Thought*. He reinterprets in this fashion empirical facts obtained by other researchers, often selecting only those that support his thesis.

Dasen, Berry & Witkin (1979) objected that cultural differences could equally well be interpreted as just differences, quite without attaching value judgments. This is certainly the case if one employs the ecocultural conceptual framework, introduced earlier in this book, according to which each society favors the development of those concepts, aptitudes, and skills that are necessary for their subsistence activities. Dasen (1975), in a study inspired by this model, predicted that the development of concrete operational reasoning in the domain of space would be particularly rapid in nomadic hunting and gathering societies because of the necessity of finding one's bearings in an extended territory, whereas quantitative concepts (for example, conservation of quantity, of weight, and of volume) would be more valued and would develop more rapidly in sedentary agricultural societies, which must deal with harvested produce in several ways, including storage and exchange or sale of surplus.

These hypotheses have been fully confirmed, and the obtained results are illustrated in Figure 7-2 for two concrete operational tasks, conservation of liquid and the concept of horizontality.[6]

In comparing graphs A and B, note that the relative order of the develop-

---

[6]This is a spatial concept. In this task, the subject is shown a bottle half filled with water, placed in various positions (tilted left or right, upside down, on its side); the subject has to draw in the water level on corresponding outline drawings. The task consists of three parts: First, the water level is hidden while the shape and the positions of the bottle remain visible. The second part provides a training opportunity; the cover is taken off, and the subject is allowed to see and copy the water level. The third part assesses performance after this training, the water level being hidden again. According to Piaget's analysis, to solve this task, the subject has to coordinate two orthogonal spatial reference systems, one internal to the bottle and one given by the box or table the bottle stands on. This is why this apparently simple task is in fact difficult. Several substages mark the development along the route.

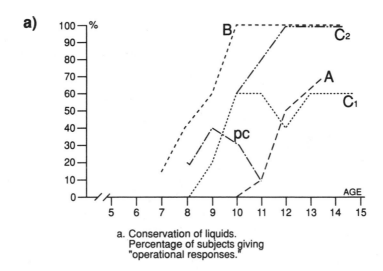

a)

a. Conservation of liquids.
Percentage of subjects giving
"operational responses."

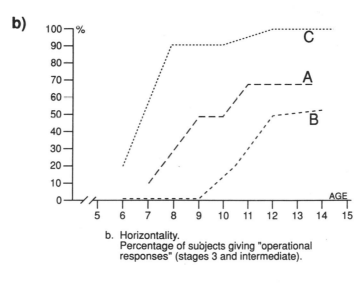

b)

b. Horizontality.
Percentage of subjects giving "operational
responses" (stages 3 and intermediate).

– – – – –	**A**	Aranda (Australian Aborigines)
– – – – – –	**B**	Baoulé (Côte d'Ivoire)
·················	**C**	Central Inuit, Cape Dorset, Canada
·················	**C₁**	performance
–··–··–··–	**C₂**	competence
–·–·–·–	**pc**	probably pseudo-conservation

FIGURE 7-2. Percentage of subjects giving operational responses

mental curves is completely reversed, as predicted by the ecocultural hypothesis. The relative order of the two sets of curves reveals cultural differences due to temporal decalages in the development of competence for these concepts. As Dasen (1984) noted, the fact of comparing developmental curves in their totality rather than treating the samples of each age group separately (cf. Irvine, 1983a) assures the reliability of these findings.

Note that the exact placement of the samples on conservation of liquids depends on whether we attend to performance (C_1) or competence (C_2) and whether we take into account the possible occurrence of pseudoconservation (pc).

These results also contributed to challenging an element of Piagetian theory, namely the idea of domain consistency (*structure d' ensemble*, in French) according to which the development of different concepts belonging to the same stage unfolds concurrently. This is the impression that one gains in reading Piaget's work, since the development of each concept is described in terms of the same schema, whereas in fact the empirical facts derive in each case from different samples. When researchers presented a large number of tasks to the same sample, it appeared that heterogeneity was the rule, even among children in Western societies. The cultural differences are only superimposed on a variability much more important than that which had been initially anticipated.

There is nevertheless a certain coherence in other respects in the development of concepts within a single domain; this has been shown by studies using factorial analyses and by training studies, in which the learning of a concept generalizes to other concepts in the same domain and sometimes even to other domains (Dasen, Ngini & Lavallée, 1979).

In summary, if the hypothesis of an absolutely homogeneous and unidimensional development in all cultures has not been verified by empirical research, neither has the converse, a complete relativity of particular concepts, each specific to a particular cultural context. *The empirical results allow us to opt for an intermediate solution, a simultaneous universality of hierarchical sequences and cultural variation in the timing of development.* In other words, the sequence of stages is the same everywhere, only the timing varies. Dasen (1980, 1983), in the model reproduced here below (Table 7-1), has called this intermediate solution "local constructivism," illustrated by the metaphor "valleys of construction" suggested by Harris and Heelas (1979). This is in contrast with the absolutist approach of orthodox Piagetian theory and its use by Hallpike (1979), on the one hand, and the extreme contextualism of Cole, which denies any structuralist construction and links between concepts, on the other.

If, between the absolutism of Piagetian orthodoxy and extreme cultural relativism we choose to take the middle ground, that nevertheless implies a

Table 7-1. Alternative Approaches to Cognitive Processes*.

	Contextualism (Cole & Bruner) (Cole & Scribner)	Local Constructivism (Harris & Heelas)	Constructivism (Piaget)
Basic Operations	invariant	constructed	constructed
Contexts	impermeable	impermeable	permeable
Models	functional cognitive systems	valleys of construction	structure d'ensemble

*Following Harris and Heelas (1979).

transformation in Piagetian theory whereby it has to be relativized as a consequence of this cross-cultural detour.

Still another question is what aspects of child development are most valued by the parents. Dasen et al.'s (1985) study, reviewed in Chapter 5, is relevant here. In the second part of their study, the researchers asked 47 sets of parents, each of whom had one child in the study, to designate, by citing some illustrative behaviors, which were the positive or negative aspects of n'glouèlê (and of its different components) that pertained to their own child. The correlations between parental judgments and the performance of the children on Piagetian tasks in the spatial domain, in conservation, and in elementary logic were, in general, close to zero. In the spatial domain, correlation coefficients with technological components ranged between −.40 and −.77, showing a very significant inverse statistical relationship. These results show the gap that exists between the Baoulé definition of intelligence and concrete operational reasoning. They also confirm Dasen's (1975) hypothesis, which we mentioned earlier, that spatial concepts will not be valued in sedentary societies such as that of the Baoulé.

In this same study, correlations between parental judgments of n'glouèlê and "natural indicators" derived from spot observations were also obtained. For the indicator "self-managed sequences" (as defined above by Nerlove et al., 1974), no significant correlations were found. In contrast, Dasen et al. (1985) found that another natural indicator, called "nondirected activity," correlated positively with parental judgments of n'glouèlê; this correlation was particularly significant for girls. This latter indicator measured initiative and responsibility-taking in those situations where children's behaviors are spontaneous and not demanded by an adult and where they are not under direct adult control or that of an older child.

All these studies reveal a coherence between parental ethnotheories and the daily activities of children. In contrast, psychological tests currently in use, whether imported or locally constructed, do not necessarily measure what is valued in societies outside Europe and America.

The Stage of Formal Operations

The conclusions that we have just reached regarding the sequence and timing of stages of cognitive development apply to the stage of concrete operations. Piaget's theory concerning the stage of formal operations has been only partially confirmed, even in single-culture studies. According to Piagetian theory, reasoning at the formal operational stage must no longer be tied to concrete content. Yet research has shown that the majority of adolescents and adults in Western societies, even those schooled at the level of high school or university, do not reason in formal operational fashion except under certain conditions and in certain domains (particularly in their professional specialization). This led Piaget (1972) to revise his position by stating that all adults have the capacity for formal operational reasoning, but that this capacity would not reflect itself in performance except under favorable circumstances.

At the moment, not enough systematic information is available to confirm the universal applicability of Piaget's conclusion. Cross-cultural studies that have employed Piagetian tasks in the formal domain have all shown that schooling up to the secondary level is a necessary but not sufficient condition for success at these tasks (e.g., Laurendeau-Bendavid, 1977; Shea, 1985). That is not at all surprising, since these tasks (even when administered in noncurriculum-related situations) relate directly to physics, chemistry, or mathematics as they are taught in school.

This does not necessarily mean that cross-cultural studies that employed formal operational tasks were uninteresting or invalid, particularly if subjects were schooled. Keats (1985), for example, administered six tasks of formal operations to high-school students 16 to 17 years of age and university students 20 to 24 years of age in Australia and also among Malays, Indians, and Chinese in Malaysia. Three of the tasks were administered in repeated fashion before and after a proportionality training session. The author concluded: "The effectiveness of the training program in removing initial differences between the groups suggests that although the initial testing did show differences in performance, these did not reflect differences in competence. . . . Evidence of formal operational thinking was found for some subjects within all groups, but not for all subjects within any group" (Keats, 1985, pp. 316–317).

Tapé (1987) used three formal-stage Piagetian tasks (the flexibility of rods, the pendulum, and permutations) in Côte d'Ivoire with secondary school pupils in urban and rural areas, and with illiterate adults. With the adults, he used group interviews, that is, social situations that are culturally more appropriate than individual examinations; this part of the study produced the most interesting results. The adults would approach the problems in a holistic fashion, clustering the dimensions into blocks of information and imparting an order of importance to the relevant factors. For example, in the pendulum problem, they asserted that the most important factor is the initial push, since without it, there would be no movement at all. They also took everyday experience into account; for example, in the flexibility-of-rods task, they did not accept the problem as it was set by the experimenter but claimed that the flexibility has to be tested over time. This, Tapé argued, results from the experience they had in using wooden rods for constructing traps. For the permutations, the illiterate adults encountered difficulties when working with more than four or five objects, since without a written record, they would lose track of the procedure.

Tapé concluded that there are two styles of thinking that become clearly distinguishable during adoelescence and that correspond to two ways of assigning meaning to nature. There is the experimental and analytic style that corresponds to formal logic, answers the question "how," and is designed to establish causal laws. The other is the "experiential" style that works through iconic or symbolic representation and corresponds to a pragmatic or action-oriented logic; it answers the question "why" and is designed to search for the ends that might be served. According to Tapé, this second style corresponds to Bantu philosophy, is produced by informal education, and was obvious in the way the illiterate adults approached and solved the Piagetian tasks.

In studying formal reasoning among nonschooled subjects, it is best not to use experimental situations, because these tend to be culturally inappropriate; as we shall see in the next chapter, experimental tasks often resemble school situations. But, observing formal reasoning in everyday situations is practically impossible. That a behavior is complex and abstract is not enough to make it formal. In addition, Piagetian criteria demand that subjects perform the task themselves without help from others, that they consider all possible combinations and control all factors, and that they be able to derive a general law. Rarely are these criteria met outside of an experimental situation. But as noted earlier, experimental situations are necessarily artificial. So what can we do?

Saxe's (1981b) research on the island of Ponam in Papua New Guinea demonstrated how it is possible to construct an experimental situation based on particular, culturally specific aspects. On the island of Ponam, the system for assigning names to children is one in which daughters receive a name according to their birth order in relation to their female siblings. Following the same rule, another series of names is reserved for sons. Figure 7-3 illustrates the task constructed by Saxe on the basis of this system.

Saxe first studied the development of subjects' (aged 8 to 23 years) under-

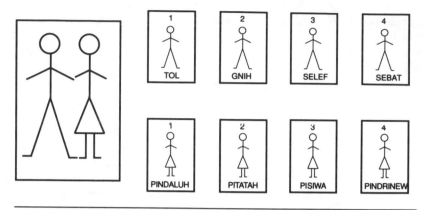

Stimulus Materials for the Birth Order Task

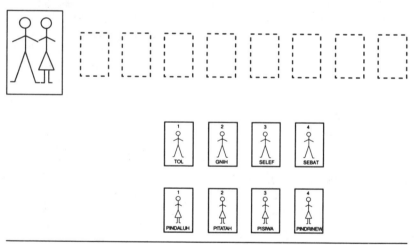

Stimulus Materials for the Task in the Family Generation Phase

FIGURE 7-3. Stimulus materials used by Saxe involving the Ponam name assignment system. Saxe, G. B., When fourth can precede second. A developmental analysis of an indigenous numeration system among Ponam islanders in Papua New Guinea, Journal of Cross-Cultural Psychology, (12) pp. 37–50, copyright © 1981 by Sage Publications. Reprinted by permission of Sage Publications, Inc.

standing of each of the two series separately. Next he assessed their under-standing of the uncertainty of the relationship between the series. He asked them to construct hypothetical families in accord with the rules concerning name attribution, asking them such questions as, "Who is the oldest, _____ or _____?"—a question that one could respond to with certitude in all cases where the children are of the same sex but to which one could respond only with respect to a particular family if the comparison involved two children of different sexes. For example, Tol is always older than Selef; in contrast, he could be younger than Pisiwa, but only under the condition wherein he has three older sisters.

Questions pertaining to each sex separately were resolved at approximately 13 years of age, whereas questions involving both sexes — which imply a form of combinatory reasoning — were not resolved until about 19 years of age. In terms of Piagetian criteria, formal operational reasoning would have been demonstrated had the researcher asked subjects to make all possible combinations, had subjects employed a systematic strategy for resolving the problem, and had they deduced from that strategy a general rule.

As Shea (1985) rightly pointed out, it would be premature to conclude an absence of formal reasoning in certain societies based on the results of a few Piagetian tasks. A more tenable hypothesis might be that this particular form of reasoning — in effect, scientific reasoning — is not what is valued in all cultures. This at least is the opinion of Greenfield (1976), who proposed that it is necessary to follow the example of Piaget himself; namely, first determine what the final stage is and then study its ontogenesis according to the particular value systems of each society. Preiswerk (1976), in his essay on the implications of Piagetian theory for intercultural relations, raised the possibility that the theory contained inherent ethnocentric characteristics:

> Does not the work of Piaget contain elements of thought deriving from rationalism, from universalism, from ethnocentrism, and from evolutionism, all elements that are central to the fashion in which the West understands other cultures? The first, rationalism, it appears to me, is very clearly a fundamental aspect of Piaget's work. Belief in decentralized Reason and in objective science are the elements which can eventually make intercultural relations difficult. With respect to the three other problems, it is necessary to procede with great care. (Preiswerk, 1976, p. 509)

It would thus be desirable, at the formal-operational stage as well as other stages of cognitive development, to proceed in a more emic fashion.

CONCLUSION

It is only very recently that cognition and cognitive development have been studied in sociocultural context. Psychologists in Europe and America have tended to study cognition as a set of internal processes, linked to brain functioning and partially, if not entirely, biologically determined. Piaget (1966), for example, while acknowledging the importance of "social factors of interpersonal coordination," basically relegated these to the same status as general "equilibration," that is, the individual's interaction with the physical environment. This interaction, be it with the physical or the social environments, follows, according to Piaget, the same patterns everywhere; it leads to universality rather than to differences. Only "factors of educational and cultural transmission" might produce sociocultural differences, but Piaget paid only lip service to these (The single paragraph on factors of educational and cultural transmission, in Piaget's (1966) 10-page-long paper, consists of all but 12 lines). Thus Piaget produced a theory of the development of an "epistemic subject", an idealized, nonexistent individual, completely divorced from the social environment.

But Piaget was not alone in disregarding the sociocultural context; most of the researchers studying cognition in the experimental psychology laboratory, be it concept formation or problem solving, or with the more recent paradigms of artificial intelligence and cognitive science, tend to study the individual in isolation from outside influences.

Challenges to this predominant line of inquiry came from social psychologists from within Piaget's own school, such as Doise, Mugny, and Perret-Clermont (1975; Perret-Clermont, 1979; Doise & Mugny, 1981), who demonstrated the importance for cognitive development of interindividual interaction. Their work was, of course, informed by the sociohistorical school of Vygotsky (1978) and Luria (1976), and by the cross-cultural research of the 1970s.[7] The so-called neo-Piagetian theories of Case (1985) and Fischer (e.g., Fischer & Bullock, 1984) refer to the same influences and allow for an integration of a structuralist emphasis on the individual with a functional emphasis on context, although none of them has so far considered links with population-level factors in their empirical implementations (Dasen & de Ribaupierre, 1987).

While cognitive psychologists have come to consider seriously the sociocultural context of individual behavior, sociologists and anthropologists have been reluctant to consider anything other than social phenomena as worthy of study. Harris and Heelas (1979) and Jahoda (1982) suggested that it has been a great fallacy to attempt to use phenomena described at the group level, such as "collective representations," to explain individual behavior; this led Lévy-Bruhl and many others, as we saw in Chapter 5, to hypothesize the existence of a primitive mentality. A more fruitful combination of anthropology and psychology has led, in more recent times, to the study of the contexts in which psychological (including cognitive) development occurs.

In this chapter we have seen how useful it is to put developmental theories to cross-cultural test. In both of the theories we have examined, basic developmental processes emerge as likely universals, whereas what we might call surface characteristics have to be adjusted to reflect cultural diversity better.

---

[7]Doise and Mugny (1981) explicitly refer, among others, to the research on psychological differentiation, to Berry's ecocultural model, and to the research in Liberia of Cole and Scribner (1974).

Most important, we have seen that the data from developmental studies had to be interpreted in light of cultural relativism to avoid the ethnocentric value judgments that tend to be attached to developmental trends.

In the next chapter, we will continue to examine cross-cultural research on cognition. Although many of the studies to be reviewed there include children as well as adults and are occasionally concerned with developmental issues, they are predominantly based on experimental laboratory paradigms. It will be interesting to see how these techniques fare when carried to the field.

Chapter 8

Cognitive Processes

WHY STUDY COGNITION CROSS-CULTURALLY?

In this chapter we examine some processes by which human beings deal with information. Obviously, information-processing mechanisms are needed by all intact human beings; in that respect, they are universal intellectual activities. This does not, however, preclude cultural differences in the way the processes are implemented, in the contents that are being processed, in the contexts in which they are called into play, or in the more complex abilities that arise from a particular combination of basic cognitive processes. To specify the conditions under which these cultural variations arise is the goal of the cross-cultural study of cognition. That they are processes serving universal functions allows us to compare them across cultures.

What are these universal intellectual activities? We all, for example, categorize—that most basic of intellectual activities. Attaching a single name to more than one object, such as calling several differently shaped objects (some soft, others hard) "chairs" is to categorize them, to treat them as exemplars of a particular category. The category itself may, however, be best represented by one particular type of chair that is taken as a standard or "prototype." Human beings everywhere use prototypes to define categories, but they may depend on environmental factors and linguistic distinctions that vary across cultures.

When we recognize and label a common attribute—for chairs, it is sit-on-ability—we are using the most important cognitive tool available to us: language. Nouns are category labels. Because every language contains thing-names, people everywhere categorize. To decide whether distinct objects should receive the same label, they must be compared and judged as to the ways in which they are equivalent or different.

People everywhere have to remember a large amount of information; otherwise they could not function. Just what kind of information they store, how they go about remembering it, and possibly how much they are able to remember, differ from one culture to another.

It must also be obvious that persons everywhere solve problems of various degrees of complexity. People everywhere are regularly confronted by practical problems; survival depends on solving them. Cross-cultural psychologists have studied problem solving, although as we shall see, not usually the kind on which survival depends, but rather the more innocuous laboratory kind.

CATEGORIZATION

Since the world consists of a virtually infinite number of discriminably different stimuli, an essential cognitive activity is the division of the environment into categories within which many nonidentical stimuli can be treated as equivalent.

Are the principles of category formation universal? According to Berlin and Kay (1969), there should be agreement on "focal points" for color among speakers of different languages, despite variation in the placement of boundaries between color terms. Thus, there should be so-called focal colors that are more salient (i.e., that stand out among others and are more easily remembered), even where there is no basic color term to designate them (i.e., even if they are not more codable).

However, codability and salience are confounded in English. Rosch (then publishing under the name of Heider, 1972 a,b,c, summarized in Rosch, 1977) designed a study to unconfound codability and salience, working in a culture where the language contains only two color terms, "dark" and "light." She presented the Dani of West Irian (Indonesian New Guinea) with a color-memory task, using focal and nonfocal colors. Since the Dani use only two basic color terms, all colors were (in their language) equally uncoded. The Dani provided an ideal opportunity to teach color names. The research question was, would the Dani remember focal better than nonfocal colors?

The results of a recognition-memory task suggest that they do. Compared with the results of the same experiment conducted in the United States, the Dani had, on average, a lower memory performance (though this could have been due to various artifacts such as familiarity with the testing situation). The absolute level of performance is of no importance to the issue; the relevant finding here is that in both cultures, focal colors were remembered more easily than nonfocal ones.

Rosch (1977) developed the following hypothesis, which she tested in an experiment that involved learning new codes in a paired associate task:

There are perceptually salient colors which more readily attract attention and are more easily remembered than other colors. When category names are learned, they tend to become attached first to the salient stimuli . . . , and by this means these natural prototype colors become the foci of organization for categories. (Rosch, 1977, pp. 10–11)

The results of the learning task supported Rosch's hypothesis. The focal-color name pairs were learned with fewer errors than the nonfocal-color name pairs. This supports the idea that perceptually focal (or salient) colors are natural prototypes (rather like Platonic forms) for the development and learning of color names (Rosch, 1977, p. 12).

Rosch also conducted child-development research in the United States to test the hypothesis that focal colors are learned first and are the prototypes around which the color domain becomes structured into categories.

Color is not the only domain in which perceptually salient, natural proto-types appear to determine the focal points of categories, serving, in effect, as their definitions. Since the Dani also do not have a terminology for two-dimensional geometric forms, Rosch produced an analog to the previously mentioned paired-associate learning task, but using form instead of color. Perfect circles, squares, and equilateral triangles were taken as the presumed natural prototypes of three form categories, in contrast to irregular figures of the same type. The results mirrored those for color.

According to Ekman (1971, 1973), facial expressions of emotion also form natural categories or prototypes. Ekman claims that there are six basic human emotions (i.e., happiness, sadness, anger, fear, surprise, and dis-gust), and that each is associated with a specific set of facial muscle move-ments. When Ekman put together sets of pictures of "pure" expressions of the proposed basic emotions, these were judged correctly not only by Ameri-cans, Japanese, and South Americans, but also by the Fore and the Dani, two New Guinea groups having minimal contact with Caucasian facial ex-pression. In this respect, Rosch makes the following methodological point:

Like color, universality was discovered in facial expressions of emotion only when an investigator thought to ask, not about all possible stimuli, but about the prototypes (best examples) of categories. (Rosch, 1977, p. 17)

On the other hand, cultural differences may occur in (a) the elaboration of language codes for the categories, (b) the organization of categories into superordinated structures, (c) category boundaries, (d) the treatment of interprototype stimuli (such as blends of emotions), and (e) the rules for the use of the categories (such as when and where emotion may be expressed).

Color, form, and the facial expression of emotion may all be structured in the same way because they are domains with a possible physiological basis. What about category formation in domains that do not have a physiological basis, like most common semantic categories (e.g., "chair")? Laboratory research within Euro-American culture has examined this question (e.g., Mervis & Rosch, 1981; Cordier, 1981), and it has been found that noun categories can be viewed as prototypes, that is, defining the category through an idea or image of the "best example."

The categorization of concrete objects may reflect the ecological structure of real-world attributes. So called basic objects (e.g., chair) are the most inclusive level of categorization at which many attributes can be common to all members of the category; categories at higher or superordinate levels of abstraction (e.g., furniture) possess few attributes common to category members, whereas categories subordinate to the basic level share most attributes with other subordinated categories. The common motor movements evoked by objects, the similarity of shapes, and the ease with which an average shape is recognizable all determine the coding of categories in terms of prototypes.

The particular choice of prototypes that define categories should vary according to ecological cue validity (cf. Chapter 4); therefore the particular prototype that is chosen may or may not be the same in all cultures. What may be universal is the mechanism through which basic-level categories are formed. In Rosch's own words, "The present theory is only a first step toward an understanding of human categorization of concrete objects. It requires cross-cultural work for its verification and further extension" (Rosch, 1977, p. 45). Not much cross-cultural replication has been carried out, however.

Bossel-Lagos (in press) studied the development of categorization behavior in two groups of 75 Peruvian girls aged 6 to 14 years. One group was Spanish speaking, with relatively rich parents of various professions, living in a town on the Pacific coast ("costena" group). The second group, in a small village in the Andes, was of modest socioeconomic conditions, the parents having had little or no schooling. This group was bilingual Spanish and Quechua, the latter being the first language of 75% of the sample. The subjects were asked to give the best examples and all other examples they could think of for the following categories presented in Spanish: illness, flower, fruit, toys, furniture, birds, fish, means of transport, vegetables, and clothing.

There were noticeable differences between the two groups in the richness of vocabulary; for some categories, like means of transport or toys, the rural group had very few examples available, and overall they produced fewer words. This probably reflects differences in the children's daily experiences, the parents' social class and education, and the bilingualism of the second group. More interesting, however, is that in both groups, the categorization changed over age from a rather diffuse definition (a large variety of "best" examples) to a clear prototypicality that comes progressively closer to the adult standard (established through repeating the study with university students in Lima). This study showed that the focal points within categories are prototypes corresponding to social conformity, established gradually through socialization. Even if particular prototypes differ between cultures, the process and the developmental trend seem to be universal.

SORTING

The principles of category formation around prototypes may be called "analog" functions; the paradigm in which categories are defined by shared attributes may be called "digital." The latter is typical of most empirical research in cross-cultural psychology and in anthropological studies of folk classifications as well. We now turn to research that is digital in this sense.

There are developmental trends in sorting behavior. Younger children tend to judge objects as equivalent primarily on the basis of striking, superficial, or even incidental perceptual properties, such as color or number. Sorting by form is considered slightly more advanced, because it requires abstraction of features from the stimuli. Older children are likely to sort on the basis of such attributes as shared function (for a bicycle and a car: "to ride") or the nominal (taxonomic) label for it ("they are vehicles" or "transportation"). Such age trends in societies with formal schooling have led developmental psychologists to speak of stages in conceptual behavior (see, for example, Bruner, Olver & Greenfield, 1966).

In studies done in some non-Western societies, especially in Africa, it has been common to find that sorting by color is most often employed, followed by sorting by form and, finally, sorting by function (with almost no taxonomic sorting). These results have emerged when children, and sometimes adults, are administered free-sorting tasks, that is, permitted to sort objects any way they like (Suchman, 1966; Price-Williams, 1962; Greenfield, Reich & Olver, 1966). In general, the African subjects have lagged behind Western subjects in their employment of form and functional sorting. But, significantly, it was found in a study done by Greenfield and her colleagues in Senegal that children with schooling tended more than unschooled children to ignore color and employ other features, especially form. The schooled children were thus seemingly performing at a developmentally more advanced stage. Still, the overriding impression left by the earlier studies done in Africa was that children were hardly able to sort by function.

Arguing that free-sorting tests, as employed in the earlier studies, revealed only habits and not abilities, Evans and Segall (1969), working in Uganda, used a learning-to-sort task rather than a free-sorting task. They believed that a particular child might be able to sort by function but might never do so if merely asked to sort. But that same child, if instructed to find the way the experimenter wanted her to sort (and rewarded for doing so), might reveal some difficulty in discovering how to do it but might nevertheless come to do it.

The Evans and Segall study addressed several questions: (1) Would sorting by color be generally easier for children than sorting by function? (2) Are there similar or different developmental trends for both types of sorting? (3) Might schooling affect performance? (4) If schooling affected the performance of children, how would adults, mostly unschooled, perform the same tasks?

The subjects in the main experiment were 302 children from three places (urban, semiurban, and rural) in the Baganda region of Uganda (see the map of southwestern Uganda in Chapter 14). They were unschooled ($N=32$) or schooled ($N=270$); the schooled were in first, third, or fifth grade. An ancillary experiment involved adults, 31 rural and 30 urban, with either zero to three years of primary education or four to seven years.

All subjects were given two sorting tasks. In one they were to find things alike on the basis of physical appearance; in the other, on the basis of function.[1] Half the subjects had to discover first that color was the appropriate basis for alikeness, and after 20 trials with that rule in effect, they had to discover that the same materials were to be sorted on the basis of shared functions. The other half of the subjects performed the same two tasks in reverse order.

On any given trial, subjects were shown a set of four pictured objects, two of which were the same color and one of which was functionally related to a third. For example, one set included two blue objects and two objects of two other colors; of the four objects, two were containers and the other two unrelated, such as a book and a hat. Subjects were told only to put together two that were alike. Subjects in the color-first sequence were told during their first 20 trials that they were correct if they selected the two objects of the same color; during their second 20 trials they were rewarded for sorting by function. For subjects in the other sequence this was, of course, reversed.

Between the two sets of 20 trials the experimenter said merely, "You have done very well. Now I am going to show you the same pictures again, and this time we want you to put them together in another way." The subjects had to discover for themselves the basis for sorting, and they had to discover both bases, color and function.

The first finding from the main experiment was that color was an easier concept for schoolchildren to discover. Using four correct trials in a row as a criterion of learning, Evans and Segall found that all but 35 reached the criterion for color, whereas 84 never reached it for function. For all nine groups of school-going children combined, the average trial on which the

---

[1]Function and naming (taxonomic classification) were not distinguished in this experiment.

criterion was reached for color was 7.5, whereas for function it was 11.3. Thus, even with a different method (concept discovery rather than free sorting), the study showed again that color is in general an easier basis for sorting than function.

Rural, unschooled children performed as well as the school-going ones on the color task but much more poorly on the function task. The unschooled children took all 20 trials (on average) to reach the criterion for function. Indeed, many of them never solved the function problem.

Children in grade one also had great difficulty with the function problem. But learning to sort by function was progressively easier with increasing grade level. Most strikingly, sorting by function was just as easy as sorting by color for fifth-graders (except in the most rural of schools). But sorting by color was generally no easier in higher grades than in grade one.

None of the adults with less than four years of school learned to sort by function, but nearly all of them solved the color-sorting problem. Adults who had had at least four years of education performed as well as schooled children on the function task and considerably better than the non-school-going children.

Clearly, then, number of years in school was the critical factor relating to manifest ability to sort objects on the basis of shared function. Schooling enabled subjects to entertain more complicated hypotheses than color and to comprehend the function-sorting task more readily than the lesser-educated children or the adults for whom schooling had been minimal and remote in time. The importance of schooling was underscored by the fact that the fifth graders (and only they) tended to sort by function on their very first trial. This tendency to search for less obvious attributes of a stimulus is what schooling may instill in children.

Taking into account findings of earlier studies done elsewhere in Africa, Evans and Segall (1969) suggested that "unless Ss are induced by the experimenter to look for some less obvious characteristic, and unless they have some countertendency established by prior experience of the kind gained in school, they will employ the most obvious one available as the basis for sorting" (p. 51).

They suggested that sorting perceptually appears early and is easy because of the salience of color. Sorting by function (when color is simultaneously available) requires being taught — as children in school are taught — to consider less obvious stimulus attributes. This was substantiated by a study done in Colombia (Evans, 1975), in which learning to sort on the basis of abstract qualities (functional or taxonomic as opposed to perceptual) was shown to be dependent on school grade level. Thus, functional sorting is at least partly a product of experience, of which schooling is a particularly influential kind. This experiment could not have been done within Euro-American culture, where nearly all children are schooled and where maturation and schooling are confounded, with age trends likely to be attributed to maturation, whereas in fact they result from experience.

Other Influences on Sorting Behavior

Okonji (1971) who compared schoolgoing children in a rural town in midwestern Nigeria with an age-comparable group of school-children in Glasgow, Scotland, found that the Nigerian children employed more accurate, inclusive, and superordinate bases for grouping objects than their Scottish counterparts (significantly so for those aged 11 to 12) when the objects to be sorted were more familiar to the Nigerian children than to the Scottish children. This occurred even though his younger Nigerian subjects (mostly between 6 and 8 years) often used color as a sorting basis, whereas none of the Scottish children did. Despite this, the Nigerian children performed overall at a level of conceptualization that at least equaled that of the Scottish sample.

Okonji attributed the high performance of the Nigerian subjects to their familiarity with the objects. A similar point had been made by Price-Williams in 1962 and recurrently by others since (e.g., Serpell, 1976), although some experiments have been reported in which familiarity with the testing materials had no influence (e.g., Dasen, 1984).

The different expectations of subjects and experimenter about the task are also possibly important. Consider the anecdote reported by Ciborowski (1980), about a study Glick did on classification behavior among traditional Kpelle rice farmers in Liberia. The procedure was a standard free-sorting task with objects. Glick found that the majority of the Kpelle made groupings based on either perceptual or functional relations among items (for example, the knife with the cassava, because it is used to cut the tubers, instead of the knife with the machette because they are cutting tools, and the cassava with the yam because they are root vegetables). When Glick probed by asking for reasons for the groupings,

> Most of the subjects replied that the groupings they made were, in the Kpelle traditional sense (Kpelle custom and culture), the clever way to do it. Glick interpreted this reply as meaning that the subjects construed his instruction to group the items as a test of their cleverness; most importantly, as test of their cleverness according to the Kpelle culturally accepted view of the term. Acting on a hunch, Glick asked a subject to do the classification task as a *stupid* Kpelle person might do it. The result was dramatic. Under the new instructions, the subject produced a perfect taxonomic grouping. (Ciborowski, 1980, p. 283)

This anecdotal report corroborates other evidence that the process of equivalence sorting occurs in much the same fashion among a wide variety of ethnic groups. Qualitative differences are found primarily among people who are tested with unfamiliar materials, who understand the task differently from what the experimenter means it to be, or who have not had certain types of experiences, such as schooling. What was once thought to be a difference across ethnic groups in the capacity to process information is better thought of as a reflection of the experiences people have and of the cultural appropriatcncss of thc way their skills are assessed. Given the right opportunities to learn to play the Euro-American psychologists' sorting games, people anywhere can come to play them well.

We have examined various findings from cross-cultural research about how people categorize or classify. How deductive logical relations between classes are established, or how we reason about the relative extensions of classes, are questions addressed mainly within the Piagetian tradition (cf. Chapter 7 and the problem-solving issues later in this chapter). Now we turn to the study of another basic cognitive process — memory.

MEMORY

If people in different cultures classify objects and events differently, do they remember them differently? Do different classification schemes assist memory? Is it possible that certain groups, especially people in nonliterate societies, have quantitatively better memories than people in societies where much of the knowledge they want to retain is available in written form?

Anecdotal evidence abounds that people with oral traditions have phenomenal memories. Many observers, in tales of their travels to exotic lands, have reported remarkable mnemonic feats. Some serious students, perhaps influenced by these anecdotes, have argued that memory skills in preliterate societies develop differently from, if not better than, those in literate societies (e.g., Bartlett, 1932). They have noted that daily life in nonliterate societies places a premium on remembering details of the sort that in literate societies are a matter of bookkeeping or other forms of written record. Thus, Cole and Gay (1972) theorized that memory skills may be reinforced in some traditional societies both by the lack of a written language and by the emphasis placed on learning tribal histories and traditions.

Some empirical evidence shows some superiority in memory among persons reared in societies with a strong oral tradition. Ross and Millsom (1970), for example, suspected that the reliance on oral tradition that is characteristic of African societies might make Africans more likely to remember details in orally presented stories than a comparable group of Americans. Both groups were university students, one in Ghana and the other in New York. The researchers tested retention of the themes contained in several stories read aloud. They found that, in general, the Ghanaian students recalled the stories better than the New York students. The sole exception was one story told in 17th-century English. The Ghanaian performance was especially impressive, since they both heard and reproduced the stories in English, which to most of them was a second language.

It may also be that people in preliterate settings exceed those in literate societies in the memory of objects and pictures. In literate societies people are practiced in coding experience into words, which may enable them to recall large quantities of coded information. At the same time, individuals in literate societies, because they can rely on memory banks such as telephone directories, history books, and computers, may have lost memory skills through lack of practice. By contrast, individuals in preliterate settings may employ modes of memory that involve less encoding. And, because there are few alternatives to storing experience in their own heads, they may be well practiced in storing images of concrete experiences.

Research on a related phenomenon called eidetic imagery is described in Box 8-1.

Cole and his colleagues (see, for example, Cole, Gay, Glick, & Sharp,

---

Box 8-1 Eidetic Imagery

A first cross-cultural study on eidetic imagery (photographic memory) was reported by Doob (1964), who tested the incidence of eidetic imagery in a sample of Ibo people of Nigeria, a haphazardly selected group of 45 persons, male and female, children and adults, urban and rural. Doob found the Ibo performance to be "dramatically higher than that normally found in the West." The study also showed significantly more use of eidetic imagery among rural Ibo than among urban Ibo. Suspecting that eidetic imagery may correlate negatively with the Western character of a community, Doob (1966, 1970) continued his search for high levels of eidetic imagery in other non-Western settings but did not find it systematically, which led him as well as Feldman (1968) to speak of a "cross-cultural will-o'-the-wisp."

Other studies of eidetic imagery are those of Levak (1969) among the Bororo of Brazil, and Sheehan and Stewart (1972) among Australian Aborigines. The latter study revealed a high incidence (50%) of eidetic imagery among an isolated group of Bamyili in Arnhem Land, whereas the incidence was similarly low (5% to 15%) in Aborigines living on a reserve near the town of Armidale, and in Aboriginal and European children living in that city. In a later study, Sheehan (1973) found the same percentage of eidetic imagery among the Bamyili using a different methodology and different experimenters which provided evidence for the replicability of the phenomenon. The incidence of eidetic imagery was found to be very low, however, in an even more isolated group of Australian Aborigines. Clearly, the dimension "level of acculturation" does not have sufficient explanatory power to explain the cultural differences in eidetic imagery. Sheehan (1976) discusses various alternative explanations and the methodological questions that such results raise for cross-cultural research.

1971; Cole & Scribner, 1974) reported a complex series of memory experiments with schooled and unschooled Kpelle in Liberia. In one experiment, Kpelle subjects heard and were then asked to recall the names of 20 common items, five each in four categories — food, clothing, tools, and utensils. They were given several trials. Compared with Americans, the Kpelle subjects remembered less and improved less over trials; there was little improvement with age; and there was almost no clustering into semantic categories, a mnemonic skill current in American children after the age of 10. Neither did the Kpelle groups seem to learn by "rote" (recalling the words in the order in which they are given).

This surprising result prompted Scribner (1974) to propose that the categories employed were inappropriate for the Kpelle. When the subjects were allowed to use their own groupings, they used clustering in their recall, although more clustering did not always lead to better recall.

The researchers subsequently did a number of other widely varied experiments. They tested both educated (in Western style) and uneducated Kpelle, as well as Vai subjects, some of whom were literate in their own syllabic script. They employed both clusterable and nonclusterable names. They varied the order of names. They used real objects, not merely their names. And they varied the conditions of presentation, among which was an ingenious procedure known as "concrete cueing" in which the objects to be remembered were given a spatial location by being held over one of several chairs. Furthermore, they embedded the words to be recalled into stories, a situation that comes closer to everyday practices than the usual laboratory-type memory experiments.

Among the diverse findings that emerged were the following:

1. Clusterable lists were more easily learned than nonclusterable lists, and even more so by educated subjects.
2. Whereas American subjects showed serial position effects — that is, they recalled items late in a list best, those at the beginning next best, and those in the middle least well — Kpelle recall was unrelated to serial position.
3. Concrete objects were recalled better than their names, but this was also true for Americans.
4. The concrete-cueing procedure enhanced recall, especially when clusterable objects were each held over a particular chair. Exactly why this procedure proved successful has, however, not been established.
5. The employment of an explicit verbal instruction such as "Tell me all the tools you remember" also enhanced semantic clustering. This was true both for Kpelle and American subjects.
6. Performance increased when the words were part of a semantic discourse.

To summarize: when allowed to use their own categories, or when they employed certain aids to clustering the material to be remembered, the Kpelle subjects, particularly those with some schooling, were able to recall in a manner and to a degree comparable to American subjects. The experiments did not reveal any superior memory skills among the Kpelle. But they did allow specification of circumstances under which Kpelle memory would function like that of Americans, who, it may be suspected, were more practiced (especially through schooling) in employing mnemonics, that is, aids to memory. Signaling categories latent in clusterable lists was the technique that aided the Kpelle most.

A major implication of the Kpelle research program was that schooling heavily influences the performance of tasks requiring memorization; poor recall was characteristic of unschooled subjects, who could, nevertheless, benefit from techniques imposed by Cole and his colleagues. The use of conceptual organization as a means to remembering was more likely to be characteristic of schooled persons.

In a comprehensive review of the Kpelle research (Cole & Scribner, 1974), it is argued that schooling teaches people to remember aggregates of material that are not at first perceived as interrelated. Thus, people become practiced in learning new organizing principles, the acquisition of which then facilitates the remembering of instances that relate to the principle.

In any event, in this research program there was no evidence of superior memory skill among the unschooled Kpelle; according to this study, memory processes are not inherently better in preliterate societies.

On the basis of research in Mexico (Wagner, 1974, 1975) and Morocco (Wagner, 1978a, 1978b), Wagner (1981) introduced the distinction between the structure or "hardware" of memory (short-term memory capacity and forgetting rate) and the control processes or "software" (acquisition strategies such as clustering and rehearsal, and retrieval strategies). Wagner's hypothesis, briefly summarized, is that the structure of memory is universal, whereas the control processes are culturally influenced.

Two experiments (short-term recall and recognition memory) were conducted in Morocco on a sample of 384 males, who differed in age (7 to 19 years), schooling, and urban/rural environment. Additional groups of subjects were tested to study possible culture-specific influences on mnemonics: pupils in Quranic schools (where the Quran is learned by rote through chanting) and rug sellers (for an experiment on the recall of oriental rug patterns).

The recency effect (the fact that the last items in a list are remembered best, a measure of short-term storage or structural property of memory) was stable and relatively invariant across all populations studied, regardless of age, schooling, and environment. The primacy effect (the fact that the first items are remembered better, which is linked to verbal rehearsal, a control process) developed with age only for schooled subjects, and to some degree in nonschooled children who lived in an urban setting. Thus, the hypothesis was supported.

Quranic students were originally thought to have special memory abilities, but in both experiments they remembered very little and made little use of memory strategies. In Liberia, Scribner and Cole (1981) found that Quranic students used mnemonics, but only when the task made use of serial ordering skills in so-called semantic incremental memory. Thus the particular task used is a determinant of memory performance; there is no general memory skill but rather different specialized memory skills.

PROBLEM SOLVING

The drawing of inferences and the predicting of future events based on an analysis of past events, processes that often require postulating causal relationships, are forms of cognitive behavior characteristic of science. By Western values, scientific thinking represents the ultimate in intelligent behavior. To behave "scientifically" is, many believe, to perceive the world "as it really is."

Drawing causal inferences and discovering general principles on which valid predictions can be based are, of course, truly intellectual activities. They are often difficult to perform well, even with training. For centuries, scholars have struggled to provide guidelines for scientific thinking. The complex statistical techniques that help guard against perceiving relationships when none in fact exist, and the frequency with which such errors are nevertheless made, testify to the difficulty of scientific thinking. Yet, even in everyday life, logical analysis, predicting, and other scientific activities must occur.

Many people who hold Western values claim allegiance to scientific thinking. Only a minority argues that other modes of knowing, for example, intuition or mysticism, is a superior way of understanding reality.[2] What is the case in non-Western societies? Is Piaget (1966, p. 30) correct, for example, in assuming that all people tend toward formal-operational (scientific) thinking, but that non-Western people fall short of its achievement? Might it be, as suggested by some of the "great divide" theories reviewed in Chapter 5, that such thinking is absent from non-Western societies? Is there some other mode so highly valued and practiced that it takes the place of science and serves as well or even better to reveal "knowledge"? Questions

---

[2]Western culture has its share of poets, mystics, and others who insist that there is knowledge that cannot be penetrated by scientific inquiry, and insights that can be obtained by other means. Still, the scientific mode of knowledge seeking is most widely acclaimed.

like these have prompted cross-cultural research, some of which we reviewed in Chapters 5 and 6. We will now consider additional relevant studies.

Inferential Reasoning

As Cole, Gay, Glick and Sharp (1971) point out, it is difficult to get clear evidence of inferential reasoning by observing naturally occurring instances, which are always open to alternative interpretations. If a person sees a black cloud on the horizon and says it is going to rain, did she make an inference, or did she simply remember a common association? If that person says it is going to rain, while using instruments to measure wind velocity and barometric pressure, did she make an inference? It is more likely, but not certain; she, too, may just have recalled an earlier experience. We need evidence that the person is using a new combination of previously learned elements. To be sure, we must study the inferential reasoning process in a new situation, where previous learning can be controlled by the experimenter, as in a laboratory.

Cole et al. (1971) presented their subjects in Liberia (nonliterate Kpelle adults and children, and schooled children and young adults) with an oblong box apparatus, divided into three parts (A, B, and C), each with its own door. Subjects were first taught that they could get a marble by opening door A only and pushing the button in the middle of panel A. Then they were taught that they could get a ball bearing by pushing the button in panel C. Then, with doors A and C closed, candy (or some other reward) could be had by putting a marble (but not a ball bearing) into an appropriate opening in panel B. Finally, all three doors were opened simultaneously for the first time and subjects told to do whatever necessary to get a candy. In other words, the problem has to be solved by combining two independently learned behaviors.

With American children, there is a clear developmental trend; young children (up to about 10 years) did not integrate the two segments of the problem, whereas older children did (Kendler, Kendler & Carrick, 1966). In Liberia, subjects of all ages experienced difficulty with this task, and there were no age differences. Only 15% of the nonliterate Kpelle adults spontaneously solved the problem, a smaller percentage than five- to six-year-old nonschooled Liberian children (of whom 30% succeeded). Schooling made no difference (30% success in both 9- to 12-year-old and 17- to 20-year-old students). Schooling did have one influence: Only educated subjects were inclined to start working immediately with the strange apparatus. Among the nonliterate subjects, there were overt signs of fear. They would play with extraneous features of the apparatus; many subjects would press both side-panel buttons, and then sit quietly, waiting for the experimenter to ask additional questions. With prompting, 60% to 80% of the subjects would end up solving the problem.

The researchers could have been tempted to conclude that the Kpelle find it difficult to make simple inferences, that they lack the capacity for logical reasoning. But Cole et al. (1971) did not; instead they designed a Kpelle version of the same problem, one that had the same logical structure but made use of familiar materials. The additional research is described in Box 8-2.

The additional experiments by Cole et al. (1971) showed that the Kpelle, schooled or not, are quite able to use inferential reasoning, but only if the conditions are right. It is this kind of finding that led Cole and his colleagues to the conclusion that the use of cognitive processes is context specific.

Verbal Logical Reasoning

Logical reasoning can also be studied with verbal problems, such as syllogisms. Consider the following example:

All men are mortal;
Socrates is a man;
Therefore, Socrates is mortal.

An early cross-cultural study with syllogisms was carried out in Uzbekistan and Kirghizia (central Asia) in the 1930s by Luria, but the report became available in Russian only in 1974, and in English not until another two years later (Luria, 1976). This was, in fact, a study of the consequences of social change; one group of subjects was composed of nonschooled, noncollectivized farmers, and the second of people from the same villages who were engaged in the collective planning of farm production and had received about one year of literacy training. Luria found striking differences in the way these two groups responded to simple verbal syllogisms.

If the problems related to the concrete, practical experience of the villagers, they were not difficult to solve. But some contained unfamiliar content, for example:

In the North, where there is snow all year, the
    bears are white;
Novaya Zemlya is in the far North;
What color are the bears there?

Illiterate peasants typically said, "How should I know what color the bear was? I haven't been in the North. You should ask the people who have been

---

Box 8-2 A Kpelle Version of the Inference Apparatus[5]

The solution was to use a locked box containing a piece of candy as the goal object. The box could be opened with a key (keys and locks are now generally available in central Liberia). At the start of the experiment, two keys were shown to the subject, one painted red, the other black. The keys were then placed in two identifiably different matchboxes. In the first phase of the experiment, the subject learned which matchbox contained which key (this is analogous to learning which panel contains the marble in the original version). Then the matchboxes were set aside, the two keys were presented, and the subject learned which key fit the lock and made it possible to obtain the candy. (This is analogous to learning that the marble and not the ball bearing produced the candy when inserted in the center panel of the original apparatus.) Finally, the subject was presented with the two matchboxes and the locked box and told to do whatever was necessary to get the candy.

The change in response to the problem was dramatic when the key-lock procedure was introduced. From 70 to 80 percent of the subjects (aged 7 through adulthood) solved the problem spontaneously and 90 percent solved it with a little prompting. This way of conducting the experiment makes it look as if the Kpelle experience no difficulty at all with a simple inferential problem—provided that they are familiar with its elements.

It is possible, however, that in choosing a new form for the problem, we were doing more than simply changing the particular elements. Consider the second form of the problem again. Putting keys in locks is almost certainly a very well learned response for subjects who know about keys and locks. In fact, a key might be defined as something that opens a lock. If this is the case, we may have inadvertently been providing our Kpelle subjects with half of the answer to their problem in the key-lock version, thus making them look more competent than they would look if they had to learn the whole problem in the situation itself.

These ambiguities led to still another experiment, this time aimed at determining whether a previously learned link between the goal and the object used to obtain the goal made it easier to solve this kind of inference problem.

(continued)

---

[5]From *Culture and Thought: A Psychological Introduction*, (pp. 158–159) by M. Cole and S. Scribner, 1974, New York: John Wiley. Copyright 1974 by John Wiley and Sons. Reprinted by permission.

there and seen them. We always speak of only what we see; we don't talk about what we haven't seen."

Luria (1976) concluded that the subjects in the two groups were using different reasoning processes: concrete, or "graphico-functional", in the case of the illiterate group; abstract, or "hypothetico-deductive", for the collectivized, literate group (cf. Table 5-1). A relatively short-term socio-

---

Box 8-2 *Continued*

In this second experiment both Kpelle and American children were studied. The two conditions of greatest interest involved combinations of the procedures (and apparatus) used in the first two experiments. In the first of these conditions, subjects obtained a red or black key from panels A or C of the apparatus . . . ; one of these keys could be used to unlock the box from the second experiment. In the other conditions the subjects obtained keys from matchboxes, one of which caused a candy to drop when it was placed in panel B of the original apparatus. The results were completely contrary to our expectations: performance was best when the keys were taken from matchboxes and dropped into the center panel of the original apparatus. Performance when keys were obtained from the apparatus and then used to open the locked box was no better than performance in the original experiment.

From this new experiment we can conclude that the difficulty that young children and tribal Liberians experience with our simple inference task is that they do not know how to begin. For some reason, the process involved in obtaining a marble or a key from the side panel of the original apparatus interferes with later phases of the response sequence. Cultural differences seem in this case to reside in the kinds of initial situations that promote a good beginning for problem solution, not in the ability to link separately learned elements in order to solve a problem.

---

historical change, he thought, was producing a completely new way of thinking. Consider his example of a student in a village school who had only a few months of schooling.

> This subject, he writes, clearly demonstrates the capacity to perform hypothetical, theoretical operations independently of his own practical personal experience. It is of considerable interest that this shift and the capacity to perform "theoretical" operations of formal discursive and logical thinking appear after relatively short-term school instruction. The significance of schooling lies not just in the acquisition of new knowledge, but in the creation of new motives and formal modes of discursive verbal and logical thinking divorced from immediate practical experience. (Luria, 1976, p. 133)[3]

An Estonian psychologist, Tulviste (1978), used syllogisms with 35 schoolchildren (aged 8 to 15 years) among the Nganassan, a formerly nomadic population living from hunting and raising reindeer in northern Eur-

---

[3]An alternative interpretation is that schooling may have had an actualizing effect. Recall how we saw in Chapter 7 that a short period of training is sometimes sufficient to actualize underlying concrete operational reasoning.

asia. Ten syllogisms were presented, half with everyday content (e.g., "Saiba and Nakupté always drink tea together; Saiba drinks tea at 3 P.M.; Does Nakupté drink tea at 3 P.M. or not?), and half with school content (e.g., "All precious metals are rust-free; Molybdenum is a precious metal; Does molybdenum rust or not?"). The subjects were asked to explain their answers.

Drawing upon definitions used by Scribner (1978), Tulviste called "theoretic" answers in which the conclusion related explicitly to the premises; statements justifying the conclusion on the basis of what the subject knows or believes to be true were classified "empiric." Twenty-two children gave both "theoretic" and "empiric" answers. Syllogisms with school content were correctly dealt with in 90 out of 110 cases, justified with theoretic explanations in 59 cases. Syllogisms with everyday premises were correctly handled in 81 cases, but only 26 theoretic explanations were given.

> Theoretic syllogistic reasoning . . . first appears in the sphere of school knowledge and only after that is also applied in the sphere of everyday knowledge. The results presented reveal that theoretic syllogistic reasoning is not a skill previously present in the subjects, which under the impact of formal education can be applied to new kinds of problems. Rather, *it is a qualitatively new skill engendered by schooling*, which later on may be also applied to everyday matters. (Tulviste, 1978, pp. 12–13; italics ours)

Tulviste considered theoretic reasoning as "absent among traditional subjects" (p. 3) and an example of the Vygotskian term *thinking in scientific concepts* that first occurred in the social and cultural situation of ancient Greece and from where, through schooling, "it has come into different cultures and changed the thinking of men" (1978, p. 20).

Syllogistic reasoning problems were also used in Liberia with Kpelle and Vai people and among Mayan-speaking and Spanish-speaking, rural and semi-urban, schooled and nonschooled, adult and child populations in Yucatan, Mexico (Cole et al., 1971; Cole & Scribner, 1974; Sharp, Cole & Lave, 1978). The results were drawn together by Scribner (1979). Overall, the performance of "traditional" or "nonliterate" subjects was little better than chance. Within each culture, there was a large discrepancy in performance between schooled and nonschooled subjects; with schooling, there are only small cultural differences in performance.

Is it that traditional people do not reason logically? Or might it be that traditional people simply do not apply their logical skills to *verbal* material? Scribner rejected both of these hypotheses, illustrating logical reasoning by an illiterate Kpelle farmer with extracts from the following protocol:

> Experimenter: If Sumo or Saki drink palm wine, the Town Chief gets vexed; Sumo is not drinking palm wine; Saki is drinking palm wine; Is the Town Chief vexed?
> Subject: The Town Chief was not vexed on that day. The reason is that he doesn't love Sumo. Sumo's drinking gives people a hard time, that is why

Box 8-3 The Empiric Mode in Answering Syllogisms[6]

Problem	Answer and Explanation

Rejection of problem information

1. All women who live in Monrovia are married; Kemu is not married. Does she live in Monrovia?

Yes. Monrovia is not for any one kind of people, so Kemu came to live there. (denial of first premise)

2. Some government officials are wealthy; all wealthy men are powerful. Are some government officials powerful?

No. Because all government officials are wealthy, but not all wealthy people have power. (denial of second premise)

Importing new evidence

3. All people who own houses pay house tax; Boima does not pay a house tax. Does he own a house?

Yes. Boima has a house but he is exempted from paying house tax. The government appointed Boima to collect house tax so they exempted him from paying house tax. (discussion indicated this was exception to rule that all people pay house tax)

Verifying a conclusion

Problem 3 above.

No. If he has a house, he would pay the government tax *as required by the Liberian government.* (factual corroboration)

4. Some people we know are not in school; all of the people we know are in Liberia. Are all of the people in Liberia in school?

No. Because you said you know some people who do not go to school and *I myself know a lot of them too.* (Corroboration of formal evidence by personal experience)

5. All schools in Vai land are in a town; I know a school in Vai land. Is it in a town?

Yes. All schools are in a town. A school *should* be, for the *fact human beings are attending it, so it can't be built in the bush.* (Corroboration by common sense)

[6]From "Modes of thinking and Ways of Speaking: Culture and Logic Reconsidered" by S. Scribner, in *Discourse Production and Comprehension* (pp. 15–16) by R. D. Freedle (Ed.), 1978, Norwood, NJ: Ablex. Reprinted by permission.

the Town Chief gets vexed. But when Saki drinks palm wine, he does not give a hard time to people, he goes to lie down to sleep. At that rate people do not get vexed with him. (Scribner, 1979, p. 228)

In this example, and others analyzed in detail by Scribner, the reasoning follows logically from the evidence used by the subject, rather than from the evidence supplied in the experimental problem. In other words, the illiterate subjects use information based on fact, belief, or opinion. While this is consonant with Luria's and Tulviste's observations, Scribner drew different implications from it. For her, the empiric mode enters the reasoning process

> primarily as selector and editor of the "evidence." Personal knowledge and experience were used as (1) the criterion for acceptance or rejection of particular information conveyed in the premises, (2) the source of new information from which to derive a conclusion, (3) "proof" or verification of a conclusion reached through use of problem information. (Scribner, 1979, p. 232)

Some examples of answers collected by Scribner among illiterate Vai in Liberia are reprinted in Box 8-3.

When the illiterate subjects were asked to repeat the syllogisms after they were read, or to recall them after they had been solved, information was systematically omitted or transformed in such a way as to change the meaning of the problems, destroying the hypothetical status of the problem.

In other words, Scribner (1979), and Cole in the introduction to Luria's book (1976), interpret the empiric mode not as the absence of logical reasoning, but "the refusal to engage in the reasoning task at all, on the grounds that the problems presented are, *in principle*, unanswerable" (Scribner, 1979, p. 23, italics in original). Verbal logical problems are a special genre, a style of discourse, that is frequently used in school contexts, which explains why the theoretic mode is common among schooled subjects; the willingness to engage in this style does not reflect a different form of thought but rather the habit of applying a common form of logical reasoning to a new context.

> The most firmly based, and perhaps the most important conclusion we can reach at the present time is that thus far there is no evidence for different *kinds* of reasoning processes such as the old classic theories alleged — we have no evidence for a "primitive" logic. To go beyond this to a positive characterization of *how* traditional people think will require a host of new techniques and a great deal of imaginative thinking on the part of psychologists. (Cole & Scribner, 1974, p. 170)

This is based on a large array of studies, only a few of which have been sampled here. Most dealt, implicitly or explicitly, with the impact on cognitive processes of literacy, or of Western-type schooling, an issue we will address more specifically in the next section.

THE COGNITIVE CONSEQUENCES
OF LITERACY AND SCHOOLING

Schooling was shown to be an important determinant of performance in studies reviewed on sorting, memory, and syllogistic reasoning, (with the exception of inferential reasoning, on which schooling had little effect). If we consider a broader array of studies on schooling and cognition, including the Piagetian ones, as reviewed by Gillet (1976), Nerlove and Snipper (1981), and Rogoff (1981), the literature clearly shows varied, substantial (and sometimes inconsistent) effects of schooling. The following summarizes many findings:

> Research suggests that schooled individuals have gained skills both in the use of graphic conventions to represent depth in two-dimensional stimuli and in the fine-grained analysis of two-dimensional patterns. They have increased facility in deliberately remembering disconnected bits of information, and spontaneously engage in strategies that provide greater organization for the unrelated items. Schooled people are more likely to organize objects on a taxonomic basis, putting categorically similar objects together, whereas non-schooled people often use functional arrangements of objects that are used together. Schooled groups show greater facility in shifting to alternative dimensions of classification and in explaining the basis of their organization. Schooling appears to have no effect on rule learning nor on logical thought as long as the subject has understood the problem in the way the experimenter intended. Nonschooled subjects seem to prefer, however, to come to conclusions on the basis of experience rather than by relying on the information in the problem alone. The results of Piagetian tests are somewhat inconsistent, but they suggest that schooled children are more likely to show conservation and that schooling may be necessary for the solution of formal operational problems. (Rogoff, 1981, p. 285)

There is some disagreement on the meaning of these results. Heuristically, we distinguish four alternative, although not necessarily competing, interpretations:

1. The first has it that schooling, and more particularly literacy,[4] produce new cognitive processes. This is how Luria (1976) and Tulviste (1978), and more generally the sociohistorical school influenced by Vygotsky, see it. Cole and his colleagues seem sometimes to share this interpretation, although they usually prefer the second and third below. Goody, Cole and Scribner (1977), for example, wrote:

> When an individual comes to master writing, the basic system underlying the nature of his mental processes is changed fundamentally as the external symbol system comes to mediate the organization of all of his basic intellectual operations. (Goody, Cole & Scribner, 1977, p. 298)

---

[4]We shall see in a little while how to distinguish between schooling and literacy.

This is because writing is a double symbolic system: The letters stand for words that stand for ideas. Writing thus allows the decontextualization and formalization of thought; it promotes abstraction and critical thinking, or rationality. Literacy is here seen as one of the prerequisites of scientific reasoning.

2. The second interpretation claims that schooling promotes the application of existing processes to a large array of contexts, including new and unfamiliar ones (Bruner, 1966; Greenfield & Bruner, 1969; Greenfield, 1972; Scribner & Cole, 1973; Gillet, 1976). Schooling emphasizes the searching for general rules and is characterized by the use of verbal instruction out of context, free from immediate social contingencies; school learning is disconnected from everyday life, happens in an artificial context, usually with an adult who is not a family member. Schooled individuals are therefore more likely (a) to use abstract principles, (b) to apply general rules to specific problems, and (c) to verbalize their actions and to explain the reasons for their behavior.

   Schooling has a homogenizing effect (Gillet, 1976); that is, all individuals are brought to a minimal level of competence that can, however, also be attained in some circumstances by other "cultural opportunities" (Nerlove & Snipper, 1981). This would explain why the effects of schooling are not always consistent; they depend, for one thing, on the type and quality of schooling and also on the type of stimulation provided by the out-of-school environment.

3. A third interpretation attributes the empirical findings largely to experimental artifacts (Cole, Sharp & Lave, 1976). The testing situations used, almost unavoidably, very much resemble the "hidden curriculum" of schools; for example, schooled individuals regularly interact with a strange adult, they dare to ask questions (instead of keeping respectfully silent), and they are used to answering questions (even when they know that the adult already knows the answers). Schooled individuals are used to tackling strange tasks and to persisting in searching for a solution. All these experiences are similar to the implicit demands of the research situations, and therefore the observed performances may have been enhanced artificially.

4. Lave (1977), considering that the skills learned in school are quite specific to the school situation, argued that these skills should therefore show up in school-like experimental studies but are likely to have little relevance for everyday life. This notion will be reexamined in the next chapter.

All four interpretations contain a germ of truth. The first one, however, is different because it seems to go somewhat beyond the facts and because it relates more explicitly to literacy than to schooling. Since literacy is typically attained through schooling, it is as difficult to study the respective effects of these two variables as it is to separate the effects of age and schooling in Western developmental studies. We now turn to this issue, relying on an excellent review by Akinnaso (1981).

Literacy or Schooling?

When considering the effects of literacy, we ought to distinguish its consequences for the individual from its impact on society as a whole. In fact, it is on the basis of a historical and anthropological analysis at the population level, comparing societies with or without writing (or, historically, the culture change when writing is invented or introduced), that Goody (1980) and his colleagues hypothesized the creation of new cognitive processes as a consequence of literacy.

Literacy is seen as a highly potent catalyst of cultural change (e.g., McLuhan, 1962; Goody & Watt, 1963; Olson, 1977). First of all, written language is different from speech. With the introduction of a writing system, the basic character of the storage and transmission of knowledge is changed. Transmission of information becomes possible beyond the limited circle of personal contacts, necessitating a more explicit, decontextualized form of language; writing also promotes the development of elaborate syntax. Written language cannot rely on the simultaneous transmission of information over other, paralinguistic channels, such as postures and gestures. In the words of Vygotsky (1962), "writing is speech without an interlocutor, addressed to an imaginary person or to no one in particular" (p. 99). The storage of information is no longer limited by human memory; knowledge becomes cumulative, even over generations, a basic condition for the development of science (Goody, 1977).

Historically, the invention of writing also allowed mass communication; the spread of messianic religions based on a revealed, holy text; and the development of institutions such as bureaucracies, allowing the administration of large and complex political entities, and schools that help to perpetuate the system.

To study the effects of literacy on individual cognitive functioning, and to distinguish them from the effects of schooling, Scribner and Cole (1978, 1981; Cole, 1978) took advantage of a "natural experiment" among the Vai people in Liberia, some of whom are literate in their own script without ever having been to school. The Vai phonetic writing system consists of a syllabary of approximately 210 characters that are combined into a text without any separations between words. The script is used for writing letters and keeping personal records, and it is transmitted entirely outside of any institutional setting through individual tutoring among friends and relatives. Approximately 20% of Vai men are literate in Vai; 16% have attended Quranic schools and are therefore more or less literate in Arabic, although that language is used only for religious purposes. Another 6% are literate in English, the official national language that they have learned in Western-style schools. Vai women are generally not literate in any script.

Scribner and Cole compared the performance of Vai men who were literate in the various scripts, and that of nonliterates, on a variety of psychological tests, including classification (sorting), memory (free and incremental recall), and logical reasoning (syllogisms), and some tasks designed specifically for the project on the basis of an anthropological analysis of the skills involved in the use of each of the scripts.

The results showed consistent schooling effects on all but two of the tasks. The effects of the other types of literacies were much less systematic, indicating that literacy per se does not produce any general cognitive effects. Rather, the specific activities involved in the use of a particular script facilitated the development of closely related cognitive skills. For example, as we have already mentioned, Quranic schooling did not improve overall memory performance, but specifically incremental recall. Vai-script literates performed well in a referential communication test, in which they had to describe a board game in its absence (but so did the schooled subjects). They also proved skillful at encoding and decoding rebuses and at integrating auditory information (understanding sentences broken into syllables that were presented at a slow rate). When the sentences were presented word by word, they had no advantage over the other literates. Their auditory information processing skill was attributed to practice with scripts without word or phrase division, where reading implies strategies for integrating syllables into meaningful linguistic units.

Scribner and Cole provided no confirmation at all of Goody's hypothesis that literacy should produce new cognitive processes. Rather, certain forms of literacy promote very specific language-processing and cognitive skills. On the other hand, the more general impact of schooling was confirmed again. Note that even this very careful research design did not allow the researchers to distinguish clearly between the second and third interpretations mentioned above.

SUMMARY AND CONCLUSIONS

We have discussed numerous studies conducted in many different parts of the world that dealt with diverse cognitive activities including classification, concept discovery, memory, logical thinking, and problem solving. We found evidence of *differences* across cultural groups, differences in habitual strategies for classifying and for solving problems, differences in cognitive style, and differences in rates of progression through developmental stages. Variations across groups in the way individuals interact with the world around them appear early in life and tend to increase throughout the life span. These differences, however, are in performance rather than in competence. They are differences in the way basic cognitive processes are applied to particular contexts, rather than in presence or absence of the processes. Despite these differences, then, there is an underlying *universality* of cognitive processes.

We found a set of ideas that might help explain cross-cultural differences in cognitive performance. The central theme is that the modes of knowing toward which development proceeds in any setting are those produced by the socialization practices that are emphasized there. The socialization emphases in turn reflect social and economic adaptations to ecological forces. Thus, individuals in all societies are heir to a culturally shaped way of conceptualizing the world and their relation to it. What is inherited tends to conserve the modes of knowing that have, over generations, permitted the society to survive in its particular habitat.

This does not mean a static adherence to tradition. Our framework is inherently dynamic and underscores the fundamental flexibility of human beings. Implicit is the expectation that as ecological or cultural forces change, so will the use of basic cognitive processes in the new contexts. From our perspective, cognitive styles are not superior or inferior; any prevailing style is adaptive, suited to the prevailing ecological and cultural context.

Therefore, any test of ability constructed in one cultural setting will, most probably, elicit relatively "poor" performances in some other culture. In general, we know this to be the case for Western intelligence tests applied to minorities within Western societies and to populations outside of a Westernized, urban, industrial world. But armed with the emphasis on learning that is at the core of the ecocultural framework, we need no longer accept the characterization of different performances by such persons as "poor."

We have come to recognize that the Western world's concept of intelligence is culture-bound, as are the tests that measure it. The Western definition of intelligence, and the tests that reflect it, relate primarily to academic performance. In other societies, the key concept will be whatever is valued, just as academic performance is valued in some. But whatever kinds of behavior are seen as intelligent, those behaviors are likely to be found in good supply.

In the last three chapters, we have come to understand human cognitive functioning as an active process dynamically influenced by cultural forces. All of us, everywhere, adapt to the world around us in ways that our cultural ancestors have found to be functional. Within any cultural setting, some individuals may be better equipped than others to apply their skills and strategies, and across cultures, the preferred skills and strategies will vary. But everywhere, humans have found ways that work. The optimistic prediction, that we will continue to find new ways, as the old ways may prove less functional, is consistent with what we have seen.

The point of departure for much of the research on cognition reported so far has been the use of tests, tasks, and experimental situations as they were first developed in Western psychology. This approach has its advantages, but it also has weaknesses; the kind of cognitive processes that are studied often bear little obvious relationship to daily life in the real world. In the next chapter, we examine a new trend common to both cross-cultural and mainstream psychology, namely, the study of "everyday cognition."

Chapter 9

Everyday Cognition

INTRODUCTION

The experimental anthropology studies of Michael Cole and colleagues (discussed in Chapter 8) demonstrated how profitably one can adapt laboratory techniques to cross-cultural research. As we saw, one must first acquire profound ethnographic understanding in order to conduct experiments meaningfully in a new cultural milieu. In experimental anthropology, one is never content simply to measure performance. Experimental procedures may have to be modified to allow subjects to display their real cognitive competence.

Despite the care taken in experimental anthropology to be culturally sensitive, ironically, the cognitive processes that the experimental anthropologist chooses to study (such as memory and syllogistic reasoning) derive from interests inherent in Western psychology.

An even more emic methodology would be to determine the cognitive processes that appear to be involved in ongoing daily activities. In everyday-cognition studies, cognitive behaviors are studied in a natural situation, usually through a combination of observational and more experimental methods. These behaviors are sometimes so banal that, until very recently, they hardly attracted the attention of researchers. Everyday-cognition research is concerned with the informal, oral, "traditional," or "popular" knowledge, meaning the knowledge of ordinary people, in contrast with school- or book-based, expert or scientific, knowledge. We are referring here to a continuum, however.[1]

---

[1]In our discussion, we employ the terms *knowledge* and *cognition* in virtually interchangeable fashion: We have in mind all the information that individuals use to understand the world

A goal of everyday-cognition studies is to maximize cultural validity; to achieve this, some experimental control may be lost. And, experimental methods must be combined with natural observation in particular cultural milieus. What makes the research cross-cultural is more the method used than the place where the research is carried out. Whereas many everyday-cognition studies employ situations that are rare in Western society (e.g., children selling produce in the market, unschooled tailors), everyday cognition is also characteristic of Western societies. Informal learning is a common phenomenon, even in complex and highly institutionalized societies. Recent research in this domain has been conducted in North American supermarkets, in factories, and in cocktail lounges (Rogoff & Lave, 1984). These studies have in common the researcher's departure from the laboratory in order to become involved in daily-life settings.

First, we will deal briefly with two approaches that are related to the study of everyday cognition — ethnography of daily life and ethnoscience.

ETHNOGRAPHY OF DAILY LIFE

By its very nature, ethnology[2] is the science of the everyday. But although it is commonplace that anthropologists describe in minute detail every twist and turn of whatever "exotic" people they have travelled afar to study, we are surprised when researchers in more industrialized societies use the same approach for the daily life that surrounds them. Such an approach, however, in *any* society could be extremely fruitful.

For example, we find work in France on "the invention of the everyday" (de Certeau, 1980), which describes and analyzes "popular culture" activities and the rituals of daily life in urban space. A finely detailed description of everything involved in cooking in contemporary French society (Giard, 1980) includes, of course, customs and mores, but also individual knowledge and know-how and the cognitive processes that support them.

> As soon as one takes a close look at the process of culinary art, it becomes obvious that it demands a multiple memory; one must remember what one was taught, what movements witnessed, what textures felt, how thick a sauce should be. . . .
> It also requires a kind of intelligence that permits planning ahead; it is necessary to calculate assiduously both preparation and cooking times and to integrate all the various sequences with each other. . . .

---

around them and the way in which they acquire or construct it. As far as possible, however, research should try to separate the acquired bits of knowledge from the cognitive processes that underlie them.

[2]For definitions of ethnography, ethnology, and cultural anthropology, Erny (1981) may be consulted.

Each meal requires inventing a mini-strategy of substitution, whenever a particular ingredient or utensil is not at hand. . . .

Thus, to undertake the art of cooking, to manipulate these mundane things, puts intelligence to practical work. It must be a subtle kind of intelligence, full of nuances, of on-the-spot innovations, an intelligence that is light-hearted and which can be devined without clearly revealing itself. It is an intelligence of the most ordinary kind. (Giard, 1980, pp. 158–159, our translation)

This report is quite phenomenological. The language is more literary than scientific; the facts are "soft," qualitative, and difficult to verify. But given the research goal, we welcome the richness of the observations. Ethnology must do more than describe and transcribe, however; the hidden meaning of the activities should be revealed. It is a form of analysis, then, in which the role of the anthropologist is substantial.

COGNITIVE ANTHROPOLOGY OR ETHNOSCIENCE

Another, slightly different, approach is cognitive anthropology or ethnoscience, which seeks to build a model of an underlying cognitive structure from systematically gathered empirical facts. Pioneering work of this kind was described by Tyler (1969), and more recent studies were covered in a critical and synthetic analysis by Gardner (1985); this approach is also discussed in Jahoda (1982) and Berry et al. (in press).

Ethnoscience tries to work emically (i.e., using a society's own category system) to ascertain the cognitive principles by which the society's members apprehend their world. Accordingly, the ethnoscientist tries to determine which aspects of the environment are considered important, what they are called, and how the local populace relate them to one another. In this manner, cognitive anthropology tries to discover how each culture creates order out of chaos.

According to Edgerton and Langness (1974, cited by Gardner, 1985, p. 246), the goal of ethnoscience is "to write a set of rules for a culture which is so complete that any outsider could use them to behave appropriately in that culture." This amounts to extracting the "grammar" of a culture or its underlying structure. As with any generative grammar, however, the model might predict what is generally appropriate in a culture but could not predict the behavior of any particular *individual* member of the society. The model must be able to explain all of the relevant observations parsimoniously, i.e., with a minimum number of necessary principles.

How to proceed? First the ethnologist, on the basis of his or her own observations and intuitions, chooses a semantic domain that appears to be important in the society being studied, for example, kinship terms. Then all the lexical elements in this domain (e.g., mother, father, sister, nephew) are collected. Next, the ethnologist looks for the dimensions or principles according to which it seems possible to organize those elements, such as sex, generation, or linearity. In this manner, a "componential analysis" is completed, the results of which are usually reported in graphic form.

Considerable attention is paid to reliability in componential analysis. The likelihood that different ethnologists would obtain the same results is assessed routinely. But the method is plagued by several difficult methodological problems, all of which pose threats to its validity:

1. The information on which the analysis is based comes usually from privileged informants. Sometimes a few informants each provide partial data. Usually there is uncertainty as to whether everybody (or even anybody) in the society actually employs the total model.
2. Interindividual variations are not often taken into account.
3. It is not clear whether the results of a componential analysis reflect a psychological reality. This problem is similar to that encountered in the study of artificial intelligence.
4. The models are based solely on linguistic facts. Nonverbal elements that might be important are missing.

Briefly, then, ethnoscience is the emic determination of domains that are generally treated scientifically; accordingly, what it produces may properly be termed ethno-botany, ethno-astronomy, ethno-medicine, and the like. Because of the methodological difficulties listed above, it is no longer widely practiced, but a combination with psychological methods attending to individual differences may enhance its potential (Wassmann & Dasen, 1989).

The relation of ethnoscience to everyday cognition is obvious, since, like it, ethnoscience tries simultaneously to determine modes of popular thought and to derive the cognitive principles that underlie them.

To review: In emic research, we try to study a culture so as to see it as its own members do. Thus, research designed to show how a particular people classifies experience, yielding the classification system they habitually employ, is a form of emic research known as ethnoscience (Tyler, 1969; Gardner, 1985; Dougherty, 1985). Ethnoscience is usually ideographic, i.e., it describes, for a particular group of people, how they understand the world, what the elements are that are considered important, what they are called, and what relations exist among them, without attempting to compare this scheme with others.

It is of course also perfectly legitimate to ask how different cultures classify their world and to produce some comparison among the different schemes. What needs emphasizing, however, is that any single culture's classification system should first be expressed in the terms employed indigenously. It is that system, after all, that makes up the cognitive map of persons in that culture, and it is that system, expressed in its own terms, that is of paramount interest to the psychologist who would seek reasons, embedded in other facts about the behavioral setting, for the presence of such a system. To understand *why* a people think the way they do, we must first appreciate *how* they think. And for that we must discover each people's own system.

EVERYDAY KNOWLEDGE OF ARITHMETIC

The contextualist school of Cole influenced numerous studies of everyday cognition. Most of these studies are described in works edited by Rogoff and Lave (1984) and Lave (1985). One well-studied domain is arithmetic, perhaps because it involves cognitive behaviors that are easily observed.

Many readers will be accustomed to thinking of arithmetic as linked with schooling and literacy. We will now look at some studies that demonstrate that the ability to read and write is by no means a prerequisite for arithmetic competence, and that illiterate persons can sometimes perform very complex mental calculations.

Everyday Arithmetic and School-Based Arithmetic

It is fascinating to travel over time and space to examine the (pre)historic development of number systems (Ifrah, 1985) and their diverse forms and uses in comtemporary societies. Every society has a number system, albeit sometimes rudimentary. The Aranda, for example, an Aboriginal group from central Australia, name only three numbers—"one," "two," and "three"—which they combine to express "four" and "five"; beyond "five," they say only "many" (Elkin, 1943). This reflects a cultural devaluing of quantification—a characteristic of nomadic hunter societies throughout the world. The production of a surplus among high-food-accumulation groups such as farmers and herders provides the motivation for the development of a genuine arithmetic, particularly where commerce is important. Recall that in Chapter 7, we reviewed the work of Saxe (among others), who combined Piagetian inquiries with the study of the numbering system of the Oksapmin of Papua, New Guinea.

The following questions will guide our comparison of everyday, informal arithmetic with its school-based counterpart:

1. Are the calculation strategies employed in the two situations the same or different?
2. How effective is everyday arithmetic and what are its limits?

Rosin (1973), in one of the first studies to address these questions, described the kinds of calculations made by an illiterate peasant in Rajasthan (India). Box 9-1 provides an excerpt from this anecdotal but nevertheless instructive account.

Knowledge of elementary arithmetic can develop without schooling, particularly if children have opportunities to practice certain fundamental concepts in their everyday activities. Posner and Baroody (1979) demonstrated this in a study of their conservation of number among agricultural Baoulé children and merchant-class Dioula children. The latter were reared in a society where quantifying is particularly valued because of the commercial activities of their parents. As expected, the Dioula children, on the whole, gave more conservation responses than the Baoulé children (on the average, for 9- to 10-year-olds, 77% vs. 52%). This difference was greater for nonschooled children than for schooled children. A similar difference between Baoulé and Dioula nonschooled children was found for counting as well.

A study of mental arithmetic among Dioula children and adults, both schooled and nonschooled, as well as among Americans (Ginsburg, Posner & Russell, 1981) showed that as age increases, schooled Dioula and Americans increasingly use school-based algorithms, whereas nonschooled persons make efficient use of number facts (subjects recall correct answers directly and quickly without calculation) and regrouping (subjects break addends into more manageable units that may then be added by using

---

Box 9-1 A Virtuoso Display of Everyday Arithmetic

Rosin (1973) made very detailed observations of some elaborate calculations by an illiterate peasant from Rajasthan (India), named Rupsingh (whose writing skill was limited to placing an X on a document as a signature). Rosin accompanied Rupsingh to a goldsmith where they bought two gold medallions, each weighing 3¾ *tola*. A tola of gold costs 6¾ rupees. A rupee is equivalent to 16 *annas* or 100 *naya paisa*. The price for each medallion came to 25 rupees and 5 anna (or 25 rupees and 31 naya paisa). Rosin did the calculations twice in writing, once using fractions and once with decimals, and he got two different solutions. Since one of them corresponded to what the goldsmith asked, Rosin was prepared to pay it, but Rupsingh proposed instead that he verify the calculation himself to be sure that the goldsmith was not in error.

Rupsingh's strategy was to triple 6¾, then to find ¾ of 6¾, and to combine the results. This he did only by multiplication and division by two. He did addition by counting on his fingers (15 finger joints) and by memorizing the intermediate results each time. The calculation took him several hours spread over several days, after which he called his younger brother and his nephew, both of them schooled, and discovered that they had not yet solved the problem even with the use of paper and pencil.

This observation is anecdotal and limited to a single example. Nevertheless, this limitation is balanced by the richness and the detail of the description.

number facts, counting, or some other procedure.). In this study, non-schooled adults did not make any more errors than schooled adults (this was not so for children). Implicitly, the nonschooled adults used decomposition, associativity, and commutativity—all while only having learned informal methods of calculation.

In contrast, Petitto & Ginsburg (1982), in another study of mental calculation among illiterate Dioula, tested subjects on all four arithmetic operations (i.e., addition, subtraction, multiplication, and division) and found that informal arithmetic skills have their limits. This study is described in Box 9-2.

Reed and Lave (1979) demonstrated how computational errors made by Vai tailors in Liberia could be explained by features of their number system. The Vai system (like that of many other societies) uses the base 5 in combi-

---

Box 9-2 How Limited Are Informal Arithmetic Strategies?

The subjects in Petitto and Ginsburg's (1982) experiment were 20 non-schooled Dioula adults, either tailors or cloth merchants, and 14 American students. The problems given to them consisted of eight pairs of calculations related to each other by reciprocity (e.g., $90 + 35$ and $125 - 90$; 100×6 and 6×100).

For addition and subtraction (treated as inverse addition), the subjects used regrouping without any difficulty, thus applying implicitly the principles of associativity and commutativity. The results were nearly always precisely correct.

For multiplication, a problem like 100×6 presented practically no difficulty. It is expressed in Dioula by "100 added six times" and is solved effectively by successive addition. In contrast, the reciprocal—6×100 or "6 added one hundred times"—becomes a practically unsolvable problem, and commutativity is not in general recognized.

Division is done by looking for a corresponding multiplication (or successive additions), sometimes employing approximations. For example, $300 \div 3$ is easily solved by adding 100 three times (and noting that that equals 300). For a problem like $300 \div 100$, some subjects first chose a small number like 2, for example, added it one hundred times, and then tried another number until they found the solution. In contrast, the schooled American subjects never, of course, had any difficulty solving this type of problem using simultaneously school-based algorithms and informal strategies, and they were also able to explain the mathematical principles involved.

The limitation of informal strategies in comparison with school-based algorithms is thus very real. All calculations are reduced to addition, and the number position is not used, despite the existence of a base 10 in the Dioula number system. But this limitation is probably of very little functional importance in the ongoing life of Dioula merchants, since the problems they have to solve never involve such large multipliers or divisors.

nation with the base 20. Schooled subjects tended to use the decimal system or to combine it with the Vai system. They made errors of place (i.e., being wrong by a factor of 10 or 100), whereas nonschooled subjects either made smaller errors (being wrong by 5, 10, or 20 units) or simply proceeded by approximation. Reed and Lave distinguish two classes of strategies for performing arithmetic operations: (1) those that deal with *quantities*, in oral arithmetic, using strategies such as counting on fingers, manipulating pebbles, or using an abacus; (2) strategies using number names, i.e., school-based algorithms designed for the manipulation of *symbols* and using a *written* numerical representation.

Brenner (1985) also worked among the Vai in Liberia, addressing the question of the efficiency of combining school-based algorithms with traditional methods. Brenner's study was based on observations of pupils (preschool, first- and fourth-grade primary) in four Liberian schools, to whom he presented an arithmetic test covering all four operations. Observations in the market place of the everyday arithmetic of tailors and carpenters revealed that everyday calculations involved diverse strategies, including breaking down a problem into the simplest possible units, counting concrete objects, reducing multiplication to addition, and the like. In class and on the test, nearly all the pupils (97%) used a combination of Vai and school-based strategies. This combined method appeared to be very powerful: Those who used the greatest variety of school-based methods and different Vai techniques did best on the test. The Vai teachers apparently accepted the use of diverse arithmetic methods.

As already noted, everyday arithmetic calls on heuristic procedures, whereas school-based arithmetic requires conventional algorithms. This was clearly demonstrated in a set of studies done in Brazil, as described in Box 9-3.

Applying these results to formal education practices, the Brazilian authors suggested that arithmetic be taught, at least in the beginning, in contexts that have practical significance, thereby taking advantage of the arithmetic knowledge children have already picked up in their daily activities. Then teachers could gradually add more powerful algorithms (instead of trying to teach them first), followed by their possible applications. The heuristic procedures are often complex and call for a surprisingly high level of skill in manipulating numbers. Furthermore, they vary among individuals and across problems. In contrast, school algorithms are general tools that may be employed in many different situations.

Arithmetic in the Supermarket

Most studies of nonformal knowledge have been carried out in Third-World settings where it is relatively easy to find nonschooled populations,

Box 9-3 Oral and Written Arithmetic

Carraher, Carraher, and Schliemann (1985) observed some schooled children in Recife in Brazil who also worked as sellers in the market. In the practical market setting, the children solved correctly 98% of some relatively complicated problems. For example, they solved the problem 35×10 as follows: $3 \times 35 = 105$; $105 + 105 + 105 + 35 = 350$. In the school situation, the same children solved equivalent calculations correctly 74% of the time if presented in problem form, but only 37% of the time when presented in the form of numerical calculations.

The authors employed Reed and Lave's (1979) formulation to distinguish heuristic arithmetic procedures from school-based algorithms. This distinction is illustrated by the following examples.

Example 1 (a 12-year-old child): 4 coconuts at 35 centavos each (4×35).

A. Nonformal situation: "3 coconuts cost 105" (here the child is using his knowledge of a frequent fact); "plus 30, that makes 135; and 1 coconut costs 35, and that makes 140."
B. School setting: "$4 \times 5 = 20$, I write down 0, and I carry the 2; $2 + 3 = 5$; $5 \times 4 = 20$. I attach the 0 and the 20, and so the answer is 200."

Example 2 (four 9-year-olds): 3 coconuts at 40 centavos each (3×40).

A. Nonformal situation: "40, 80, 120."
B. School setting: "40×3, I take the 0 down; $4 + 3 = 7$; I attach the 0 to the 7, and my answer is 70."

In these two cases, the market child proceeded by successive addition and, in the first example, employed an already memorized quantity (105) and also used a decomposition ($35 = 30 + 5$). In the school situation, by contrast, the child tried to use the multiplication algorithm but erred because he added the 10s before multiplying them. From all the evidence, it appears that the child learned a routine without understanding it and wasn't surprised by an erroneous result because it didn't represent anything in terms of money.

In a follow-up study, Carraher, Carraher, and Schliemann (1987) gave some arithmetic problems to 16 children, aged 8 to 13 years, in the third primary grade in Recife. These problems included all four operations and each in three different situations. In one, the child took the role of grocer, and the experimenter was the customer; real objects were available. The same calculations were presented in the form of meaningful problems and as written calculation exercises. The three series of 10 problems were administered by the same experimenter in a systematically varied order.

The authors discovered that the children tended more to use oral, heuristic procedures in the first two situations and school-based algorithms in the third.

(continued)

Box 9-3 *Continued*

On the whole, the oral procedures led to more correct responses than the written procedures. This was clearly so for subtraction, multiplication, and division (on average, 65% to 75% correct responses with oral procedures, and 40% to 44% for written procedures). Thus it was not so much the formality or nonformality of the situation that mattered but the choice of procedures.

The oral procedures rested on decomposition or regrouping, or both, which allowed working with quantities that are easier to manipulate and can then be part of a calculation of an iterative nature, such as successive additions or successive divisions by 2.

thereby guaranteeing that the knowledge being studied could not have been acquired formally. Still, in industrial societies there are many everyday situations that call on know-how and problem-solving skills (often requiring arithmetic calculations), and in such settings we can study the degree to which subjects use school-based skills or other more specific strategies.

The everyday situations studied in North America include calculations made by shoppers in a supermarket (Lave, Murtaugh & de La Rocha, 1984; Murtaugh, 1985), computations made by weight watchers following a strict diet (de La Rocha, 1985), and problem solving in an industrial dairy (Scribner, 1984). These studies all revealed competencies that often exceed purely school-based techniques in efficiency and accuracy. The basic difference between the two types of situations is that in practical settings, subjects must frame the question themselves, deriving it from a meaningful reality. They have to be able to simplify the problem and to be satisfied with a functionally acceptable approximation. Reed and Lave (1979) found that reasoning by quantities often led to better solutions than reasoning by symbols.

Murtaugh (1985) and Lave, Murtaugh and de La Rocha (1984) systematically observed 24 adults shopping in a supermarket, following them and asking them to explain their various selections and to describe the kinds of calculations they needed to perform. Since products were packaged in nonmetric sizes (involving numbers like 24, 32, and 64, for example, in ounce- and pound-denominated weights) and often lacked unit price markings, rather complex calculations were required.

Of a total of 803 purchases, 312 required an explicit decision, either based on brand preferences (reflecting habits, tastes, and advertisements) or taking into account such factors as package size in relation to family size. For another 125 of the products purchased, 213 calculations were performed. In 30% of these cases (i.e., 65 cases), "best buy" calculations were performed. Of these, 16 involved simply using unit prices that were provided on the packages. In the other 49 cases, the buyers rarely tried to determine the precise unit cost but simply multiplied the price of one item to compare it roughly with another of equal weight. They tried to find out simply which was more advantageous (but not by how much) and often employed simplification and approximation. Exact calculations were performed in only 5% of the cases.

Still, the calculations performed were correct 98% of the time, even though the same persons who participated in the supermarket study solved, on the average, only 59% of the items on an arithmetic test. These percentages are not really comparable, however, because unlike the Brazilian study described in Box 9-3, the problems presented were not the same in both situations.

The author concluded that in everyday situations, one has not only to *solve* problems but to *frame* them as well. This must be done in practical terms and often requires simplifying the problem. "Problem formation and problem solving are very likely to be integral parts of a single process in many real-world environments" (Murtaugh, 1985, p. 192).

Newman, Griffin and Cole (1984) also noted that in everyday situations, people first have to define a problem before being able to solve it. Moreover, these real-life situations are typically ones involving social interaction. In contrast, in psychological laboratory situations, the task is usually defined by the experimenter while the subject (often an isolated individual) attempts to solve the problem alone. Classroom situations tend to fall somewhere between these two extremes.

To summarize: Everyday arithmetic has both strengths and weaknesses. Because the strategies employed are so varied, everyday arithmetic often leads to more correct solutions than school-derived algorithms. These strategies often involve decomposition and regrouping, which are based on principles of associativity and commutativity. On the other hand, the reciprocity of two operations is not always recognized. The four operations are, in general, reduced to successive addition. This underscores the limits of everyday arithmetic, particularly with large numbers.

The characteristics of everyday arithmetic most often demonstrated are:

1. Quantities are manipulated rather than symbols.
2. Problems must be redefined in order to simplify them.
3. Solutions tend to be idiosyncratic; they vary across both individuals and problems.

TRANSFER AND
GENERALIZATION

Is everyday knowledge transferable to new situations? Is it generalizable[3] or is it inextricably tied to the contexts in which it was learned?

At the end of Chapter 7, we touched on the specificity-versus-interdependence controversy with respect to cognitive mechanisms. We noted that Cole and his followers adopt an extreme contextualist viewpoint whereby each aptitude is treated as independent of the others yet tied to the context in which it is functional (LCHC, 1983). They would expect a minimum of transfer from one context to another. At the other extreme are researchers (often using factor analysis) who postulate the existence of a very general aptitude (the "g" factor), a position similar to that of Piaget's theory, in which, prior to cross-cultural and differential studies, a certain homogeneity of behaviors within any given stage was assumed (see Dasen & de Ribaupierre, 1987). From this perspective, one would expect a certain "permeability of contexts" and thus relatively easy transfer.

A third alternative is intermediate and is exemplified by "local constructivism" (Harris & Heelas, 1979; Dasen, 1983) and "cognitive styles" (Berry, 1984), both of which postulate a functional connection between the contextual system (such as the ecocultural dimension) and cognitive domains within which transfer would be possible. We will shortly examine some empirical facts relating to these alternatives.

Transfer of School Knowledge

Transfer is obviously a phenomenon of considerable importance in education. One of the goals of schooling is to prepare children for their lives as adults, but the classroom situation and the skills acquired there are not necessarily those of adult careers and occupations. So we should ask whether school-based learning is actually useful later on. This question is especially important in societies undergoing rapid change, where the role of the school should be to prepare young people to deal with a multitude of

---

[3]Experimental psychologists study transfer by measuring the effects of prior learning on performance (Postman, 1971). Learning is a cumulative process. The more information acquired, the greater the probability that new learning experiences will be affected by prior experiences. An adult never learns anything entirely from scratch; even when confronting unknown tasks, accumulated information and habits are involved. Piéron (1957) offered the following definition: "one says that there is transfer when the progress obtained in the course of learning a certain form of activity involves an improvement in the performance of a different, more or less related, activity" (p. 370). If there is a strong effect on relatively far-removed tasks, one speaks of generalization rather than of transfer.

new and unanticipated situations. There are diverse opinions. Some argue that subjects like Latin and mathematics (to use examples most often cited) "shape the mind," thus claiming their profound generalization value. Others argue that whatever leads to success in the real world of adult occupations must be learned outside of formal school settings (e.g., Cador, 1982). In Third-World contexts, the gap between school and the world of work makes transfer even less probable. Paradoxically, Third-World schools are also the principle sites of sociocultural change and, thus, potentially the best locales for learning how to deal with novelty.

When we examined in Chapter 8 the cognitive effects of schooling, we saw that these might be characterized as, at one extreme, the acquisition of narrow bits of knowledge (tied specifically to school situations per se) and, at the other, the creation of new cognitive processes. In fact, most studies seem to indicate that schooling encourages the application of learned cognitive aptitudes to a variety of situations, even new or artificial ones. Thus, the data support a generalizability hypothesis.

Transfer of Everyday Cognition

In research on the transfer of everyday cognition to new situations, the following research design is typically used: An everyday cognition is studied, first of all, in its own context using participant observation. Then, test situations are constructed by varying the degree of familiarity of the context to which the knowledge is to be applied. One chooses tasks that are very similar to daily activities and then gradually departs from these, finally reaching situations that are completely artificial. Such studies ought to (but don't usually) include a detailed analysis of the strategies employed for solving the different problems in order to be able to specify what in fact was transferred and to eliminate alternative explanations (Ginsburg, 1977).

Tailors in Liberia

Lave (1977) tried to implement a design like this in her research with tailors in Liberia. The subjects were 33 master tailors and 30 apprentices. About one half of the two groups had never been to school. The schooling of the rest ranged from 1 to 10 years, and their tailoring experience ranged from a few months to 25 years. After observing their work in the tailor shops, Lave administered two kinds of arithmetic problems: a set of 16 reflecting in a very direct way the practice of tailoring and 16 analogous problems, of the same level of difficulty and requiring the same algorithms for solution, but with no obvious relation to tailoring.

With the first type of problem, practical experience as a tailor had a greater influence on performance than did schooling (which had practically no effect). But the success rates were so high (87% to 95%), it is possible that the problems in this set were all too easy for a schooling effect to show up. By contrast, there was a marked effect of schooling on performance of the second type of problem. The subjects who had had 5 to 10 years of schooling were correct 91% of the time, whereas those with less (or no) schooling achieved a 74% success rate. Nevertheless, even on these problems, practical experience related significantly to performance as well.

Lave concluded that "the inductive teaching/learning techniques of apprenticeship training do not prevent the formation of general problem-solving principles" (p. 179). Her second hypothesis is that "like tailors' arithmetic, school-learned arithmetic is a functional system in which certain kinds of problems are familiar and easily solved while others are not" (p. 180). In other words, the second set of problems were familiar specifically to schooled tailors, and schooling would not strongly facilitate out-of-context problem solution.

In another report of this research (Greenfield & Lave, 1982), Lave describes using a third problem type (the matching of drawings of trousers according to the proportions of waist to length) with a multiple-choice format. Here, the problem content is close to that of tailoring, but the task format is school-like. Hence this task had some features that were relatively unfamiliar from both tailoring and school points of view. On these problems, performance was not affected by schooling or by experience as a tailor. The authors concluded from this that "it appears that neither schooling nor tailoring skills generalize very far beyond the circumstances in which they are ordinarily applied. . . . The ability to generalize cognitive skills to unfamiliar but related situations may be heavily constrained" (Greenfield & Lave, 1982, p. 199).

Weaving in Mexico

Greenfield and Childs (1977), in a study of the learning of weaving among young Zinacanteco (Mexico) girls (also discussed in Childs & Greenfield, 1980; Greenfield & Lave, 1982) explored the cognitive effects of weaving on the representation of patterns similar to those that are used in traditional fabrics (always involving alternating red and white bands of varying size). The two tasks employed in this study involved (1) copying two familiar figures with sticks of colored wood, and (2) completing six incomplete figures, varying both in complexity and familiarity, with the wooden sticks. The subjects, between 13 and 18 years of age, included nine nonschooled, female weavers, and 18 nonweaving boys, half of them schooled, the others not.

In the first task, the girls used the wood sticks as if they were threads, whereas the nonschooled boys dealt with the figure as a whole. The girls were thus able to transfer their practical knowledge to a different material. But the schooled boys were also proceeding analytically. The authors explained the boys' performance not as a consequence of familiarity with the figures but of a general ability acquired in school to move from one content to another. Greenfield and Lave (1982) note that reading and writing require movement between the visual and auditory domains.

On the second kind of task, which involved a problem that is truly novel with respect to traditional weaving, one could have reasonably expected to find good performance only among the schooled boys. In fact, it was all the boys, schooled or not, who outperformed the weaving girls. The authors explained this result as a gender-role phenomenon, related to the fact that in this society, boys are the predominant participants in the money economy and make frequent trips to urban centers, where they have ample opportunity to see a great variety of fabrics.

The lack of generalization from weaving to these test situations demonstrates the specificity of this kind of know-how, at least in cultural contexts in which innovation is not valued. In effect, the Zinacantecos, at the time of this study, used to weave only two or three designs and did not consider variations.[4]

The study by Childs and Greenfield (1980) is not beyond methodological criticism. The number of subjects was very small and the design incomplete; the observational part of the study was done with only eight dyads (mothers and one of their daughters), and the more experimental study used nine unschooled girl weavers and 18 boys, all nonweavers, half of whom were schooled. There were no schooled girls included in the study, and no weaving boys.

Now, there are very good reasons for these choices: Among the Zinacantecos, only girls learn to weave and only boys go to school; weaving skill and sex are always confounded in that society, just as schooling and age are confounded in others. Taking a video camera to the field, especially at the time this study was carried out (the early 1970s), and recording such behavior observations even on only eight dyads, takes an enormous amount of time and effort. These, then, are some of the limitations of this study, and some of the reasons for them. In a typical study of mother-child teaching styles carried out in a laboratory in a European or American university,

---

[4]Greenfield & Lave (1982, p. 201) refer to two other studies (without details or references), one by L. Aronson among the Ibo of Nigeria, the other by M. Loukey and J. Loukey in a Mayan community in Guatemala, where girls first learn to weave on miniature looms with small pieces of thread or grasses. Later, when they begin to weave with real equipment and material, they can manage by themselves. In these two societies, weaving is not constrained to traditional designs, and the creation of original designs is encouraged.

many more subjects are easily included. Were not the trade-offs for doing the study in Mexico worthwhile?

Of course they were. Working with nonschooled teachers (the mothers) and nonschooled pupils, the authors were able to discover the informal but quite systematic pedagogy of errorless learning, uninfluenced by schooling. Observing naturally occurring events (even though the use of a video camera was unfamiliar in that setting) increased the validity of the findings, as against the contrived situations where mother and child are set up for the observation and given a task to do. Furthermore, producing a data set of precise observations, amenable to quantification, presented an advance over most previous studies of informal education that had relied only on less systematic ethnographic observation. In the more experimental part on pattern reproduction, the tasks that were used may have been awkward (weaving with sticks), but at least they were designed locally on the basis of previous observations, and were not imported tests.

Transfer of Formal Operations in Brazil

A series of studies by a team of researchers from Recife in Brazil demonstrate the presence of combinatory and proportional reasoning (assigned by Piaget to the stage of formal operations) among minimally schooled adults, who use it in the practice of their craft, and its transfer to new problems. Brazilian foremen, observed on building sites, are capable of calculating proportions by using the scales of their plans. They are also able to transfer their knowledge to the use of unfamiliar scales (for example, $1/40$ and $1/33.3$, whereas they normally use $1/20$, $1/50$, or $1/100$). In this study reported by Carraher (1986), 60% of the subjects gave evidence of transfer by using their knowledge in a flexible manner, but their performance was not directly related to their degree of schooling (which varied from 0 to 11 years). A similar result was found with fishermen (Schliemann & Carraher, 1988) who were accustomed to using multiplication for price calculation and for estimating the proportions of processed to unprocessed fish and shellfish. The problems given to them required that they invert the normal procedures; they had to calculate the unit price from the price of a large amount or calculate the amount of fish that had to be caught in order to obtain a given weight of filets. The most difficult problems were solved at a 57% success rate, and again, problem solution was not correlated with amount of prior schooling (which varied from one to nine years).

In contrast, amount of schooling was shown to be an important factor in a study of combinatorial reasoning (Schliemann, 1988). Daily experience with betting in a number lottery was another factor that favored this kind of reasoning. This study also demonstrated transfer from an everyday situation to the solution of new problems. The proportion of formal reasoning shown in this study, however, was very weak: 0% for a control group of adults from a very low socioeconomic level, 15% among adults from the same level but involved in betting, and only 25% for first-year university students.

Carraher, Schliemann and Carraher (1988) conclude from this whole set of studies that everyday activities foster the development of transferable, flexible knowledge, which is therefore conceptual and not merely procedural.

Conceptual and Procedural Knowledge

Like Ginsburg (1977), who distinguishes strategies from principles, Hatano (1982) contrasts "procedural skill" and "conceptual knowledge." The former is a routine procedure for rapidly and efficiently solving problems in a specific context. It would be efficient only if external constraints do not change. Procedural skill is often specific to a society and goes unquestioned; it is institutionalized and is considered necessarily "the best" method. For example, Hatano points to the Asian cultural tradition of counting with an abacus, internalized for the purposes of mental counting in the form of a "mental abacus" (Hatano, Miyake & Binks, 1977; Stigler, Barclay & Aiello, 1982; Stigler, 1984). The performance by some experts was astonishing—calculations involving 15 digits, sometimes performed more rapidly than on an electronic calculator! On the basis of earlier work, however, Hatano suggested that this procedural skill does not transfer to other forms of calculation, such as those with numbers to the base 10 or those requiring comprehension of the remainder principle. Neither did it transfer to problems requiring the memorization of information other than numbers.

It thus appears that procedural-skill transfer is limited when unaccompanied by conceptual knowledge. Conceptual knowledge involves the mental representation of a procedure's meaning, an understanding of why and how it works and some notion of what its variations might be. Transfer, and hence flexibility, adaptiveness, and innovation, are possible only with this kind of understanding. Conceptual knowledge will be more easily acquired if external constraints change, if the situation demands procedural variations, if procedural skill is put into some doubt (either by the user or the user's companion), and if the user is encouraged to *think about* the procedure rather than *execute* it as rapidly as possible.

Most instances of everyday cognition are of the procedural kind. Insofar as people live in a stable cultural setting, procedural skill is enough to ensure production. The culture provides the procedural model, but only rarely is this accompanied by an explanation for its use.

> In conclusion, we assume that though practice in most culture-specific procedural skills tends to produce routine experts, with developed special processes involved in their performance, it usually doesn't facilitate development

of the corresponding conceptual knowledge, nor competence under a new set of constraints even in the same domain. (Hatano, 1982, p. 17)[5]

Conclusion Regarding Transfer

What may we conclude from the various studies of transfer of everyday cognition? Certainly the findings are not definitive and we cannot yet state precisely when transfer will occur. A series of studies seems to show that everyday cognitions are most often tied to the context in which they are usually applied. This specificity excludes transfer beyond situations relatively close in all respects. In contrast, Lave (1977) provided evidence of the transfer of arithmetic skills acquired by tailors to problems of the kind used in school, and Pettito (1982) found that fabric sellers could solve analogous problems with nonfamiliar content (oranges). Even more convincing are the Brazilian studies reported above.

For those studies that did not find transfer, one could object that the generalizability of everyday cognition was not demonstrated because the test situations were often artificial (e.g., weaving with little sticks or pipe cleaners, choosing designs in a multiple-choice format) and were therefore inherently strange. Might not transfer be more easily demonstrated in situations that were new but, at the same time, not so foreign, such as those used in the Recife studies?

As regards knowledge acquired in formal schooling, we tend to believe it automatically generalizable. Even if it is more generalizable than everyday cognition, we saw that it, too, has limits. Increasingly, school is seen as simply another context for learning, with specific cognitive outcomes.

LEARNING PROCESSES

According to Greenfield (1984), a value system oriented toward the maintenance of traditional ways would be congruent with learning by observation, scaffolding, and shaping (learning processes to be defined and discussed below), in other words, errorless learning. Trial-and-error learning would be associated with a greater ease of transfer and would be found in societies that value innovation more. In this section, we will examine in more

---

[5]Hatano allied himself with Piaget, who was always more interested in the underlying structures (the basis of understanding) than in performance itself. Hatano also distanced himself from the American empiricist tradition, which he considered too restrictive. Nevertheless, Hatano's notion of conceptual knowledge is vague and will no doubt be difficult to operationalize. This notion underscores the entire problem of subjects' awareness of their own functioning. In any case, it is a direction to pursue.

detail the different learning mechanisms that occur in informal education, in formal traditional education, and in schooling.

Greenfield and Lave (1979) distinguished three types of learning processes: (1) trial and error, (2) shaping, and (3) scaffolding. In the first, which Piaget called "operative learning," the learner is confronted by a new situation constituting a conflict with what he already knows; he then tries different approaches, succeeding only after making successive adjustments. In this type of learning, motivation is seen as internal to the learner, and the conflict and the errors made are, theoretically, positive features.

Shaping is a process where the learner's responses are controlled by a teacher, who organizes problems according to a sequence designed, insofar as possible, to avoid errors. Correct responses are reinforced by external rewards.

Learning by scaffolding also involves an adult and also tries to avoid errors, but the whole problem is presented immediately in its entirety. The expert provides support to the novice, furnishing information and intervening when some step appears to be too difficult. Scaffolding involves adjusting the demands of the task to the ability level of the learner. The expert's intervention diminishes in the course of the apprenticeship. Scaffolding allows the novice eventually to do alone what at the beginning could be done only with help from the expert. Thus, scaffolding is a learning process that always involves social interaction.

This model illustrates Vygotsky's concept of a "proximal zone of development." In contrast to Piaget, Vygotsky asserts that there is always sociocultural mediation in individual development, with every function appearing twice, first at the "intermental" (or social) level, then at the "intramental" (or individually interiorized) level (Rogoff & Gardner, 1984; Wertsch, Minick & Arns, 1984; Schneuwly & Bronckart, 1985).

In their study of weaving apprenticeship among the Zinacantecan girls in Mexico and that of the tailors in Liberia, Greenfield and Lave (1982) found that the masters "use scaffolded intervention to achieve developmental sequencing within chunks. This results in relatively errorless learning under circumstances where errors would cause considerable economic harm to the teacher's household" (Greenfield & Lave, 1982, p. 207).

Greenfield (1984) proposed that the concept of learning by scaffolding characterizes especially those situations where the economic stakes are high. By contrast, where cost doesn't matter or where there is not a real task being done, as in many school-based situations, trial-and-error learning would be more common. Shaping could be combined with either of the other learning processes in both situations.

These three learning processes do not relate cleanly to the distinction between formal and informal education. In fact, Greenfield and Lave indicate that weaving apprenticeship may be accomplished either by scaffolding (as among the Zinacantecos) or by trial and error (as among the Mayas of Guatemala).

In learning to drive a car, trial-and-error learning would be hazardous, and so it is usually done by scaffolding (or thorough prolonged observation). By contrast, when learning to master a video game, no harm comes from proceeding by trial and error. Greenfield and Lauber (1988) found that students with little or no experience with video games significantly improved their ability to solve problems relating to the logic of electronic circuits after two and one-half hours of practice with a multistaged game, where new goals and procedures had to be discovered for each stage.

We suspect that cultural differences with respect to these three learning processes consist primarily of the degree to which they predominate in any particular society, and this would depend on their respective economic implications.

Greenfield (1984) also hypothesized that learning by scaffolding would tend to inhibit generalization, where trial-and-error learning would facilitate it. Thus, everyday cognitions acquired by scaffolding would often be tied to very particular contexts, whereas school-based knowledge acquired through trial-and-error learning would easily transfer to new problems, but we saw in Chapter 8 that empirical support for this hypothesis is still very weak. Here is a domain in which future research could well be very fruitful.

Figure 9-1 depicts these different learning processes, following a scheme proposed by Strauss (1984) and including elements proposed by Chamoux (1981) and Greenfield (1984). On the left side of Figure 9-1 are the mechanisms that predominate in informal education, and on the right side, those of formal education (although, as stated earlier, the mechanisms do not divide cleanly across the formal-informal dichotomy). Chanting is characteristic of formal, traditional education. The important difference between observation and imitation is that in the former, action is deferred, sometimes for years, whereas imitation takes place in the presence of the model. The distinction between well-defined and ill-defined procedures does not imply a value judgment but derives from studies on artificial intelligence and problem solving. Well-defined procedures are those in which the necessary information is fully laid out, and the steps to be taken and the goals to be attained are completely specified, whereas in ill-defined procedures, the learner is confronted by considerable uncertainty, which requires proceeding by trial and error.

EDUCATIONAL APPLICATIONS[6]

Brenner (1985), in a study of arithmetic in Liberian schools, demonstrated the value of a combination of traditional strategies and school-based

---

[6]Applications to teaching theory and practice are implicit in most of the studies we have already reviewed in this chapter, but in very few of them did the research lead directly to educational applications.

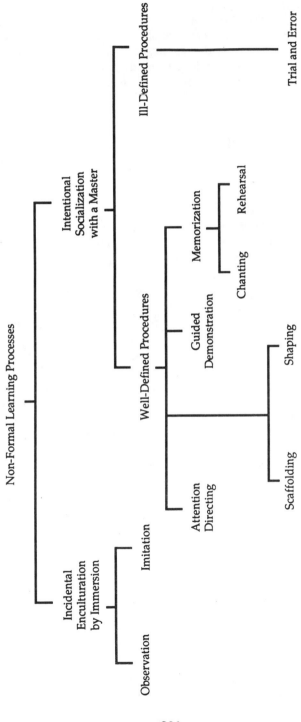

FIGURE 9-1. Learning processes

algorithms. Some other studies indicate possible pedagogical applications. For example, Carraher, Carraher, and Schliemann (1985) suggest that teaching arithmetic would be easier if it could be built on knowledge already established by everyday learning. This implies that teachers should accept the use of individual strategies, like counting on the fingers or successive addition. In other words, they advocate teaching arithmetic by starting with practical concerns, before presenting it as an abstract system. Nevertheless, they are careful to point out that the use of street arithmetic in school would make only the beginning easier. They do not doubt that algorithms, offered later, provide more powerful tools and that "mathematics taught in schools has the potential to serve as an amplifier for thinking processes" (Carraher, Carraher & Schliemann, 1985, p. 29).

Ginsburg and Allardice (1984) identified two systems of informal arithmetic knowledge:

1. Intuitive mathematics concepts, which develop before school begins. Examples include understanding comparatives (more or less) or Piagetian concepts of conservation and classification. (Note that Ginsburg and Allardice seem to believe that these understandings are "natural," linked to biological development, which is an exaggeration, albeit a common one, of the maturational component in Piaget's theorizing.)
2. Counting, and the solution of addition with real objects, which depend on informal cultural transmissions (by adults, by television, etc.) during the preschool years.

These informal understandings serve as the prerequisites for school-based learning; one may hypothesize that those pupils who have difficulty with arithmetic, particularly those labeled "culturally deprived," might be handicapped because their home environment doesn't provide them with those informal understandings that are useful for school. This argument inspired the compensatory education movement in the United States and elsewhere, of which we spoke in Chapter 5. Ginsburg and Allardice are skeptical of this hypothesis.

Ginsburg and Russel (1981), in a study in which young American children had to solve informal arithmetic problems, found very little effect of such factors as race, social class, or family structure. Rather, the principal determinant of performance was simply age. Among the younger children, there was a difference in favor of middle-class children, but this difference no longer existed once the children were in nursery school.

According to Ginsburg and Allardice (1984), the only social-class or cultural differences are in age of acquisition of particular skills and not in competence per se. "Schooling and middle-class American culture are not necessary for the development of understanding, even though they can accelerate its appearance" (p. 201). Still, we must not belittle the significance of these temporal gaps that ought to be taken into account in schooling. Nevertheless, these studies show that difficulties in school cannot be explained solely by weaknesses in informal mathematics knowledge.

The writers refer to Ogbu (1978) to suggest that the difficulties instead result from a lack of motivation stemming from socioeconomic discrimination; because these pupils know that they have no access to economic success, they are not motivated to make a full-fledged scholarly effort. In school-based arithmetic, these pupils have specific difficulties with the "third system," that of "imposed algorithms," of written and of explicitly expressed mathematical principles. It is a "schooling culture" to which they don't adhere that hinders them. They know that they are failing, and repeated failures produce a cumulative deficit.

The pupils studied by Ginsburg and Allardice (1984) would often succeed much better in oral calculations, inventing their own strategies, but believing that the algorithms were completely arbitrary and detached from reality, they were ready to accept aberrant results uncritically. The authors of this study speak of a kind of "cognitive schizophrenia": a complete dissociation between informal and invented strategies, on the one hand, and formal understanding and written calculations, on the other.

The cause of learning problems in school is to be found in the educational system itself, say Ginsburg and Allardice, and not in a cognitive or cultural deficit. It would be necessary, then, to find an educational context that would permit all pupils to use their potential for learning. This would probably be a context that encourages independent thought before insisting on the rigid application of standard algorithms.

None of this, of course, is entirely new. For a long time, educators have been trying to use everyday knowledge and concrete ideas from the local environment as the departure place for schooling. Certainly this has been the case for mathematics (Meljac, 1979; Vergnaud, 1983), notably in the Nuffield Program (Nuffield, 1970, 1972; Dumont, 1977). Nevertheless, even if the principle is widely acknowledged, to put it into practice requires detailed documentation of relevant nonformal knowledge. Much research remains to be done in this regard. For the teaching of children coming from a social or cultural background marked by a lack of coherence between the school-based and real-world cultures, research on informal knowledge would be exceedingly useful.

Research on transfer and generalization provides other potential applications to teaching. Despite the embryonic state of this research domain, we know enough to suggest that schools ought explicitly to train students to apply their newly learned skills in as large a variety of contexts as possible. It ought not be assumed that the implications of school-based knowledge will be used spontaneously in everyday life. A real effort is called for to seek reciprocal relation between school and the real world, especially when the two are rooted in different cultural traditions, as in many non-Western societies (Mukene, 1988).

CONCLUSIONS

Research on everyday cognition is a field that has emerged in the last decade and illustrates well the interdisciplinary nature of cross-cultural psychology. It is an attempt to study cognition in its sociocultural context, that is, culturally relevant cognition. Through the emphasis on specific contexts, the particularities of knowledge in action may have been overemphasized, as well as the lack of transfer to new problems. Lave (1988) recently called into question the whole paradigm of transfer research, pointing out how its basic assumptions are linked to laboratory procedures. Further research should look for the common threads across situations and develop a stronger theory of everyday cognition. To do this, attention to recent developments in mainstream cognitive psychology will be in order, in particular the research in artificial intelligence and cognitive science, and the so-called neo-Piagetian theories (Dasen & de Ribaupierre, 1987). It is through the mutual interaction between mainstream and cross-cultural psychology that we can expect the most promising results.

Part III
PERSONALITY AND SOCIAL BEHAVIOR

The most obvious differences among peoples of different societies are in life-style. Travelers to a foreign land are likely on their first stroll down an unfamiliar street to notice new sights, sounds, and smells and to remark on the clothing, the babbling of a foreign tongue, and the aromas of the exotic foods.

Soon after, they will become aware that something more profound separates them from their hosts. That something, hard to put into words, includes a difference in priorities, a departure from the importance that they would attach to events and experiences. Such differences, not directly observable, become obvious through numerous behaviors that reflect values, goals, and aspirations that are central to one social group but that may be merely peripheral to another. It is common for visitors to sense not only different life-styles but also different attitudes toward life itself.

Sometimes the visitor exaggerates or otherwise misperceives values inherent in another culture because novel patterns of behavior mask an underlying similarity of values. In like fashion, true value differences may be missed; similar behaviors may be taken as indicative of similar values when, in fact, they express different ones. Both errors are possible because the assessment of values requires inferences from observed behavior, and overt acts can have diverse meanings. Still, the prevailing impression a foreign observer usually forms is that "they" don't believe in X the way "we" do, or "they" don't care about Y to the degree "we" do. And, as we shall see, such impressions are likely to be essentially correct, but only in some respects.

It is virtually intrinsic to the concept of culture that different peoples will possess different values, beliefs, and motives. To delineate such differences as they are manifest in behavior is one of the enterprises that engages cross-cultural psychologists. In Chapter 10, we will consider that enterprise in some detail.

In Chapter 11, we will pay particular attention to relations between the sexes, with respect to which values indeed vary across cultures, nevertheless finding widespread consistency in gender roles and related consistencies in characteristic behaviors of males and females.

One behavioral difference that exists between the sexes all over the world is in the degree to which aggression is used to resolve conflicts. In Chapter 12, we will see that males are far more likely than females to display behavior that does harm to other people. There we will also examine variations in aggression across cultures and consider what these variations suggest regarding theories of the causes of aggression and strategies for controlling aggression.

Whether the next few chapters leave you with a sense that societies are very different from each other or, on the contrary, that they are very much alike in their social behavior remains to be seen. Perhaps both impressions are accurate!

Chapter 10

Cultural Differences in Motives, Beliefs, and Values

INTRODUCTION: WHY STUDY VALUES CROSS-CULTURALLY?

Cross-cultural research on motives, beliefs, and values has several objectives. One is simply to describe them, which is not easy, because they are never directly observable; they may only be inferred from behavior. Another objective is to find the ecological and cultural forces with which the traits may be correlated and to make sense out of such links. To do this, we assume that the behavioral dispositions of the members of any cultural group will be consistent with, reflective of, and supportive of the culture's social-economic-political system. A final objective is to describe the mechanisms that produce these links, usually in the socialization emphases of the society.

We answer the somewhat rhetorical question, "Why study values cross-culturally?" by saying, "Because they are interesting." Like Mount Everest, the values that underlie the behavior of various human groups invite the curious to explore them. Second, to study the values of others is to search for universal values, motives that transcend cultural differences in behavior settings. The discovery of such universals would reveal characteristics shared by all human beings and thereby enhance our self-knowledge. Finally, an examination of the values of others may reveal attractive alternatives to our own, wherever we might live.

We will begin with some reflections on the value system of contemporary Western culture, because aspects of Western culture impinge on many persons everywhere. Moreover, as was stated in Chapter 2, cross-cultural psychology is in part a reaction to Western ideas.

215

A Brief Exposé of Western Values

Numerous scholarly analyses of some of the more salient Western values have been published, but none is more thought provoking than that by the eminent American economist Robert Heilbroner, whose *An Inquiry Into the Human Prospect* (1975) startled a good many readers with its grim predictions and Malthusian warnings.

The Heilbroner Thesis

This economist's ideas are not explicitly related to any psychological theory nor have they directly influenced psychological research. Psychological issues are implicit in Heilbroner's thesis, however.

Heilbroner saw several concrete threats facing mankind: (1) the accelerating population overload, particularly in the poor nations; (2) an ominous spread of nuclear weaponry and other potentially coercive power to heretofore exploited nations; and (3) the technologically developed world's continuing, excessive demands on environmental resources. These threats, accompanied by the emulation of profligate Western life-styles by Third-World societies striving for "growth" and "development," make the survival of mankind a dubious proposition, in Heilbroner's view.

The behaviors that alarm Heilbroner reflect some of the most basic, cherished Western values that are present in both of "the two great socio-economic systems that influence human behavior in our time: capitalism and socialism" (Heilbroner, 1975, p. 63). He characterized these two fundamentally Western social systems in two stark sentences. "Each has been marked with serious operational difficulties; each has overcome these difficulties with economic growth. Each has succeeded in raising its level of material consumption; each has been unable to produce a climate of social satisfaction" (p. 75).

Common to capitalist and socialist societies is an industrial civilization, built on scientific technology and stressing such values as hard work, efficiency, production, management, the taming and exploitation of the environment, and material (as opposed to spiritual) achievement. Although the two systems differ from each other in some values pertaining to the individual and the society, it is this common industrial civilization that Heilbroner labels a "root cause" of the dangers to humanity. Industrial civilization clearly dominates the world as it approaches the 21st century, and it stresses, above all else, growth. It is this dominant orientation of economic growth that must give way, because such strategies are no longer feasible, given dwindling reserves of economic resources. "In place of prodigalities of consumption must now come new frugal attitudes" (p. 94).

To save ourselves, Heilbroner argued, we must transform our industrial civilization into a postindustrial society that no longer emphasizes growth. He turned toward preindustrial societies for guidance:

Some human societies have existed for millennia, and others can probably exist for future millennia, in a continuous rhythm of birth and coming of age and death, without pressing toward those dangerous ecological limits, or engendering those dangerous social tensions that threaten present-day "advanced" societies. In our discovery of "primitive" cultures, living out their timeless histories, we may have found the single most important object lesson for future man. (Heilbroner, 1975, p. 141)

Human beings — whom Heilbroner, like Becker (1973), recognizes as the only animals that contemplate their own death — have constructed a variety of life-styles in an attempt to distract themselves. In Western societies, their distractions consist of work, achievement, striving after efficiency, and acquisition and consumption of material goods as rewards. As we shall see in detail in Chapter 13, much of the world is adopting these same distractions. But the whole world had better, in Heilbroner's view, move away from the work ethic and the values that sustain it.

The Heilbroner thesis provokes the thought that the core values of Western civilization, reflecting science, technology, and industry, however much they have contributed to material well-being, have not produced comparable psychic well-being and may propel us toward our own doom. In terms of the ecocultural framework employed in the present text, it is obvious that the changing ecological circumstances confronting industrial society have made less functional those cultural and behavioral patterns that must once have been adaptive. Ecological changes have produced the need for new coping strategies. For example, we can no longer use fossil fuels at the level of carelessness that characterized the period of industrial growth in the West. It is also ironic that as industrialized nations move away from some of the habits of their recent past, other nations are beginning to industrialize. A very provocative book that echoes some of Heilbroner's ideas and satirically dissects one of the sacred cows of Western cultural evangelism — the concept of economic development — appeared in French in 1987 bearing the amusing title "Once Upon a Time . . . Development" (Rist & Sabelli, 1987).

In any case, there is something to be learned from a study of the values of existing, nontechnologically oriented societies.

The Plan of This Chapter

We will try to (1) describe variations in values, motives, and other behavioral dispositions that have been recorded systematically by cross-cultural psychologists; (2) relate such variations to ecological and cultural differences or other features of the behavioral settings in which the variations have been noted; and (3) explain the mechanisms by which the behavioral dispositions that seem to "fit" with certain cultural factors come to be learned by the individuals who possess them.

We will find few facts that go beyond description and few relationships for which a particular explanation must be favored. For explanation, we will frequently rely on social-learning theories within which socialization is seen as the mediating link between ecocultural forces and human values.

Most of the available studies are done by cross-cultural psychologists who have been reared or trained in Western societies; the studies have mostly involved values that are deeply rooted in Western culture. Ironically, then, in this chapter on cross-cultural studies of human values, much of the content is fundamentally culture-bound.

INDIVIDUALISM/COLLECTIVISM
AND DISTRIBUTIVE JUSTICE

We have already noted that the stressed values of industrial civilization include individual hard work, achievement, and concern with self and self-improvement; all of these values could be summarized as reflecting individualism. Focusing on work-related values, Hofstede (1980) studied employees of a multinational firm with units both in established industrial nations and in newly industrializing nations and found the value of individualism to be less characteristic in the less industrialized nations. (A more detailed treatment of Hofstede's study is given in Berry et al., in press.)

Triandis (1983) initiated a research program dealing with individualism and collectivism as two poles of a dimension along which societies might vary. Hui and Triandis (1984, 1985) produced a scale to measure individualism and collectivism, which Hsu (1981) had suggested was a salient difference between Americans and Chinese. Collectivism, as defined by this scale, involves being concerned with others, considering the implications for others of one's decisions, and the sharing of material resources.

Hui (1984) showed that collectivism was more likely to be valued by Chinese college students than by American college students. Hui and Triandis (1984) conducted a scenario study both in Hong Kong and in Illinois (United States), wherein students allocated money to themselves and to partners. In such studies, alternative principles of reward allocation are possible, most notably "equity" (reward based on quality of performance), "equality" (equal rewards to all regardless of performance), and "need" (unequal rewards reflecting differential needs). Hui and Triandis found that the Chinese students were more equality-oriented and more other-serving than their American counterparts.

The question of what is fair is likely to come up in any society whenever resources have to be allocated. The resources may be positive, such as a financial reward, or negative, such as a salary cut or a tax levy. Which allocation principle seems most fair may depend on whether a positive or negative resource is being contemplated. Thus, cultural norms might favor assigning a positive resource to the most productive persons (an equity principle) while protecting poor people from a negative resource (a need principle). Moreover, since the norms that govern resource allocation are, as we have just said, cultural norms, definitions of fairness might well vary from culture to culture.

Some evidence suggests that even Western cultural groups differ in what they believe is fair. Tornblom and Foa (1983) detected some differences between Sweden, West Germany, and the United States by reviewing separate studies conducted in those three Western nations, but because procedures employed in these separate studies differed, it is difficult to interpret the findings. A clearer picture emerges from studies conducted simultaneously in two or more societies, e.g., Japan and the United States (Mahler, Greenberg & Hayashi, 1981), and the United States and India (Berman, Murphy-Berman & Singh, 1985). In the latter one, students of psychology at universities in both nations considered twelve hypothetical distribution problems (presented as vignettes written in English and Hindi, with back-translation to make them as similar as possible), half of which involved positive distributions and half negative, with target persons either an excellent worker who was economically comfortable or an average worker in economic need.

Respondents in both samples had to decide whether to distribute the resource ($200 or its purchasing power–equivalent in rupees, described as a bonus in the positive instance and as a pay cut in the negative one) in one of five ways: (1) all to the needy person, none to the meritorious one; (2) $3/4$ and $1/4$; (3) $1/2$ and $1/2$; (4) $1/4$ and $3/4$; and (5) none to the needy, all to the meritorious person.

Classifying the first two responses as a "need" decision, the middle one as an "equality" decision, and the last two as an "equity" decision, the psychologists found that for the American respondents, "equity" was the most popular decision when there was a positive resource (a bonus) to distribute (49%, with 16% saying "need"), whereas for the Indian respondents, "need" was the most popular decision (52%, with only 16% saying "equity"). When a pay cut was the resource in question, both samples of respondents favored need, but this decision preference was more marked for the Indians (65% made the need decision for allocating negative resources, compared with 41% of the Americans). Clearly, for the Indian sample, need was the preferred mode of assigning distributive justice; in contrast, for the American sample, while need mattered when taking resources away, merit prevailed when assigning rewards.

Viewing the same data differently, both the Indians and the Americans chose the need principle more often when taking away than when giving (65% vs. 52% for the Indians, 41% vs. 16% for the Americans). Despite other cultural differences in concepts of distributive justice, both cultures distinguish between what is fair when giving and what is fair when taking away.

The authors attribute the overall tendency of the Indians to favor need over merit to the fact that "need is so much more visible and such a salient part of the Indian experience" (Berman, Murphy-Berman & Singh, 1985, p. 63). An alternative suggestion focuses on the fact that the Indians were less sensitive to merit, because in India family background and social status, including caste, are often more important in determining how one is evaluated than one's achievements are. Either or both of these interpretations account for the pattern of findings and reflect a more general argument that concepts of distributive justice are influenced by norms rooted in the economic and social characteristics of societies.

Leung and Bond (1984) suggested that in collectivistic cultures "equality and need rather than equity [merit] will be more influential in reward allocation" (p. 5), but they expected this relationship to hold only when the target person is an in-group member, particularly so among collectivists. Leung and Bond (1984) found support for their hypothesis that Chinese subjects would allocate more equitably than American subjects with out-group members. In a second study, experimenters manipulated the group membership of the recipient, the input of the allocator, and the allocation principle to test for differences between Chinese and American subjects' judgments of fairness of an allocation and likability of an allocator. They found that "compared with American subjects, Chinese subjects liked an allocator who divided the group reward equally with an in-group member more, and regarded such an allocation as fairer" (p. 793).

Social Loafing

How much do people actually contribute in a work-sharing situation? Does the typical contribution vary between individualistic and collectivistic cultures?

A phenomenon first established in laboratory studies done in the United States (e.g., Latané, Williams & Harkins, 1979; Latané & Nida, 1981) is that people exert greater effort when they work individually than when they do in a group in which individual outputs of each member are not visible. Termed "social loafing," the phenomenon has also been reported in several non-Western societies, including Thailand (Latané, 1981), India (Weiner, Pandey & Latané, 1981), Malaysia (Ward, 1982), and Japan (Williams, Williams, Kawana & Latané, 1984).

The tasks employed in these studies included sound production (shouting alone or in psuedogroups), idea production, typing, and signal detection. Subjects in the various studies have included preschool and school children, university students and postgraduates, and working adults. Given the range of tasks and subjects, plus similar findings in several cultures, social loafing would appear to be a candidate for a universal feature of social behavior. When Gabrenya, Latané, and Wang (1983) used the sound-production task with graduate students in China, however, they found that these subjects worked harder in groups. This was the sole exception to otherwise consistent findings of social loafing, at least with these kinds of relatively meaningless tasks.

Gabrenya, Wang, and Latané (1985) did a study in Taiwan and Florida (United States) with school children, working alone and in pairs, performing a somewhat more meaningful, skill-related task that required discriminating stereo-broadcast tones from tones presented only to one ear. No cultural differences in social loafing occurred among sixth-graders, but among ninth-graders, the Americans loafed more than did the Chinese. The American ninth-graders performed in pairs at 88% of their alone level whereas the Taiwanese ninth-graders performed in pairs at 109% of their alone level (thus displaying what might be termed social striving).

The Chinese scored higher on a group-orientedness questionnaire, and whereas they were more group-oriented in the ninth grade than in the sixth, the Americans were *less* group-oriented in the ninth grade than in the sixth.

Clearly, then, social loafing cannot be considered a cultural universal. When a relatively meaningful task is performed, persons with relatively high group orientations, such as collectivistic Chinese, seem to care very much about how their group will be judged. Rather than loaf, they strive even harder and perform even better.

COOPERATIVENESS AND COMPETITIVENESS

Whether one person strives with or against another in circumstances where limited resources are being sought is probably determined by a complex of factors, including the nature and degree of scarcity of the resources in question, the kind of affiliation that prevails between one person and the other, and the prevailing cultural norms that govern such potentially competitive situations.

When in Doubt, if American, Compete

Much research on cooperation and competition has been conducted in the United States employing one or another variation of the so-called Prisoner's Dilemma game (Luce & Raiffa, 1957). Each of two players must choose one of two moves, with the rewards on each trial contingent on four possible joint choices. If one player chooses the move that offers the maximum possible personal payoff, the payoff will occur only if the other player simultaneously chooses the move with the lesser payoff. If both players simultaneously choose the maximum possible payoff move, they will both, in effect, be penalized by gaining less (or losing more) than they would have if both had chosen the lesser-payoff move (in which case they would each have received a moderate reward).

It would be to both players' advantage to make the lesser-payoff move consistently. Any rational player would do so, provided he or she expected the other player to do the same, rather than expecting the other player to take advantage of his or her good will. If players tend to make the lesser-payoff move, it would constitute evidence of mutual trust, mutual expectation of cooperation, and a shared predisposition to cooperate. The general finding in U.S. studies, however, has been that competitive responses (choosing the maximum possible payoff move) predominate.

Gallo and McClintock (1965) reviewed many of these U.S. studies. Clearly, the typical U.S. player of this game tends to compete. This tendency is found over a wide variety of payoff arrangements and with players of diverse personality profiles (and of both sexes). Even though a confederate of the experimenter may shame a real player into cooperating by doing so consistently, competition prevails even when a confederate makes a high proportion of cooperative responses. Clearly, the prevalent tendency among U.S. players of Prisoner's Dilemma is to attempt to win as much as possible by taking advantage of the other player, however the other plays.

It is possible, of course, that there are other shared values in U.S. culture that influence behavior in situations that are epitomized by this game, such as being "fair" or reluctant to "take advantage" of another human being.

When Values Conflict

A study by Oskamp and Perlman (1966) illustrates how conflicting values might interact. American male college students played a 30-trial game with cash payoffs. The players were paired on the basis of degree of friendship: pairs were either best friends, acquaintances, nonacquaintances, or mutually disliked persons, as determined earlier by sociometric questioning. The study was done in both a liberal arts college and a business-training school.

In the former setting, best-friend pairs made an average of 22 cooperative responses; acquaintances, 20; nonacquaintances, 14; and mutually disliked pairs, 11. Clearly, liberal-arts students' cooperativeness was enhanced by the closeness of their relationship. By contrast, best-friend pairs in the business school averaged only six cooperative responses, and all other kinds of pairs made about 14! Thus, while friendship encouraged cooperation among the liberal-arts students, it had just the opposite effect among the business-school students.

It seems that the values governing behavior toward friends and the values governing individual assertiveness interacted in very different ways in the two settings. In an atmosphere like that of an American business school, competitiveness may be so highly valued (and justified as leading to some greater good such as economic progress) that competitive behavior will emerge especially when a player is interacting with a person whose approval he or she seeks or respects. A good businessman, like a good poker player, may actually enhance the bond that exists between himself and a good friend by taking advantage of him!

Cultural Roots of Competitiveness

It appears that competitiveness is such a strong value in some places that it will override other values. In societies in which the socioeconomic system encourages individual initiative, competitiveness may emerge as a dominant life-style.

In any society, however, there are likely to be individual differences. Thus, Albert Pepitone, an American psychologist working with colleagues in France and Italy (Pepitone et al., 1967), found some consistent evidence, at least in the United States and France, that individuals high in self-esteem compete more than persons low in self-esteem in a version of the Prisoner's Dilemma game. (For some unexplained reason, the reverse was true for a sample of Italian university students.) But overriding whatever individual differences might exist within societies, we can expect to find intersocial differences that correspond to prevailing cultural values that are consistent with the socioeconomic characteristics of the societies.

And so we do. Madsen employed a mechanical gadget that is functionally similar to the Prisoner's Dilemma game. Marbles are spilled, rather than won, if two players pull strings simultaneously. But both players can gain marbles if they take turns pulling. In Box 10-1, we learn what some children living in the United States and in Mexico did with this game.

Munroe and Munroe (1975) suggested that urban, industrial societies such as the United States, the Soviet Union, Germany, and Japan, are often stereotyped as "driven" by individual competitiveness. They note that these four societies even dominate in the Olympic Games, winning gold medals to a degree that is highly disproportionate to their numbers. "East Germany had less than half the population of France (in 1972) but won ten times as many gold medals" (Munroe & Munroe, 1975, p. 137).

So, modern, urban, industrial societies—whether capitalist or socialist— appear to encourage more individual competitiveness. Within traditional, rural, subsistence-level societies, what do we find?

Some Sketchy Evidence Relating to Food Accumulation

Because low-food-accumulating societies (hunting, fishing, and gathering groups that are nomadic rather than sedentary) stress training for achieve-

---

Box 10-1 Picking Up the Marbles

Madsen (1971) found American 8-year-olds from Los Angeles averaging only .3 marbles won on an initial 10-trial exposure to the game. But 8-year-old Mexicans from a small town averaged 6.9 marbles in the same situation. Training in cooperation, which was introduced by the experimenter before a second 10-trial round, led to perfect cooperation among the Mexican children but to about 50% cooperation among the Los Angeles children. With 12-year-old children, cooperation was less in both societies, but the intersocietal difference that had been found for 8-year-olds recurred. Hence, it does appear that different behavioral dispositions regarding competitiveness exist in different societies.

In the Madsen (1971) study, society was confounded with the rural/urban dichotomy. (Recall that the U.S. sample was from a major urban center and the Mexican sample from a small town.) This rural/urban dimension may have been crucial for the behavioral differences noted in the study, for Madsen himself (1967) had found relatively high competitiveness in a sample of urban Mexicans. Munroe and Munroe (1977) found 5- to 10-year-old Kikuyu children in a periurban community in Kenya to be considerably more cooperative on a Madsen-type task than a comparison group of suburban American children. In other studies that involved rural/urban comparisons (see, for example, Shapira & Madsen, 1969, in Israel; Miller & Thomas, 1972, in Canada) the findings have indicated more competitiveness among urbanites. Since urban settings anywhere are places in which the values of industrial society are likely to prevail, it seems reasonable to attribute the motive power of competitiveness to the values of industrial society.

---

ment, self-reliance, and independence, such societies *should* value individual competitiveness.

There is some indirect evidence that involvement in high-food-accumulation activities leads to lowered individual initiative. Whiting and Whiting (1971) compared herd-boys of between 5 and 11 years of age in the Kisii district of Kenya (and in some other societies in which herding is an important subsistence activity) with nonherding Gusii[1] schoolboys. They found that the herd-boys (1) were more frequently told what to do by their mothers, (2) were more frequently punished for disobedience, (3) more frequently issued commands and "responsible suggestions" to their peers, and

---

[1]*Kisii* is a place name; *Gusii* is the name of the people who live there. These are African words. In several African languages, prefixes vary to indicate noun classes; places and people are different classes.

(4) were less often boastful or otherwise likely to call attention to themselves. In short, prosocial behavior was more prevalent among boys assigned the traditional task of caring for the valuable accumulated food that meat on the hoof constitutes in Kisii society than among boys who spent their days in Western-style schools where, according to Whiting and Whiting, "each individual is out for himself and his goal is individual achievement" (Whiting & Whiting, 1971, p. 36).

On that note, we shift our attention from competitiveness per se to individual-achievement orientation.

ACHIEVEMENT MOTIVATION

Need to achieve is the class of motives that has been most intensively studied, both within and outside the United States. Before examining some findings pertaining to achievement motivation, let us recall that "motives" per se are not accessible to direct observation. In a very real sense there is no such thing as a motive, except as a construct used by psychologists to characterize differences in behavior.[2]

At the human level there are many ways of collecting data that might be employed to infer motivation. One is simply to ask people what they want. One can offer people choices and determine their preferences. From the choices made, one can then infer differences in needs, wants, and motives. But there are problems with such a direct approach. Ever since Freud, psychologists have tended not to trust self-reports on the grounds that individuals may themselves not be aware of their own motives or may be inhibited from revealing them directly.

The Indirect Approach

Not surprisingly, then, psychologists have invented a number of indirect verbal techniques for eliciting behavior from individuals whose motives they want to study. Among these are projective techniques, like the Thematic

---

[2]When working with nonhumans, for example, a psychologist might observe that some animals will tolerate high levels of electric shock while crossing the grid to reach a sexual partner, whereas others will cross the grid only at lower levels of shock. To summarize this observed behavioral difference, the psychologist might very well speak of differences in level of sexual motivation. The psychologist would be particularly likely to do so if she had differentially deprived her laboratory animals of the opportunity to engage in sexual intercourse and had found that those who tolerated high shock levels to reach a sexual partner were the very animals that had been most deprived.

Apperception Test (TAT). In this test relatively ambiguous pictures are displayed to respondents, who are instructed to tell aloud the stories that the pictures suggest to them.

Imagine a TAT picture of a shadowy figure holding aloft a misty object shaped somewhat like a figure eight. To this, a person tells a story about a young man who practices the violin six hours a day in anticipation of his concert debut before a wildly cheering audience and enthralled music critics. One might infer that this person attaches high importance to individual achievement, particularly if most other people who are shown the same picture tell stories that lack such individual-achievement themes.

Research on achievement motivation undoubtedly began with the common observation that individuals vary in the degree to which they strive. To summarize such observations, McClelland invented the concept "achievement motivation" in the United States in the 1950s. Often called achievement need, it is designated by the symbol N_{Ach}. Then, psychologists had to construct an instrument for assessing it. A set of pictures that potentially elicits stories about striving to meet standards of excellence was a promising candidate.

In the early stages of research on achievement motivation the reliability and validity of the instrument were established. The fantasy productions elicited by TAT cards were found to be consistent and correlated with achievement-oriented behavior in the real world (Atkinson, 1958).

Frequent studies, primarily with U.S. males as subjects, have used TAT-elicited stories that are scored according to an achievement-theme manual (McClelland, 1958). These stories have been found to predict performance on a variety of other tasks that can reasonably be taken as indexes of persistence, the willingness to take risks, and the pursuit of difficult-to-attain goals. Accordingly, the employment of fantasy-eliciting instruments like the TAT as a measure of achievement motivation has become standard practice.

What Produces the Need to Achieve?

McClelland and his colleagues then searched for experiential antecedents of different levels of this motive. Focusing on differences in childhood experience within U.S. culture, they found that males who scored high on N_{Ach} were products of homes in which mothers had been warm and encouraging and fathers nonauthoritarian. Males who scored low had, during childhood, been dominated by respect-demanding, authoritarian fathers (Rosen & D'Andrade, 1959).

The research program was expanded to other societies. The aim was simply to determine whether similar patterns of antecedents could be found in non-American settings. Working in Brazil, Rosen (1962) found that families with highly authoritarian fathers tended to produce sons with relatively low levels of N_{Ach}. In Turkey, a society in which the typical father tends to be very authoritarian, even with adult sons, Bradburn (1963) found that individuals who had grown up relatively independent of their fathers scored relatively high on N_{Ach}. Rosen's and Bradburn's findings confirmed the existence of similar patterns of antecedents to N_{Ach} in at least three different societies.

Assuming that on the average, Turkish fathers are more authoritarian than American fathers, Bradburn predicted — and found — lower mean scores on N_{Ach} for his Turkish sample than for a sample of American graduate students. (The Turkish sample was composed of individuals participating in a management-training program.) Rosen's (1962) Brazilian study also showed lower levels of N_{Ach}.

Cross-cultural variations in modal levels of N_{Ach} should lead to a search for both societal antecedents and consequences. We next consider the ecocultural forces that are likely to produce the kinds of socialization practices that instill varying levels of N_{Ach}. Later in this book, we will consider the economic consequences that might flow from a society's particular level of N_{Ach}.

Sources of Achievement Motivation

Weber's (1904) thesis attributed to Protestantism the sociopsychological impetus for the capitalist spirit that arose in some European countries from the 17th through the 19th centuries. From this thesis McClelland (1971) fashioned a consistent, but more general, argument. He asserted that the key factor in instilling achievement motivation in significant members of a population is the existence of a religious, or ideological, belief. This belief holds, according to McClelland, that one's own group is superior to groups that invest more authority in institutions than they do in individuals. Many analyses of groups differing in characteristic levels of N_{Ach} have resulted in findings that are consistent with this argument. Let us examine one of the most thorough of these analyses, summarized in Box 10-2.

We have learned from our review of cross-cultural research on achievement motivation that modal levels of N_{Ach} vary considerably and relate in systematic ways to child-rearing practices and the values they reflect. The existence of such differences is probably a good thing. (As always, differences across cultures in performance on some trait may reflect the nonuniversality of the trait itself, or of the instrument used to measure it. In other words, the very concept of individual achievement may not be pertinent in some societies.) Later in this book, we will review — and criticize — some efforts by McClelland to promote increased levels of N_{Ach} in India.

Box 10-2 Nigerian Dreams

LeVine (1966) collected dream reports from secondary-school boys in Nigeria. The boys were either Hausa (the predominantly Moslem tribe from northern Nigeria), Yoruba (the politically dominant, relatively Westernized tribe from western Nigeria), or Ibo (the economically dominant, also relatively Westernized tribe from eastern Nigeria, the part of the country that temporarily seceded from Nigeria just a few years after LeVine's study to form the short-lived nation of Biafra).

Before considering his results, let us note that LeVine's method for obtaining N_{Ach} scores was to ask individuals for a report of a recent or recurring dream and to score the obtained reports just as if they were stories told after viewing a TAT card. The stimulus employed—the request to tell a story—is far more likely to be culture free than a TAT card, which, however ambiguous, contains some content that is potentially misinterpretable. So LeVine's data-collection method is certainly worthy of note—and of emulation—in future cross-cultural studies of achievement motivation (or other behavioral dispositions, for that matter). And, of course, the fact that a given dream report may be fictional would matter not at all. In any case, a fantasy production would have been elicited, with a minimum of stimulus direction.

With blind scoring of the dream reports, the Ibo sample very decidedly outscored both the Yoruba and the Hausa (especially the latter) on achievement motivation. Ibo performance in this regard fit well their actual achievements as an ethnic group in this large, developing nation. Their reputation as hard-working, money-saving individuals, who wandered over all parts of Nigeria, earning the envy and enmity of local people who competed too little or too late for the same jobs, has spread well beyond Nigeria. That Ibo schoolboys should outscore their Hausa and Yoruba peers on N_{Ach} corresponds to much of what is known about the three ethnic groups. The really interesting question posed by LeVine's study concerns the reasons, both social and psychological, for the apparent acquisition of different levels of N_{Ach} by the three groups of boys.

Analysis of the anthropological and historical facts pertaining to the Hausa, Yoruba, and Ibo societies led LeVine to formulate a "status-mobility" hypothesis. By that term, LeVine was referring to differences among the three societies in their traditional socioeconomic, and related political, practices. At one extreme was the Hausas' centralized and hierarchical system, within which authority trickled down through subservient layers. Power tended to be inherited, although it might shift as the result of warfare. Class status was relatively unchanging, so that a young man not well born might hope to improve his lot only by choosing to serve a powerful leader. At the other extreme, Ibo society was quite decentralized, with a variety of activities leading to wealth and, hence, local power, provided they were well performed and recognized. Such contrasting possibilities for status mobility, LeVine argued, would result in differences in values held by parents. These differences, in turn, would lead to differing child-rearing practices and, finally, to personality differences, probably along several dimensions but certainly including achievement motivation.

LeVine's study stands on its own as a demonstration of how interdisciplinary (psychological/anthropological) research can produce impressive, cohesive findings. It serves also to support McClelland's notion that an individualistic, high-self-esteem ideology can provide the psychological underpinnings for high levels of achievement motivation.

EXPECTATION OF REWARD AND
OTHER TEMPORAL VALUES

Both within and across cultures, individuals differ in their tendencies to wait for rewards. Some seem quite able and willing to tolerate delays in reward. Perhaps they anticipate larger ones if they wait. And they have probably learned to trust that the rewards, however delayed, will in fact be forthcoming. Others prefer immediate rewards, however small. Perhaps these people have little reason to expect the rewards to be larger if delayed. And perhaps they lack trust. By this reasoning, preferences for immediate or for delayed reinforcement would be seen as manifestations of variations in expectations. Such variations, in turn, might be expected to vary systematically with childhood experiences with reinforcing agents, most notably parents. To the extent that such experiences vary across cultures, we should anticipate cultural differences in preference for delayed reward.

A series of studies focusing on reward preferences are by Mischel (1958, 1961a, 1961b), whose most provocative findings relate to father absence. In his 1958 study, done in Trinidad with rural children between the ages of 7 and 9 years, children from father-absent homes were most likely to choose an immediate reward (a small piece of candy) than to wait a week for a promised larger one. In his 1961 study, Mischel found a greater preference for delayed reinforcement among Grenadian Negro schoolchildren as compared with Trinidadian Negroes, but within both Trinidad and Grenada, for children aged 8 and 9, father absence was related to individual preference for immediate reward. Mischel (1961a) presented evidence that ability to delay gratification in the United States is also related to strength of achievement motivation, long-term goal direction, and other indexes of individual autonomy.

Price-Williams and Ramirez (1974) found white American fourth-grade schoolchildren to prefer delayed gratification more than Mexican-American children, with black Americans generally intermediate. Wober and Musoke-Mutanda (1972), working with Ugandan primary-school children, found differences between the sexes and between social classes. In neither of these studies, however, was it possible to relate the performance differences to other possible cultural determinants.

Time-Related Values

Doob (1971) has appropriately warned that findings relating to delay of gratification must be cautiously interpreted. He notes that persons "choosing the lesser of two . . . rewards [may have] intended, not to obtain gratification immediately, but to use the sum to invest in a small business and hence to obtain greater rewards in the future" (p. 100). That warning is contained in a major work by this pioneer cross-cultural psychologist enti- tled *Patterning of Time*, in which numerous temporal motives and other time-related behaviors are examined in light of both anthropological and psychological insights.

Doob's book is replete with ideas from which testable hypotheses about cultural influences on time-related behavioral dispositions can be derived. Only a brief sample can be presented here: Social life requires regulation of behavior, and regulation requires a system of time reckoning. Every society will therefore keep track of time and organize activities within time frames. Activities and events will everywhere be subject to scheduling. Hence, delay, waiting, postponing, remembering, anticipation, expecting, abandoning, and similar time-related processes will occur everywhere. All of these tem- poral matters, however, will relate to the modal beliefs and attitudes that prevail in any society and that each individual acquires by socialization. Subjective estimates of durations may thus be expected to vary not only among individuals but also across groups. So must all motives and values that relate to time.

In a section of the book that is most directly relevant to cross-cultural psychology (Doob, 1971, pp. 52–100), there are numerous propositions per- taining to differences between traditional and industrial societies. For ex- ample, "Traditional peoples are likely to pay relatively little attention to the future" (p. 52). This may be a bit too sweeping. We know, for example, that in some hunter-gatherer societies, adults consider themselves to be the stew- ards of their territory for future generations.

Doob also suggested, "The modal temporal perspective of a society re- flects and affects a modal philosophy of values pertaining to other be- havior" (p. 56). The complex of values known as "modernity" (to be dis- cussed in Chapter 13) includes, according to Doob, a heightened concern with being on time and with advance planning (p. 81). The more a society's essential activities require coordinated efforts by several persons, the more scheduling and planning will occur (p. 82).

In another section of the book that is relevant to our present concerns (pp. 332–346), it is noted that age grading is a universal dimension of social organization. Thus, reference groups (groups to which individuals relate themselves or that serve as a standard of comparison), status, and roles all vary with age and are, therefore, basically temporal values. Individual be- havior, then, will vary with age in ways that reflect cultural values. And cultures will vary in the different degrees of prestige attached to various age statuses. This variation, in turn, may relate to modal tendencies to be either tradition-oriented or future-oriented.

OTHER BEHAVIORAL
DISPOSITIONS

In this chapter we have already ranged widely over a variety of motives, values, and behavioral dispositions, seeking cross-cultural differences and pancultural factors that might contribute to their acquisition. Our review was by no means exhaustive. It dealt with certain classes of behavior (autonomy/conformity, cooperation/competition, achievement motivation, and time-related behaviors) that have long been of interest to Western psychologists. But there are other classes of behaviors — which presumably reflect important human dispositions, subject to cultural influence — that have attracted some attention from psychologists working in more than one culture. In this section a few of these will be briefly noted.

Morality, Humanism, and Kindness

Morality is a very difficult topic to study cross-culturally. Nevertheless, some scholars have attempted to study those behaviors that are considered morally and ethically desirable in at least some societies, in part to see how universal they might be.

Compliments: Is "Being Nice"
the Same Behavior Everywhere?

Later, in our chapter on aggression, we will consider cultural differences in reactions to insults. Now, let's focus on more prosocial behavior, namely, complimenting others. Are there cultural differences in complimenting behavior and in reactions to compliments? One might expect that people everywhere enjoy being complimented, and that is probably true, but the conditions under which compliments are welcomed and perceived as such (rather than as unwelcomed flattery) might vary from culture to culture, because cultural norms govern their use.

Within U.S. culture, for example, Pomerantz (1978) found a highly consistent pattern (and very narrow range) of compliments, with deviations therefrom not always understood by their recipients. These findings were confirmed by Wolfson (1981), who recorded hundreds of instances of American compliments and found that two thirds of them were composed of only five adjectives!

Noting that Wolfson also considered some Indonesian and Japanese compliments, after which she was moved to speculate that "what counts as a compliment may differ very much from one society to another" (Wolfson, 1981, p. 123), an American and Japanese pair of social scientists (Barnlund & Araki, 1985) studied the relative frequency of compliments, their topical themes, the preferred manner of expressing them, and their relationship to the status of the givers and receivers of compliments in both Japan and the United States.

Barnlund and Araki found that (a) compliments occur with far greater frequency in the United States than in Japan; (b) in Japan, there is a wider variety of themes than in the United States; (c) Americans employ a wider variety of adjectives and more superlatives than the Japanese; (d) Americans are more likely to accept compliments; and (e) Japanese are more likely to employ compliments in interactions involving nonintimates, whereas Americans are more likely to do so with close friends. Beyond these differences across the two cultures compared, there were also several similarities. Thus, in both societies, females were more often recipients and givers of compliments and, in both societies, nearly everyone studied reported "feeling good" about receiving and giving compliments. Barnlund and Araki concluded that this pattern of findings was consistent with the individualism/collectivism differences between Japan and the United States. "A society founded on the group rather than the individual, that stresses harmonious relations, is not likely to encourage comparisons that inherently weaken group membership" (Barnlund & Araki, 1985, p. 25).

Morality and Ethics

Traditionally subjects of philosophy, morality and ethics may also be studied from a psychological perspective by focusing on what individuals actually say or do about situations that pose dilemmas because of conflicting values. Psychological morality may be studied developmentally, by examining changes in solutions to moral dilemmas as people grow older and presumably learn their culture's values. A developmental approach to the study of morality is exemplified by some of Piaget's work (1932) and by the work of Kohlberg (1969a, 1969b, 1970). These two psychologists offered stage theories of moral development that could be taken as possible models of the universal unfolding of morality.

Against these models can be measured the developmental trends revealed by empirical research with persons of various ages in any society. Various standardized tests of behavior in situations that pose dilemmas can be administered, and differences in response as a function of age can be compared across cultures. Such research can have several worthwhile ends. It can test the universality of the stage theories. It can reveal possible cultural differences in the definition of moral behavior. And it may demonstrate similar adult-level definitions of morality, accompanied by different rates of progress over age toward the incorporation of that definition in actual behavior. Alternatively, one might find different definitions of morality, as was demonstrated by Mundy-Castle and Bundy (1988).

We might expect all societies to recognize behavior that serves others (rather than self-serving behavior) as morally desirable. And one could add that, in one manner or another, a central concern of child rearing in each society should be to instill in children this concern for others. But societies also teach respect for authority, obedience, and some self-aggrandizing behaviors (for example, individual achievement), such that competing behavioral tendencies are likely to emerge among individuals in any society. The particular mix of competing behaviors is likely to vary from society to society. Hence, the prevailing moral dilemmas and their characteristic modes of solution are also likely to vary across societies.

There has been less research done than this argument might suggest. For the most part the research to date is descriptive, revealing similarities or differences in moral behavior across a small number of societies, with minimal efforts to explain those similarities or differences.

An aspect of Kohlberg's model of moral development inspired a cross-cultural study by Bloom (1977), who administered questionnaires to French and American university students and to a sample of adult residents in Hong Kong. Kohlberg had postulated a necessary link between "moral autonomy" (referred to by Bloom as "social principledness" and meant to denote a readiness to differentiate between a conventional and a personal standard of morality) and "social humanism," or a readiness to give priority to human welfare over other, potentially competing, values. Bloom found instead that in all three cultural settings these two dimensions were independent of each other. In short, in all three societies some persons scored high on both dimensions, but many others were high scorers on only one or the other.

There is considerable interest in studying moral development cross-culturally, with some studies done in Israel, where the Kibbutz ideology was shown to be related to moral reasoning (Snarey, Reimer & Kohlberg, 1985; Fuchs, Eisenberg, Hertz-Lazarowitz & Sharabany, 1986). Nevertheless, it may well be the case that the Kohlbergian model of moral development applies mostly, if not exclusively, to urban, middle-class groups, as Snarey et al. (1985) suggested and involves a gender bias, as Gilligan (1982) asserted.

More work needs to be done, especially studies that go beyond attempts to measure moral beliefs or attitudes. We would welcome some cross-cultural replications of field experiments in helping behavior. (See, for example, Feldman, 1971, for a report of real-life tests of honesty conducted in the streets, shops, and taxis of Boston, Paris, and Athens.)

Romantic Love and Affective Relationships

In a very thoughtful essay dealing with certain patterns of personality found to prevail in many subsistence-level societies in Africa, LeVine (1973) contrasted an African pattern of seemingly unemotional behavior toward intimates with the importance Westerners attach to emotional relationships.

Rosenblatt (1966) has shown, for a sample of 18 traditional societies, considerable variation in the importance attached to romantic love. A few African societies were included; they scored low on romantic love as a basis for marriage. His study also provided empirical support for a Freudian-based hypothesis that initial oral indulgence and later severity of oral socialization (because oral needs are presumably related to a general need for affection) would covary with the importance of romantic love in adult life. Rosenblatt found that romantic love was more likely in societies that did not orally indulge their infants and that did severely socialize childhood orality. In short, where oral needs were more frustrated, romantic love was more likely to be employed as a basis for marriage.

Beliefs About Illness

Freudian hypotheses, modified to make them more compatible with American learning theories and sharpened so that they might be subjected to empirical examination, were tested by Whiting and Child (1953) in their classic study of relationships between child-training emphases and adult belief systems. The Freudian concept that attracted the attention of Whiting and Child was fixation, or as Freud originally viewed it, arrested development at one or another putative stage of psychosexual development. In his own treatment of fixation, Freud argued that it could result either from "overindulgence" or frustration. Thus, a child might become orally fixated as a result of an extremely permissive feeding schedule or as a result of a too-rigid one. Whiting and Child, members of a generation of social scientists whose immersion in behavioristic learning theory made them acutely aware of the contrasting effects of reward (indulgence) and nonreward (frustration), found it desirable to modify Freud's fixation notion by postulating opposing effects of indulgence and frustration.

Hence, their learning-theory modification of Freud's ideas produced the two concepts of positive fixation and negative fixation. They argued that the former, a product of indulgence, should lead to a positive evaluation of relevant behaviors. The latter should lead to a negative evaluation. In adulthood, then, behaviors like those that had been subjected to much reward during childhood would be strong and accompanied by positive feelings. But behaviors associated with earlier punishments should be anxiety-provoking and otherwise accompanied by negative feelings.

Although they assumed such mechanisms to occur at the individual level, the authors actually tested their modification of Freudian theory at the societal level of analysis. They reasoned that positive or negative aspects of shared belief systems would reflect, respectively, childhood indulgence or severity of socialization of behaviors related to the beliefs. The belief system they investigated had to do with illnesses, their suspected causes, and their preferred therapies. They further reasoned that what a whole society mod-ally tends to believe makes one ill is a good index of anxiety surrounding certain activities, whereas what the society tends to believe can cure illness is an index of behaviors that are surrounded by positive feelings. Thus, Whiting and Child had to predict that in societies in which feeding training (oral socialization) is strict and severe, oral activities would be likely to appear in the belief system as an illness-causation factor. But in a society in which children are orally indulged, oral activity would more likely be viewed as therapeutic.

Employing data from the Human Relations Area Files, the authors found much stronger evidence for negative fixation than for positive fixation. And the predicted correlations between aspects of child training and illness belief varied in magnitude for the various behavioral arenas studied. The strongest relationships involved severe and sudden weaning and oral explanations for illness (Whiting & Child, 1953).[3] A reanalysis of their data, completed almost 20 years later and employing more sophisticated statistical tech-niques and computer technology (Guthrie, 1971), has produced questions about the meaningfulness of the relationships uncovered by Whiting and Child. But their study stands as a pioneer example of a cross-cultural ap-proach to the study of shared beliefs.

Death Concepts

Children develop an understanding of what death is in much the same way that other ideas develop (Koocher, 1974); the process may involve devel-opmental stages, similar to those formulated by Piaget (1955). If this is so, the development of the concept of death may be influenced by experiences provided by children's cultural environments. Hence, cross-cultural differ-ences in the ages at which children reach particular conceptions of death, and qualitative differences in conceptions, seem likely. In fact, they have been demonstrated.

A comparison between American, British, and Israeli Jewish children (Smilansky, 1980) found that the Israelis understood death's nonreversa-bility, finality, and inevitability at a younger age than the American and British children. So did children in Northern Ireland (McWhirter, Young & Majury, 1983). In both Israel and Northern Ireland, where these studies were done, political insecurity and awareness of violent death were characteristics of daily life and might well have contributed to the relative maturity of the concept of death among children living there.

---

[3]A somewhat fuller account of this classic cross-cultural study of child rearing and adult beliefs may be found in Berry et al. (in press).

Beyond such influences, ideas about death are a central feature of religious teachings to which children are exposed. Therefore, it would be interesting to determine whether children who live in the same political environment, but who belong to different religious groups, develop their understandings of death in different ways, and with different results. This question was investigated in Israel by Florian and Kravetz (1985), who used Smilansky's (1981) questionnaire with four samples of 10-year-old schoolchildren, either Jewish, Christian, Moslem (predominantly Sunni), or Druze. The Jewish and Christian groups revealed more so-called scientific (Western) understandings of death, and the Jewish children, in some respects, were more scientific than the Christian children. (What the authors called "scientific" was a set of ideas related to a Western biomedical model.)

Florian and Kravetz's (1985) findings are subject to diverse interpretations. They might reflect differences in exposure to Western ideas generally, or differences in socialization emphases, or differences in the specific teachings about death that are presented by the religions to which the four ethnic groups belong. Whatever the explanation, this study suggests that various factors associated with culture influence both the rate and the nature of development of the concept of death. On the other hand, as the authors were careful to note, their findings do not imply that "any one of the groups of children lacks the capacity to develop the Western scientific and technological concept of death" (Florian & Kravetz, 1985, p. 187).

Another treatment of conceptions of death as cultural product is Becker's (1973), an account of which appears in Box 10-3.

SOME CONCLUDING OBSERVATIONS

Perhaps the single best generalization that can be made from the material reviewed in this chapter is that in any society there is likely to be a meaningful relationship between child-training emphases and adult behavior. This generalization has guided research since Whiting and Child's study in the early 1950s. It is clear that ecological and economic factors are also important, so that our generalization is probably best expressed in these terms: Children are likely to be induced to behave in ways compatible with adult roles that they will have to assume, with those roles in turn reflective of socioeconomic complexity and social organization. This generalization applies to nearly everything we have covered in the present chapter.

Future cross-cultural research on behavioral dispositions, to be fruitful, should be of a systematic, hypothesis-testing kind; should focus attention on ecological and economic variables, child rearing, child behavior, and adult behavior; and should seek interrelationships among all of these. Conducted in such a manner, the research is likely to succeed in filling in many

Box 10-3 A Psychoanalytic Approach to Death

The psychoanalytically oriented anthropologist, Ernest Becker (1973), in his remarkable book *The Denial of Death*, built on the ideas of numerous psychoanalysts and philosophers, but especially Rank (1931, 1941), Kierkegaard (1844, 1849), and Brown (1959). Becker asserted that human beings' ability—obviously mediated by language—to contemplate and fear their own death propels them to deny their mortality, to run from their animalness, and to invent ways of making themselves appear meaningful to themselves and others. Stating it poetically, each of us strives to be a hero. To Becker, society is a "codified hero system, . . . a living myth of the significance of human life" (1973, p. 7). Because we are both animal and symbol user, our terror of death moves us to create institutions, both religious and secular (to Becker, "every society is a religion" [p. 7]), that allow us to repress the unavoidable fact of our impending death. "All culture, all man's creative life ways, are in some basic part of them a fabricated protest against natural reality, a denial of the truth of the human condition, and an attempt to forget the pathetic creature that Man is" (Becker, 1973, p. 33).

Because humans have language, they can give names to experiences and can manufacture and manipulate symbols. They can transmit, receive, and process information, not only about the here and now but also about the there and then. They can even contemplate the merely possible. Using these tools of language, humans become conscious of self and others and aware of their mortality. They come to realize their dependence on others and their need to relate to others in order to live a meaningful existence. Because people start life as helpless, dependent animals, they must learn from others the meaning-imposing myths of human existence. They learn those behaviors that others before them have invented to make them seem more god-like than animal-like. Each personality—or, as Becker terms it, "the lie of character"—is "built up because the child needs to adjust to the world, to the parents, and to his own existential dilemmas" (p. 73).

Thus, propelled by the anxiety of impending death, anxiety that only a linguistic creature can possess, we allow self-shaping largely in terms of the image of parents and peers. Whereas prelinguistic children may be in some sense aware of their animalness, their developing humanness involves, in Becker's terms, a "fall from natural perception into the artificialities of the cultural world" (p. 65).

However artificial, culture gives meaning to human life, and it is only in culture that we find the forces that shape human nature. Whether or not Becker was correct in his view of culture, he succeeded in demonstrating the futility of explaining human behavior as the outward manifestation of instincts. Becker's point of view is compatible with and underscores the need to recognize culturally mediated learning as the process that sets humans apart from other animals. In short, it is the unique nature of humans to be conscious and wary of their animalness and to learn to live as if they were not animals. To live as human, man acquires a socially conditioned identity that allows him to "feel that he controls his life and his death, that he really does live and act as a willful and free individual, . . . that he is somebody" (Becker, 1973, p. 55).

Human nature, then, is a seriously misleading concept. It is the nature of humans as sociocultural creatures to learn to behave in ways that their predecessors have found useful as defenses against despair, as Becker saw it, and in ways that enhance their existence.

details, as yet unrecorded, of the network of relationships expressed in this now well-supported generalization.

An implication of the generalization is that motives, beliefs, and values are nowhere static. As ecological systems and social structures change, we might expect the associated child-rearing systems and the behavioral dispositions they instill to change also. The degree to which this is so and the intergenerational conflicts this might induce are issues that we will examine in detail in Chapter 13, where we will consider cultural change.

But first we must deal with some very important matters concerning sex (Chapter 11) and violence (Chapter 12).

Chapter 11

Males and Females and Relations Between Them

INTRODUCTION: WHY STUDY SEX AND GENDER CROSS-CULTURALLY?

We devote a whole chapter to matters relating to sex—including differences between the sexes in behavior, the development and change of gender roles, and relations between the sexes—because none of these issues can be understood without taking into account the ways in which cultural variables affect them. While sex itself (i.e., membership in one of the physiological/anatomical subgroups of humankind) is biologically determined, behaviors that are characteristic of the two sexes ("masculine" and "feminine" behaviors), however much *influenced* by biology, are *not* biologically determined. We must consider the accumulating evidence that although males and females differ behaviorally in some ways everywhere,[1] they don't always differ in the same ways or to the same degree (and, as we shall see, there are also similarities across cultures in sex differences). The mere fact that behavioral differences between the sexes are not the same in every society is enough to suggest that culture plays a role in shaping them.

The variation across cultures in the differences in behavior between the sexes might even be interpreted as evidence that nurture and not nature is responsible for them. Ember (1981), however, warned that "the available evidence does not warrant any strong conclusions" (p. 531) because biolog-

---

[1] Men and women are also behaviorally similar in some respects everywhere. Social scientists have found sex differences more intriguing, however, in part because how they are explained has potential social significance.

ical sex *and* differences in experiences differentially available to men and women are always confounded. The fact that they are confounded in different ways in different cultures could give cross-cultural research a theory-testing role. To date, however, little systematic theory testing has been done. Nevertheless, we will advance some theoretical ideas in this chapter.

Sex and Gender Distinguished

Whereas "sex" is biological, "gender" is psychosociocultural. Gender refers to the meanings attached to being male or female, as reflected in social statuses, roles, and attitudes regarding the sexes. When we speak of gender, we have in mind such issues as (a) *gender role* (culturally rooted definitions or prescriptions of male and female behaviors, e.g., division of labor by sex), (b) *gender identity*[2] (how one perceives oneself with respect to sex and gender roles), and (c) *sex-role ideology* (sex stereotypes, the attitudes governing relations between the two sexes, and their relative statuses). Such matters are not inherently biological; they are, in fact, inherently cultural.

For example, sex-role ideologies vary across cultures. In most societies, there is a power differential in favor of males, but the extent and nature of this differential is not the same everywhere. In some societies, the power differential is large and relatively stable, whereas in others it is breaking down. Later in this chapter we will examine in some detail cross-cultural similarities and differences in sex-role ideology.

Moreover, all of these things — gender roles, gender identity, and sex-role ideology — are intertwined. For example, the way the two sexes characteristically behave and define themselves is partly a cause of, and partly a result of, the way they relate to each other. With changes in the role of women come changes in behavior in *both* sexes. Since each and every part of this complex set of facts is influenced by culture, so is the whole set.

Accordingly, gender must be studied from a cross-cultural perspective. Some recent efforts to develop instruments to measure gender identity, as described in Box 11-1, point in this direction.

PSYCHOLOGICAL DIFFERENCES
BETWEEN THE SEXES

Sex and Culture as They Relate to Cognition

It is widely believed that males and females have different cognitive skills. In the United States, where the testing of cognitive aptitudes for selection into educational programs and jobs is a culturally sanctioned practice that

---

[2]In the psychological literature, gender identity has often been termed "sex-role orientation."

Box 11-1 Can Gender Identity
Be Measured Cross-Culturally?

Interest in gender identity has been spurred by the availability of instruments to measure it, such as the Sex-Role Inventory developed initially in the United States by Bem (1974). Essentially, such an instrument measures the degree to which individuals identify themselves as masculine, feminine, or androgynous (i.e., having both male and female sex-typed traits). Using the Bem Scale with university students of both sexes in the United States and Israel, Maloney, Wilkof, and Dambrot (1981) found that whereas the two female samples were similar in their degree of femininity, the males differed across the two societies; Israeli men were less sex-typed (less "masculine") than the American men. *If we assume that the Bem Scale is equivalent in the United States and Israel,* these results suggest that Israeli culture provides experiences that shape male identities differently from the way they are shaped in the United States.

Some researchers have developed translations and revisions of the Bem Scale for use in particular areas of the world, for example, the Spanish language Latin American Sex Role Inventory (Kaschak & Sharrat, 1983). Others (e.g., Diaz-Loving, Diaz-Guerrero, Helmreich & Spence, 1981; Kranau, Green & Valencia-Weber, 1982; Soto & Shaver, 1982) have employed similar scales for use with Hispanic peoples.

---

touches hundreds of thousands of people every year, reports of differences between the sexes in performance on tests of verbal and quantitative skills have regularly been published. The nature and magnitude of these differences has changed over time, but males sometimes earn higher average scores on some tests than females, and vice versa on others. For example, in the United States, there have been consistent sex differences in scores on quantitative and verbal-skills tests, with males outperforming females in the first, and vice versa for the second. Irvine (1983b), reviewing studies done over the years in various African countries, noted frequent but not entirely consistent sex differences favoring males in performance on tests that employ figural test items (like Kohs Blocks and the Ravens Progressive Matrices). But test-performance differences across the sexes could very well reduce to nil.

In most if not all cultures, task assignments to the two sexes reflect beliefs that the assignments are appropriate because they reflect inherent sex differences in skills. But surely, the opposite is possible — that the division of labor by sex sets up social forces leading to differential socialization of the sexes during childhood, *as a result of which* they learn different skills to different degrees. Consider, for example, what we know about sex and cognitive style.

Sex Differences in Cognitive Style

In research on cognitive style in the United States, many hundreds of studies have revealed sex differences in degree of psychological differentiation. Males are more field independent, although this sex difference is not so reliable until adolescence. Recently, cross-cultural studies have partly confirmed the American findings but have also produced other findings that throw light on the mechanisms that probably produced the sex differences first noted in the United States.

Employing three perceptual-cognitive tests (the Embedded Figures test, Kohs Blocks, and a visual-discrimination task) in 17 societies, Berry (1976a) found a considerable cross-cultural variation in sex differences on these tasks that was correlated with an index of cultural complexity.

By 1978, Mary Stewart Van Leeuwen could review 30 studies done outside the United States, employing various measures of psychological differentiation. When significant sex differences were found, they were nearly always in the direction of males' earning scores closer to the differentiated end of the scale (Van Leeuwen, 1978). Although this clear trend is consistent with a hypothesis of universality of sex differences, Van Leeuwen, like Berry before her, properly noted that the *variation* in the magnitude of the sex differences was more intriguing. An effort to explain this variation — from minimal to large — might reveal the social and cultural forces that impinge on psychological differentiation generally, that is, for individuals regardless of sex, and an understanding of the sex differences as well.

Van Leeuwen adapted the ecological framework to encompass the findings from a number of the studies reviewed, including all those done in non-Western societies engaged primarily in subsistence-level economic activities.

Van Leeuwen's Theoretical Approach:
An Application of the Ecological Framework

This application of Berry's (1966, 1971) framework points to economic conditions in subsistence-level societies that can produce sex differences in psychological differentiation through socialization practices that may differentially influence the two sexes.

The framework includes the idea that the degree of food accumulation in a subsistence-level society will influence its level of psychological differentiation. It is in low-food-accumulating societies like the Inuit's that the environment demands very sharp perceptual articulation for survival. Berry's framework and Van Leeuwen's use of it are consistent with earlier work done by Herbert Barry and colleagues (see, for example, Barry, Child & Bacon, 1959). These studies showed that socialization for obedience and responsibility was stressed in high-food-accumulating societies, whereas socialization for achievement, self-reliance, and general independence was more likely to be stressed in low-food-accumulating societies.

Taking into account the findings of Barry and his associates, Berry's ecological hypothesis, and some additional information (to be described below at appropriate points in the argument), Van Leeuwen formulated her argument. That is, "The relatively greater freedom of women in more no-madic hunting-gathering societies will result in lesser sex differences in per-formance on differentiation tasks, whereas the restrictiveness of agricultural groups will produce greater sex differences in performance" (Van Leeuwen, 1978, p. 96).

It is, in fact, low-food-accumulating groups — for example, Inuit, Au-stralian Aborigines, and some Canadian Indian groups — that show minimal or even no sex differences in psychological differentiation. And high-food-accumulating groups — for example, the Temne, Ibo, Zulu in Africa, and Maori in New Zealand — show significant sex differences.

Barry, Bacon, and Child (1957) found that high-food-accumulating so-cieties where large animals were domesticated emphasized the compliance training of girls. Barry, Child and Bacon (1959) also found that in cultures where nurturance, obedience, and responsibility training are stressed (high-food-accumulating societies), they are stressed more strongly for girls.

Thus, Van Leeuwen's use of the framework is consistent with reliable correlations between degree of food accumulation and magnitude of sex differences in psychological differentiation. The balance of her argument is more theoretical and is concerned with possible mechanisms for these em-pirical relationships. Among them are the following:

1. That men have greater physical strength and that women are the child bearers led to a specialization of labor by sex in large grain-crop or large animal-husbandry subsistence societies. Family-maintenance tasks were relegated to women, and hence, compliance, dutifulness, and nurturance are stressed for girls.
2. Greater role specialization in sedentary groups led to a more exclusively female preoccupation with child-related activities. Hence, girls receive more training in social sensitivity (a characteristic of the so-called undif-ferentiated cognitive style).
3. The low role diversity in hunting-and-gathering groups led to a higher valuation of women's activities. In sedentary, agricultural groups, where women's roles are more diverse, the role of women is more likely to be regarded with contempt (possibly feigned). Male activities are more likely to be accorded inflated prestige, and male adults tend to scorn participa-tion in child-rearing activities. All of these contribute to a preponderance of maternal child rearing, considerable paternal absence, and measures to keep women "under control." Maternal dominance and father absence contribute to an undifferentiated cognitive style in general, and the con-trol of women contributes to the even less differentiated cognitive style characteristic of women in such societies.

Any or all of these mechanisms can account for variations in degree of sex differences in psychological differentiation in essentially subsistence-level societies. For Western or Westernized societies, Van Leeuwen notes, variations in sex differences may reflect such variables as degree of obedience, conformity, family and religious loyalty, and mother salience in early childhood. Once again, those societies that stress such socialization practices stress them more for girls than for boys. Hence, she postulates a "social-conformity model" to encompass the pattern of sex differences found in studies done in industrialized societies. This is consistent with and incorporable within the ecological model. Whether in subsistence-level societies or in societies in which food getting is less of a preoccupation, the socialization practices that tend toward compliance and conformity, and that contribute to greater field dependence, are applied more to females than to males.

Thus, variations across societies in the degree of sex differences in cognitive style result in part from differential socialization with regard to compliance. Cross-cultural differences (regardless of sex) in cognitive style are also a partial product of varying degrees of compliance training. Van Leeuwen's application of the ecological model shows how cognitive style is shaped by culture, through socialization, with culture in turn at least partly shaped by ecological and economic factors.

Gender Roles: Some Characteristically Masculine and Feminine Behaviors

Besides differing in cognitive behaviors, males and females differ in additional ways, some of which involve values, attitudes, and other behaviors of social significance.

With few exceptions anywhere in the world, males are more likely than females to initiate sexual activity. Males are more likely to be physically aggressive. Males are more likely to express dominance over females, rather than vice versa; females are more likely to conform, defer, comply, and otherwise submit to an authority figure of either sex, but especially to a male.[3] These generalizations derive from many publications, including sev-

---

[3]Of course, there are many individuals of both sexes whose behavior departs from these roles. For a thorough review of empirical research findings on differences as well as similarities between the sexes in social behaviors such as aggression, conformity, and helping, see Eagly (1987). In her book, Eagly argues that sex differences reflect primarily gender-role differences, or what she calls "the differing social positions of women and men" (p. 9).

eral from the Six Cultures study (Whiting, 1963; Whiting & Whiting, 1975; Whiting & Edwards, 1973).

Whiting and Edwards report observations of children of both sexes in two age groups (3 to 6 years and 7 to 11 years) in Okinawa, India, the Philippines, Mexico, Kenya, and New England. Among the behavior classes for which boys generally outscored girls in these six diverse societies were (1) expressing dominance, (2) responding aggressively to aggressive instigations, and (3) manifesting aggression both physically and verbally. Girls outscored boys on two subclasses of dependency, "seeking help" and "seeking or offering physical contact," but not on a third subclass, "seeking attention," which was found to be mostly a male form of dependency. A female superiority in nurturance was found, but only among the 7- to 11-year-olds.

The tasks assigned to girls provided the best predictor of the degree to which girls exceeded boys in displaying "feminine" behavior. For example, in the Kenyan society, some child-care and other domestic tasks are assigned to boys, and in the New England town, tasks assigned to girls are not exclusively stereotypically feminine ones; in these two societies, sex differences in behavior were smaller or less frequent than in the others (Whiting & Edwards, 1973).

Sex Differences in Achievement

Until recently, nearly all of the research on achievement motivation has been done with males. What little had been done with females yielded either inconsistent findings or some provocative facts about females' achievement motivation that makes them appear strikingly different from males. And the psychological literature contains much about additional differences in motivational patterns, life-styles, and other behavioral dispositions. We will inquire into those sex differences and consider possible explanations, rooted in cultural forces, for them.

Differences in Attitudes Toward Success. Little was known about women's achievement motivation until Horner's research program with U.S. university students in the late 1960s. The outcome was striking. Horner interpreted her findings to mean that these women — of above-average intelligence and education, reared and living in one of the most achievement-oriented societies in the world — were typically burdened by strong *fears* of success!

Horner (1969) administered a standard stimulus, analogous to a TAT picture but in the form of a beginning of a story, to be completed as one saw fit. The stimulus sentence read, "After first-term finals, Anne found herself at the top of her medical school class." Stories were scored as expressing a success/fear disposition if they contained any references to negative consequences of doing well. Of the 90 stories obtained from the women, 59 contained such references.

The fears expressed in the 59 stories were varied in content. They included expectations of social rejection: "She will be a proud and successful, but alas a very lonely, doctor." They also included doubts about femininity: "Anne no longer feels so certain that she wants to be a doctor. She is worried about herself and wonders if perhaps she isn't normal." Some of the stories revealed what appears to be an attempt at denying the very possibility of success: "It was luck that Anne came out on top, because she didn't want to go to medical school anyway" (Horner, 1969, pp. 36, 38).

Horner's findings are all the more striking when contrasted with the behavior of a control group of 88 male university students who responded to an identical stimulus sentence, except that the subject was "John." Among these 88 stories, only eight could be scored as containing fear-of-success themes.

There is, however, some ambiguity in Horner's findings. It is not clear whether the women were expressing (by negative-consequence stories) an internalized fear of success or merely a cultural stereotype that surrounds feminine achievement. In other words, were Horner's female subjects projecting their own motives on Anne or reacting to Anne in the way their culture had taught them to respond to a woman occupying a heretofore male-dominated role? These are, of course, closely related phenomena, but it is worth the effort to distinguish them, if possible. This is the objective of the research project described in Box 11-2.

Horner's (1969) study and the clarification provided by Monahan et al. (1974) together showed that U.S. values toward success are contaminated by attitudes toward the sexes. Whereas success for males is generally viewed as a positive goal, success for females is not an unqualified good. At least for persons who hold a traditional, sexist orientation, female success in a traditionally male role is viewed negatively. People who have adopted a less sex-linked sense of role demands (who do not perceive one sex or another as more qualified for a particular occupation) should view success for females in "male" roles more positively.

Competing Values in Kenya. Kenya, by the 1970s, had clearly chosen a Western, free-enterprise path of development of its modern sector. A small but visible group of career women had begun to emerge in this East African nation.[4] Beatrice Whiting (1973) observed that Kenyan career women, who are encouraged and expected to be independent and competent in their work roles outside the home, behave very submissively in their relations to their husbands. This may reflect negative reactions to success by females that may

---

[4]Most employed women in Kenya, however, have low-paying jobs. Kariuki (1983), in a study of single-women abuse, described the oppressive circumstances of teen-age rural women employed as house servants.

Box 11-2 Cultural Stereotypes and Reaction to Success

A study by Monahan, Kuhn, and Shaver (1974) made such an effort. They modified Horner's research design by assigning the "Anne" story to both male and female respondents. Similarly, they gave the "John" story to two additional groups of respondents, one male and the other female. Monahan and colleagues reasoned that if negative-consequence responses occurred only, or predominantly, among female respondents and to either the John or Anne cue sentence, this would be strong evidence for an internalized motive among females. But if only the Anne cue sentence elicited negative-consequence responses from both males and females, this would be evidence that the stereotypes surrounding women's achievements are negative and are learned and accepted by both sexes.

The researchers also used younger subjects than Horner had studied. They employed 120 6th- through 11th-grade students in a middle-class urban school, of whom 52 were boys and 68 girls.

The Monahan team's first finding was a replication of Horner's. They found that a majority of the female respondents (51%) confronted by the Anne cue told stories with negative content, but only 21% of the male respondents who were given the John cue did so. Their most important finding, however, was that for both sexes of respondents, the Anne cue elicited a higher proportion of negative stories. Coupling that finding with the fact that boys responded to the Anne cue even more negatively than the girls did, the authors properly con cluded that the sex of the actor in the cue was a more critical variable than the sex of the respondent. The cultural-stereotype hypothesis had to be favored as an interpretation of the reaction-to-success phenomenon.

be manifestations of role conflict to which successful, "modern" Kenyan women are subjected. Whiting also noted that Kenyan men, with considerable regularity, express outspoken criticisms of successful women. In the Kenyan case the ambivalence surrounding success for women probably reflects conflicting values — one set traditional, the other modern — that apply to the female role. A relevant Kenyan study is described in Box 11-3.

Ambivalence as we have seen in the U.S. and Kenyan studies is a likely consequence of competing values and of differing definitions of success. In both of these cases, there is probably a positive evaluation of individual success for people in general and a negative evaluation of female self-assertiveness in situations where it is traditionally unwelcome. To varying degrees in both of these societies, the traditional role definition for females includes submissiveness, subservience, and deference toward males. In that setting, a "successful" female would be one who strove, effectively, to meet that role expectation.

Box 11-3 Ambivalence Toward Success in Africa?

Evidence that these competing values impinge on Kenyan women has been obtained by Fleming (1975). She had 123 University of Nairobi students (44 females and 79 males) and 143 secondary-school students (87 females and 56 males) write stories to Horner's cue sentence concerning success in medical school. The sex of the actor and the sex of the respondent were the same. Although the frequency with which both sexes cited negative consequences for success was lower than in the U.S. studies, it was substantially higher for females than for males, especially among the secondary-school students. In the university-student sample, 36% of the stories about females contained negative imagery, whereas 20% of the male stories did. In the secondary-school sample, 41% of the female stories did, compared with only 9% of the male stories. Fleming also administered a female-success cue to 51 male university students; of these, 31% produced negative stories. This latter finding was similar to that of Monahan and associates (1974), which had shown that both males and females in the United States react negatively to success by a female.

More Evidence for Cultural Differences in Attitude Toward Success by Males and Females. That the critical values are cultural (or at least not universal) is shown by studies that assess individual attitudes toward certain values held by both males and females in different cultures. Peck (1967) presented male and female students at the University of Mexico and the University of Texas with a list of 15 value terms, for example, love, career success, freedom, and wealth. These terms were to be rank-ordered according to the importance the students would personally attach to them.

For the most part, Peck found that the two sexes in each culture agreed with each other in their rankings. For career success, however, there was a striking departure. Among the Mexican respondents, career success was ranked first by males and second by females, whereas among Texas respondents, it was ranked fourth by males and 12th by females!

The consistent cross-sex behavior of the Mexican respondents may relate to some findings of Diaz-Guerrero (1987), who suggested that many kinds of individual behaviors in Mexico reflect the historical sociocultural premises (HSCPs) that are shared by most members of the society. He defines HSCPs as those "cultural traditions concerning values, beliefs, and behaviors" (1987, p. 239) that are held by more than 50% of the individuals in a culture. Through an extensive examination and factor analysis of the sayings, proverbs, and dictums of the Mexican people, Diaz-Guerrero came up with nine factors or HSCPs that are characteristic of a Mexican belief system. When these Mexican HSCPs were applied in questionnaire form to Mexicans, Mexican-Americans, and Anglo-Americans, it was found that Mexicans endorsed the HSCPs to a greater extent than did the Mexican-Americans, and they in turn more than the Anglo-Americans. He also noted that the tendency for Mexican-Americans to endorse these HSCPs to a lesser extent than Mexicans did may be because the Mexican-Americans have greater economic resources and opportunities than Mexicans have. Of course, so do Anglo-Americans.

Success for women in the United States (and presumably in some other societies as well) is, as we have now seen in several studies, obviously a mixed blessing. It is not valued in the same way that success for males is valued. Conflict surrounds it, and the stereotype of the successful female is hardly flattering. Stereotypes often function as self-fulfilling prophecies. So we should not be surprised to discover that in cultures where this negative stereotype exists, females react quite differently from males to situations in which they can accept or reject an opportunity to succeed.

Risk Taking by Males and Females

Slovic (1966) found this to be the case for children ranging in age from 6 to 16 years with a game that he had set up at a county fair in the United States. Slovic's game involved a free vending machine with ten switches. Players were told that pushing any but one of the switches, one at a time, would result in their winning candy. But if the one "disaster" switch were pushed, the game would be terminated and all winnings forfeited. From the player's vantage point then, the game offered an opportunity to be successful, but it also presented an element of risk.

In several respects, female performance showed less risk taking than male performance. First, whereas 735 boys volunteered to play the game, only 312 girls dared to enter Slovic's tent. This particular sex difference increased with age. Second, far more boys than girls played the game to its theoretical limit of nine trials. This sex difference also increased with age. In fact, the difference in style of play did not exist at all for children between 6 and 8 years, but it increased in magnitude until it reached statistical significance at about age 11. Somehow, it seems, American girls acquire different dispositions toward risk taking than do American boys. This acquisition requires some years of rearing in a culture that possesses a negative stereotype about female achievement and that apparently treats the two sexes differently during the child-training years.

DIFFERING SOCIALIZATION FOR BOYS AND GIRLS: WHY AND WITH WHAT CONSEQUENCES?

If you consider what we have seen already in this chapter about sex differences and what anthropologists tell us about division of labor by sex, you might conclude, as did Munroe and Munroe (1975, p. 116), that

(1) there are modal sex differences in behavior in every society and (2) every society has some division of labor by sex. These two phenomena, besides being universal, are also probably interrelated in a functional way. Let us now see how.

Earlier, we learned that Barry, Bacon, and Child (1957) had found rather consistent differences in the way many societies discriminate between the sexes in childhood-socialization emphases. A later publication by the same team of cross-cultural psychologists (Barry, Bacon & Child, 1967) was based on ratings of reports in the Human Relations Area Files for 45 societies. The team reported sex differences in every society in nurturance, responsibility, and obedience (with females displaying more of those classes of behavior) and in self-reliance, achievement, and independence (with males displaying more of those).

The correspondence between sex differences in socialization emphases and sex differences in behavior is virtually perfect. That the two sexes behave in ways they are taught to behave is, of course, not surprising, but it still raises some interesting questions. For example, have all these societies observed different inborn behavioral tendencies in males and females and shaped their socialization practices to reinforce such biologically determined tendencies? Or are societies' socialization practices merely influenced by certain physical differences between males and females, with those practices responsible for behavioral differences?

Risking oversimplification, we can summarize the picture of sex differences in behavior that is presented by anthropology and cross-cultural psychology as showing males to be more self-assertive, achieving, and dominant and females to be more socially responsive, passive, and submissive. How best might this be explained?

Economic and Biological Roots

One key to the explanation is the fact that the behavioral differences just summarized, although nearly universal and almost never reversed, range in magnitude from quite large down to virtually nil. A satisfactory explanation, then, will account both for the universality of *direction* of difference and for the variation in *magnitude* of the difference.

Such an explanation takes into account economic factors, including division of labor by sex, and socialization practices. Key contributors to this explanation have been Barry, Bacon, and Child (1957); Barry, Child, and Bacon (1959); and Van Leeuwen (1978). Their arguments were reviewed at the beginning of this chapter in the context of a discussion of sex differences in field independence/dependence, but they can now be amplified and generalized.

The argument begins with an early anthropological finding (Murdock, 1937) that a division of labor by sex is universal (or nearly so) and quite consistent in content. For example, food preparation is done predominantly by females in nearly all societies. Child rearing is usually the responsibility of females. Sometimes it is shared, but in no society is it the modal practice for males to assume the responsibility themselves. Although there are many cross-cultural variations in the content of sexual division of labor, there are, once again, hardly ever significant reversals.

Barry, Bacon, and Child (1957) suggested that this consistent pattern of sex-role differentiation during adulthood represents a set of solutions that societies have invented to deal with what were, for subsistence-level societies, practical problems. These problems are viewed as arising from biologically based physical differences (and not behavioral ones) between the sexes, especially the female's lesser overall physical strength and — most of all — her child-bearing function. Different economic roles for males and females, with the latter consigned mostly to close-to-home activities, would have been a functional response.

It is likely that differential socialization of the two sexes evolved as a means for preparing children to assume their sex-linked adult roles. Then, the behavioral differences are a product of different socialization emphases, with those in turn reflective of, and appropriate training for, different adult activities.

Consistent with this argument is Barry, Child, and Bacon's (1959) finding that large differentiation between the sexes in socialization tends to occur more often in societies with "an economy that places a high premium on superior strength, and superior development of motor skills requiring strength" (p. 330). Also consistent with the argument is the finding that if sexual differentiation occurs during socialization, girls nearly always receive more training in nurturance, obedience, and responsibility than boys do and less in assertiveness, achievement, and independence (Barry, Child & Bacon, 1959).

The ecological framework expands the argument so that it can accommodate numerous details about the subsistence mode and variations in degree of sex differences in behavior. Thus, in sedentary, high-food-accumulating societies, not only will females be subjected to more training to be nurturant and compliant, but the degree of the difference between the sexes' training will also be very high. In low-food-accumulating societies, such as gathering or hunting societies, there will be less division of labor by sex and little need for either sex to be trained to be compliant. Often in such societies (at least in gathering societies, if not hunting ones, as we will see shortly), women's contributions to the basic subsistence activity are integral to it. Hence, women's work is valued by the men, who are then not inclined to denigrate women or to insist on subservience from them.

Some related findings have been reported by Schlegel and Barry (1986) that expand our understanding of some of the consequences of division of labor by sex. One of the ways in which division of labor by sex varies across cultures is in the degree to which women contribute to subsistence, or food-getting activities. This varies, depending on the activity. For example, if food is gathered, women's participation is usually high; in 79% of 14 gathering societies for which ethnographic reports were coded by Schlegel and Barry (1986), women were high contributors. By contrast, in only 13% of 16 hunting societies did women make a high contribution. (Schlegel and Barry defined high contribution as any percentage above the mean contribution for their entire sample of 186 nonindustrial societies, which was about 35%.)

Percentages of societies with above-average contributions by females for other types of subsistence were as follows: fishing, 29%; animal husbandry, 46%; incipient agriculture, 77%; extensive agriculture, 72%; and intensive agriculture, 33%. Thus, women are more likely to contribute relatively highly to subsistence where the main activity is either gathering or agriculture (other than intensive agriculture), and less highly where the activity is animal husbandry, intensive agriculture, fishing, or hunting. (Schlegel & Barry, 1986, p. 144).

Does this variation in the subsistence role played by women have any consequences? Schlegel and Barry (1986) found that it did, indeed, on such aspects of social life as sexual and marital relations, pregnancy norms, certain child-rearing practices, values accorded to females, and the amount of personal freedom enjoyed by them. Associated with high female contributions to subsistence were (a) polygyny, (b) bridewealth (gifts from the groom to the bride's family), (c) exogamy (going outside the immediate society for mates), (d) long post-partum sex taboos (which results in fewer and more widely spaced pregnancies), (e) more industriousness-training for girls, (f) higher valuation of females, (g) more permissiveness with respect to premarital sexuality, and (h) lower probability of rape.

Schlegel and Barry (1986) thus found that two sets of cultural features — adaptive and attitudinal — are associated with female contribution to subsistence. Where women play a relatively large subsistence role, the adaptive features of polygyny, exogamy, brideprice, birth control, and work-orientation training for girls prevail. And under these same conditions (high contribution by females to subsistence), females are relatively highly valued, allowed freedoms, and are generally less likely to be perceived as objects for male sexual and reproductive needs. Needless to say, the behavior of women will vary across societies as a consequence of their role in subsistence activities. So, not only do women behave differently from men, both men and women behave differently in different societies, and the two sexes relate to each other differently in different societies.

What we have seen in this section is that females do indeed have some behavioral dispositions that are different from those of males. But, thanks primarily to cross-cultural research, it is clear that these sex differences are the product of cultural forces, operating through socialization practices and reflective of ecological factors. Both the consistencies in the cross-cultural data and the variations from society to society help us to understand how cultural values have been defined differently for the two sexes and how individuals come to behave in accord with them.

We have just reviewed studies that describe and explain behavioral differences between the sexes. There are also similarities in behaviors across the sexes, however. That is, in some ways men and women are alike. In the following section, we examine a study by Williams and Best (1989) that found evidence of *both* cross-cultural similarities and differences in the ways that males and females in many societies perceive or define themselves.

GENDER IDENTITY: SELF-PERCEPTIONS OF MEN AND WOMEN ACROSS CULTURES

Self-perceptions—how we perceive ourselves in relation to other people and situations—are inextricably linked to cultural prescriptions concerning male and female behavior. In every one of 25 countries included in a study by Williams and Best (1989), the sex stereotypes that generally exist in the world (as revealed, for example, by Williams and Best, 1982, and discussed in the next section of this chapter) are reflected both in how people describe themselves and in their ideal selves. For example, in all countries, the ideal-self descriptions of men (and, of course, their perceived selves) were more stereotypically "masculine" than those of women. By the same token, for *both* men and women, the ideal self was more "masculine" than the described self. Indeed, men and women generally were more similar in their ideal selves than in their perceived selves. Moreover, with regard to the affective meaning of both perceived-self and ideal-self concepts, in most countries these were both "stronger" and more "active" for men than for women.

It was also the case that in most countries women were more diverse in their self and ideal concepts than men were. In other words, generally, in the countries studied by Williams and Best (1989), women were more "androgynous."

SEX ROLE IDEOLOGY: CROSS-CULTURAL PATTERNS OF MALE-FEMALE RELATIONSHIPS

Stereotypes About Males and Females

Whatever the *real* differences in behavior between the sexes may be, there are widely shared *beliefs* about those differences. As Williams and Best (1982) have shown, children in many Western countries (for example,

France, Germany, Norway, the Netherlands, Italy, and the United States) and a few non-Western nations as well (e.g., Malaysia, Nigeria, and Peru) behave very similarly in the way they differentially ascribe patterns of traits to men and women. These consensual stereotypes, although held even by 5-year-old children, were more pervasively shared among 8-year-olds. Generally, with Norway and Germany as exceptions, children of each sex knew their own sex stereotype better than that of the other sex. These differences aside, the most striking finding of this project is the prevalence across cultures of sex stereotypes (stereotypes about the two sexes, like any other stereotypes, may of course include beliefs about real differences).

Williams and Best (1982), having studied 100 university students in each of 25 countries, found some general agreement across countries in differentially attributing 300 traits to men or women. Some of the notably widely shared, if not universal, stereotypes were that dominance, autonomy, aggression, exhibition, achievement, and endurance were traits ascribed to males, whereas abasement, deference, succorance, nurturance, and affiliation were traits ascribed to females. Generally speaking, men are perceived to be stronger and more active.

In their later (1989) study, Williams and Best found that the self-perceptions of men and women were less stereotypical in more economically and socially developed countries. Indeed, the most interesting of all their findings relate to sex-role ideology.

Changing Sex Role Ideology

In more highly developed countries (where higher proportions of women are gainfully employed, where women attend universities in relatively high numbers, etc.), ideology regarding the status of women is more egalitarian. In such countries, Williams and Best (1989) found that men and women perceive themselves in a more similar fashion.

As sexual-equality ideals spread, behavioral differences may diminish and so may the prevailing sex stereotypes. There is evidence that the ideology of sexual equality is spreading, but it is still more acceptable to females than to males. In most countries in the Williams and Best (1989) study, the women subjects were more liberal than the men. Similarly, Kalin, Heusser, and Edmonds (1982) found that females were more egalitarian than males in Canada, England, and Ireland. Whether the prevailing ideologies in these three countries were more egalitarian than in the past was not addressed by this study. Scher, Nevo, and Beit-Hallahmi (1979) also found Israeli female students to be more egalitarian than their male counterparts. On the other hand, Scher et al. found that Israeli respondents of both sexes were more egalitarian than their U.S. counterparts. Israeli males in particular were more likely to endorse sexual equality than American males.

Sex-role ideology was found by Williams and Best (1989) to be more egalitarian in predominantly Christian societies than in predominantly Moslem societies. In another study, Furnam and Karani (1985) compared the attitudes toward women of three different religious groups (Hindus and Parsis in India, and British Christians). They found that men in all three groups were more conservative than women in their attitudes toward sexual equality. Furnam and Karani reported that regardless of religion or culture, men in this study were more likely than women to believe in a just world (i.e., to believe that one gets what one deserves) and that these beliefs were related to their conservative sex-role attitudes. Women, on the other hand, who held more liberal attitudes toward sexual equality, attributed more to chance and to powerful others (i.e., an external locus of control) and held more *unjust* world beliefs. These results suggest that the persistence of sex stereotypes may be closely linked with a cross-cultural power differential that accords one sex more privileges and power than the other. Whether men support or resist changing women's roles may in part reflect the extent to which they experience this power differential as unfair and are willing to give up some of the privileges and controls that greater male prestige has afforded them in the past.

Many social scientists interested in changing sex roles assume that male-female equality and societal modernization are closely linked. Indeed, as Williams and Best revealed, changes in the roles of women in a given society may be one indicator of that society's level of modernization. In many societies, as modernization proceeds, traditional patriarchal patterns of female seclusion and male dominance are gradually replaced by women's greater civil equality and political participation.

A study by Biri, Pendleton, and Garland (1987) focused on men's attitudes toward changing women's roles in Libya, where the effects of modernization on the family and society are becoming increasingly evident, particularly as more and more Libyan women seek gainful employment outside of the home. The Biri et al. study is discussed in more detail in Box 11-4.

Toward Equality of the Sexes

Awareness of a movement for equality of the sexes probably exists worldwide, as indicated by the 1985 international conference held in Nairobi to mark the end of the United Nations' Decade of Women. Still, it is probably no accident that the movement for equality of the sexes took root and flourished effectively in industrial nations. In industrialized nations, division of labor by sex is not nearly so functional as it is in predominantly subsistence-level societies. Modern technology has produced numerous labor-saving devices, which make possible unprecedented leisure time and make differences in physical strength between the sexes virtually irrelevant.

Box 11-4 Men's Attitudes Toward Changing Women's Roles in Libya

In the United States, sex roles are related to age, education, socioeconomic status, and religion. Biri, Pendleton, and Garland (1987) searched for a relationship between these characteristics in Libyan men and their attitudes toward women's changing roles.

Biri et al. defined traditional attitudes as "those which encourage male dominance and a subservient role for women within the home and discourage women's participation in political and economic activities outside of the home," and modern attitudes as "those which encourage women's participation in decision making within the home as well as their active participation in political and economic activities outside the home" (p. 297). The social characteristics on which their study focused were age, education, socioeconomic background (urban vs. rural), religiosity, social status, mother's employment, and family type (extended vs. nuclear).

They hypothesized that men most likely to hold modern attitudes would be ones with an urban background, who grew up in a nuclear family with a mother who worked outside the home, who are young, highly educated (high school or above), of high social status (as measured by family income), and without a strong commitment to religion. Interviews were conducted (in Arabic) with 200 Libyan men in Tripoli, using scales of attitudes toward (1) division of labor within the household, (2) women's participation in family decision making, (3) women's political participation, and (4) women's participation in the labor force.

The results confirm the investigators' hypotheses concerning age, education, and mother's employment. That is, *young, educated men whose mothers worked outside the home generally showed more modern attitudes toward all four dependent variables.* With the exception of those urban men who had a modern attitude toward women's participation in the labor force, however, there were no significant bivariate relationships between religiosity, income, and urban/rural background and degree of modernity in attitude. Contradictory to the investigator's hypotheses, they found that *men who came from extended families showed more modern attitudes toward division of labor at home and toward women's participation in family decision making than did men from nuclear families.*

The authors explained that high social status, though not an influential variable by itself, is closely linked with educational level. Furthermore, in Libya, those families with higher incomes have better access to educational opportunities, and these families are most likely to be extended families. Thus, the modern attitudes of Libyan men from extended families seem to be a function of the higher educational level of those men.

Males who tend to be principally employed outside the home, in fact, have many hours available each day to spend at home. Hence, they are available to perform domestic tasks, including child rearing. Similarly, women in modern societies are no longer so tied to such tasks. Furthermore, family-planning technology, very pervasively employed in industrial societies but not yet very widely accepted elsewhere, has drastically reduced the time and attention that must be devoted to infant care, traditionally the most time-consuming and restricting activity of female adults.

Hence, it is no surprise in industrial societies that sexual differentiation during childhood socialization is minimal (Barry, Bacon & Child, 1957) or that sex differences in behavior among children are minimal (Whiting & Edwards, 1973). A visitor from Mars dropping into most nonindustrialized nations would have little difficulty detecting the existence of two sexes (how could she fail to note differences in hairstyles, dress, and so on?). But if the visitor arrived in some American or European university classroom, utter confusion might result. If warned in advance to look for men and women, the visitor might expect the men to be the short-haired ones wearing blue jeans and using four letter expletives! These and other once-reliable sex-distinguishing characteristics would mislead our visitor as often as they would help. Clearly, a degree of gender homogenization has emerged, albeit with constraints and countertendencies.

In these same societies where a blurring of sex differences in child rearing and in behavior has begun, inequality of economic opportunity remains as an anachronism. Not surprisingly, these societies have seen the emergence of feminist movements as an inevitable response to that inconsistency. No such inconsistency characterizes mostly subsistence-level societies. Where tradition prevails, adult roles remain sex-linked, and socialization practices include clear and effective efforts to produce behavioral differences between the sexes that are for the most part accepted as normal, natural, and appropriate.

Of particular interest in this regard are those nonindustrial societies in which certain cultural facts may contribute to an unanticipated blurring of sexual distinctions. For example, since in most societies both boys and girls are reared primarily by female caretakers, there is the likelihood that young boys will have available adult role models who are preponderantly female. Practices that enhance the probability of maternal predominance in rearing include polygyny, exclusive mother/child sleeping arrangements, and matrilocal residence patterns, all of which enhance father absence and reduce male salience. If these societies also accord social dominance to adult males (as is clearly the case in high-food-accumulating, subsistence-level societies), they are in addition very likely to have severe male initiation ceremonies during adolescence, including circumcision (Burton & Whiting, 1961; Harrington, 1968; Whiting, 1962).

A persuasive interpretation of the cross-cultural correlation between low male salience during infancy and male initiation ceremonies during later childhood is that the ceremonies represent an institutional response designed to overcome cross-sex identification tendencies in young males.

Munroe and Munroe (1975) provided a thorough review of studies bearing on cross-sex identification and other social responses to it. These responses include the couvade ("male pseudopregnancy," an institutionalized set of practices whereby an expectant father is treated like an expectant mother) and still other institutions that permit males to display "feminine" behaviors in societies that do not structurally emphasize maleness. Munroe and Munroe (1988) reiterated that the couvade was more likely to be present in societies where mothers and their infants sleep together and in societies with a high frequency of matrilocal residence. On the other hand, when societies are scored on "defensive masculinity" (a concept similar to Broude's notion of hypermasculinity, which will be discussed below), the couvade is found disproportionately often in societies that are low on this variable.

Societies differ in the value attached to the maintenance of differences between the sexes. Some sex distinction is universal, but the content of the distinction and its perceived desirability vary across cultures. With the spread of feminist ideology, in many societies, gender role boundaries are actively being blurred. In others, they are being reinforced, and in still others there is conflict between pressures to diminish them and institutional practices that reinforce them. How and to what degree societies struggle against, tolerate, or even celebrate sex distinctions reflects the perceived functionality of adult division of labor by sex. Where the economic system functions more smoothly with such a division of labor, acceptance of longstanding sexual inequalities is likely. Where a sexual division of labor is largely irrelevant to the economic system (as is probably the case in postindustrial societies), sharp distinctions between male and female roles become less functional and sexual equality is more likely to be present as a social norm.

It might also be the case that little boys and little girls will increasingly be treated alike. But for the moment, as we saw in an earlier section of this chapter, there remain some sharp differences in socialization for males and females.

A SOCIOCULTURAL THEORY OF HUMAN SEXUALITY

Now we turn our attention to sexual behavior itself, surely a critically important aspect of interpersonal relations. Our perspective on human sexuality emphasizes that it, too, has social and cultural meanings.

In his book *Journey Into Sexuality: An Exploratory Voyage*, sociologist Ira Reiss (1986) cross-culturally examined patterns of sexual behavior, relying heavily on anthropological data from the Human Relations Area Files. Interpreting these data, Reiss offered a view of human sexuality that sees sexual practices and customs as linked to other features of a society such as kinship patterns and power structures.

For Reiss, human sexuality practices follow "shared cultural scripts" that promote specific types of sexual behavior while discouraging others. All groups attach great importance to sexual scripts, but these vary greatly between ethnic groups, social classes, age groups, and societies. *All* societies have the need to regulate sexual behavior in some way, so the existence of sexual scripts constitutes a cultural universal.

Whether sexual scripts restrict and control sexual behavior or encourage sexual promiscuity (and both kinds can be found), it is these sexual scripts, and not biological stimuli, that determine what people will find erotically arousing. Thus, according to Reiss, sexual arousal is a learned response to social and cultural stimuli. Of course, sexual arousal has biological underpinnings, so it might be more complete to say that sexual arousal is a product of an interaction between biological forces and what Reiss has termed sexual scripts.

In order to explain why certain sexual scripts exist in some societies but not in others, Reiss examined cross-cultural patterns of sexual activity as they relate to specific social systems. He found sexual practices to be closely linked with the kinship system, power structure, and ideological beliefs of a given society. Based on these findings, Reiss proposed a sociological theory of human sexuality that understands these links as initially stemming from the potential of sexual bonding to create lasting human relationships and a support system that will provide for the needs of the newborn infant. From these kinship ties emerges a pattern of task assignment that is typically based on gender. These gender-based task assignments, as we saw earlier in this chapter, are the basis for a power structure favoring men, both within the kinship system and in the wider society. Where women's kinship ties are strong, however, such as in matrilineal societies, female power is also likely to be greater, and women will experience less sexual abuse. The greater the power of one sex, the greater that sex's ability to control sexuality and define sexual scripts.

In Reiss' view, members of the more powerful sex not only secure control of major social institutions, they can also shape gender roles in ways that accord themselves greater sexual privilege. Thus, the sexual scripts and erotica preferences of a given culture may reflect a power differential that favors one sex (typically males) over the other.

As noted above, relations between the sexes are influenced by gender roles, gender identity, and sex-role ideology. Broude (1983) explored cross-culturally the relationship between these variables and male-female interaction, using coded data for 201 societies listed in the Standard Cross-Cultural Sample (a portion of the societies listed in the Human Relations Area Files). Prior research (e.g., Whiting & Whiting, 1975) had suggested that male sex-role ideology and gender identity (labeled "hypermasculinity" by Broude) may be related to both the quality of sexual relationships and nonsexual intimacy. Broude expected that heightened masculinity (as indicated by such cultural features as "male boasting" and a double standard governing extramarital sex) would be reflected in (a) sexual hostility, (b) repressive attitudes toward female sexuality, (c) less sexual intimacy, and (d) greater husband-wife aloofness.

Seeking evidence for such relationships, Broude included three categories of variables in her study: measures of hypermasculinity (e.g., male boasting), of sexual intimacy (e.g., frequency of extramarital and premarital sex), and of nonsexual intimacy or husband-wife aloofness (e.g., the extent to which husbands and wives eat, room, and spend leisure time together). Various patterns of intercorrelations emerged, leading Broude to several conclusions, including the following.

First, Broude did not find that hypermasculinity relates to sexual intimacy or marital aloofness to the extent that the earlier literature had suggested. However, Broude's various indices of hypermasculinity did correlate highly among themselves.

Second, although Broude reported that hypermasculinity was not *directly* related to degree of cross-sex intimacy, her findings suggest that male self-concepts and attitudes toward women and sex influence certain behaviors affecting marital stability. That is, where the frequency of extramarital sex is high for men but low for women (i.e., the double standard), marriages are more likely to end in divorce. Conversely, where women have some degree of premarital sexual experience (i.e., where attitudes toward female sexuality are less repressive), marriages tend to be more stable.

Broude suggested that male behaviors such as boasting, sexual hostility, and marital infidelity may best be understood as attempts by men to overcompensate for underlying insecurities about their masculinity.[5] These findings replicate an earlier study by Broude (1980) in which she found the extramarital double standard to be significantly related to boasting, machismo, men's houses, segregation of the sexes in chore assignments, and father absence—all components of the pattern of male protest behavior.

The works of Reiss (1986) and Broude (1980, 1983), which deal primarily with sexual behavior, dramatically suggest that even one of the most biological acts human beings perform is embedded in culture.

---

[5]In the next chapter, we will consider some important implications of this idea for our understanding of aggressive behavior.

CONCLUSION

We have now completed our discussion of cultural differences in values, attitudes, and behavior relating to the sexes. We have seen a considerable amount of consistency around the world in the ways in which the sexes differ from each other in characteristic behaviors and in the ways that socialization practices instill those behaviors.

We have also seen that these consistencies are probably linked to division of labor by sex, so that if adult sex roles remain stable, so will socialization practices and behavioral differences. There is reason to believe, however, that the (a) division of labor by sex, (b) gender roles, and (c) related sex-role ideologies are changing, and as they change, so might socialization practices and the behaviors that characterize the two sexes. Still, in the world today, there are some tenacious differences between the sexes in behavior. One of these is aggression, to which we turn in the next chapter.

Chapter 12

Culture and Aggression

INTRODUCTION:
WHY STUDY AGGRESSION
CROSS-CULTURALLY?

One of the sex differences noted in the last chapter is that around the world, on the average, males consistently commit more aggressive acts than do females. This is probably a cultural universal. Later in this chapter we shall examine this sex difference very closely because it may be crucial to our understanding of aggression per se. We must first put aside sex differences and ask some fundamental questions about aggression and culture.

Do we find aggression everywhere and to the same degree, or do societies vary in their typical levels of aggression? If they do vary, is the variation systematically related to certain aspects of culture? Do these relationships reveal how aggression is both caused and controlled? Until we can answer these cross-cultural questions, we cannot claim to understand human aggression.

THE CROSS-CULTURAL
RESEARCH STRATEGY
APPLIED TO AGGRESSION

As stated often before, the overarching goal of cross-cultural psychology is to understand how factors in the natural and man-made environments influence our behavior in more-or-less adaptive ways. The ultimate goal of cross-cultural research on aggression is to understand why human beings behave aggressively. That they do so in differing degree, in different ways, and for different reasons is clear. These differences exist at the individual level within societies as well as across societies. Both individual and social differences may reflect some universally applicable principles concerning aggression's causes that cross-cultural research should help us discern.

The antecedents of aggressive behavior are ecological and structural. They include the probability of conflict over resources, the probability of frustrations of various kinds, norms governing conflict resolution, child-rearing emphases, and the kinds of behaviors displayed by persons who might serve as models to be emulated. All of these antecedents exist in every culture but they vary in kind across cultures. So, cross-cultural research on aggression is both possible and essential.

A Conceptual Framework for Aggression Research

A comprehensive review of alternative theoretical perspectives on aggression, including psychoanalytic, biological, and social-learning approaches, can be found in Siann (1985). The following account is our own. More than other approaches, it stresses ecocultural forces.

The way diverse variables interact to influence aggressive behavior is shown in diagrammatic form in Figure 12-1,[1] where we can see many possible contributing factors that bear on an individual's likelihood of behaving aggressively.

The diagram illustrates possible links between ecocultural forces, socialization practices, individual experiences, and individual behavioral dispositions when persons find themselves in situations in which frustrations need to be overcome or conflicts need to be resolved.

Definitions

To read the diagram, some definitions should be kept in mind. Terms relating to aggression, including *aggression* itself, have diverse meanings in popular discourse.

To begin, let us make clear what *we* mean by aggression. Following Dollard, Doob, Miller, Mowrer, and Sears (1939), who worked together at the Institute of Human Relations at Yale University, many behavioral scientists define aggression as "a sequence of behavior, the goal response of which is the injury to the person toward whom it is directed" (p. 9). Implicit in this classic definition is that the "injury" may be physical or psychological

---

[1]From "Aggression in Global Perspective: A Research Strategy" by M. H. Segall, in *Aggression in Global Perspective* (pp. 1–43) by A. P. Goldstein & M. H. Segall (Eds.), 1983, Elmsford, NY: Pergamon. Copyright 1983 by Pergamon Press, Inc. Adapted by permission. The present version of this figure also appears in Segall, 1988, p. 75.

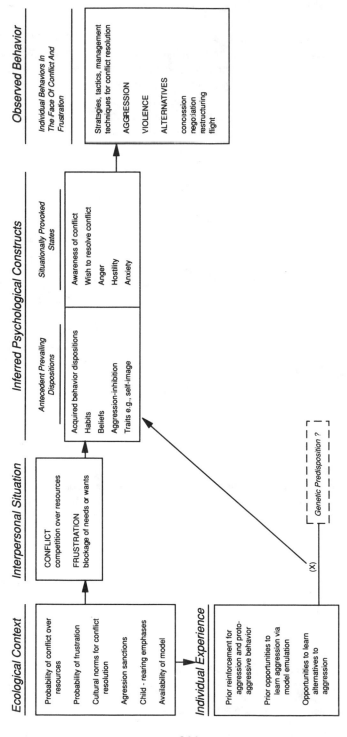

FIGURE 12-1. A conceptual framework for the study of aggression

and that the "response" is an overt manifestation of an inferred behavioral disposition, which may or may not include an intention to harm. By *aggression*, then, we mean simply any behavior by a person that inflicts harm on an other.

By *conflict* we mean any situation involving a disagreement about the allocation of resources, with the added implication that participants in a conflict are motivated somehow to resolve it.

Frustration, often a feature of a conflict, is defined as a barrier to satisfaction of a need or want. Frustration can lead to anger or hostility (defined below) and can increase the probability of aggression.

Anger is an inferred state of an individual denoting a feeling that often accompanies conflict or frustration. A short-lived state, anger is usually provoked by the behavior of another person, toward whom it is directed (although it may be displaced onto others).

Hostility is a longer-lived state, inferred from behavior, usually less intense than anger, and frequently directed diffusely to a collective target, as in cases of enduring ethnic hostility. It is often shared by many people, who learn hostility by emulating others, as when one group of people feel hostile toward a group of "foreigners" whom they have never met.[2]

Why these particular definitions? We deliberately stress aggression's overt behavioral quality in order to avoid unnecessary problems that surround notions of behavioral intent. Particularly when dealing with aggression in a cross-cultural context, inferring correctly the intent that may underlie a particular aggressive act is very problematic.

By recognizing that anger and hostility are never directly observed but only inferred from observed aggression, we emphasize that not all aggressive acts are caused by anger or hostility. Aggression occasionally reflects other motives, possibly more so in some cultures than in others.

We also wish to distinguish aggression from the popular, quasi-psychiatric notion of "aggression" as a drive or an instinct, the blockage of which might result in some psychic harm.

Aggression, as defined here, is also to be distinguished from assertiveness, with which (in popular American English usage and perhaps in other languages as well) it is often confused. The difference between aggression and assertiveness is that assertiveness need not inflict harm, whereas aggression, by definition, always does. Thus, whereas one can readily approve of assertiveness, it is difficult ever to applaud aggression.

There are, of course, individual differences in attitudes about aggression.

---

[2]In this chapter, we will not discuss intergroup hostility or aggression directed to out-groups, as in discrimination against minorities within a society or warfare across societies. These topics will be treated in Chapter 13, where they will be given the detailed exposition they require.

The same aggressive acts may be approved by some persons and strongly condemned by others. Whole groups, too, (such as ethnic groups or socio-economic groups) may vary in their judgments of aggressive acts, particularly when they are expressive of political acts, as when one group's "freedom fighters" are seen by another group as "terrorists." Some groups have no moral objection to police actions that target groups consider examples of "police brutality" (Kahn, 1972). On the other hand, social psychological research, most of it done in the United States, has revealed some widely held values with respect to aggression. For example, the more harm producing an aggressive act, the more it is disapproved of by children; adults, on the other hand, apply moral judgments to aggressive acts on the basis of perceived intentions (Rule & Nesdale, 1976). After reviewing numerous laboratory experiments in which various kinds of aversive events increased aggressiveness, Carlson and Miller (1988) concluded that social provocation increased aggressive responding (of a retaliatory nature) to a very high degree. In Western cultures, then, according to Carlson and Miller, the "dominant response" to an insult or a criticism is "to counteraggress" (1988, p. 157). Do some of these generalizations hold across cultures? Are there cultural differences in attitudes toward aggression? Are there both communalities and differences? A few comparative studies address these questions.

Fraczek (1985), replicating an earlier questionnaire study done in Finland (Lagerspetz & Westman, 1980), studied samples of adults in Poland. They resembled comparable samples of Finns in the combinations of aggressive acts and "justifications" that they found acceptable. The Polish sample, however, was generally more accepting of aggressive acts than was the Finnish sample. In particular, the Polish sample gave higher approval to acts of torturing, killing, verbal abuse, ironic comments, and fits of rage and gave higher ratings to justifications of aggression such as in self-defense, on behalf of others, as a punishment, in defense of one's property, and to overcome communication difficulties (Frazcek, 1985, p. 48). Differences in both the legal codes and the current living conditions in these two European societies (e.g., capital punishment is legal and used in Poland; in Finland it was long ago abolished) may well underlie the differences in attitudes reported by Frazcek.

THE CENTRAL THEME: AGGRESSION'S MULTIPLE CAUSES

Now that the meaning of the key terms in the diagram has been made clear, its central theme should be obvious. Aggressive behavior is a product of cultural influence, acting largely through culturally mediated childhood experiences. Where, then, do we stand on possible genetic and other biological influences on aggression?

Our framework acknowledges the possibility that some genetically based dispositions, products of human biological evolution, interact with experience-based dispositions to produce aggression as one of several reactions to frustration or as a conflict-resolution strategy. But we do not label these genetic dispositions "instincts"; we use a question mark in the diagram to indicate that we do not know the precise nature of these genetic factors.

Why Not Aggressive Instincts?

The one biological argument applied to human aggression for which we have no regard is instinct theory (and associated notions of catharsis), in which expressions of aggression are seen as natural, necessary, and even therapeutic. Such theories, which attempt to account for the pervasiveness of aggression by viewing it as an instinctive, wired-in, primal feature of human nature (e.g., Lorenz, 1963; Ardry, 1966; Morris, 1967; Storr, 1968) are grounded in distortions of reality. That instinct theories are so popular is a phenomenon in its own right, one that cries out for explanation. Could their popularity reside in the justification they offer us when we in fact aggress? Don't these theories allow us to say, "I'm sorry I hurt you but I couldn't help myself"? We agree with Carr (1981) who, after a careful review of instinct theories of aggression concluded, "They have little to recommend them and in fact may be pernicious."

That aggression is pervasive does not require that we consider it instinctive. Other biological and cultural forces could be common enough to contribute to aggression everywhere. Various social-learning theories that stress the importance of socialization (e.g., Freud, in some but not all of his discussions of aggression; Dollard et al., 1939; Berkowitz, 1958; Bandura & Walters, 1963) can also explain the pervasiveness of aggression.

Biological Possibilities

We do not exclude biology from our effort to understand human aggression. There are many ways in which biology may be implicated. For example, there are possible dietary factors involved. One of a growing number of anthropologists to stress biological factors in human behavior, Bolton (1973) linked hypoglycemia (problems related to glucose metabolism) to homicide among the Qolla, an Amerindian group living in the Andes. Many anthropologists, however, says Bolton (1984), "still think they can exclude biological factors from their attempts to understand social and cultural phenomena" (p. 2). We concur with Bolton, who asserted, "Only by integrating social and cultural factors with psychological and biological ones will it be possible to solve some of the most significant anthropological puzzles" (1984, p. 2). Human aggression is surely one of those puzzles.

A second biological approach to understanding aggression, one that we find less compelling, is described in Box 12-1.

Another way in which biology might affect aggression is through androgen or testosterone levels. Reason to consider hormonal factors resides in the fact that for nonhuman animals, castration (which dramatically lowers androgen levels) lowers aggressiveness (see, e.g., Hutt, 1972; Moyer, 1974) but, at the human level, research results are contradictory; Mazur (1976) reviewed six relevant studies and found that in only two of them was there a relationship between androgen level and aggression in humans. Human studies among adult males of individual differences in circulating testosterone levels, however, show correlations with (a) various physical characteristics and (b) acts of dominance. Both of these might in turn correlate with aggression. (Then again, they might not.) Whether they do may well depend on how those physical characteristics or tendencies to strive for dominance interact with cultural determinants of behavior. For example, in some societies, physically strong, dominating individuals may be rewarded for behaving aggressively. Nevertheless, some students of aggression are very impressed by the role of testosterone in aggressive behavior. For example, Konner (1988), in a research summary which was published in a widely read newspaper, argued that degree of exposure among female mice to intra-

---

Box 12-1 Genetics and Crime

Wilson and Herrnstein (1985) conceive of criminal behavior as "criminality"—a syndrome of traits thought to characterize persons who commit crimes—and then inquire into the factors that are correlated with it. They concluded from a review of over a thousand diverse studies (done mostly in the industrialized part of the world) that genetic and biopsychological variables are at least as important as sociological ones in predisposing individuals to become criminal. Specifically, they spotlight low intelligence and "impulsivity" as predisposing factors, arguing, for example, that individuals of low intelligence are less aware of long-range consequences, less willing to defer gratification, and less able to restrict impulsivity, and, hence, more likely to tend toward criminality. The Wilson and Herrnstein argument is one version of a biological explanation of aggressive behavior in which intelligence and impulsivity are construed as genetically determined characteristics that in turn predispose individuals to commit criminal acts. But the mere fact that IQ scores and crime are correlated is, of course, subject to several possible explanations, many of which have little or nothing to do with genetics.

uterine testosterone related to their tendency to fight. Acknowledging that comparable experimental evidence for humans does not exist, Konner turned instead to "clinical studies" involving human fetuses exposed to hormones "that have effects similar to those of testosterone" that showed that they are "more aggressive than their same-sex siblings, as indicated by a paper and pencil test." We will return to this particular set of biological factors later in this chapter.

By including a concern for biology in our conceptual framework, we mean that it is reasonable to expect that certain biological factors, including but not exclusively genetic ones, will predispose individuals to react in particular ways to particular runs of experiences they might have in their lifetimes. But this makes it all the more important to conduct research on those experiential factors. The known biological facts regarding aggression cry out for elucidation through research on the cultural factors that mediate between biology and aggressive behavior.

Social-Learning Possibilities

In any social-learning theory, aggression is considered an outcome of learning from others, primarily through socialization and enculturation, involving both teaching and learning by observation. Systematic variations in aggression that relate to specifiable ecocultural variations would support social-learning theories, but such support would not constitute evidence against biological contributions to aggression. The issue is not one of nature versus nurture, since both biology and learning can interact and contribute singly or jointly.[3]

A social-learning approach predicts cross-cultural variation in parental responses to infants when they display—as do all infants—what has been termed proto-aggressive behavior (Segall, 1976, p. 201). Such behavior includes the intense, diffuse thrashings about, crying, and struggling that are characteristic of the relatively helpless infant's mode of signalling needs. When those needs (for water, food, relief from discomfort, etc.) are tended to, the infantile behavior that induced the parental caretaking is also rewarded and thereby strengthened. If infants in some societies receive more reinforcement for their proto-aggressive behavior, and if such variation is correlated with variation in strength of aggressive behavior in older children, social-learning theory thereby garners support.

Variations in the training of older children also interest social-learning

---

[3]See the discussion in Chapter 1, based on the work of Boyd & Richerson (1985) and Campbell (1965, 1975), of the analogous features of biological evolution ("nature") and cultural evolution ("nurture").

theorists. If cultural differences in degree of parental consistency in social-ization are correlated with variations in overt aggression by the children, this would be in accord with a social-learning theory that views inconsistent reinforcement schedules as frustrating and, consequently, aggression in-ducing. Because of the well-established empirical link between frustration and aggression (Caplan & Paige, 1968; Dollard et al., 1939; Miller, 1941; and Miller & Bukelski, 1948), differences across cultures in their character-istic levels of inequality of opportunity would also reveal a social-learning mechanism working at the social level.

Even more to the point are cultural variations in the use of punishment as a socialization tool. Social-learning theory and research indicate that pun-ishment, although effective in suppressing the responses that are punished, inadvertently sets the stage for subsequent aggression. Sometimes this ag-gression is directed against the punishers themselves, but more often it is against surrogate authority figures or relatively weak scapegoats. The theory predicts that cultural variations in punishment relate to cultural variations in overt aggression.

The Six Cultures study stands out as a rare, systematic cross-cultural study of aggression. It included observations of aggressive behavior by chil-dren and their parents' means of socialization of aggression, issues like those we have just reviewed.

Research in Six Cultures

Lambert (1971) reported differences across six communities (U.S., Kenyan, Indian, Mexican, Okinawan, and Philippine) in degree of parental punishment for aggression by children against other children. The Mexican parents were maximally strict, whereas the U.S. (a New England village sample) parents were maximally tolerant. This difference in socialization of childhood aggression reflected the presence or absence of close relatives. Lambert suggested that the more nearby persons with whom a family is interdependent, the less is aggression by the family's children allowed.

With regard to punishment by mothers of childhood aggression toward adults (especially toward mothers themselves), the Kenyan, Philippine, and Mexican samples scored high; the Okinawan and U.S. samples were mod-erate; and the Indian sample was relatively low. The variable that related the most strongly to variations in control of adult-directed aggression was the presence of other adults in the household.

Neither control of peer-directed aggression nor control of adult-directed aggression predicted manifest aggression by children in these six societies, however. To account for aggression, Lambert (1971) offered a two-stage theory of the shaping of aggressive dispositions. Applied to peer-directed aggression, for example, the first stage presumably makes some children in any culture more active (high social interactors) than other children. Then, in stage two the more active ones acquire whatever cultural values pertain to aggression in their particular society. Hence, in Mexico the more active children should tend to be less aggressive, but in the United States the more active children tend to be more aggressive (Lambert, 1971, p. 58).

What happens in the presumed second stage is, according to this theory, a function of the need to control aggression under conditions of high-density living. Harrington and Whiting (1972, p. 481) reiterate this idea. But, as Munroe and Munroe noted (1975, p. 103), this finding and its interpretation clash with most findings from Western settings that punitiveness breeds rather than diminishes aggression. Munroe and Munroe then reexamined findings from the Six Cultures study and were struck by the fact that in the three societies with extended-family households, children displayed more aggression. Although this fact eliminates the clash with Western findings, it raises some fascinating questions. As Munroe and Munroe aptly put it:

> The extended family not only treats aggression harshly, but also breeds aggression. Is this because, as first assumed, high density cannot easily tolerate aggression and punishes it on appearance, but the high density is stressful and produces aggression anyway? Or is it because high density cannot tolerate aggression and punishes it, and then the punishment produces aggression? Or is it perhaps because the density first produces the aggression, and the punishment is a reaction to it? [Munroe & Munroe, 1975, p. 105]

In each of the six cultures, samples of children, usually twelve boys and twelve girls, half aged 3 to 6, half aged 7 to 10, were observed in five-minute episodes outside their homes, interacting with others. Among hundreds of such episodes available for analysis, many consisted of what Lambert and Tan (1979) termed "retaliatory aggression" (responses to provocation) and many others termed "self-instigated aggression" (no apparent provocation). In all of the six cultures, approximately 30% of the children's aggressive acts were retaliatory.[4] This is true of both age groups and is consistently more true of boys than of girls. On the average, boys retaliated one third of the time when provoked; girls, one fourth of the time. Because boys tend to display retaliatory aggression more than girls, they display a higher rate of overall aggression while receiving no more attacks than girls do.

Lambert also noted that most aggressive acts by children seem instrumental in gaining some objective other than merely to hurt and that generally, except for hitting, aggressive acts do not decline with age during child-

---

[4]In an unpublished paper written in 1983, entitled "Some strong strategies in the aggression of children in six cultures," Lambert argued that children everywhere tend to learn a tit-for-tat strategy and that this accounts for the prevalence of retaliatory aggression.

hood (but as children get older, they are less likely to be aggressive in the presence of people who are older than themselves). On the other hand, there is a culture-by-age interaction, with some cultures showing less and others more overall aggression as children approach puberty (Lambert, 1981, p. 157), but this intriguing fact remains to be explained.

Such facts as these, derived from the Six Cultures study, suggest that a social-learning theory of aggression, whatever its details, is likely to be needed to account for variations in aggression across societies and, hence, for variations in individual aggression within societies as well.

Aggression and Power and Status

Many seemingly "aggressive" behaviors might better be thought of as attempts to exercise social control by means of coercion, according to an argument by Tedeschi and colleagues (Tedeschi, Smith & Brown, 1974; Tedeschi, Gaes & Rivera, 1977; Tedeschi & Melburg, 1983). If coercive acts are considered unjustified and committed with an intent to harm their target, they are likely to be judged "aggressive," but similar acts when committed by an acknowledged superior toward a subordinate might well be seen as legitimate exercise of authority and not as aggression. Since societies vary in the extent to which subordinates accept their lower status (Hofstede, 1980, 1983), cross-cultural differences in the judgment of the aggressiveness of coercive acts may be anticipated.

This line of reasoning led Bond, Wan, Leung & Giacalone (1985) to predict that Chinese students in Hong Kong and American students in Albany, New York, would respond differently to verbal insults delivered by a superior to a subordinate, with the Chinese students (whose culture, in Hofstede's [1980, 1983] terms is characterized by relatively high "power distance") less likely to characterize the insults as aggressive acts. Bond et al. (1985) also expected that because Chinese culture is more collectivistic (Triandis, 1983) than U.S. culture is, the Hong Kong students would differentiate more between in-group and out-group sources of insults, negatively sanctioning in-group insulters more than out-group insulters to a greater extent than would the students in New York.

Bond et al. (1985) presented male undergraduates in both Hong Kong and Albany with a scenario in which a manager in a company board meeting insults either a superior or a subordinate either within or outside his own department and had the undergraduates rate both the legitimacy of the insult and the personality of the insulter. These ratings were obtained both as unstructured responses (e.g., free responses describing actions that should be taken before the next meeting and characterizations of the insulter's behavior) and as structured responses to a 16-item bipolar rating scale.

The hypothesis that markers of status and group membership would be more influential in determining the response of the higher power distance/ higher collectivism Chinese students was confirmed. For example, for the Chinese students, the high-status, in-group insulter was perceived as less unlikable and his acts as less illegitimate than the Americans perceived them. The prediction, however, that among the Chinese, insults from in-group members would be disparaged more than those from out-group members was not confirmed. In this high collectivist society, it appeared that insults within the group are acceptable whereas insults directed beyond the group are not. Most important, however, among the Chinese subjects in this study, insults from a higher- to lower-status member of a group are not seen as aggressive but rather as justified, legitimate, and acceptable.

This brief review of some relevant studies suggests that systematic cross-cultural analysis of socialization practices, ecocultural antecedents, institutionalized expressions of aggression, and other potentially related variables is necessary if we are to understand aggression.

Cultural Factors Relating to Crime

One manifestation of aggression that has received some attention cross-culturally is crime. Criminal behavior includes many kinds of acts and reflects many different motives, including greed, genuine need, compensation for low self-esteem, and probably many others. But most acts that are socially defined as criminal involve the infliction of harm on others, so they satisfy our working definition of aggression. Like other aggressive behaviors, criminal acts occur in all societies.

Landau (1984) examined statistics on criminal acts of violence in Interpol reports, UN documents, and various national statistical yearbooks relating to a dozen nations (Austria, Denmark, Finland, India, Israel, Japan, the Netherlands, New Zealand, Norway, Sweden, Switzerland, the United States, and West Germany) for more than a decade spanning the mid-1960s through the late 1970s. During that period, all but one of these nations reported either stable or increasing homicide rates and robbery rates (Japan was the exception, about which we shall comment later). Landau's primary use of these data was to provide a preliminary test of a sociological-level model derived from frustration-aggression theory, involving social stressors, measures of social support, and measures of violence and aggression. The model predicts that the probability of violence and aggression as reactions to stress will increase when social-support systems fail or malfunction. Using inflation rates as his major measure of social stress (he also used psychiatric admissions for the few countries for which information was available), and ratio between marriage and divorce rates as a social-support/

stress measure (another was rates of births to unmarried mothers, available for only five countries), Landau (1984) found parallels in changes of these various indices in every country but Japan, which led him to conclude, "Over the time period covered by this study, the increase in social stress (as measured by inflation rates) and the parallel weakening of the family as a social support system, was accompanied in almost all the countries by an increase in most measures of violence and aggression" (p. 152).

In Japan, which deviated from this finding, an increase in social stress (as indexed by inflation) and a decrease in the strength of the family was accompanied by a considerable increase in suicide. Landau suggested that strong social-control mechanisms beyond the family exist in Japan, notably in schools, local communities, and work places. He also cited the fact of much citizen participation in crime prevention in collaboration with professional law enforcement agents in Japan, and three important social-control mechanisms embedded in Japanese cultural phenomena: a strong sense of shame, a sense of duty and loyalty, and respect for human relations. Switzerland was another partial exception in this sample; there, whereas measures of aggression and violence also increased, the greatest increase was in suicide rate.

Although Landau's primary interest in this (1984) study was his model linking stress, social control, and aggression, we can find in his data some notable differences across the sample countries in levels of crime rates. These cross-country differences, of course, must be interpreted very cautiously, since record keeping varies so much across countries. Still, information provided by Landau's data sources is very interesting. For example, some countries had relatively high and fairly consistently increasing homicide rates (Finland, Israel, USA, and West Germany), whereas others had relatively low and stable homicide rates (Austria, Switzerland, England, Netherlands, Sweden, Norway, Denmark, and India), and Japan had both a low and declining homicide rate. So, as noted earlier, although criminal acts occur in all societies, it is also true that societies vary in their crime rates. That this appears even in a sample like that used by Landau (1984), composed primarily of industrialized nations, all containing similar social stressors and experiencing declines in certain social-support systems, suggests that other variables must be implicated in the story of cultural influences on crime. As we move on, it might be well to keep in mind that what Landau called social stress was really a measure of family strength (the ratio of marriage to divorce rates), for we are about to see that whether a family is intact or broken may have much to do with crime and other forms of aggression.

The Landau (1984) study of crime concerned contemporary industrial nations. What do we know about crime in nonindustrialized societies? Bacon, Child and Barry (1963), beginning with a sample of 110 mostly nonindustrial societies, found 48 for whom ethnographic information in the Human Relations Area Files was adequate to permit reliable ratings of criminal behavior. They examined correlates of crime in general, correlates of theft, and correlates of crimes against persons. Their most striking finding was that both subcategories of crime — and hence crime in general — were more frequent in societies in which opportunity for contact between child and father is minimal (for example, societies with polygynous mother/ child households).

The Bacon team related this finding to the tendency of most crimes to be committed by males and to findings (Whiting, Kluckhohn & Anthony, 1958; Burton & Whiting, 1961) concerning cross-sex identification problems in "low-male-salience" societies. They offered their finding as support for a hypothesis that crime is partly a defense reaction against initial feminine identification in males. Such a hypothesis has been favored by several students of crime and delinquency in the United States (see, for example, Glueck & Glueck, 1950; Rohrer & Edmonson, 1960). It is impressive to find supportive evidence for such a mechanism in a broad cross-cultural sample.

Other findings of Bacon and associates were concerned with the distinguishing correlates of theft on the one hand and personal crime on the other. Three social characteristics — "level of political integration, social stratification, and elaboration of social control" (all considered to be indexes of a highly differentiated status system) — were positively correlated with theft and unrelated to personal crime. Also, the greater the value attached to personal property in a society, the more likely was the occurrence of theft (Bacon et al., 1963, p. 297). Personal crime was found to be correlated with several child-training emphases, for example, severity of punishment, that together the authors viewed as indexes of childhood experiences conducive to the development of attitudes of rivalry, distrust, and hostility (p. 298). Thus, two different forms of crime were shown over a sample of 48 societies to have their unique correlates as well as a common relationship with factors likely to encourage compensatory efforts to establish masculine identity. The Bacon et al. study, then, yielded support for a social-learning interpretation of aggression, one that takes into account some possible consequences of gender.

GENDER, SOCIAL LEARNING, AND AGGRESSION

In the preceding section of this chapter, we found reason to expect that a social-learning theory would contribute to our understanding of aggression. We also learned some facts from cross-cultural research about maleness and aggression and we were introduced to the idea that masculine identity (how manly one considers oneself to be) may play a role in aggressive behavior. In this section, we shall concentrate on material that relates to the social learning that leads to gender identity and to possible linkages between gender and aggression.

As we recalled at the very outset of this chapter, on the average around the world, males consistently display more aggression than do females. Let us now take a closer look at this phenomenon.

In her review of many cross-cultural studies dealing with sex differences, the anthropologist Carol Ember (1981) noted, "The most consistent and most documented cross-cultural difference in interpersonal behavior appears to be that boys exhibit more aggression after age 3 or so" (p. 551). This is true in the United States (Maccoby, 1966; Maccoby & Jacklin, 1974), in the several societies studied in the Six Cultures study (Whiting & Whiting, 1975), and in 10 of 14 societies for which ethnographic reports on aggression by young children (2 to 6 years) were examined by Rohner (1976). In fact, in Rohner's survey of these societies, either males clearly out-aggressed females or no difference was detectable. It is virtually impossible to find a society in which young girls are more aggressive than young boys.

With regard to criminal behavior, the findings are consistent with the conclusion that males are the more aggressive sex. As we saw in the preceding section, Bacon et al. (1963) presented data from 48 nonindustrialized societies showing that males commit the preponderance of criminal acts. In the United States, it has long been the case that the best predictor of fluctuations in crime rates is the proportion of adolescent males in the population. As Goldstein (1983) has noted, "The 1960–1975 increase in violent crime and the stabilization of the crime rate since 1975 parallel directly the number of 14–24 year-old males in the United States" (1983, p. 439).

So, there is a correlation between sex and aggression and it exists across most societies. There is also a relationship between age and aggression. The quote from Goldstein's (1983) paper not only says that males account for a disproportionate number of violent crimes, it also singles out a particular age group — 18- to 24-year-olds. So the perpetrators of most crimes in the United States are best described as male adolescents. In at least one other industrialized society, Japan, we find the same phenomenon. There, from 1966 through 1979, 14- to 24-year-olds outnumbered 25- to 39-year-olds by between three to one and four to one in arrests (Goldstein & Ibaraki, 1983, p. 317). Similar findings prevail in other industrialized societies, as summarized in Newmann's (1979) profile of the most typical violent individuals: 15- to 30-year-old males, with lower socioeconomic status, living in urban areas, and disproportionately likely to be a member of an ethnic group that is low in the social hierarchy in the country. Naroll (1983) compiled "Juvenile Criminal Ratios" for 42 such societies (e.g., West Germany, New Zealand, Australia, etc.). In all of these societies, at least a quarter and as many as half of all reported crimes were committed by adolescent males (Naroll, 1983, p. 389).

Thus we have cross-cultural evidence for a pan-species generalization about aggression. Males of the species perform most aggressive acts and they are most likely to do so as they move from childhood toward adulthood. What should we make of this?

A Biosocial Answer

A biological fact that may be very relevant to our understanding of the high frequency of aggressive behavior among male adolescents is that (as we saw earlier in this chapter) circulating testosterone is related to dominance behavior (Mazur, 1976). In a later paper, Mazur (1985) explicitly linked testosterone to male adolescent behavior: "As young primate males pass through adolescence, they often become more assertive with posturing and strutting that may be labeled "macho" in human terms. . . . they move rapidly up the group hierarchy, taking their place among the adult males. These changes may be a consequence of the massive increase in testosterone production that occurs during puberty" (p. 383). Since there is a surge of male testosterone at adolescence, that alone may produce an intensification of dominance-striving behavior among male adolescents, and if that behavior includes aggressive acts (which constitute one possible form of asserting dominance over others), then a sex-linked, age-related hormonal phenomenon could account for male adolescent aggression.

The validity of this answer depends on how closely dominance and aggression are linked. Konner (1988) argued that the link is very close. "It has become increasingly obvious that male-female differences in tendency to do physical harm are intrinsic, fundamental, in a word, biological" (1988, p. 33). But we don't believe that it is as simple as that.

Mazur's (1976) review included some evidence that testosterone-produced differences in early development made males both more dominant and more aggressive, but Mazur (1985) concluded that dominance and aggression are not inextricably linked. In the course of presenting a model of competition for status, which emphasizes long-term changes in testosterone, Mazur (1985) noted that the literature links testosterone and *dominance* behavior and that it is important to distinguish dominance behavior from aggressive behavior, a distinction that is particularly important for humans, "who often assert their dominance without any intent to cause injury" (p. 382).[5]

---

[5]Mazur also notes that at present there are no firm data on the effect of testosterone on dominance in humans. Also, the causal link between testosterone and dominance behavior may be in the opposite direction, with success in status competition producing an increase in testosterone. So, he refers to the relationship between testosterone and dominance behavior as "reciprocal" (1985, p. 383).

Like Mazur, we believe that dominance striving by male adolescents includes many nonaggressive behaviors (e.g., displaying expertise at games, problem-solving, acquiring valued goods, demonstrating sexual prowess, and more) and that whether it includes aggressive acts probably depends, in the end, on cultural norms. Even Konner grants a role to culture, when he says, "Is there no contribution of culture, then, to the consistent male excess in violence? Of course there is; but it acts on an organism already primed for the sex difference. Cultures can dampen or exaggerate it. The role of modeling in encouraging aggression is well proved" (Konner, 1988, p. 34). Later, we will develop our own version of an explanation for the sex difference in aggression that involves an interaction between biology and culture.

Concerning modes of communicating dominance, Mazur notes that among humans, "violent threat and attack is discouraged in most modern societies as a mode of allocating status, but it is still common among certain subgroups, such as adolescent males, where there are culturally specific norms that govern fights" (Mazur, 1985, p. 390). In any event, whether testosterone produces both dominance and aggression or merely dominance that is sometimes socially encouraged to be expressed through aggression, there is good reason to consider biological (more specifically, hormonal) forces as being implicated in male adolescent aggression.

A Strictly Cultural Answer

There would be a very simple answer to the question of why most aggressive acts are committed by male adolescents (an answer that leaves out biology altogether) if cross-cultural research showed that in most societies boys are encouraged more than girls to behave aggressively. Then we could say that male adolescents are more aggressive simply because they have been taught to be. But, as we shall now see, this answer is too simple.

Barry, Josephson, Lauer, and Marshall (1976) scored nearly 150 societies drawn from the Standard Cross-Cultural Sample (Murdock & White, 1969) on inculcation (deliberate teaching and encouragement) of aggression among children. They found a sex difference on the average over all of these societies—more inculcation of aggression for boys than for girls—with this average sex difference more marked during later childhood. But the sex difference was significant in only one out of five of these societies when they were examined singly; in the others it was either very small or nonexistent. So we cannot account for the cross-cultural consistency in greater male aggressive behavior *solely* on the basis of differences in inculcation of aggression.

Other factors must be implicated in the phenomenon of greater aggressive behaviors among males than merely their hormones or the fact that generally they are subjected to more inculcation of aggression than are females. It is to these other factors that we now turn.

An Expanded Biocultural Model

Earlier, when we considered the role of testosterone and dominance in the story of male aggression, we suggested that whatever biological mechanisms are involved, they probably interact with cultural mechanisms. Now, we shall consider some of these cultural mechanisms. As already noted, they must be more complex than inculcation alone. They include (a) division of labor by sex, (b) gender identity, and (c) aggressive behavior that serves a gender-marking function. Each of these, and the relationship among them, will be dealt with in turn.

Division of Labor by Sex

Every society has some division of labor by sex. We saw this in Chapter 11, where we considered some of the implications of this cultural universal. Recall that every society has not only some kind of division of labor by sex but also some modal sex differences in behavior (Munroe & Munroe, 1957, p. 116) and that these two phenomena are linked in many ways. Most pertinent is the notion, expressed most clearly by Barry, Bacon, and Child (1957), that the division of labor by sex sets the stage for differentiation between the sexes in socialization emphases and that this differentiation in turn functions as a means for preparing children to assume their sex-linked adult roles. Thus, the relationship between (a) division of labor by sex and (b) differentiation across the sexes in socialization emphases is a reciprocal one.

The clearest (and most nearly universal) of all sex-linked adult roles is child rearing itself. During socialization, females are taught traits that are compatible with child rearing and are later encouraged to assume that role. Males, on the other hand, are taught other traits during childhood, like independence, and are encouraged later to assume roles (e.g., food-getting) that are largely incompatible with child rearing. Consequently, females do most of the child rearing in most societies and virtually all of it in some.

Whatever the reasons for this (see Chapter 11), there results, in many societies — and perhaps in all in varying degree — a paradoxical state of affairs. Young males have somewhat restricted opportunity to observe adult males at home, since their fathers tend to be nonparticipants in the child rearing. To the extent that gender-role learning involves modeling (or learning by observation), boys will have restricted opportunity to acquire a masculine identity early in life.

Cross-Gender Identity

The cutting edge of this paradox is that father absence is most marked in societies with the sharpest division of labor by sex. Thus, precisely in those societies in which the two sexes are expected to have the most distinct gender identities, young males have restricted opportunity to acquire their masculine identity by emulation of male models!

In societies with a particularly distinct division of labor by sex (as discussed in Chapter 11, sedentary societies, those cultivating large grain crops, and those raising large animals [Van Leeuwen, 1978]), there is therefore a likelihood that young males will acquire a cross-sex identity. How ironic this is, considering that in societies where there is a relatively sharp gender-role distinctiveness, the role of women is often regarded with contempt by males, whose own activities are accorded higher prestige. Consider the pressure that adult males in such societies must face to avoid behaving "in womanly fashion." Yet their sons, we are here suggesting, are likely, during childhood, to acquire a predominantly female identity.

Gender-Marking Aggression

Recall now that the Bacon et al. (1963) study of crime was cited above as a primary source of evidence for the masculinity of aggression, showing, as it did, that males commit the preponderance of crimes in most societies. This same study also revealed that aggressive crimes, such as assaults, rapes, and murders, were more likely to occur in societies that provided exclusive mother-child sleeping arrangements, which prevail, of course, in societies where fathers are not active participants in child rearing. Bacon et al. related this finding to the idea of "cross-sex identity" that had been introduced earlier (e.g., by Whiting, Kluckhohn & Anthony, 1958, and Burton & Whiting, 1961) as a likely problem to be found in "low male-salience" societies. Applying this idea to crime, Bacon et al. offered the hypothesis that aggressive crimes are part of a defense reaction against initial feminine identification in males. Long ago, a similar hypothesis was hinted at by students of crime and delinquency in the United States (see, for example, Glueck & Glueck, 1950; Rohrer & Edmonson, 1960).

Extending the Bacon et al. hypothesis, Beatrice Whiting (1965) suggested that males reared primarily by females would be more susceptible to envy of powerful adult males but could not become like them until escaping somehow from the early influence of their mothers. Examining her anthropological field notes (which later became part of the Six Cultures study, Whiting & Whiting, 1975), she found two of her societies, Khalapur in India and Nyasongo in Kenya, to be particularly interesting. In both of these societies, husbands and wives do not regularly eat, sleep, work, or relax together. Both societies are characterized by relative father absence and higher male prestige. Both have a tradition of extolling warriors and cattle raiders, and, most important, both have high rates of physical assault and homicide.

Whiting linked the young males' status envy to what she called "protest masculinity." Observantly she suggested, "It would seem as if there were a never-ending cycle. The separation of the sexes leads to a conflict of identity of the boy children, to unconscious fear of being feminine, . . . exaggeration of the difference between men and women, antagonism against and fear of women, male solidarity and hence to isolation of women and very young children" (Whiting, 1965, p. 137).

What do societies that produce this identity conflict do about it?

Making Men Out of Boys

The identity conflict designated by Whiting would obviously constitute a problem for societies that encourage sharply distinguished gender roles. In some such societies, the problem is dealt with in an institutionalized manner, namely, by male initiation ceremonies. Severe male initiation ceremonies at puberty, often including tests of endurance and manliness, were found by Whiting, Kluckhohn, and Anthony (1958) to be correlated with exclusive mother-son sleeping arrangements and postpartum sex taboos, both indices of father absence. The interpretation of this finding that is pertinent to our present discussion is that such ceremonies serve the function of stamping in masculinity for boys who need it because of inadequate opportunity to acquire it in childhood.

What happens, however, in societies which have this identity conflict but lack the initiation ceremony? To answer this question, let us now pull together most of the ideas we have discussed on the last few pages.

Compensatory Machoism

We suggest that in societies that have the preconditions requiring a stamping-in of masculinity, but which don't achieve this through initiation ceremonies or other institutionalized practices, adolescent males will try on their own to assert their masculinity. They may do so in a variety of ways, but one of them might well be to behave aggressively. If a society is one in which aggressiveness and such allied traits as fortitude and courage are an integral part of the definition of manliness, boys approaching manhood will wish to display these characteristics.

They may have been taught and encouraged to behave this way, but as we have seen, in addition to whatever inculcation may have occurred during childhood, a structural feature of such a society can set the stage for the boys' need to acquire these behaviors and traits during adolescence. This structural feature is a sharply defined division of labor by sex, with child rearing assigned primarily or even exclusively to mothers, resulting in relative father absence during the boys' childhood. That in turn leads to cross-sex identity during childhood that has to be undone by displays of "manly " behaviors and traits, notably fortitude, courage, and aggression.

We call the resultant aggression "compensatory machoism" to underscore that it is rooted not in anger but in a felt need to escape from womanliness and to mark one's masculine gender.[6] In other words, such aggression has the function of displaying that the actor is behaving like an adult male, in accord with that society's definition of the masculine gender.

An Illustration of Compensatory Machoism in the United States

We can find what is perhaps the most striking example of compensatory machoism as a cultural phenomenon in the United States. In the mid 1980s, the American Bureau of Justice reported statistics that revealed that a black man in America stands a 1-in-21 chance of being murdered in his lifetime (compared with 1 in 131 for white men and 1 in 369 for white women). And, as one reporter who defined himself as a black male in his twenties and hence "part of the endangered group" noted, "Currently, about 95% of murdered black males between 15 and 34 are killed by other young black males" (Sargent, 1986).

Trying to make sense out of this epidemic, for that it surely is, with murder being the leading cause of death of young black males in America, Sargent pointed to conditions that prevail in inner-city neighborhoods, where "impoverished, idle, hostile and ill-educated" young men must exhibit anger or toughness as a "primary survival technique." "You must walk angry, talk angry, think angry." In these urban ghettos, notes Sargent, "you're either a chump or a champ. . . . You're macho or gay."

The young males who seem so predisposed to kill can be characterized, according to Sargent, as unemployed, poor, and subscribing to the ideology that masculinity means having a dominant male social role. Among the many things that need to be done to solve this problem, including, of course, teaching conflict resolution skills, improving access to meaningful education, and providing attractive employment, Sargent gives prominence to, as we would, the need to "change conceptions of masculinity." But since conceptions of masculinity are rooted in the culture and reinforced by economic and social conditions such as unemployment, educational deficits, and racial discrimination, all of which contribute to a prevalence of broken homes, with female-headed households almost a norm in some ghettos, it is clear that compensatory machoism will prevail until, as Sargent put it, people in the United States "look at the tragedy as the national crisis that it is."

The ways in which cultural norms regarding "manly" behavior can affect an individual in the United States was revealed in a poignant account by a journalist who described himself as an only child in an upper-middle-class

---

[6]This concept, compensatory machoism, is clearly derived from Whiting's notion of "protest masculinity", which was discussed earlier in this chapter. Both concepts are concerned with attempts to resolve cross-sex identity problems. Compensatory machoism further specifies that these attempts will include aggression by adolescent males, especially in societies lacking gender-marking rituals.

black American family. "Why didn't I fight back?" he asked himself repeatedly about an incident during his youth when, as an army private he was
viciously attacked by a white soldier while lying asleep in his barracks bunk
(Wormley, 1985). Although he didn't fight back (because, he stated, he had
been raised in a "sheltered world" of middle-class culture, in which violence
was deplored), the author offered the opinion that the majority of American
men would have because, as he suggested, "The ability and the will to fight
back are integral parts of our society's conception of manhood. . . .
Fighting back . . . involves the adoption of an attitude that one's retribution is morally justified — or even, at times, morally obligatory."

Wormley further suggested that this attitude is especially salient for members of minority groups. Reflecting on how he had been contemptuously
confronted by a fellow black soldier on his failure to retaliate, Wormley
commented, "To Morris, I had disgraced the entire black American population." When, many years later, he hit a man who had made a racist remark
in a roadside restaurant, he first sensed a "feeling of exultation," but this was
followed by "shame and sadness" that he, too, had succumbed to the cultural norm that encourages manly retribution. Wormley's article was a contribution to *The New York Times*' regular feature column "About Men."
That this important American newspaper runs such a feature is evidence
that gender is a significant concern in contemporary American culture.

Other Cultural Contributions to Aggression

The social-learning approach to aggression that we are taking in this
chapter attributes much to learning by observation, or modeling. Obviously,
then, those societies that provide more aggressive models should, according
to this theoretical approach, encourage more aggression.[7] This proposition
has received much study, particularly in the United States, where many
social scientists have addressed the question of the impact of violence in the
media, especially films and television (see, for example, Chaffee & McLeod,
1971; Eron & Huesman, 1982; Lefkowitz, Eron, Walder & Huesman, 1977;
Liebert, Neale & Davidson, 1973; and Milgram & Shotland, 1973). The
prevailing view among social scientists who have studied the effects of the
massive diet of violence that exists in the American media is that those
viewers who are most prone to aggression (such as the young males we have

---

[7]Some thoughtful readers might detect an apparent contradiction in our argument in this
chapter. If the availability of aggressive models increases aggression, why did we argue earlier
that the *absence* of adult males can increase aggression in their sons? The contradiction is
removed when it is recalled that the father absence of which we spoke occurs during early
childhood and that its effect is to set the stage for later learning of aggression by various means
including, as we are now stressing, emulating aggressive models.

described above) find encouragement and tutelage from television and films. Those who control the media in that culture, the television network executives and the film producers, tend to resist the conclusion that the media make a causal contribution to the problem of aggression in America and wherever else American films and television programs appear, but that conclusion is hard to avoid.

Groebel (1986) has reviewed studies done in other societies where media effects on aggression have been examined. Groebel found in a study done in Australia, where government officials monitor television programs in an effort to minimize violent content, that although there was evidence of overall smaller effects than typically found in U.S. studies, boys who identified with aggressive male television characters were those who themselves displayed aggressive behavior. In Finland, where no locally produced programs contain any violence but imported U.S. programs do, it is generally the case, according to Groebel, that viewers perceive what violence they see as characteristic of the United States but not of Finland and are therefore less likely to emulate it. But again, Groebel finds evidence in some Finnish data provided by Lagerspetz and Viemero (1986) that boys who identify with male television models find encouragement to develop their own aggressiveness. Groebel also cited data from Israel, Poland, the Netherlands, and West Germany, and concluded that in all of these societies the impact of media violence on aggressive behavior is less than in the United States because other factors (e.g., cultural norms, parental training) interact with the medial violence to produce varying degrees of inhibition of aggression.

It appears to be the case, then, that whereas media violence can contribute to aggression in any given society, the extent to which it does depends on the cultural context in which the media violence is made available. Like any single cultural variable, media violence interacts with other cultural variables to produce a complex effect. To understand its effect, additional cross-cultural research is clearly needed.

CONCLUSIONS

In this chapter, we presented a framework for studying human aggression cross-culturally. The several studies we described that we believe fit into this framework make it clear that we cannot understand human aggression without viewing it from a cross-cultural perspective. Although biology is surely implicated, it is dangerously incorrect to conclude that aggression is simply instinctive. Our biology interacts with our culturally shaped experiences to lead us to react to frustration, to assert dominance, and to attempt to resolve conflicts in a wide variety of ways.

We saw in this chapter that societies vary in their characteristic levels of aggression. We saw, too, that individuals vary in their aggressive habits. A pan-species generalization concerning individual variation is that male adolescents tend to be the kinds of individuals who aggress the most. Because the evidence reviewed in this chapter does not support the view that it is inevitable that male adolescents will aggress, there is hope that the pervasive amount of aggression that presently characterizes the world may be reduced, but only if we become more knowledgeable about the experiential factors, rooted in culture, that presently encourage so many people to aggress.

Part IV
CULTURES IN FLUX AND CULTURES IN CONTACT

In the research reviewed in previous chapters, culture was, for the most part, treated as if it were merely "there," one culture per society, serving as an unchanging context in which individual behaviors are acquired and shaped, through socialization and enculturation. Viewed as such, culture—we must now confess—is a convenient fiction.

As we have seen throughout the earlier parts of this book, it is useful for psychologists to treat a particular complex of cultural facts as if it were a fixed state of affairs, a particular ecocultural setting, influencing the behavior of all persons living in it. Most of the principles thus far stated in this book linking culture and behavior are exemplified by such statements as, "If a society *has* a particular set of values, then certain behaviors are likely to be characteristic of its members." But the fact is, all cultures are continuously in flux. Values and other culturally based social stimuli don't stay put anywhere. Every culture is ever changing.

In much of the research examined earlier, the pictures of culture that we employed were mostly stills, which froze the action, enabling the researcher to relate some cultural facts to some behavioral phenomena. Now our interest shifts to what might be revealed by motion pictures, which would enable us to relate changes in culture to changes in behavior. Rather than depicting *states*, our intent now is to focus on *process*.

In the course of examining the process of cultural change, we will consider some of the forces that produce it. Some of those forces derive from contact between cultures. Of these, many are embodied in educational systems in both Third-World countries and industrialized nations.

The story of changing cultures, in contact with each other, and the effects of education in reshaping societies will be told in the two chapters that constitute Part IV of this book.

Chapter 13 will deal with the psychological antecedents and consequences of culture change in a broad, general, and comprehensive manner. In Chapter 14, we will consider how societies relate to one another and how those relations might, according to cross-cultural psychological theory, be improved.

Finally, Chapter 15 offers some conclusions derived from all that has been presented in this introductory text in cross-cultural psychology.

Chapter 13

Cultural Change and Modernization

WHY STUDY CULTURAL CHANGE?

In this chapter we will discuss the potentially modernizing impact on individuals of changes in their sociocultural environment. In Chapter 1, we encountered *en*culturation — the process that links developing individuals to their cultural contexts. Here, we introduce *ac*culturation to indicate the influences on individuals of *changing* cultural contexts. The term *acculturation* often implies contact with other cultures. The causes of cultural change are both internal and external, however. Contributing factors include intercultural contact, diffusion of ideas and artifacts across cultures (when technologies or institutions that began in one culture spread to others), and innovation and invention within a single culture. This chapter deals with individual reaction to cultural change, whatever its origins.

The study of cultural change and modernization needs no lengthy justification. Because the goal of cross-cultural psychological research is to discover how human behavior is shaped by culture, study of the impact of *changing* cultures on individuals could be a fruitful strategy for testing basic propositions relating culture and behavior. (It is noteworthy that when the *Journal of Cross-Cultural Psychology* published its first special issue devoted to a single topic [Vol. 8, No. 2, June 1977], that topic was the psychological aspects of culture change.) Furthermore, because a majority of the world's societies (the so-called developing nations) are undergoing rapid social and economic change, much of it planned and striven for, it is of obvious practical interest (as well as theoretical) to study how people bring change about and adjust to it.

As Kelman (1968) argued, social change should be studied also in industrial societies "because the forces toward social change . . . manifest themselves wherever there are populations that have been excluded from effective participation in the political process, from a share in the benefits of the national economy, and from meaningful roles in the social structure" (p. 15). Moreover, all societies experience economic and social changes that may require adjustments from everyone.

PRELIMINARY GENERALIZATIONS CONCERNING INDIVIDUAL REACTIONS TO CULTURAL CHANGE

All cultures are always changing, sometimes rapidly, sometimes imperceptibly. Though we may speak of modern nations on the one hand and developing nations on the other, all societies are modernizing. Institutions change, technologies are modified, ideologies are amended. As these change, so do the persons who both invent and respond to them. Hence, acculturation is as fundamental a phenomenon in human existence as is enculturation. Not only is every one of us shaped by the traditional norms and teachings that prevail in our culture (socialization and enculturation), each of us is subjected to lifelong changing influences.

Most research on how cultures change has been concerned with effects that spread across cultures. Acculturation in the context of intercultural contact is covered in detail in Chapter 12 of Berry et al. (in press), but a brief summary of some important generalizations about such acculturation is included here.

Individuals within the culture in which some innovation was born *and* individuals in other societies to which it may have diffused are both subject to acculturation. Our first generalization, then, is that *cultural change and acculturation are universal and may be studied anywhere.*

All societies in the world today are in contact with other societies. None exists in complete isolation from ideas, institutions, technologies, or values that originated elsewhere. All such cultural aspects are widely dispersed by immigrants, tourists, missionaries, business people, guest workers, diplomats, films, literature, and numerous other culture carriers. Our second generalization is that *culture contact is a major source of acculturation everywhere.*

The spread of cultural elements among societies is a two-way process. Host cultures influence their visitors and are influenced by them. A study of acculturation should take into account the reciprocal influences that result from cultural contacts. Therefore, our third generalization is that *cultures influence each other.*

Although societies in contact influence each other, the influence is usually uneven. Often, one society dominates. If there is a power differential, influence is relatively one-sided. In interactions between societies in recent centuries, power has resided mostly with Western, industrialized nations. Consequently, as Berry et al. (in press) show, studies of acculturation have concentrated on the influence of industrialized societies on subcultural groups within them and on persons in nonindustrial nations. Our fourth generalization, then, is that *acculturative pressures flow in an unbalanced way, reflecting power differences across cultures.* Hence, many acculturation studies are done in Third-World settings and are conceptualized as studies of behavioral changes moving from "traditional" to "modern."

The precontact characteristics of a society may condition its members' typical response to acculturative pressure. Whether (and, if so, why) some societies are more resistant to cultural contact than others has been a major topic in acculturation studies. The fifth generalization is that *among relatively low-power, so-called traditional societies, some may be more susceptible to acculturative pressures than others.*

A corollary to the fifth generalization concerns individual differences within societies in susceptibility to acculturative pressures. Not all individuals in societies experiencing acculturative pressures are equally affected by them. Nor is it the case that among those who are affected all of their behavior changes. Much of the research discussed in this chapter consists of efforts to measure and account for such individual differences.

AN ACCULTURATION MODEL AND SOME THEORIES OF THE MODERNIZING PROCESS

Figure 13-1 depicts key variables that are typically examined in the study of cultural change and modernization. This framework provides a way of conceptualizing the complex relationships among ecological, social, cultural, and behavioral variables involved in these processes. The focus of the framework is the individual whose *psychological acculturation* consists of behavioral changes and adaptations to the sometimes competing forces impinging on him or her. Psychological acculturation is a term coined by Graves (1967) to refer to the changes that an individual experiences as a result of participating in the process of (societal-level) acculturation that his cultural or ethnic group is undergoing.

This framework distinguishes between two levels: the *population* (ecological, cultural, social, and institutional at the left) and the *individual* (the behaviors and traits of persons, at the right). At the population level, ac-

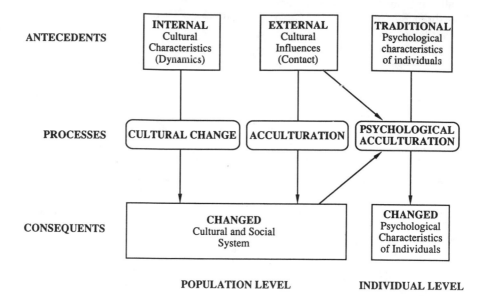

FIGURE 13-1. Relationships studied in acculturation research

culturation consists of changes in social structure, economic base, and political organization, and at the individual level, psychological acculturation involves changes in identity, values, attitudes, and behaviors. Moreover, not every acculturating individual participates in the collective changes that are underway in his group to the same extent or in the same way. So, to understand the psychological concomitants and consequences of cultural change, we need to assess population-level acculturation, participation in it by individuals, and the psychological impact it has on them.

The framework distinguishes also between antecedents and consequences, which are shown in the framework as the outcomes of events flowing downward from the antecedents. Reverse influences can and do occur, as when individuals change and by so doing influence their society to change further, but these are assumed, rather than depicted, in Figure 13-1.

Although many disciplines (including anthropology, international-development studies, rural sociology, economics, and political science) have been working for a long time at the population level of Figure 13-1, the task has fallen mainly to cross-cultural psychology to study the individual level, and its relationship to the population level.

Culture Contact

An emigrant going to set up a new life in another country offers an example of external cultural contact followed by both cultural and individual changes. The decision to emigrate is often based on some prior contact with and knowledge of the target country. Perhaps members of the person's own family have already settled in the new country and have written home about it. Perhaps its language is being taught as a foreign language in the home-country schools, and perhaps, through the mass media, depictions of the way of life in the new country have become familiar. So, even before leaving home, the individual is changing because of contact with aspects of another culture, at least with respect to motivation, as reflected in the decision to migrate. Upon actual immigration, once in the new country, there can be some dramatic contact experiences and subsequent, far-reaching psychological reactions.

Consider next the case of a person whose country and culture have been colonized. Here, there is no choice to enter or not enter into cultural contact. Thus, motivation to acculturate before the contact very likely was not present. Once the contact starts, individuals (and, indeed, whole communities) may vary in how they deal with it. Some may turn their backs, others may embrace the colonial culture (or whatever part of it is made accessible), whereas yet others may selectively engage the new, while merging it with the old.

In these, and in many other kinds of cases, the intercultural contact and the individual psychological responses will be related to each other. Cross-cultural psychology examines these relationships, seeks to understand them, and aims to produce empirically supported generalizations about the processes involved in psychological responses to culture contacts. Research on the psychological effects of culture contact, as was noted earlier, is discussed in detail in Chapter 12 of Berry et al. (in press). Research on the effects of cultural change, whatever its origins, is our concern in the present chapter.

Cultural Change

Individual behavior and personality changes constitute the internal dynamics of cultural change. Numerous studies have tried to measure the degree to which individual behaviors in the context of a changing culture are either traditional or modern in character. Other studies treat individual traits as qualities that predispose individuals either to change or to resist it. We will review some studies, arranged according to theoretically different ways of thinking about relations involving individuals and cultural change.

Some Modernization Theories

Theories of modernization are attempts to conceptualize, in greater detail than we did in the model shown in Figure 13-1, the relationship between cultural and individual changes. Godwin (1974) noted that the theories employed in modernization studies tend to treat individual personality traits either as independent, mediating, or dependent variables in the process of societal modernization. In other words, some theories consider the individual primarily as a contributor to cultural change, others as an intermediate actor between prior cultural forces and subsequent cultural changes, and still others as the recipient of the effects of cultural change. Of course, all three of these are part of the total picture; we will examine examples of each kind.

Personality as the Independent Variable in Modernization

Some theorists emphasize the presumed necessity for certain individually held attitudes, values, motives, or other dispositions to exist before modernizing behavior — and hence societal modernization — can occur. Such theorists usually acknowledge the need for certain economic resources before modernization can occur. But they stress that without certain psychological attributes in good supply, modernization will not take place.

Achievement Motivation. McClelland (1961) argued that a society must have a sufficiently high level of N_{Ach} for economic development characteristic of modern industrial society to take place. He initiated a program of research, resulting in considerable support for his contention. Early findings showed successful entrepreneurs to have been high in N_{Ach} years before their business success was noted (see, for example, McClelland, 1965). McClelland then predicted that any society should develop economically to the degree that it possesses persons with high N_{Ach}. Research by McClelland and others that examines this idea is described in Box 13-1.

McClelland found support for his proposition that a high level of achievement motivation precedes economic growth. The data, derived from analyses of such diverse collective products as literature and ceramics, at least suggest that the production of achievement themes does precede economic growth, in some places at some times. Whether high levels of achievement need are either necessary or sufficient is not so clear (in an elaboration of McClelland's theory, Pareek (1968) suggested a somewhat more general paradigm in which development is the result of achievement motivation plus a concern for others).

Efforts to Instill "Modern" Attitudes. Need to achieve and other individualistic ideologies, as we saw in LeVine's Nigerian study (described in Chapter 10), seem to require a whole complex of socioeconomic and political circum-

Box 13-1 Folktales as an Indicator

To test the notion that a society needs high-need achievers before it can develop economically, McClelland first turned to fantasy productions (popular stories) of various societies in order to assess their collective levels of N_{Ach}. He could then report, "Of the twenty-two cultures whose stories were high in N_{Ach}, 74 percent were observed to have at least some men engaged as full-time entrepreneurs, whereas for the twenty-three tribes below average in N Achievement, only 35 percent contained any full-time entrepreneurs, a difference that could rarely have arisen by chance" (McClelland, 1971, p. 8). McClelland considered this finding to have at least established the fact that collective fantasies, as in folktales, could be employed as a measure of N_{Ach}. The folktale scores related to societal-level entrepreneurial activity just as TAT scores had predicted individual entrepreneurial behavior.

Analysis of the content of textbooks, folktales, and other literary products as an assessment of prevailing motivational structures in various societies has become a popular and sometimes fruitful enterprise. Child, Storm, and Veroff (1958) related achievement themes in folktales of various societies to socialization practices in those societies. Zimet, Wiberg, and Blom (1971) did a multi-theme content analysis of primers employed contemporaneously in 13 (mostly industrialized) nations in an attempt to gain insight into some of the values that are stressed in socialization. They found numerous differences and similarities among these nations' first-grade-textbook themes.

Beshai (1972), working in Egypt, assessed the magnitude of themes relating to N_{Ach} in stories produced during three recent historical periods—the 1920s, the mid-1950s, and the late 1960s. He found a significant increase in N_{Ach} imagery from the earliest to the latest period. He also discovered the overall incidence of N_{Ach} imagery in Egypt to be lower than that reported in the United States and some developing nations, a fact he attributed to the traditional Moslem ethic of egalitarianism and success within the confines of group sanctions. The increase from 1920 to 1970, however, he attributed to the Western-influenced industrial development now under way in Egypt. These and similar studies illustrate the potential usefulness of written materials as a source of inference about shared motives and values relating to achievement.

Berlew (cited in McClelland, 1961, 1971) followed McClelland's lead and analyzed Greek literary documents from three distinct historical periods: one of growth, one of climax, and one of decline economically. Scoring them for achievement themes, without knowing from which period they had originated, Berlew found such themes to have peaked well before the economic growth peaked and to have declined in advance of the economic decline. A similar finding for 15th- through 19th-century England, based on street ballads and other literary products and relating the times at which achievement themes were high to temporal fluctuations in coal imports, was reported by Bradburn and Berlew (1961). These two studies lent support to the proposition that some sufficiently high level of N_{Ach} needs to exist in a society as a prerequisite for economic growth.

In what was perhaps the most fanciful set of studies to test this proposition,

(continued)

Box 13-1 *Continued*

ceramic designs were used as the source of inferences about N_{Ach}. Inspired by a finding that male U.S. college students with high N_{Ach} doodled in more orderly fashion than those with low N_{Ach} scores (Aronson, 1958), the McClelland team turned to designs on ancient Greek pots. They found that on that basis they could also predict the waxing and waning of Greek economic activity (McClelland, 1971, p. 9). Davies (1969) found the same for the Minoan civilization.

For contemporary nations, McClelland (1961) used children's readers from about 1925 as the source of collective fantasy from which N_{Ach} was assessed. And he used gain in electric-power consumption from about 1925 to 1950 as indicative of economic growth. McClelland found that the former predicted the latter.

However, Finison (1976), who focused on industrialized nations, found no correlation between N_{Ach} in 1950 and growth in electrical production between then and 1971. Finison also reported a negative correlation between N_{Ach} and national-income growth. This failure to replicate McClelland's earlier work casts doubt on his model of development, on its applicability to the time period studied by Finison, or on the measures employed. (As usual, negative results are ambiguous.)

---

stances, exerting their influence through the expression of values reflected in child-rearing practices. If so, then nations left to their own devices would experience economic development only to the extent that their traditional values were appropriate to the inducement of achievement motivation in some critical number of individuals who could serve as agents of development.

What about those nations whose traditional structures—and hence their traditional values—are antithetical to the emergence of N_{Ach}? Are they doomed to economic stagnation? McClelland, perhaps reflecting a characteristically American optimism and a faith in the ability of the expert to intervene effectively to influence human events, apparently thought not. He undertook a program to enhance achievement motivation in some individuals in developing nations in an effort to stimulate economic growth.

McClelland's own account (1971) of this effort is interesting:

> McClelland reasoned that if ideology was important in raising achievement motivation levels, one could perhaps start up economic development in a society by directly increasing the achievement motivation of a number of its key business leaders. So he arranged to have courses, designed to develop achievement motivation, given to a number of men in two small cities in the

south central part of India. Their business activity records before and after the courses were compared to similar records of men who were just like them but who had not been trained in achievement motivation. McClelland and Winter (1969) reported that the trained men were considerably more active: 51% of them had definitely improved their businesses in the two-year period after the course, contrasted with only 25% of the untrained men. Furthermore, trained men had invested, on the average, about twice as much money in expanding their businesses and had added twice as many new employees as the untrained men. Two or three years later, there was, however, no evidence that the city as a whole from which the trained men came was markedly more economically advanced than a comparison city. Perhaps the time period was too short for a general economic improvement to be observed or the number of people affected too small. Or perhaps ideological change by itself, without institutional or structural change, is insufficient [pp. 16–17].

This account reveals some success in enhancing the entrepreneurial efforts of persons already so oriented. But it reveals little else. Moreover, the validity of that small success is questionable. Did the enhanced activity of the trainees stem from the content of the training (instruction and encouragement in the production of achievement-oriented fantasies) or merely from the fact that they had been singled out for attention? Ever since the classic industrial-psychology studies conducted in the Hawthorne, Illinois, plant of the Western Electric Company (which showed enhanced production among workers selected for various programs, regardless of the content of the programs) psychologists have had to be wary of what has come to be known as the Hawthorne effect. One must suspect such a phenomenon among the Indian trainees.

Possible Negative Consequences. McClelland (1971), in a summary of research on achievement motivation, cited Southwood's cross-national analysis, which found that economic development efforts were correlated with various indexes of domestic disorder and authoritarian, undemocratic politics, at least among poorer nations with relatively low proportions of schooled individuals. So, McClelland expressed wariness about circumstances in which numbers of achievement-motivated individuals are confronted with a "low opportunity structure," circumstances that are likely to produce domestic turmoil. His solution would be to enhance opportunity through increased openings in education and employment. "The moral is not that achievement motivation should remain low, if one wants to avoid violence. Rather, high N Achievement and greater opportunity to achieve must go together" (McClelland, 1971, p. 13).

This prescription is a good generalization of the Protestant ethic, of the "American dream," and of the dreams of many others to acquire the material comforts that an environment that richly rewards hard work can provide. It is a principle that has inspired and justified technical-assistance programs mounted by wealthy industrial nations ostensibly to spur the economic growth of poorer nations.[1]

Whether or not one advocates organized efforts to encourage economic growth, it is well to know what might foster it. Others, for example, Lerner (1958) and Hagen (1962), also suggested psychological preconditions.

Empathy. Lerner (1958) argued for the central importance of a psychological disposition that he terms "empathy." This is a personality trait that presumably enables newly mobile individuals to operate efficiently in a changing social environment. Through empathy, transitional individuals are able to imagine what life is like outside the restrictive realm of their traditional surroundings. Their empathy leads to the desire to experience what has been imagined and to become participating members of the transitional society. For Lerner, participation is shown by holding opinions on public matters. To the degree that such overt behavior is present in a population, the society will be able to modernize.

Innovativeness. Another theory that treats personality as the independent variable in social change is that of Hagen (1962), who assumed that economic development requires individual movement away from authoritarian, noninnovating personality. Trained as an economist, Hagen turned to psychology for an understanding of why "people of some societies entered upon technological progress sooner or more effectively than others" (1962, p. ix). He considered that "the differences were due only in very minor degree to economic obstacles, lack of information or lack of training" and so he turned his attention "to other possible causes of differences in human behavior—to differences in personality, and hence personality formation and the social conditions affecting it" (p. ix). His overall scheme is represented by a model of society "which stresses the chain of causation from social structure through parental behavior to childhood environment and then that from childhood environment through personality to social change" (pp. 8–9).

Hagen concentrated his psychological study on "the first half-dozen years of life" (p. xii), leading him to rely heavily on the psychoanalytic literature.

For Hagen, economic and technological growth occurs only gradually in agricultural societies. "Contact with technologically advanced societies is a necessary condition" (pp. 34–35), but it is not sufficient. Material resources and social and psychological factors must also be present. The key to growth "seems to be largely internal rather than external" (p. 55).

In traditional societies, "behavior is governed by custom, not law. The social structure is hierarchical. The individual's position in the society is

---

[1]For a dramatically critical assessment of development projects, see a book by Rist and Sabelli (1986) poetically entitled *Once Upon a Time . . . Development.*

normally inherited rather than achieved. And, at least in the traditional state so far in the world's history, economic productivity is low" (pp. 55–56). "We may conclude that the structure of traditional society has lasted so long as it has because the personalities of the simple folk are authoritarian" (pp. 73–74).

Hagen defined the contrasting "innovational personality" as involving creativity, positive attitudes toward working in novel fields, and openness to new experience. The resultant innovators, finally, are viewed in this theory as the necessary agents of economic development. For Hagen, "social change will not occur without a change in personality" (p. 86). The personality change this requires is from authoritarian to innovational.

Personality as the Mediating Variable

Modernization theories that propose that the primary thrust toward modernization comes from changes in the opportunity structure usually treat personality variables as mediating between such changes and the resultant modernization. In most such theories, shifts in the economic and political environment are viewed as providing opportunities for individuals to "modernize." But it is only those individuals with the appropriate attitudes, values, and beliefs who can and will respond gainfully to those opportunities. Thus, one or another set of personality traits is seen as facilitating profitable adjustment to changing external conditions. In the mediating-variable theories the importance of personality resides in the ability to exploit opportunity, an ability that is conditioned by the existence of personal characteristics.

The mediating-variable approach to acculturation is exemplified by the theories of Kahl (1968), Inkeles and Smith (Inkeles, 1969; Smith & Inkeles, 1966), Doob (1960), and Dawson (1967, 1973). All of these theorists tend to treat the modernizing personality as a complex of values, attitudes, and beliefs. And, in most applications of their theoretical position, they have concentrated on efforts to measure that syndrome of modernization-tending traits. We will consider some of these efforts later, in a section on the measurement of modernism/traditionalism.

Personality as the Dependent Variable

A dependent-variable approach to the study of acculturation is advocated by Godwin (1974). Instead of viewing "modern" attitudes as causing or helping the individual to produce social change, the attitudes and behaviors are seen as *consequences* of structural and cultural changes. The conception advocated by Godwin is consonant with a policy of restructuring the social environment so as to induce modern behaviors, with the expectation that the appropriate attitudes will subsequently emerge.

These three approaches to the study of modernization vary only in the

Box 13-2 Diversity of Terms in Acculturation Research

A wide variety of terms have been generated to describe social change, particularly that occurring among so-called developing nations. Terms such as *acculturation, civilization, Europeanization, Westernization, economic development, urbanization, industrialization, detribalization, assimilation,* and *modernization* have particular connotations. But they have all been used to refer to changes in social, political, and economic environments. Often, the same terms are employed to refer to the behavior of individuals who live in those changing environments, and again the term employed carries with it certain emphases.

Some of the terms—especially *civilization, Europeanization, Westernization,* and, to a lesser extent, *modernization*—have a decided aura of ethnocentrism about them, used as they are primarily by Western social scientists studying the behavior of peoples "becoming like us." Similarly, the concept *detribalization* conveys negative affect to people living in some societies. These people contend that the concept *tribe* did not exist until anthropologists visited and—refusing to recognize nations because the societies had features different from those of the anthropologists' own nations—called them tribes. Terms such as *urbanization* and *industrialization,* though neither very ethnocentric nor offensive, seem limited and specialized in meaning. *Assimilation* also has a special usage, limited primarily to studies of immigrants becoming integrated into a host society. Hence, these various terms are employed by some and shunned by others. If used, they are differentially employed in different kinds of situations.

Yet there is a common thread running through them. At the social level of analysis the terms refer to changes that we will henceforth in this chapter call *modernization.* These changes will include industrialization, urbanization, and other concomitants of sedentary, high-food-accumulating, cash-economy societies. A formal education system, mass communications, and a transportation network are all rapidly appearing nearly everywhere in the world and at an accelerating pace. The fact that such social and cultural features appeared earlier in Western societies is irrelevant for our present purposes. That they are replacing—for better or for worse—nonindustrial, rural, subsistence economies enables us to label the newly appearing features as modern. Our use of the concept of modernity is meant to convey only the temporal fact of their recent appearance and spread. We do not consider modern as necessarily better, however much those people who are themselves modernizing might believe it to be.

When employed at the individual level of analysis, all of these terms refer to changes in behavior (and presumably underlying attitudes and habits) among people confronted with relatively far-reaching changes in their environments.

role they assign to the individual in the modernization process. Whichever approach is employed, psychological research on modernization will focus on individual behavioral variables—treating them either as independent, mediating, or dependent—that need to be measured. A fundamental problem in all modernization research, then, will be the measurement of modernity, and it is to this problem we now turn.

THE MEASUREMENT
OF MODERNITY

There have been several attempts to define and measure individual differences in acculturation, concentrating on variations in individual responses to cultural change. Because the variations are so often treated as degrees of modernity, we shall use this term. The research literature, however, employs diverse terminology, as is detailed in Box 13-2.

Modernization can refer, in a value-neutral way, to *social* change resulting primarily from cultural contact. We will use *modernity* to refer to *individual* behavior that contributes to and reflects social modernization. How people move from traditional to modern behaviors is the concern that has led to efforts to measure modernity.

Four Approaches to the Measurement
of Individual Modernity

Two efforts to assess modernity stem from a sociological interest in economic development (Kahl, 1968; Smith & Inkeles, 1966), and two were originated by cross-cultural psychologists (Doob, 1957, 1967; Dawson, 1967, 1969).

Kahl's "Modern Values"

This approach derives from several assumptions about values: (1) Traditional and modern societies differ in many aspects, including division of labor, state of technology, degree of urbanization, type of economy, system of social stratification, education and communications, and—most significantly—values. (2) Values either affect the social and economic development of a nation as a whole or influence the behavior of upwardly mobile individuals. Of particular interest are work-related values. (3) Values, properly assessed, can differentiate among social groups and can predict behaviors in particular situations. (4) Each traditional/modern value can be treated as a continuous variable that ranges from extreme traditionalism to extreme modernism, and each individual can be located on this continuum.

Kahl's values came from sociological theory, for example, Talcott Parsons (1951) and Florence Kluckhohn (1949–1950), and from his own interviews with 25 Brazilians who were either traditional farm laborers or modern office managers. Some of his modern values (with their traditional counterparts in parentheses) are as follows:

- Activism (fatalism). Humans, through science and technology, can control and change the world around them.
- Occupational primacy (the primacy of other activities such as recreation). Career success is the highest goal.
- Individualism (need for security in the form of close ties with work mates). Independence from work mates is stressed.
- Participation in mass media (dependence on local gossip).

Kahl's questionnaire reflects 14 value domains. One item designed to tap activism reads, "The secret of happiness is not expecting too much out of life, and being content with what comes your way." Strongly disagreeing with this statement constitutes the most "modern" response to it.

Employing specific subgroups, for example, factory and white-collar workers, Kahl administered his questionnaire to more than 1,300 male respondents in Brazil and Mexico. Seven of the original 14 modernity values intercorrelated in nearly identical fashion in both Mexico and Brazil.

Inkeles and Smith's "Overall Modernity"

Alex Inkeles and David Smith (Inkeles, 1966, 1969, 1975; Smith & Inkeles, 1966; Inkeles & Smith, 1974) attempted to relate modernism to certain institutional and experiential variables. They began with a conception of modern society as characterized by a complex of traits, including urbanization, high levels of education, and industrialization. The modern individual has acquired behaviors that permit effective participation in such a society. Inkeles and Smith considered 20 potentially relevant themes reflecting a "thoroughly elaborated theory as to the qualities which modern settings are likely to generate, as well as considerations of personal attributes which are likely to best adapt a man to life in such institutional settings" (Smith and Inkeles, 1966, p. 359). They considered the industrial factory to be the most influential of these settings. In *Becoming Modern* (1974), Inkeles and Smith detailed how the factory is an agent in the socialization of the individual from traditional to modern.

They identified several additional modernism themes, including attitudes toward the family, religion, and social stratification. They also attempted to tap individual modernity by including questions on what the respondents knew (information presumably acquired from having behaved in modern ways) and what they did (self-reported modern or traditional behavior). For example, respondents were asked to name three newspapers and to demonstrate their ability to read.

Inkeles and Smith sampled men, aged 18 to 32, in six "developing" countries: Argentina, Israel, Chile, India, East Pakistan, and Nigeria. In each country, subsamples were chosen to represent degrees of exposure to presumed modernizing influences. Two major groups were cultivators still living in a traditional rural community and former rural dwellers who had had at least three years of experience working in urban industrial factories. A third sample was composed of migrants from the countryside who had just arrived in the city and who were not yet integrated into factory or bureaucratic work settings. A fourth sample, urban nonindustrial workers, was added to test for the effects of simply living in the city versus working in a factory. Additional subsamples based on varying factory experience, amount of education, and type of factory were employed in an effort to permit diverse tests of hypotheses about determinants and consequences of modernity.

They concluded that there is "a general factor or syndrome of individual modernity which influences or is reflected in the individual's response to the particular issue with which he is confronted in many different realms of life and in many diverse social relations" (Inkeles & Smith, 1974, p. 98). Central to this syndrome are the following values and behavioral tendencies listed by Inkeles (1975): (1) Openness to new experience; (2) the assertion of increasing independence from the authority of traditional figures, and a shift of allegiance to leaders of government, public affairs, trade unions, cooperatives, and the like; (3) belief in the efficacy of science and medicine and abandonment of passivity and fatalism in the face of life's difficulties; (4) ambition for oneself and one's children to achieve high occupational and educational goals; (5) preferences for punctuality and an interest in carefully planning one's affairs in advance; (6) strong interest and an active participation in civic and community affairs and local politics; and (7) a striving to keep up with the news and a preference for national and international news. Inkeles and Smith asserted that this modernity syndrome was remarkably similar across their six national samples.

To validate their scale, they used the criterion-group method.[2] By this method, the scale is found to be valid if it discriminates accurately between men who are known to be modern and those known to be traditional by some other independent criterion of modernity. According to their theory, men are made modern by certain experiences and exposure to certain influences. The authors could independently identify men who had had more and less of this exposure and experience.

Inkeles and Smith (1974) devised a summary index of modernization composed of ten independent variables: years of education, years of urban residence, home/school modernity, mass-media exposure, consumer goods

---

[2]A good discussion of this method and its application to acculturation research may be found in Kim (1984).

possessed, months of factory experience, father's education, residential urbanism, objective skill, and a number of factory benefits. Men with higher scores on this summary index earned higher scores on the scale, both within each country and across the six countries.

Doob's Modernization Scales

In his book entitled, with wit and irony, *Becoming More Civilized* (1960), Leonard Doob reported research on acculturation in rapidly changing African societies.

Three questions guided Doob: (1) What differences can be identified among people in the old society who are having varying degrees of contact with the representatives of a new society? (2) What accounts for these differences? (3) Do these differences stem from psychological differences that were present before contact began, or is it the contact itself that produces such differences?

Doob (1957, 1960) asked how the conditions of culture contact and the characteristics of individuals experiencing it might influence them. Contact was defined operationally as having had Western education or being a leader among one's people. An illustrative hypothesis: Individuals with greater contact show antagonism to traditional authorities and are able to postpone gratification for the sake of future rewards. In these early studies Doob found support for such hypotheses.

Later (1967) Doob offered a set of eight scales devised to measure opinions and attitudes dealing with modernization: (1) *temporal orientation*, an emphasis on the future rather than the present or past; (2) *government*, the belief that the country's present legal government has important beneficial functions to perform for its citizens; (3) *confidence and optimism*, the feeling that life in general is pleasant and that to a significant degree people control their destiny; (4) *patriotism*, strong feelings of attachment and loyalty to the country; (5) science and *determinism*, "correct" knowledge from a scientific viewpoint, and the conviction that phenomena are intelligible; (6) *conception of people*, a nonparanoid, generous, trusting conception of human nature; (7) *politics and leaders*, approval of the country's leaders and their specific policies; and (8) *nontribalism*, a tendency to deemphasize or discredit traditional values and practices.

Doob's eight scales were administered to 14 African samples characterized by various tribal affiliations, rural or urban residence, and differing educational experiences. Scores on the scales related primarily to education.

Dawson's Traditional Versus Modern Attitudes

Dawson (1973) proposed a multifactor theory of how attitudes change from traditional to modern. These factors included (among others) the environment and related subsistence economy, the type of socialization (severe or permissive), the degree of social stratification, and the degree of cultural tolerance for cognitive inconsistency. Dawson viewed change from traditional to modern attitudes as an adaptive process in which the individual in a changing society tends to achieve consistency. He assumed that attitudinal inconsistency is maladaptive and needs to be reduced.

To measure attitude change in transitional situations, as in Sierra Leone, the site of some of his research, Dawson developed the Traditional Versus Modern Attitude Scale (1967). He expected that individuals would be affected by Western-influenced education, economic change, and medicine. For 18 themes pertinent to Sierra Leone, Dawson constructed four-statement sets reflecting traditional, semitraditional, semimodern (semi-Western), and modern (Western) attitudes.

Dawson administered his scales to three samples of Sierra Leonean men who had varying exposure to Western influences—illiterate villagers, illiterate mine workers, and mine apprentices with a secondary-school education. A fourth group of university students was also tested. As expected, the scores for the illiterate villagers were high on the Traditional subscale and progressively lower on the Semitraditional, Semi-Western, and Western subscales. By contrast, the university students obtained low Traditional subscale scores and progessively higher scores on the others. The two intermediary groups tended to score in between the villagers and the university students.

In later studies (1969, 1972, 1973) Dawson and his associates constructed similar traditional/modern scales for use with Australian aboriginal, Chinese, Japanese, and Eskimo respondent groups. For them, traditionalism/modernism comprised somewhat different sets of attitudes. The traditional/modern scales were constructed anew for each cultural group. This culture-specific approach of Dawson reflects his concern with the ecological and economic environments as factors influencing attitudes and values. Inkeles and Smith and Kahl, in contrast, seem more concerned with the influence of certain modernizing institutions, which can, in a sense, be transported across cultures. Dawson's study of traditionalism/modernism, then, is restricted to comparisons among subcultural groups within national and cultural boundaries and does not involve comparisons across countries.

Similarities and Differences in Definitions of Modernism

There are similarities among the several separate research efforts in which modernity has been operationally defined. The similarities are spelled out in Box 13-3.

Two other conceptions of modernism are a bit different. Foster (1967) presented a limited-good model of the traditional peasant, who sees all

---

Box 13-3 Similarities in Operational Definitions of Modernism

Some common elements in modernism definitions (and the researchers who have identified them):

- Independence from traditional authority figures (Inkeles and Smith, Dawson)
- Belief in the efficacy of science (Inkeles and Smith, Doob, Dawson)
- Activism—abandonment of passivity and fatalism (Inkeles and Smith, Kahl, Adinolfi and Klein, 1972, Kiray, 1968)
- Ambition for oneself and one's children (Inkeles and Smith, Kiray)
- Interest in civic affairs (Inkeles and Smith, Schnaiberg, 1970)
- Mass-media participation (Kahl, Schnaiberg)
- Low integration with extended relatives (Kahl, Schnaiberg, Dawson)
- Individualism (Kahl, Adinolfi and Klein, Dawson)
- Emphasis on the future (Doob, Kiray)
- Trust in one's fellow humans (Kahl, Doob)
- Low valuation of traditional beliefs and practices (Doob, Dawson)
- Egalitarian attitude toward family role structure (Kahl, Schnaiberg, Dawson).

---

desirable things in life as existing in absolute quantities that are insufficient to fill the needs of everyone. This world view inhibits development. In contrast, there are those individuals who are innovators (who have done new things, such as buy a sewing machine or use chemical fertilizer). Innovators are motivated by the desire for economic profit and for new forms of prestige and status. Triandis (1973) holds that modernity involves a relatively complex view of one's environment. More specifically, the modern individual is sufficiently differentiated in the universalistic forms of exchange (information, money, goods) and relatively less differentiated in the particularistic forms of exchange (love, status, services).

Thus, we have seen both diversity and communality in various definitions of modernism and differences and similarities in approach to measuring it. Modernity is most often viewed as a syndrome of attitudes.

Behavioristic Approaches to the Study of Modernization

Measuring modern behavioral tendencies indirectly by the measurement of modern attitudes may be a less promising strategy than was once thought. With reference to determining the causes of development-related behavior, Guthrie (1970) wrote:

Faced with the unproductive activities of many individuals in a poorly developed area, one is often prompted to ask, "Why don't they . . . ?" The answer often comes in a form which describes the behavior under consideration or invokes an inferred inner quality, "They don't because they are conservative, or ignorant, or poor." When they examine the matter further, we are led to conclude that there is no satisfactory answer to, "Why don't they . . . ?" There is no way to rule out alternative answers. A question which can, at least theoretically, be answered is "What changes need to be made so that they will . . . ?" In this way we are looking at behavior as determined by factors in the individual's history and his present environment. The latter, at least, can be manipulated in various ways to test the validity of an assertion that change in a given factor can lead to change in a specific cultural practice.[3]

Guthrie argued in favor of an experimental approach to ferreting out the causes of individual behavior that contribute to development. He proposed, for example, that Philippine barrios be randomly assigned to various types of development programs in order to determine which external conditions and reinforcement contingencies lead to particular forms of "modern," or "adaptive," behavior on the part of residents. Research that focused on behavior other than verbal expressions of attitude would be welcome.

Concluding Comments on the Measurement of Modernity

After reviewing many of these attempts to measure individual modernism, Brislin, Lonner, and Thorndike (1973) commented that the modernism measures "dealt with a 'traditional-modern' continuum as if everyone knew what it is" (p. 199). Our own review suggests that this is only partly true. Although many students of modernity indeed began with a priori conceptions of the characteristics of modern men and women, the scales they have emerged with were largely empirically determined. We saw that some reliably measurable aspects of modernity were unique to particular groups; we also saw considerable communality in the content of modern values and attitudes, including independence from traditional authority figures, belief in the efficacy of science, personal ambition and achievement motivation, a future-looking temporal orientation, and similar points of view. That is an encouraging state of affairs to those who conceive of modernity as a pancultural dimension and who would try to measure it anywhere

---

[3]From The Psychology of Modernization in the Rural Philippines, Institute of Philippines Culture Papers, No. 8 (p. 110) by G. M. Guthrie, 1970, Quezen City: Aleno de Manila University Press. Copyright 1970 by the Ateneo de Manila University Press. Reprinted by permission.

with a more or less standardized instrument. But even this empirical success must be viewed with caution. "Even the most rough instrument can yield data which can potentially force people into categories of [the investigator's] convenience, and not necessarily into categories that reflect reality" (Brislin, Lonner & Thorndike, 1973, p. 200).

The measurement of modernity is only a tool for the investigation of substantive hypotheses about the individual behavioral changes that accompany modernization. In the next section of this chapter we will consider some studies that have this more substantive focus.

SOME EMPIRICAL STUDIES
OF MODERNIZATION

On the Maintenance of Traditional
Beliefs by Modernists

Not surprisingly, people who are becoming more modern in some ways retain many traditional behaviors and beliefs. This phenomenon has been demonstrated in a study of supernatural beliefs (witchcraft, ghosts, spirits, and so on) among Ghanaian university students (Jahoda, 1970). On seven of ten items designed to assess acceptance of such beliefs, a clear majority of 280 students expressed at least qualified acceptance.

But even more interesting were Jahoda's findings relating acceptance of supernatural beliefs to age and to individual differences in modernism and field independence. Younger students (less than 25 years of age) were found to hold more supernatural beliefs than older ones. Among the younger students modernism was not correlated with holding such beliefs. But among the older students the less modern ones were more likely to hold the traditional beliefs. Also, among the younger students the holding of supernatural beliefs was not correlated with field independence. But among the older ones, the more field-independent individuals were the ones who most often subscribed to traditional beliefs.

This complex pattern was explained by Jahoda as follows: First he noted that the older students, whose entry into the university was delayed, had received their earlier education at a time in Ghana's development when anything traditional was evaluated negatively by the modernizing elite. Hence, in that generation of modernizing Ghanaians only field-independent (nonconformist) individuals might be expected to hold on to traditional "superstitions." With a general increase in self-confidence in the next generation of Ghanaians, there developed a partial rejection of foreign values and a reassertion of indigenous ones. The intellectual climate changed, enabling younger Ghanaians, including more conformist ones, to express approval of traditional beliefs. In short, for the younger students, whether individually more modern or not, the holding of a belief in supernatural phenomena, provided the belief was perceived as traditionally Ghanaian, would be merely to subscribe to a prevailing norm.

Jahoda's observations and findings are a clear demonstration of what may be a pervasive phenomenon of modernization. Earlier, less sophisticated modernity may involve rejection of anything that smacks of tradition, whereas later, more sophisticated modernism may include a reassertion of indigenous values.

On the Key Role of Formal Education

Participation in a formal educational system is so obviously a means for acquiring modern behavioral dispositions that there can be little doubt that formal education is a key factor in individual modernism. Many other factors contribute, but no other single one is of similar import.

In their thorough review of psychological development in diverse cultures, Munroe and Munroe (1975) give prominence to the contrast between traditional and modern societies. They especially note developmental differences in cognition, competitiveness, achievement, and self-orientation, all of which they attribute to purposeful training. Much of this training occurs in socialization; but they note that socialization practices are supported by "special institutional arrangements," one of which is a formal educational system (p. 150).

The amount of schooling thus far completed is often employed as an independent variable in research on individual differences in modernity. In Doob's (1960) series of hypotheses comparing three categories of persons in modernizing nations—"the unchanged, the changing, and the changed"—the categories were in fact defined by amount of education.

In most so-called developing nations, whether a child enters the formal schooling programs (and in most such nations participation is both optional and costly) and how far the child progresses virtually determine which of two contrasting life-styles—traditional or modern—will be pursued during adulthood. Aspects of modernity impinge on nearly everyone in a modernizing society. But for those persons with little or no formal education, such aspects remain essentially foreign. And for those with larger amounts of education almost the reverse is the case; for them, traditional practices are likely to seem foreign.

Generational gaps, although present in all societies, are nowhere more dramatic than in the developing nations, where it is common for students to report that it is nearly impossible to communicate with their uneducated parents.[4] In such settings school vacations are in many respects like a trip to a foreign land.

Thus, it may be merely documenting the obvious to demonstrate that the amount of formal schooling correlates with individual modernity, but such documentation has been provided by several studies. LeCompte and Le-Compte (1970) found that first-year secondary-school students in Turkey expressed more traditional attitudes than third-year students. Feldman (1972) reported a similar finding from Kenya. Dawson (1967, 1969), working with Sierra Leonean persons no longer in school, found that those who expressed the most traditional attitudes were those who had the least amount of education. Traditionalism declined as educational accomplishments increased, but only up through secondary education. Individuals who had been to college expressed more traditional attitudes than those who had stopped at secondary school, a finding that is interesting to relate to Jahoda's Ghanaian findings reviewed above.

It would obviously be reasonable to expect that if a school in a developing country were managed and staffed by persons from a more modern one, the impact of education on the students' modernity would be enhanced. Le-Compte and LeCompte in their (1970) study in Turkey compared girls attending an American missionary school with girls attending a Turkish government school and found higher scores on a modernity scale among the former.

Sex Differences

Some provocative sex differences in modernity and some interesting interactions between sex and education have also been reported. To understand them, it is perhaps well to note first that females in developing countries are in general more sheltered than males and less likely to be schooled, or if schooled, more likely to drop out at a lower level. By the same token, a modernizing experience, as is epitomized by formal education, is likely to be a more dramatically liberating experience for females, provided that the effects of the education are not effectively counteracted by traditional, authoritarian upbringing.

Some relevant findings include those of Omari (1960), who found female secondary students in Ghana to express more modern attitudes toward marriage and family than male students. Doob (1960) reported more modern attitudes among females than among males for both Zulu and Jamaican respondents. Feldman (1972), working among the Gusii in Kenya, also

---

[4]Even within generations, communication difficulties between formally educated and nonformally educated individuals create striking problems of human relations. See, for example, Okot p"Bitek's (1966) dramatic poem Song of Lawino for an artistic insight into such problems in an East African setting.

found that female secondary-school students expressed more modern attitudes.

On the other hand, in a study of "superstitions" among Lebanese Arab students in Beirut, Za'rour (1972) found female secondary students to be more superstitious than male students, particularly among those of the Moslem faith. Za'rour suggested that these sex differences could be explained by the fact that girls are more exposed than boys to traditional beliefs and practices maintained by uneducated female elders and that all women, even educated ones, remain largely under male domination in this essentially conservative and authoritarian culture.

Language as a Factor

Formal schooling usually employs a Western language (notably English or French) as the medium of instruction. Thus, modernizing is produced not only by the content of education but also, perhaps, by the language in which it occurs. When individuals acquire the modern language while retaining their traditional one, they may even hold contrasting sets of attitudes, each couched in a different language.

Indeed, there is some evidence, not wholly consistent, that educated persons express different degrees of modernity depending on the language of the questionnaire by which their attitudes are assessed. This was the case in a study by Doob (1957) of bilingual Ganda, Luo, Zulu, and Afrikaaner respondents in Uganda and South Africa. When queried in their native language (as were a randomly selected half of Doob's respondents), individuals in all four of these ethnic groups assented more to questionnaire items designed to tap traditional values. Doob (1958) did not replicate this finding in Jamaica, however. Botha (1968) found the language-of-questionnaire effect for bilingual Arabic-French students in Lebanon but did not find it for bilingual Arabic-English students in the same country. Feldman (1972) found among the more modern of his Gusii secondary-school students in Kenya that those who received a questionnaire in their traditional language expressed more traditional attitudes. This was not the case for less modern-scoring students, however, for whom the language of the questionnaire did not matter.

While these findings concerning the language of the modernity questionnaire are primarily of methodological interest, they do support a substantive hypothesis suggested by Botha (1968) that language carries with it a set of cultural values that the language user necessarily adopts, even inadvertently, whenever the language is used. Hence, not only what is learned in school but also the language in which it is learned may contribute importantly to the modernizing effect of formal education. In any event, there can be little doubt that formal education is a key factor in individual modernity. Many other factors contribute, but no other single one is of similar import.

SUMMARY AND CONCLUSIONS

In this chapter we have been concerned primarily with the influence of cultural change on behavior. All cultures are constantly changing, and all people are thus faced with the need to adapt their behaviors to suit new conditions in their social environment. Our focus was on developing modernism, that psychological process by which individuals acquire behavior patterns that seem necessary for coping in the technologically developing nation-states in which more and more of the world's population lives.

We considered some basic generalizations about cultural change and some theories of the psychological changes that accompany it. We examined several approaches to the measurement of individual modernity and reviewed a few examples of empirical research relating individual differences in modernism to education and other potential modernizing forces.

If there is a central theme in the diverse content of this chapter, it is that human beings are remarkably flexible. Although their personalities are shaped from early childhood by socialization, with the result that they internalize the values and norms of their own more primary groupings, they can also acquire new responses as the culture around them changes. As was true of the Ghanaian university students (Jahoda, 1970), there is apparently room in any person's psychological makeup for alternative values, ideas, and attitudes, just as long as the alternatives are not unavoidably conflicting.

Chapter 14

Intercultural Relations
in a Shrinking World

INTRODUCTION:
THE DUBIOUS DISTINCTION
BETWEEN IN-GROUP
AND OUT-GROUP

Photographs of a tiny Earth taken by cameras borne aloft into space have made us aware that all who inhabit this globe share a single fate. Resource depletion, environmental degradation, and the need for more equitable economic development can be confronted effectively only if viewed as worldwide challenges. Yet an outmoded consciousness persists, fueling a loyalty to ethnic or national segments. Although the most pressing problems confronting humankind are global in scope, most people identify primarily with relatively small groups. All too often, the world is divided into "us" and "them."

Most people relate most positively to their own cultural groups. Why this is so has been implicit in all the previous chapters. Our views of the world, our values, and our life-styles are largely conditioned by our particular cultures. Much cultural content is internalized by each of us; we are, in a sense, our own cultures. That we identify with our cultures is thus not surprising.

Does it necessarily follow that we must relate negatively to cultures other than our own? Must we live in a world characterized by in-groups and out-groups? Inherent in at least one definition of ethnocentrism is a discouraging answer to this question.

ETHNOCENTRISM

The core concept in our attempt to understand in-group and out-group attitudes is ethnocentrism, first employed in an analysis of individuals' links with their own and neighboring groups by William Graham Sumner (1906) in his classic sociological treatise, *Folkways*. The concept embraces both positive feelings toward one's own group (the in-group, in Sumner's terminology) and negative feelings toward others (out-groups); indeed, in Sumner's insightful theorizing, each feeds on the other.

> The relation of comradeship and peace in the we-group and that of hostility and war toward others-groups are correlative to each other. The exigencies of war with outsiders are what make peace inside, lest internal discord should weaken the we-group for war. These exigencies also make government and law in the in-group, in order to prevent quarrels and enforce discipline. . . . Ethnocentrism is the technical name for this view of things in which one's own group is the center of everything, and all others are scaled and rated with reference to it. . . . Each group nourishes its own pride and vanity, boasts itself superior, exalts its own divinities, and looks with contempt on outsiders. Each group thinks its own folkways [the contemporary equivalent is customs] the only right ones, and if it observes that other groups have other folkways, these excite its scorn. (Sumner, 1906, pp. 12–13)

Thus Sumner postulated a universal syndrome of behavioral dispositions in which positive links with the in-group are reinforced by negative attitudes and behaviors toward out-groups. Cross-cultural research can test the universality of such a syndrome and can illustrate how behaviors directed toward the in-group and out-groups interrelate. Conversely, Sumner's theory can help interpret whatever findings emerge from cross-cultural research on intergroup relations.

Although, as Sumner suggests, ethnocentrism is difficult to overcome, we *must* become more than loyal members of our own societies. To avoid impending ecological catastrophes, more of us must learn to transcend our own cultures. We must develop — at a minimum — empathy with others. Ideally, we ought to identify with the whole human race as enthusiastically as we presently do with our own tribes.

Research into individuals' relations with in-groups and out-groups can illuminate the magnitude of the problem and may even facilitate the difficult process of enhancing global consciousness. We shall examine psychological ties that bind individuals to the smaller groups to which they belong and from which they derive much of their sense of self. Among these groups, of course, is the nation. We will examine the process whereby people can move from tribalism to nationalism, overcoming impediments to identifying with groups initially perceived by us as not us. Later, we will examine those impediments and search for ways of moving beyond nationalism.

PSYCHOLOGICAL CONCOMITANTS OF NATIONALISM

Kelman (1976) defined nationalism as an ideology that provides justification for the existence of a nation-state, a definition of its particular population, and a prescription of the relationship of its included individuals to that state. Kelman recognized that often a population is considered a nation only because it is part of the state, not because the population is an interrelated group of people aware of their interrelationship. When the population is ethnically diverse, a process of nation building[1] must go on. Moreover, as Kelman put it, "The mere existence of common cultural elements among members of a collectivity is not enough to define them as a nation. They must also have the consciousness that these common elements represent special bonds that tie them to one another" (Kelman, 1976, pp. 9–10).

In this, Kelman echoed views expressed years before by one of the founders of social psychology, Floyd Allport, who asserted, "The main criteria of nationality are psychological. There are certain traditions, historical perspectives, and principles possessed in common by the members of every national group which are both the evidence and the substance of their nationality. If an individual shares these ideas with the others of his group, and like the others is loyal to them, he belongs to their nation" (Allport, 1933, p. 138).

The psychological counterpart to national ideology is national identity. What are the social forces required to stimulate national identity and the psychological forces it taps? Kelman (1976) proposed that two powerful psychological needs — for self-protection and for self-transcendence — constitute the motivation for identification with a nation-state. Political leadership is required to mobilize these motives and to mold them into national consciousness, particularly in new nations.

After World War II, many new nation-states were created. These were often composed of smaller, "tribal" units. As Doob (1962) pointed out, Africa contains approximately 700 traditional societies integrated into fewer than 50 nations. For citizens to function effectively in such nations requires the acquisition of behaviors different from those that led to adaptive functioning as members of small traditional societies, where they were linked by kinship, language, and common life-styles.

---

[1]Nation building, as a sociopolitical process, merely begins with the declaration of national independence. It also requires a psychological process that must take place in the minds of many individuals. Less obvious perhaps than the political and economic aspects of nation building, its psychological components are nevertheless fundamental. A nation is not merely a geopolitical fact; it is also a state of mind.

One desideratum is a sense of loyalty to the nation and an identification with it. Doob (1962) suggested "it is most difficult to create this psychological groundwork for nationalism, for distinctive qualities must come to be associated with the synthetic entity of the nation, loyalty must be aroused and deep convictions must be stirred" (p. 152). Such feelings exist in traditional societies comprising a single ethnic group whose members easily identify with each other. Most new nations are composed of several ethnic groups, and their boundaries — in many cases drawn by outsiders meeting in political conferences — cut across ethnic territories. Identification with the nation, then, takes time and requires individual changes in attitudes.

A Case Study of Nationalism in Sub-Saharan Africa

Individual reactions to nation-building efforts in one new nation were studied by Segall, Doornbos, and Davis (1976) during Uganda's first decade of national independence. (Uganda is an East African nation that attained its political independence from Great Britain in 1962). The study examined the possible emergence of national identity. It focused on the self-identification patterns of several hundred Banyankore men, members of a traditional society in Uganda. The Banyankore constitute a distinct Ugandan subgroup united by language (one of many spoken in Uganda) and customs (some of them unique to Banyankore). Throughout most of their history, the Banyankore had been subjects in a traditional kingdom called Ankole, which during the colonial era the British considered a district of the Uganda Protectorate.

The research addressed several questions: What changes in self-perception occur as the Banyankore become integrated into Uganda? What personal events correlate with the acceptance of national citizenship? What tactics available to central-government leaders foster national integration? Is suppression of traditional identity frames, as in the abolition of a so-called tribal monarchy, effective? Does national integration require a decline in "primordial" group identity?

Between 1965 and 1968, when the study was done, Uganda's central government enacted a new constitution. This event, in 1967, provided an opportunity for a natural experiment — a chance to measure the effects of the new constitution by comparing data from before and after its enactment.

The study involved two waves of comparable face-to-face interviews with samples of Banyankore men, 227 before the 1967 event and 115 after. Respondents were given several opportunities to reveal how they thought of themselves through both open-ended and highly structured questions. "Munyankore" (a person of Ankole) was a consistently popular response over all item formats.

The Primacy of Banyankore Identity

At the outset of the interview, respondents were asked simply, "What are you?" Approximately 40% first said "I am a Munyankore" (34% in the first survey and 46% in the second). The only response to exceed "Munyankore" in popularity was "I am a person," and then only in the pre-1967 survey.

When asked "How *should* the Banyankore think of themselves?" most respondents (over 60%) said "as Ugandans." Still, about 25% of them said that they should think of themselves as Banyankore (24% in the first survey and 27% in the second). Clearly, more Banyankore think of themselves as Banyankore than as anything else, and a good many thought they should.

When asked to rank all applicable descriptive terms, Munyankore earned the highest composite rank in both surveys. Regardless of how the question was posed, Munyankore is what more people seemed to consider themselves.

Few Banyankore by 1968 had come to think of themselves as Ugandan. Hardly anyone said that he was a Ugandan in response to "What are you?" The phrase "I am a Ugandan" can hardly be said to have been on the tip of the tongue of the typical Munyankore.

On the other hand, it is equally clear that the Banyankore knew that they were Ugandan, that they ascribed "importance" to that status, and that most of them acknowledged the propriety of thinking of themselves as Ugandan. About two-thirds of all respondents said that Banyankore should think of themselves as Ugandan, and both samples gave high ratings to Ugandan on both ranking and pair-comparison tasks. Indeed, these ratings were about as high as those given to Munyankore. So, the typical Munyankore man seemed to know that it was appropriate to identify as a Ugandan and value his Ugandanness as a status to be accorded value, but he had yet to think of himself as a Ugandan.

The study also looked into individual variations in the ways members of the East African society identified themselves. Findings regarding individual differences are reported in Box 14-1.

Persistence of Banyankore Identity

Next we ask about the impact of the constitutional change. If the abolition of the Ankole monarchy and other features of the 1967 constitution were intended to lessen the Banyankore's sense of identity as Banyankore, those tactics failed. The salience of Munyankoreness (as assessed by first responses to "What are you?") was even greater after 1967 than before. The salience of Ugandanness remained low. The awareness of the desirability of "thinking Ugandan" (as assessed by responses to "How should the Banyankore think of themselves?") was no greater after 1967 than before.

Ranking and pair-comparison data revealed no inter-wave differences, either. Munyankore was ranked highest in both waves, with Ugandan ranked

---

Box 14-1 Individual Differences in Identity in Ankole

It appeared reasonable to the authors of this study that "sense of Ugandan-ness" might be positively correlated with educational level. But Ugandan was not systematically related to educational level. Rather, the better educated Banyankore were more personalistic. In response to "What are you?" lesser educated respondents tended to say "I am a Munyankore" and better educated respondents said either "I am a person" or cited their occupations. With increasing education there was a decline in salience of Munyankore but no change in salience of Ugandan. It was concluded that the more exposure a man has to broadening influences, the less investment he makes in his corporate identity—whether tribal or national—and the more he thinks of himself as a unique personality. Accordingly, it appears that education per se cannot be expected to make national identity more salient.

Education related to rankings in some surprising ways. Ugandan was ranked higher by better educated respondents than by lesser educated respondents, but so was Munyankore. Thus, a sense of Munyankoreness and a sense of Ugandanness seemed not to be in psychological opposition. With increased levels of education, both terms were given higher rankings.

The authors concluded that education enhances awareness of the importance of the nation but doesn't reduce the judged importance of the tribal reference term. Educated persons do not trade one group identity for another but, rather, discover themselves in the process of becoming educated. This might be due to the fact that education as practiced thus far in developing nations like Uganda has been a privilege enjoyed by a select few, one that drastically enhances one's economic and social potential. High achievement academically has meant entry into the elite, and the prestige accompanying that status would, not surprisingly, reinforce personalistic thinking. And, schooling itself fosters individualism.

---

near it both times. There were no significant differences in scale values across the two waves.

Thus, there was no evidence that Banyankoreness declined or that Ugandanness increased during the months following the enactment of the 1967 constitution. The removal of the tribal king did not result in a decline of traditional identifications.

Implications for Nation Building

Nothing in the data suggested that the Banyankore will ever become anything but Banyankore-Ugandans. But the strength of their identity as Banyankore is not necessarily an impediment to national integration. As the one grows, so might the other. This conclusion suggests some propositions for leaders who would seek to encourage nationalism without conflicting with the dynamics of personal identity in a new nation composed of salient, tribal subgroups.

Group attachments are mirrored in the social self. Any relationship in which an individual is involved—whether with family, fellow congregationists, co-workers, nation, or language group—contributes to self-identity. But some attachments are more meaningful than others.

Subnational identities are often considered to be of considerable tenacity. This proved to be the case for the Banyankore, whose identities are deeply rooted. One might therefore fear that subnational units will outlive the national structures superimposed on them in Africa and Asia. Europe, too, has cases where such ethnic attachments have continued to be of pervasive impact—in Northern Ireland, for example—and there is no a priori basis for ensuring that the process will be any different elsewhere.

One can challenge the view, however, that primordial attachments must be severed in order to produce integration into new membership units. Leaders of many new states encourage their people to think of themselves as citizens of these states *rather than* as members of particular sectional groups. But the potency of ethnic identities is justification enough for questioning these strategies. To argue that it is necessary, or even possible, for any ethnic group to lose its identity in order to become part of a larger social entity is probably wrong. The Uganda research suggests that it would be wrong to opt for assimilation (which presupposes a blurring of constituent cultures) instead of integration (which does not).

OUT-GROUP RELATIONS

Ethnocentrism in the Ugandan Case Study

Some findings from the Uganda study have to do with Banyankore attitudes toward other Ugandan groups. The authors adopted the Sumnerian position that a social group acquires part of its definition in reference to other groups from which, in one way or another, it is subjectively set apart. Significant other groups for the Banyankore include traditional tribal groups residing on Ankole's borders: the Baganda, Batoro, Bakiga, and Banyarwanda. Nearby are other groups, including the Banyoro, and slightly farther away are sets of groups known collectively as the Congolese and Nilotics. All of these groups except for the Banyarwanda and Congolese are part of modern Uganda.

Within Ankole itself, complicating the picture of in-group/out-group definition, there is the historically significant distinction between Bairu and Bahima (singular, Mwiru and Muhima). In Ankole, Bairu make up more than 95% of Ankole's population, with the balance being Bahima. Bairu are traditionally agriculturalists; Bahima are herdsmen. These subgroups differ in geographic origin, physical type, and ethnolinguistic category (Bahima are classified anthropologically as Nilo-Hamitic, Bairu as Bantu). They also differ in political status, because the Bahima were traditionally overlords and the Bairu serfs. Data pertaining to this microlevel intra-Ankole relationship are provided in Box 14-2.

Banyankore Attitudes Toward Out-groups

We now turn to data that reveal Banyankore perceptions of and attitudes toward their neighbors. Respondents were asked to indicate the names of people who are most like the Banyankore, people whom the Banyankore like best, people whom the Banyankore dislike, and people with whom the Banyankore intermarry.

Likes and Dislikes

Many respondents cited more than one group in response to the questions about groups liked and disliked. The name mentioned most often in response to both questions was Baganda. Slightly more than a quarter of all respondents in both waves cited the Baganda first as the group liked best; and 20% and 33%, in the first and second waves respectively, mentioned the Baganda as the people whom the Banyankore disliked. The Bakiga was the only group mentioned more often as best liked, and no other group was mentioned as often as disliked. It would have to be concluded, therefore, that the Baganda are the most salient out-group. There are approximately as many Banyankore who think of them as the best-liked out-group as there are those who think of them as a disliked out-group.

There was a clearly positive attitude toward the Bakiga. They were by far the most often cited first as best liked (by 38% and 37%, respectively) and were almost never cited as disliked. The Batoro were also rather popular (best liked by 21% and 17%) and almost never disliked. Thus, the Bakiga, Baganda, and Batoro stand out as groups cited first as best liked. Only one of these, the Baganda, was cited with any appreciable frequency as disliked. Interestingly, the positive responses toward the Baganda came mainly from lesser educated men; most of the negative answers were from better educated respondents.

At the other end of the scale were three out-groups that were relatively frequently cited first as disliked. These were the Nilotics, a category that included several northern Ugandan groups (25% and 13%), the Banyarwanda (18% and 19%), and the Congolese (5% and 10%). Hardly anyone mentioned any of these groups as best liked.

Perceived Similarity of Various Out-Groups

We turn now to evidence about how similar various out-groups appear to the Banyankore themselves. The Bakiga stand out. Half of the first-wave respondents and 60% of the second wave cited them first as the people who are most like the Banyankore. Counting second and third responses, eight out of every ten named the Bakiga as most similar to themselves. The only

Box 14-2 Banyankore Attitudes Toward Their In-group

Given this complexity, Segall, Doornbos, and Davis (1976) were interested not only in the Banyankore's attitudes toward non-Banyankore out-groups but also in the way in which they defined their in-group. Toward this end, the men in both sampling waves (before and after the 1967 constitutional changes) were asked five preliminary questions, purposely redundant, in order to elicit as full a picture as possible about Banyankore as an in-group. The five questions were asked in sequence to create a probing effect.

The first question was "What does the term Munyankore mean?" The form and content of this question was expected to produce a straightforward reply, such as "Someone who lives in (or was born in) Ankole," because the literal translation of the term is "a person of Ankole." In fact, 85% of the first-wave sample and 86% of the second wave so replied.

The second question was "Who are the Banyankore?" To this, 46% and 71%, respectively, responded "Natives (or inhabitants) of Ankole"—the same kind of response made frequently to the earlier question. But 42% in the first wave and 21% in the second singled out particular people, saying either "Bairu," "Bahima," or "Africans." Of these discriminative responses, "Africans" is of marginal interest since so few non-Africans (primarily Asian shopkeepers) live in Ankole. Responses of major interest, given the concerns of this research, were "Bairu" and "Bahima". These were given by 34% in the first wave and 16% in the second. Because no one responded in terms of religion, occupation, or any other intra-Ankole subgroup, it is striking that so many respondents, particularly in the first wave, said that Bairu or Bahima are the Banyankore.

If this question (Who are the Banyankore?) may be considered a semiprojective test—one that provided an occasion for Bahima/Bairu ethnocentrism to emerge in a not very subtle, but nonetheless indirect, fashion—then these responses may be interpreted as indexes of intra-Ankole ethnocentrism. To say that only Bairu or Bahima are the Banyankore, when Banyankore, objectively defined, includes both, is to express decidedly parochial attitudes. But in general, intra-Ankole ethnicity was found not to be salient or subjectively very important. That only 16% of respondents singled out Bahima or Bairu as Banyankore after 1967 (compared with 34% prior to 1967) suggests that intra-Ankole ethnocentrism was on the wane.

"How does someone (a stranger) recognize a Munyankore?" The third question, because it asked how, might have been expected to elicit descriptions of a Munyankore—how he looks, how he speaks, or how he behaves. In fact, in the first wave 53% said "By the language he speaks," and 24% said "By the way he looks" (and 11% rather evaded the question by stating that although a native could recognize a Munyankore, a stranger could not). The remaining 12% of responses were scattered among dress, diet, occupation, and behavior. In the second wave, the percentage specifying language as the essential cue rose to 72%, and the percentage specifying physical appearance remained near 25%. Clearly then, language, which is shared by Bahima and Bairu and distinguishes them from non-Banyankore, was thought of by most people as the distinguishing characteristic of a Munyankore. But nearly one quarter replied in terms of physical features, which distinguish Banyankore from some of their out-group neighbors but also Bahima from Bairu.

(continued)

Box 14-2 *Continued*

This last point also suggests that intra-Ankole ethnocentrism, although increasingly countered by interethnic tolerance, was not laid to rest in 1967. Differences in stature and physiognomy, which distinguish Bahima from Bairu, were frequently cited by informants. That such responses were no less frequent in the second wave than in the first, coupled with the interwave increase in language responses, suggests a continuing ethnic awareness accompanied by a spreading tendency to grant full Munyankore status to both ethnic categories, in spite of the ethnic awareness.

Respondents were then asked "Is anyone who lives in Ankole a Munyankore?" Most respondents said "Yes": 92% of the first wave and 70% of the second. The negative replies (contributed by 8% and 30%, respectively) were hardly ever accompanied by specifications of who the non-Munyankore residents of Ankole might be. Moreover, no one singled out Bahima or Bairu as non-Munyankore.

"Precisely what does a man have to be to be called a Munyankore?" was the final in-group question. Most responses in both waves belonged in the categories "native born", "Runyankore speaker", and "resident." These three categories accounted for 80% of the first-wave and 87% of the second-wave responses.

Considering responses to all five questions, it was found that (1) nearly everyone in both samples defined a Munyankore as a person who was born or lives in Ankole, with some stress—more so in the second wave—on birthplace as the defining characteristic; (2) although most people repeated these definitions when asked who the Banyankore are, a few specified Bahima or Bairu; (3) language (and, to a lesser extent, physical features) was most often cited as the distinguishing characteristic of a Munyankore; and (4) a few people, particularly better educated ones, recognized that not all Ankole residents were Banyankore, and, when pressed, most respondents stated that one had to be born a Munyankore (or its functional equivalent, a speaker of Runyankore) to be considered a Munyankore. Thus, although the responses revealed a lingering consciousness of intra-Ankole ethnicity, there were widely spread expressions of a growing willingness to grant Munyankoreness to all Banyankore.

---

other group that was anywhere nearly as often cited was the Batoro, named by nearly half (but by fewer than 20% as a first response). When persons did make multiple responses, they tended to say "Bakiga, Batoro, and Baganda" in that order.

The hierarchy of perceived similarity that resulted was Bakiga, Batoro, Baganda, and Banyoro, with Banyarwanda and Bahima following, but not very closely. The first four are, in fact, not only the Banyankore's closest neighbors but also culturally and linguistically most closely related to the majority Bairu population of Ankole.

When asked to name the groups with whom they intermarry, the men most frequently said again "Bakiga, Batoro, and Baganda." The results of this question, then, confirm the results of the more direct effort to secure subjective estimates of similarity.

So, the Bakiga were not only the best-liked group but were also perceived as most similar and were thought to provide more marriage partners than any other out-group. The latter two points may be redundant; they might also explain why the Bakiga are the best liked.

We conclude on the basis of responses to several different questions that the Banyankore have revealed that they perceive their closest neighbors as similar, likable, and marriageable. Their favorite neighbors in all three respects are the Bakiga. Toward the Baganda there is ambivalence at the societal level, in that lesser educated Banyankore like them and see them as similar and marriageable, whereas better educated do not. The Batoro are viewed in much the same way as the Bakiga, but by fewer people. The Banyoro, farther away geographically than the Bakiga, Batoro, or Baganda, are also liked and thought of as similar but hardly ever cited as marriage partners. Other groups, more distant (but known) and culturally less similar—the Nilotics, Congolese, and Banyarwanda—are far less often seen as similar and seldom thought of as marriage partners. This pattern of attitudes and perceptions is summarized in the map and chart in Figure 14-1.

With one notable exception, proximity seems to be the key to how out-groups are perceived and reacted to. The exception is the Baganda; the attitude toward this group probably reflects not proximity but the history of contact between the Baganda and the Banyankore. Once the Banyankore's overlords (during the early 20th century, when Baganda were employed by the British colonial authorities as "chiefs") and once the Banyankore's enemies in territorial warfare, the Baganda seem to enjoy the respect of the elderly (and lesser educated) and the resentment of the young.

With the special case of the Baganda aside, the people best known are the people best liked, perceived as most similar, and most often taken as marriage partners. Those peoples who live one group removed are the negatively valued out-groups. What should be underscored is that the pattern is probably no different from the one found practically everywhere. Typically, one's closest neighbors—unless seen as enemies, troublemakers, or the like—are one's positively valenced out-groups. And negative attitudes are more likely to be applied to well-known, but more distant, neighbors. The really distant ones, hardly known and historically insignificant, are usually spared both negative and positive affect. The only people who, in this sense, matter to the Banyankore are those people whom they know. Among these, the ones they perceive as most like themselves are liked. Those whom they perceive as different from themselves, they dislike.

Nilotics

Banyoro

Congolese

Baganda

Batoro

Ankole

Bakiga

Banyarwanda

Best liked	*Disliked*	*Similar*	*Intermarry*
1. Bakiga	1. Baganda[b]	1. Bakiga	1. Bakiga
2. Baganda[a]	2. Nilotics	2. Batoro	2. Batoro
3. Batoro	3. Banyarwanda	3. Baganda	3. Baganda[a]
4. No clear choice	4. Congolese	4. Banyoro	4. No clear choice

[a] Mostly by lesser educated respondents
[b] Mostly by better educated respondents

Ankole and neighboring peoples

FIGURE 14-1. Intergroup attitudes in Western Uganda

Intergroup Attraction and Perception on a Broader Canvas

The Uganda case study, a particular instance of intergroup relations, cannot serve to test general hypotheses; studies employing a large number of groups are required. One excellent study by Brewer and Campbell (1976), involving 30 groups in East Africa (Uganda, Kenya, and Tanzania), includes groups already familiar to us—the Baganda, Banyoro, Batoro, and Banyankore in Uganda, the Kikuyu in Kenya, and the Masai in Kenya and Tanzania.

Ethnocentrism in East Africa

The Brewer and Campbell study was designed to test hypotheses concerning the characteristics of out-groups that are most likely to be targets of hostility, the role of proximity and cultural similarity in shaping attitudes toward out-groups, the content of stereotypes that are likely to develop for particular in-group/out-group pairs, and the significance of contact between groups as a determinant of mutual perceptions and attitudes. These were derived from Sumner's (1906) theory of ethnocentrism.

Other theories of intergroup relations provide more hypotheses. In a systematic compilation, LeVine and Campbell (1972) listed 331 testable propositions, including 253 correlational hypotheses derived from Sumner. Many refer to attitudes and behaviors that in a strict reading of Sumner would be thought to be universally present and interrelated.

Data were collected in 1965 among 30 East African societies, 10 each in Uganda, Kenya, and Tanzania, with 50 individuals questioned in each society by a native speaker. Respondents were queried about their own group and 13 others, nine living within their country and four from neighboring countries.

The interview contained (1) questions relating to social distance (Bogardus, 1925, 1928), for example, "Would you willingly agree to become related to a _____ by marriage?" (2) questions on familiarity, for example, "Do you know any _____? Do you speak their language?" (3) open-ended questions eliciting "good" and "bad" traits about 13 out-groups; (4) a structured list of traits to be assigned to the one group that the respondent thought each trait fit best; and (5) direct questions seeking the most liked, the most disliked, and the most and least similar out-group.

The findings provide the best available information on the dynamics of intergroup attraction and perception yet assembled. They permit us to consider the fundamental features of intergroup relations.

Affect Between Groups. Brewer and Campbell found, over all 30 societies, that measures of liking for particular groups, of social distance assigned to them, and of familiarity toward them were highly intercorrelated. Specifically, liking correlated .63 with social distance and .54 with familiarity, and social distance correlated .77 with familiarity. This pattern of intercorrelations justifies a single dimension of intergroup affect, described by the authors as "desirability of close interpersonal relations" and presumed to underlie the three separate measures of liking, social distance, and personal familiarity.

The four-item scale of social distance was of interest in its own right. In most of the 30 societies the items "scaled" in the following order: (1) willingness to share a meal with; (2) willingness to work with; (3) willingness to have as a neighbor; and (4) willingness to become related by marriage. In other words, in these East African societies the least degree of intimacy, subjectively speaking, is offered by sharing a meal and the most by permitting intermarriage. That the items scaled means that an individual who named an out-group in response to the intermarriage social-distance item probably named that group in response to the three other items. If a group was named in response to only three items, it was probably to the items other than the intermarriage one.

Most individuals followed this orderly pattern of responding to the four-item set, so that the scale proved to be highly reliable and valid. Part of this success stemmed from the fact that many respondents gave all-yes or all-no answers to the entire set, but this does not detract from the detection of a consistent pattern of social-distance attitudes. And, as we have just seen, the measure of social distance correlated highly with both liking and familiarity, adding further credence to the social-distance measure as an index of inter-group affect.

Brewer and Campbell asked what characteristics of out-groups seemed to determine scores on this index of intergroup attraction. The scores covaried mostly with opportunity for contact with out-group members. High scores (that is, low social distance and high liking and familiarity) were most likely to be assigned to groups that were similar in culture and language to the in-group and that enjoyed geographic proximity to it. Most individuals in any group felt closest to those groups that were nearer, better known, and cultur-ally most like their own group.

Highest affect was attached to groups with whom traditionally there had been much contact. Even when overt conflict had recently occurred between two "familiar" groups, the psychological distance was relatively small and the mutual attraction high. So contact matters.

Another variable was the perceived (and actual) level of modernity of particular out-groups. Groups perceived as "backward" were generally as-signed high social distance and were otherwise treated as unattractive. High-status groups such as the economically favored Chagga of Tanzania, Ba-ganda of Uganda, and Kikuyu of Kenya, toward all of whom *respect* was high, were found to earn high *or* low attractiveness scores depending on their cultural similarity to a particular in-group. Brewer and Campbell sug-gested that high-status groups may serve either as "models of a desired status" or as "visible targets for resentment" (or both). "Modern" groups will be emulated and found attractive if they are culturally similar but resented and rejected if not, underscoring once more the overriding importance of similarity.

Within each in-group, while there were individual differences relating to education and urbanization, the norms of attractiveness toward out-groups were found to be widely shared. This suggests that attitudes towards out-groups are acquired through socialization and enculturation early in life and are relatively immune to subsequent individual experience.

The Reciprocity of Intergroup Affect. It was generally found that if group X liked group Y, group Y liked group X. Intergroup attraction, and lack thereof, were usually reciprocated. This follows from what we have already learned; because attraction appears to be determined primarily by cultural similarity, similar groups will be attracted to each other and dissimilar ones will find each other relatively unattractive. The empirical finding of reciprocity also suggests that a group that feels negative toward another group is not necessarily being perverse or hostile in a willy-nilly fashion. It is likely to be the target of similar feelings directed toward it from that other group. It is further likely to find "justification" for its own negative feelings toward that group in its "mistreatment of us." The mutuality of negative intergroup affect thus makes the negative affect virtually self-reinforcing and hence rather tenacious.

The Brewer and Campbell findings reveal a process in which cultural similarity (both perceived and actual) generates in any given pair of groups shared, reciprocated feelings—positive for similar groups, negative for dissimilar ones. An intriguing implication of this process may be that to reduce intergroup negative affect would require changes in the behavior of both groups, each toward the model provided by the other, together with a mutual perception of increasing similarity.[2] As long as either perceives the other as different, it will not like the other, the other will reciprocate the dislike, and the affect will remain negative. Thus, cultural contact and modernization might improve intergroup relations. As we saw in Chapter 13, these processes tend to produce cultural homogenization. We shall return to this speculative point later in this chapter.

Intergroup Perceptions. Although one might expect liked groups to be perceived as possessing mostly positive traits and disliked groups negative ones, the facts were not that simple. The contents of intergroup perceptions, unlike intergroup attraction, could not be represented by a single dimension of "acceptability/rejection;" Brewer and Campbell needed three dimensions to account for intergroup perceptions, which they labeled trust/conflict, attraction/repulsion, and admiration/disrespect. On this three-dimensional map, the distance between any two groups varied, depending on which dimension was salient at the time.

Sumner's (1906) model of intergroup perceptions, "convergent ethnocentrism," must be altered. Whereas Sumner held that each in-group and its allies would be perceived as positive in all respects, Brewer and Campbell found this to be true only when "all bases of distinction between 'us' and 'them' are highly correlated" (1976, p. 144). Sumner's model occurs only when (1) contact opportunities are low, (2) environmental survival threats require extremely high internal cooperation and in-group loyalty, or (3)

---

[2]In this regard, it is interesting to think about changes in relations between the so-called superpowers, the Soviet Union and the United States, over the periods of the Cold War and detente. Increased friendship and perceptions of enhanced similarity seem to have gone hand-in-hand.

ethnic discrimination is legally or otherwise encouraged. In the absence of such conditions, which is most often the case, there is "flexibility in adapting patterns of alliance to correspond to differing functional requirements" (p. 145).

Consistent with these findings is the likelihood that an individual in any in-group can like a particular out-group at certain times or in certain respects and negatively evaluate it at other times or in other respects. Cognitive consistency seems not to be necessary in intergroup attraction and perception. For many people, of course, such consistency will prevail. But the findings of this study suggest that many other individuals, perhaps those who generally reveal a high degree of psychological differentiation, are equipped psychologically to handle complex, inconsistent intergroup attitudes.

Contact was also related to the content of intergroup perceptions. For individuals with little or no familiarity with an out-group, the perceptions of it tended to be more simplistic, consistent, and based largely on reputational stereotypes. Individuals better acquainted with an out-group held more idiosyncratic, less consistent — but not necessarily more positive — perceptions.

Perceptions of the In-Group Itself. The aspect of Sumner's theory that was more clearly supported concerns high self-regard: "Each group nourishes its own pride and vanity, boasts itself superior, exalts its own divinities" (1906, p. 13). Negative perception of out-groups is not universal, but positive perception of in-groups may well be. Brewer and Campbell found that all in-groups in their study rated themselves more favorably than they were rated by others. Specifically, "The facet of ethnocentrism that comes closest to universality is the tendency to regard own group members as more honorable and trustworthy than others" (1976, p. 143).

Positive self-regard was maximal for groups granted either high *or* low respect by other groups, and it somewhat diminished among moderately respected groups. That especially low- and high-status groups should hold themselves in such high self-regard led the authors to hypothesize that these Sumnerian ethnocentric feelings may reflect "high self-esteem associated with achievement and positive regard from others, or a defensive self-esteem associated with rejection and/or threat" (p. 143).

A Recapitulation

The data from 30 East African societies allow one to conclude that (1) persons generally like their own groups best and perceive them in a most positive light; (2) the degree of attraction felt toward other groups is fundamentally a cultural fact, internalized by individuals early in life; (3) intergroup attractiveness tends to be reciprocal; (4) intergroup attraction depends on opportunity for intergroup contact, which, in turn, reflects cultural similarity and proximity; (5) out-groups perceived as "backward" are generally unattractive, whereas groups perceived as "advanced" enjoy high attractiveness if they are culturally similar to the in-group of the perceiver; (6) outgroup perceptions cannot be predicted solely on the basis of attractiveness (trustworthiness and achievement also matter); and (7) opportunity for contact relates to intergroup perceptions but in a complex manner: the perceptions tend to be stereotyped for individuals with little opportunity for contact, but varied and idiosyncratic among individuals who know more about the out-groups in question.

All of this is more or less consistent with Sumner's ethnocentrism theory; "more," regarding in-group perceptions and intergroup attraction, "less" with regard to intergroup perception. The importance of intercultural similarity was clearly shown by this study.

These findings, involving 30 distinct ethnic groups, ought to be replicated, preferably in some other part of the world. We can tentatively conclude that intergroup attraction and perception are products of cultural similarity and status, with the former more important than the latter.

Additional Insights From Other Cross-Cultural Studies

Thus far we have dealt with one case study and one hypothesis-testing study. There are several theories about intergroup relations and many studies inspired by them. Taylor and Moghaddam (1987) summarize six major theoretical approaches, including realistic-conflict theory, social-identity theory, and relative-deprivation theory. They see several European theories (e.g., Tajfel, 1982) as placing greater emphasis on social factors than was characteristic of North American social psychology.

Taylor and Moghaddam (1987) also noted growing interest in multicultural policies in countries where minorities are manifesting enhanced efforts to improve their status. As this phenomenon grows, we will surely need to understand better the dynamics of intergroup relations. Berry (1984) provides a discussion of multicultural policy in Canada.

Taylor and Moghaddam (1987) consider stereotyping as a process central to social psychology and relevant to all theories dealing with intergroup behavior. We will now examine a few studies in which stereotyping is of primary concern.

Stereotyped Out-Group Perceptions

Sumner's ethnocentrism theory also serves as a source of hypotheses about stereotyping, the psychological process by which out-groups are ascribed characteristics that serve to justify the social distance at which they are held. In Sumner's view, because out-groups are treated badly, verbal descriptions of them should be dominated by negatively valued characteristics, to legitimize the hostility. To make an out-group appear deserving of animosity, one might even invent negative characteristics. Such invention, however, is seldom necessary, because one can always find some difference in "their" behavior as compared with "ours"; and because ours is moral and good, theirs must be immoral and bad.

Since, as we have seen, not every out-group is held at a large social distance, Sumner's view is exaggerated. Not every out-group will be characterized by negative stereotypes. But such stereotyping is common, particularly with relatively unknown and culturally different groups.

Ethnocentrism theory also predicts that stereotyping will be a mutual, reciprocal process between any two groups aware of each other. The stereotypes may reflect real, noticed, and acknowledged differences in modal behavior patterns, with the differences described in positive terms for each in-group and in negative terms for each out-group. Because every language is rich in both positive and negative adjectives, it is usually possible to treat any noticed difference between us and them in our favor. On the one hand, if they appear typically to work harder than we, we can describe them as "compulsive." They, in turn, can describe us as "lazy." If, on the other hand, we work harder than they, we can describe ourselves as "industrious," and they can describe themselves as "relaxed." Finally, the theory predicts a tendency to exaggerate the degree to which any negative trait is possessed by out-group members, attributing it to all or most. These ideas lead to a set of expectations about the content of stereotypes; in recent years, these have been subjected to cross-cultural empirical tests. Many of these are essentially replications of early studies done in the United States. A few of these are described in Box 14-3.

Cross-Cultural Studies: No Black and White. In Hawaii, Kurokawa (1971) administered an 84-item checklist to 100 white, 100 black, and 100 Japanese-American respondents (adults, college students, and schoolchildren), who were to select five terms that best applied to each of those ethnic groups. There was high agreement that whites are materialistic and pleasure-loving; blacks, musical, aggressive, and straightforward; and Japanese-Americans, industrious, ambitious, loyal to family, and quiet. Kurokawa derived a hypothesis from Katz and Braly (1933) that the dominant whites would be endowed primarily with positive traits, whereas both minority groups would be ascribed predominantly negative traits. The hypothesis was not fully supported. In some settings, at least, positive traits are assigned to minority groups.

The Influence of Contact on Stereotypes. Contact may influence the clarity and valence (positive/negative) of stereotypes. Triandis and Vassiliou (1967), working in Greece with both Greek respondents and Americans living there, found trait attributions of Greeks and Americans that could be compared

---

Box 14-3 A Classic U.S. Study of Stereotyping

Katz and Braly (1933) did the classic study in the United States with college students, who selected terms from an adjective checklist and assigned them to numerous out-groups, some known, some not. The Katz and Braly findings were dominated by much agreement in the assignment of negative traits to any but the core-cultural white Protestant in-group. Other U.S. studies over the years showed similar patterns (see, for example, Blake & Dennis, 1943; Gilbert, 1951; Schoenfeld, 1942; Vinacke, 1956). By 1971 a review of the literature spanning more than four decades (Cauthen, Robinson & Krauss, 1971) could conclude that in the United States the content of stereotypes remained very stable, with most groups described in much the same way they had been described by Katz and Braly's respondents. Another consistency in findings was that the greater the social distance between any two groups, the greater the difference between self-stereotype and out-group stereotype. Still another was that individuals who are members of groups stereotyped by others accept at least part of the stereotype as characteristic of their own group, if not of themselves personally.

---

with attributions made by persons living in their own country and having little contact with nationals of the other country. They found that Americans living in Greece had clearer stereotypes of Greeks than did Americans who had little contact with Greeks. Also, the American respondents were more likely to describe the Greeks as similar to themselves if the Americans were living in Greece and thus enjoying contact. But the same did not hold for Greek respondents, for whom contact with Americans did not correlate with higher clarity or increased "correspondence" of stereotypes.

However, Reigrotski and Anderson (1959), in a report of a multinational study of stereotyping, showed that both clarity and content of national stereotypes may be determined by international contact. Respondents from nations that enjoy much contact with other nations were found to be less likely to bias their own-group descriptions in a favorable direction, more likely to attribute favorable characteristics to members of other nations, and more likely to describe their own group in ways that corresponded with descriptions provided by outsiders.

There may well be circumstances under which sociopolitical factors matter more than contact. Following the Nigerian civil war, Ogunlade (1971) had 100 university students from western Nigeria assign 10 adjectives from a list of 63 to each of 10 national groups (Americans, Russians, French, Chinese, and so forth), some of which had supported the federal Nigerian government (as did most people in western Nigeria) and some of which had been supporters of the secessionist Biafrans. Quite clearly, the nations that supported the federal side were described predominantly by positive adjectives, whereas the reverse was true for nations thought to have supported the rebels.

In a study by Nichols and McAndrew (1984) that also examined the effects of contact on stereotyping, rather small groups of college students (47 Americans in the United States who had never lived abroad, 19 others from the United States studying in Spain, 18 Spaniards with whom the second group of Americans were co-students, and 14 Malaysian students attending the American liberal arts college from which the American student samples were drawn) chose polar adjectives to describe their conationals and the other two groups. Whereas the Americans who were studying at home revealed the most negative view of others (including members of their own group), the Americans in Spain did not share this outlook on the world. Whether this was a consequence of studying abroad or a reflection of a preexisting disposition that also led them to study abroad is, of course, not clear. Generally, however, the strongest trend in the data relating to contact was that respondents with more intercultural contact expressed stronger stereotypes with more confidence, including negative ones. A curious qualification to this was that guests (Malaysians studying in the United States and Americans in Spain) perceived their hosts as relatively friendly, whereas the host group (Americans in the United States and Spaniards in Madrid) perceived their guests as relatively unfriendly. Might this finding suggest that persons in a less powerful position, like students abroad, look more kindly on more powerful others, in this case, their hosts?

The Role of Power. Lindgren and Tebcherani (1971) argued that relative power influences the accuracy of intergroup perceptions. The authors suggested that relatively low-power Arabs would be more sensitive to, more aware of, and more accepting of the Americans' views of themselves than the Americans would be of the Arab self-perceptions. On a measure of empathy in which Arab and American male students at the American University in Beirut described themselves and a "typical" member of the other group, Arab students described the typical American more as the American students described themselves than vice versa. (The authors acknowledged that their finding could be accounted for by a tendency for the Americans to be more open and self-revealing, thus giving more accurate self-descriptions and permitting the Arab observers to predict better how the Americans would describe themselves.)

A kind of parallelism in stereotypes is also found. Particularly when two groups are in a state of conflict, each tends to hold a view of the other that contrasts markedly with the view each holds of itself. Bronfenbrenner (1961) documented this for the United States and the Soviet Union at a time when the Cold War was intense, and he called the phenomenon the "mirror-image hypothesis." Haque (1973) applied the Katz and Braly technique with Indian and Pakistani respondents and found another example of parallelism. Specifically, *both* the Indians and Pakistanis tended to describe themselves as peace loving, trustworthy, religious, kind, idealistic, democratic, and hospitable. And *both* described the other as cruel, threatening, selfish, war mongering, greedy, and cheating. It may be that the mirror-image phenomenon is stronger when two groups are in a heightened state of intergroup tension.

The Relationship of Stereotyping
to Other Dimensions of Intergroup Attraction

Social Distance. In theory, the content of stereotypes should be predictable. Groups that like each other should tend to hold relatively favorable stereotypes of each other. Social distance and stereotyping should be correlated. But the data do not always confirm this expectation. Thus, in their East African study, Brewer and Campbell (1976) reported, "Although disliked outgroups are generally distrusted and negatively evaluated, outgroups given positive attraction ratings are not consistently assigned positively evaluated characteristics" (p. 143).

Sometimes the situation is complicated by existing social norms governing interactions among groups. Consider a circumstance where legal sanctions prevail, as in South Africa with its apartheid laws. Viljoen (1974) examined the relationship between stereotypes and social distance that prevailed for African and Indian students toward English-speaking whites, Afrikaans-speaking whites, "coloreds," Jews, and their own two groups. The students held an overall positive stereotype for the English-speaking whites and asserted that they would welcome relatively close social contact with them. For the Afrikaans-speaking whites, an overall negative stereotype was accompanied by remote social distance.

Thus, social distance and stereotyping were correlated for the two white groups. But the students revealed greater liking for other non-white ethnic groups than for the English-speaking whites, even though the stereotype of that group was more positive than those of the non-white groups. In this respect, then, the correlation between stereotype and social distance broke down.

Prejudice and Authoritarianism. Data from South Africa are also relevant to the issue of the relationship between prejudice and the personality trait known as authoritarianism. Adorno, Frenkel-Brunswik, Levinson, and Sanford (1950) found prejudice and authoritarianism to be correlated in the United States. Individuals who scored high on measures of authoritarianism (approving of rigid moral standards, strong policing, and the like) tended to express high degrees of prejudice against minority groups.

This led some theorists to argue that prejudice is an outward manifestation of a personality syndrome, indexed by scores on the authoritarianism measure, the F-scale. Pettigrew (1959, 1960) challenged this notion, at least for settings in which discrimination is sanctioned, as in the southern states in the United States and South Africa. In these settings, Pettigrew found what he termed "other-directed" prejudice, behavior that is best understood as conformity with prevailing norms. In his U.S. study, Pettigrew (1959) found that manifest prejudice against blacks by whites was not correlated with F-scale scores any more highly than in other regions. But it was correlated highly with measures of generalized tendency to conform such as regularity of church attendance. Nor was anti-black prejudice correlated with anti-Semitism in that setting, as authoritarianism theory would predict (and is, more generally speaking, the case in other parts of the United States).

In South Africa, where sanctions against blacks were even more rigid than in the southern United States during the 1950s, Pettigrew (1960) again found that anti-black prejudice was not highly correlated with F-scale scores. Lambley (1973) confirmed Pettigrew's findings with a sample of 190 white undergraduates taking introductory psychology at an English-speaking university in South Africa. He found only moderate positive correlations between authoritarianism and anti-black prejudice, between authoritarianism and social distance, and between prejudice and social distance. Also working among English-speaking whites in South Africa and using similar measures, Orpen (1971) found no significant correlations among the measures. Orpen's study was done in a setting where, as he put it, "the prevailing cultural norms explicitly sanction prejudiced ideas" (p. 301) and where individuals are encouraged to be intolerant, irrespective of personality.

Dogmatism. Another personality dimension that, in the United States at least, correlated with ethnic prejudice is dogmatism, as measured by Rokeach (1960).[3] Orpen and Rookledge (1972) administered Rokeach's Dogmatism Scale, a measure of anti-black prejudice, and a social-distance scale to 72 white English-speaking secondary school students of urban, middle-class background in South Africa. They found that only about 5% of the variance in prejudice in this sample could be accounted for by individual differences in dogmatism. Instead, political-party preference predicted prejudice, with respondents who preferred South Africa's white-supremacist party scoring more anti-black on both the prejudice and social-distance scales than respondents who preferred either of two integrationist parties, even though party preference was not related to dogmatism scores. Once again we see that in settings characterized by sanctioned discrimination and other norms

---

[3]This hypothetical personality trait is meant to characterize an individual whose cognitive processes tend to be "rigid" and who thus might be expected to be prone to simplistic, stereotypic thinking and to other symptoms of prejudice.

that encourage prejudice, sociocultural factors outweigh personality factors in shaping individual intergroup attitudes.

Agreement on Beliefs. Rokeach argued that perceived dissimilarity of belief systems is a root cause of ethnic prejudice. Research done in the United States demonstrated that acceptance of an individual sometimes depends on one's perception of the other's alleged values (see, for example, Rokeach, Smith & Evans, 1960), sometimes more on ethnicity (Triandis, 1961), and often on both.

Stein, Hardyck, and Smith (1965) presented white American high-school students with either white or black stimulus persons who held beliefs that were either consonant or not with the respondent's own beliefs. They found that belief consonance determined the perception of the stimulus person more than race. But allegedly "Negro" stimulus persons with consonant beliefs were described by respondents as less like themselves than were allegedly white stimulus persons of similar beliefs. When no information about beliefs was provided, acceptance of stimulus persons was based on race. Thus, while perceived belief congruence seemed to be of primary importance in this U.S. study, race was also salient, perhaps serving as an assumed indicator of different beliefs.

Social Norms. In South Africa, where racial discrimination is sanctioned, belief congruence/dissonance might be expected to be less important when compared with race. To test this hypothesis, Orpen and Pors (1972) administered a personal-values questionnaire to 54 white middle-class Afrikaans-speaking teenage schoolchildren in South Africa. Based on the results, a set of four stimulus persons was created, two white and two non-white, whose values were either consonant or dissonant with those of the respondent. Two months later, respondents were asked to complete a social-distance scale for each of the four stimulus persons and indicate the extent to which each was similar to themselves.

Both the consonant stimuli were perceived as more similar than either of the dissonant stimuli, indicating that the experimenters' manipulation of attributed values had been successful. The main findings, however, showed race to be more important than belief congruence in determining social distance. In fact, degree of liking for a stimulus labeled "Colored Teenager," with *no* description of beliefs provided, did not differ from the liking rating for the two non-white stimuli for which belief attributions were provided.

Rokeach's hypothesis that the perception of others as different from self is a root cause of prejudice needs qualifying. The Orpen and Pors (1972) results suggest that the social setting modifies reactions to both race and belief. The basic psychological determinant of social distance is perceived similarity but, when racial discrimination is officially sanctioned, this masks individual psychological tendencies.

Racist norms may not be strong enough to override perceived similarity. Even in Zimbabwe (then Rhodesia), where there was a heightened sense of race, Orpen (1972) found that white teenagers (about 40 each of both sexes) evaluated a stranger's desirability as a work partner largely on the basis of attitude similarity, regardless of the stranger's race. Thus, the initial contention that groups perceived to be similar to "us" will enjoy greater acceptability remains a powerful principle of the psychology of intergroup relations.

What Is an In-group?

Asserting that "each culture cuts the pie of experience differently," (or, has its own "subjective culture") Triandis has explored the likelihood that definitions of an in-group member will vary from culture to culture. Triandis, Vassiliou, and Nassiakou (1968) described the Greek definition of the in-group as more personal in character than an American one; the former includes family members, friends, and even foreign tourists, but not persons one doesn't know, even if they happen to be Greek. By contrast, Americans do not typically consider foreign tourists part of the in-group; but all Americans, even those unknown personally, are usually included.

This is not to say that co-nationality doesn't matter to Greeks. In an earlier study (Triandis & Triandis, 1962), a part of which focused on norms governing social distance, whereas Americans emphasized race to a degree not present in Greece, the Greeks emphasized religion and nationality.

The detailed content of in-group definitions and the guidelines of behavior toward persons so defined vary across cultures. A relationship that is considered intimate in one culture and available only to a highly valued in-group member may, therefore, be considered more casual in another culture and available to a larger category of persons (Triandis, 1975).

SOME CONCLUSIONS AND
TENTATIVE PRESCRIPTIONS

Our review of cross-cultural studies of intergroup relations has not been exhaustive but contains enough to permit conclusions and tentative suggestions about how intergroup relations might be improved. What surely stands out is the importance of perceived similarity and of opportunities for equal-status contact in enhancing intergroup attraction and diminishing intergroup social distance. Also, however much psychological factors (e.g., authoritarianism, dogmatism, field dependence) influence intergroup relations, behavior toward out-groups is subject to institutionalized norms and other forms of social control.

We have also seen that in-group identification and intergroup distance tend to be dynamically related parts of a whole syndrome of ethnocentric behaviors, much as Sumner argued in 1906. In this light we can better understand the Ugandan case study with which we dealt so intensively. The cultural identity of the Banyankore that we found to be so strong can now be recognized as socially functional, as it is for any in-group, in that it provides a psychological home base and a sense of belonging. By the same token, when individuals locate themselves in a relatively small collectivity that has meaning as an in-group, they can probably also identify comfortably with a larger collectivity that includes the smaller one.

But ethnic-group identification also has a potential for divisiveness and alienation from other groups. For the Banyankore, we found likability to be correlated with cultural similarity, proximity, and opportunity for contact. From the Brewer and Campbell (1976) study and from the other cross-cultural studies we reviewed, we can draw consistent conclusions. People everywhere hold their own group in highest regard, and social distance increases as perceived similarity diminishes.

If these findings tentatively answer the question "Why do we persist in behaving ethnocentrically?" a prescription for breaking down the barriers to a more global consciousness follows clearly. Ways must be found and efforts expended to increase equal-status contacts and to maximize the probability of experiences that will demonstrate and accentuate similarities rather than differences.

But, of course, equal-status contacts are not very likely between groups of unequal status. Katz and Taylor (1988) provide a book-length compilation of papers revealing the complexity of the situation in the United States, where debate still prevails among social scientists regarding the efficacy of desegregation efforts. It is not at all clear that these efforts have had the anticipated positive outcome. More equitable distribution of opportunities is probably a prerequisite for equal-status contacts. The relatively deprived (groups within multiethnic societies and economically less-developed nations) must be assisted in their efforts to "close the gap." In short, they must become less deprived and, as a consequence, more similar. Until that happens, such groups will continue to be perceived as different, and hence less good, thereby "deserving" to be held at large degrees of social distance.

In settings where ethnic discrimination is institutionally sanctioned, one of the effects of that discrimination, of course, is to accentuate and even exacerbate economic, social, and cultural differences. So, in such settings political and legal changes are absolutely necessary. Laws that force groups to remain separate from, and hence different from, their neighbors must be replaced by laws that force the opposite. Experience has shown that initial opposition to such reversals in the law is soon replaced by acceptance of them, just as Pettigrew's concept of the other-directed nature of much prejudice would suggest.

Leadership of an enlightened nature must accompany such legal changes, of course. The Kenyan case, to cite only one example, bears this out. Prior to the attainment of independence from Great Britain, Kenya was torn by racial strife. With insistence from the late President Jomo Kenyatta, himself detained in prison for years by the British for his alleged role in the Mau Mau emergency, Kenya became a model of a multiracial, multiethnic African society; although tribal identities remain salient in Kenya (recall Brewer & Campbell's 1976 report), tolerance prevailed within a few years of independence. Just as people accepted, believed in, and behaved in accordance with a "color bar" before independence, many Kenyans came to accept, believe in, and behave in accordance with laws that prohibit racial or ethnic discrimination.

It was suggested at the outset of this chapter that parochial loyalties are tenacious and not easily modified, as they will have to be if we are to contend with our global survival problems. It was also suggested that cross-cultural research into intergroup relations can both illuminate the magnitude of this difficulty and offer some guidelines for dealing with it. The research we have reviewed has served both those functions. What we have seen is the potency of cultural forces in shaping human behavior. It is cultural identity that binds individuals to their own groups; it is cultural similarity that permits those same individuals to accept and interact with persons from other groups. Just as persons within groups can deemphasize existing differences and instead emphasize what they have in common with other individuals, so can they do with other groups.

This will require a quantum leap in good will, accompanied by enlightened leadership and social policy that provide the requisite economic and normative settings in which such good will can flourish. Should this state of affairs come to pass, a new, global culture will be created, one to which an increasingly large portion of humankind will relate. But even this need not destroy loyalties, allegiances, and identifications based on small, traditional cultures. Complete cultural homogenization need not be feared. In any event, it is nowhere near as fearsome as the cultural parochialism and ethnocentrism from which we, hopefully, are departing.

Chapter 15

Conclusions

ON THE IMPORTANCE OF THE SOCIOCULTURAL CONTEXT

We asserted when this book began that to understand human behavior, it must be viewed in the sociocultural context in which it occurs. Having examined a variety of psychological topics, we can now ask whether we have demonstrated the validity of this assertion. By recalling a few examples of topics dealt with earlier, we can perhaps appreciate how attending to the sociocultural context was repeatedly shown to be essential.

Contextual Variations in Father/Son Relations

Recall some of what we learned about relations between fathers and sons, a topic that came up more than once in this book. It was first raised in Chapter 2, where we discussed a famous idea in Western psychology, Freud's notion of the Oedipus Complex. We saw that its central idea—that adolescent males feel hostile toward their fathers because of sexual jealousy—is probably a culture-bound idea and very likely incorrect! Malinowski's data from the Trobriand Islands were needed, however, before we could challenge Freud's late 19th-century Viennese thinking. Merely to test Freud's sexual jealousy hypothesis, we had to find appropriate data in a cultural setting other than the one in which the idea was spawned. Armed with Malinowski's Trobriand data, we could indeed point out a more parsimonious interpretation of young boys' hostility toward adult males (fathers included, but not only fathers), namely, that it reflected resentment by the boys of the harsh discipline to which they were subjected during their youth.

Later, in Chapter 11, where we examined the differing socialization patterns for boys and girls and some of the sex differences in behavior that exist around the world, we saw that boys are indeed treated more harshly than girls (in some respects, at least) in most societies and that they are also more subject to aggression inculcation. Thus, by surveying what has been learned regarding males and females (and relations between the sexes) in a variety of societies, we gained an even broader context in which to consider some popular, but difficult to maintain, ideas about how the personalities of both men and women are shaped by parental and other influences, all of which are embedded in culture. For males particularly, there are many factors that instill in them a tendency to display hostility and aggression, especially when they reach adolescence.

In Chapter 12, our focus was on aggression per se, and there we developed a biocultural theory of male adolescent aggression, one that attributed much of its underlying dynamics to father absence rooted in the division of labor by sex. On the basis of that theoretical argument, we suggested that "compensatory machoism" may appear during adolescence wherever boys grow up in societies with a sharp division of labor by sex and consequent low participation by fathers in child-rearing, resulting in cross-sex identification among young boys, and assertion by adolescent males of their "manliness" by behaving aggressively.

In three separate chapters, then, we found it necessary to subject ideas about relations between fathers and sons to cross-cultural scrutiny, because, it seemed, this question could be explored fully *only* by doing it that way. Whatever else resulted from that line of inquiry, we certainly moved well beyond the old Euro-centered notion of the Oedipus Complex, and far away from theories that would attribute the characteristic behaviors of males and females to sex-linked biological determinants.

Justice, Fairness, and Ethnocentrism in Cultural Context

A very different kind of question came to light in Chapter 10, where we reviewed studies relating to values, attitudes, and motives. There we saw that we had to attend to sociocultural contexts in order to comprehend the underpinnings of world views of even the most fundamental kind. One of these was the very concept of "fairness." The norms of distributive justice that prevail in different parts of the world were seen to relate systematically to the degree to which societies are collectivistic or individualistic in orientation, and this, in turn, was related to a number of fundamental ecological, economic, and political characteristics of societies. We also saw in Chapter 10 that whatever the prevailing allocation principle within a given society, how persons distribute rewards and punishments is also affected by the cultural identity of those who are to receive them. In-group members, we saw in a study of Chinese students (Leung & Bond, 1984), were likely to be preferred recipients of rewards. Thus, ethnocentrism interacts with norms of distributive justice.

To review what is known about ethnocentrism, its origins, and its manifestations, we filled a whole chapter. Chapter 14 revealed that empirical support exists for the Sumnerian view of the universality of ethnocentrism, at least in bold outline. In all societies, it seems clear, we are most likely to treat with justice members of our own groups. We bestow our best on those others whom we perceive as most similar to ourselves.

The Roots of Ethnocentrism in Socialization

We argued in Chapter 14 that the pervasiveness of ethnocentrism is best explained as a consequence of socialization. Since in all societies children are taught to value the norms of their own society, they are also taught, either explicitly or inadvertently, to value less the norms (and related behavior patterns) of other societies. Hence, the foundations of negative affect toward outsiders are laid early in life in all societies. So, of course, are the foundations of positive affect toward the in-group. Loyalty to it and conformity to its norms are transmitted over generations everywhere through socialization practices.

Issues to which questions of right and wrong pertain are many and diverse. How to treat persons as a function of their status is a paramount example. Consequently, we have prevalent notions in all societies about how to interact with persons of various ages, roles, and, of course, the two sexes.

The content of these notions varies across cultures. Often in this book, we saw how the contents depend on fundamental features of societies, such as the form of subsistence economy that characterizes them. One of the most striking examples of subsistence economy affecting human social life was studied in detail in Chapter 11, where expectations regarding the two sexes and the ways in which they relate to each other were repeatedly shown to vary with the way in which the societies sustained themselves. Again, we saw that different socialization practices, particularly the kinds of distinctions made between boys and girls in socialization emphases, reflected the sexual division of labor that may have been a functional invention within a given subsistence mode.

That behavior requires a cultural context in order to be understood is a proposition that is easily defended when the behavior in question involves attitudes, values, and intergroup processes. What is the case for more basic processes, like cognition and perception?

Context Effects on Cognition and Perception

Cognition

On the very fundamental issue of human competence, its assessment, its sources, and its manifestations, we spent several chapters reviewing data from non-Western societies that force us to rethink the notion of "intelligence." When we dealt with "everyday cognition" and informal education, we saw that we cannot understand intelligent behavior apart from the context in which it occurs.

Cross-cultural psychology, reflecting the cross-fertilization of anthropology and psychology, now takes the *individual in context* as the unit of analysis, as illustrated by the metaphor of the developmental niche. Some achievements of the approach that this concept epitomizes were illustrated in Part II. We also saw there how research in the area of "culture and cognition" has progressively shed some of its early Western ethnocentrism. We are still seeking a balance between the search for universal processes and cultural differences, and between experimental control and cultural validity.

Perception

If thinking is culturally influenced, so is perceiving, as we saw in Chapter 4. Our review in that chapter of research done cross-culturally on visual perception concluded with the assertion that "people perceive in ways that are shaped by the inferences they have learned to make in order to function most effectively in the particular ecological settings in which they live." This is a prime concrete example of the abstract ideas conveyed by the ecocultural model that informs all of the topics covered in this book.

THE ECOCULTURAL FRAMEWORK REVISITED

Illustrated in Figure 1-1, the ecocultural framework encompasses the processes of socialization and enculturation, to which we refer repeatedly in this book, as well as the concept of developmental niche, which we used in describing how early childhood development is environmentally influenced.

The framework reminds us that culture (or the "man-made" part of the environment) is not all that matters. So does the natural environment, which shapes human behavior both indirectly (that is, *through* culture) and directly, as when ecological factors relate to biological characteristics of populations.

Ecology and Cognition

The model suggests that ecology influences cognitive behavior indirectly in ways illustrated in several chapters. The work on degree of food accumulation and cognitive style is particularly illustrative of the connections that are explicit in the ecocultural framework.

Berry's research on Witkin's psychological differentiation also illustrates the dynamic interaction between theory building and empirical research.

While Berry's (1966) initial research design was originally based on an early version of the ecocultural model, it evolved as a consequence of empirical findings into the version used in this book. Although there was once faith in the universality of Witkin's theory (Witkin & Berry, 1975; Berry, 1976), it is now obvious that a cultural adaptation of the theory is needed (Okonji, 1980; Berry et al., 1986). This requires more research on the socialization practices that mediate the group-level variables (e.g., ecological pressures leading to differences in food accumulation; the sociohistorical impact of acculturation) that determine individual cognitive functioning.

The same observation holds for cultural differences in the development of concrete operations in the domains of quantification and space (Dasen, 1975). Future research needs to document more fully those aspects of the developmental niche, the social contexts, the child-rearing practices, and the parental ethnotheories that mediate the influence of the group-level factors on individual cognitive development. We covered some of the research that provides this kind of documentation (e.g., the culture-specific definitions of intelligence, in Chapter 5, and the study of informal education and everyday cognition, in Chapters 6 and 9).

What is needed is a research program that covers all aspects of the sequence portrayed in the ecocultural framework. In research with individual subjects, only Berry's long-term research program comes close to a complete design, although, as we have mentioned above, the socialization component of it is the least well documented.

Climate and Child-Rearing

In contrast, in research linking infant-mother body contact to sex identity, the child-rearing antecedents have been described in detail. Starting with climate as the ecological constraint, Whiting (1981) was able to show that infant-carrying practices are related to the mean temperature during the coldest months of the year; carrying infants in cradles is predominant in cold climates, carrying them on the body (using arms, a sling, or a piece of clothing) is significantly more frequent in warm climates. The latter carrying technique is linked to other child-rearing practices such as the sleeping arrangement (the infant sleeps near the mother at night), the post-partem taboo (the rule of avoiding sexual intercourse for some months after the birth of a child), and late weaning, all of which contribute to a close infant-mother body contact and the predominance of female role models.

We also saw in Part III how these features of child-rearing practices may lead to a feminine sex-identity, which, under some circumstances, may lead to problematic compensatory aggressive behavior in boys and young men. This research also illustrates our ecocultural framework. Most of the research contributing to this topic has been holocultural, involving the HRAF ethnographic data base, with cultures rather than individuals serving as the units of analysis. We also need more data collected on individuals in various societies.

Sociopolitical Variables

The ecocultural framework also calls for attention to the sociopolitical context. In this book, we paid attention to sociopolitical variables mostly when we discussed cultural change in Chapter 13 and intercultural relations in Chapter 14. Our analysis of acculturation in Chapter 13 revealed that individuals change over time as their cultures change and that these changes are often shaped by political forces of various kinds. Regarding "modernization" and nationalism in various parts of the world, we saw that political and economic forces affect the ways people identify themselves and how those identities both remain stable and change. In Chapter 14, we saw that political forces — for example, the behavior of leaders, who can shape widely held perceptions of outgroups — effectively influence the ways members of one society relate to another.

So, the ecocultural framework, with its call that we attend to both natural and culturally shaped environmental influences on all aspects of human behavior, has been illustrated throughout this book with examples ranging from behavior of a seemingly very individualistic and personal kind (e.g., visual perception) to such "macro" phenomena as cultural change and intercultural relations. We do indeed believe that what we have covered in this book justifies our insistence on using an ecocultural framework to understand human behavior.

RELATIONS BETWEEN CROSS-CULTURAL AND MAINSTREAM PSYCHOLOGY

In an ideal world, there would be no need for a psychological specialty called "cross-cultural psychology." If the literature of psychology included studies done in a culturally sophisticated manner in a wide variety of societies, the literature of psychology would be inherently cross-cultural. Then psychology — and not just a specialty within it — would be cross-cultural, for all its readers at least some of the time. Everyone would perforce learn about persons not like themselves. During its first hundred years, however, the literature of psychology has been produced predominantly by and about people who inhabit a few European and American societies. So whenever that work was being read by students in non-Western societies, they alone were reading cross-cultural psychology, since the behaviors described were those of unfamiliar persons inhabiting exotic settings! Western students were cheated, since they were being taught only about themselves! The real problem, of course, as we have tried to make clear many times in this book, is that all students of psychology were led to believe that they were learning universal laws about *human* behavior. And so everyone was deceived, including many psychologists themselves, who thought that what they were producing was not culture-bound, overly generalized psychology, but a purportedly universally applicable mainstream psychology. (An exciting symposium on the cross-cultural challenge to mainstream psychology was published in *The Cross-Cultural Challenge to Social Psychology* edited by M. Bond, 1988.)

Cross-cultural psychology is somewhat like a development aid project; it will be perceived as truly successful only when it is no longer needed. It will succeed when it has been absorbed into (and in the process, transformed) mainstream psychology. Since the cross-cultural approach is more a method than a set of unique problems (as one finds in certain branches of psychology like social psychology or cognitive psychology), it is quite likely to be incorporated into general psychology as simply one of the necessary methods available to students of behavior. As Heron and Kroeger stated in 1981, "Any serious and systematic attempt to study human behavior and experience must, in the very nature of things, be both developmental in depth and *cross-cultural in breadth*. In other words, general human psychology may not validly be approached as a branch of scientific inquiry in any other way" (p. 1, italics ours).

With such obviously important constraints on psychological theorizing brought to light by cross-cultural psychology, why has it so far had so little impact on mainstream psychology?

On the Failure to Penetrate the Mainstream

Of course, the authors of that pungent sentence are themselves cross-cultural psychologists. A harsh reality is that many psychologists still ignore such assertions. Lonner (1988) reported results of a content analysis on the treatment of cross-cultural psychology in the 35 most widely used (accounting for approximately 75% of sales) introductory psychology textbooks published in English in the years 1986 to 1988. He concluded that the use of cross-cultural material was "variable, limited and predictable." Whereas one textbook included five full pages on cross-cultural psychology (even that strikes us as amazingly little), others ignored it completely. Overall, only a very few topics were covered, and these tended to be the same ones. Problems connected with IQ testing, the universality of facial expressions of emotion (Ekman), the linguistic relativity hypothesis (Whorf), and some aspects of social psychology (prejudice and stereotypes) were each covered in only one quarter of the textbooks, whereas other topics were mentioned far less often.

Lonner attributed the apparent dismissal of cross-cultural psychology by the textbook writers to a prevalent belief in the universality of the findings of mainstream psychology and to space constraints that might argue against including qualifiers and other complicating issues in an introductory course. The result is an introduction that misleads.

In another survey, Dasen (1988) contacted 32 developmental psychologists spread over both anglophone and francophone areas of the world (and in Germany and the Soviet Union as well) with a small questionnaire on the impact (or lack thereof) of cross-cultural psychology on their work. All of the 20 who replied said that they had taken cross-cultural psychology into account, either in their research and writing or in their teaching,[1] but only half of them thought that cross-cultural psychology had made an important impact on general developmental psychology; the others felt that the impact was nil, limited, or just beginning to be felt.

Those who judged that cross-cultural psychology had some impact thought it to be mainly methodological. They noted that the cross-cultural method guards against unwarranted generalization, challenges the universality of psychological theories, provides "experiments in nature" that serve the unconfounding function, and, as one of the respondents said, "it thus leads to a more sophisticated and more fundamental understanding of psychological development."

Possibly more original and more interesting were the reasons given for the failure of cross-cultural psychology to make an impact. These included:

1. Cross-cultural psychology has not proved useful because it is mainly empirical and lacks a theoretical base (the theoretical model used as a background to both this volume and to Berry et al. (in press) should help to discard this objection).
2. It is always lagging behind mainstream psychology and does not easily integrate new theories.
3. Experimentally minded researchers hesitate to leave the well-controlled laboratory because they are afraid to be criticized for a lack of rigor.
4. They may also be afraid of the political overtones that cross-cultural research often has, and of possible ideological misunderstandings.
5. Cross-cultural psychology is insular, isolated in its own institutions (associations, meetings, and publications).

---

[1]Admittedly, the selection of the sample and the disciplinary affiliation of the investigator may have biased this answer.

6. Cross-cultural psychology may be resented as a threat, because it tends to be critical of mainstream psychology and associates happily with the other, nonpsychological disciplines.

That cross-cultural psychologists are comfortable with anthropologists, other social scientists, and other nonpsychologists is, of course, a positive characteristic in our opinion, but it may explain why so few psychology departments have positions for cross-cultural psychologists.

In any case, several of the reasons suggested for cross-cultural psychology's failure to break into the mainstream need to be taken seriously by cross-cultural psychologists.

Methodological Difficulties

Cross-cultural psychology is one of the newest branches of psychology (some scholars might prefer to state that cross-cultural psychology is one of the most recent *methods* that mainstream psychology now has at its disposal.) Cross-cultural psychology, as goes a popular phrase, has a long past but a short history. We saw in Chapter 2 especially, and also in Chapter 5, that its roots extend, together with those of anthropology, into the centuries during which Europe "discovered" the rest of the world, and in particular to the so-called enlightenment of the 18th century.

As part of its developmental dynamics, cross-cultural psychology has had its teething problems and childhood illnesses, from which it has only partly recovered. During much of its history, cross-cultural psychology's typical research project consisted of taking a favorite test to some exotic place, comparing the obtained results with those of the homeland "norms," and thereby "discovering a cultural difference" that either remained unexplained or was fitted with some post-hoc interpretation selected uncritically from among many uncontrolled alternatives. (This practice was discussed under the heading of "imposed etics" in Box 3-3.) This "safari-style" research was typically carried out by psychologists from Western countries on leave from their home universities, doing short-term field work, or through correspondence with a colleague in a foreign country. As this book will have made plain, we do not advocate this kind of research and we believe that enhanced publication standards will eliminate it.

A recurrent, albeit muted, theme of this book is that cross-cultural research is fraught with methodological difficulties. In Chapter 3, we discussed some of these problems and some of the solutions, and throughout the book we pointed out questions of method in connection with particular studies. But we lacked enough space to describe, for every study, exactly how it was carried out. All of the included studies, in our judgment, contribute valuable knowledge, but not all of them are beyond criticism. Indeed, cross-cultural research is so difficult to carry out that there almost always remains some point of contention, some uncontrolled variable, or some doubt because the study was done with a small number of subjects and no other researcher has attempted to replicate it.[2] In other words, cross-cultural research tends to be "soft," in comparison with the so-called "hard" data of experimental psychology.

Some mainstream psychologists simply ignore cross-cultural psychology because of its "softness." Should they? We think not. Alternative methods always have trade-offs. We are ready to weigh experimental control against the advantages to be gained from the cross-cultural approach, including the ability to unconfound variables that are always linked in single societies and the possibility of increasing the variance in a crucial variable. We are not saying that methodological rigor is unimportant; we are saying that one cannot always have it both ways, and that one occasionally has to make a choice, for example, between experimental control and validity. Although we have not tried in this book to teach how to do cross-cultural research,[3] we hope to have enabled students to assess cross-cultural studies critically. We saw in several examples throughout the book the numerous and difficult methodological decisions that cross-cultural researchers have to make. Assessing the gains in cultural validity against the loss in experimental control is part of the skill to be acquired, even though it may be difficult to specify objective rules for doing so.

LOOKING TO THE FUTURE OF CROSS-CULTURAL PSYCHOLOGY

We need cross-cultural research that is carried out with a profound knowledge of the cultural context, a cross-cultural psychology that spends as much effort on specifying the (independent) cultural variables as it does attending to the (dependent) psychological outcome measures (see LCHC, 1979). Such a research program usually requires extensive and long-term field work and an interdisciplinary approach between anthropologists and psychologists; we have covered in this volume several such large-scale efforts by expatriate psychologists. Such major research efforts needed extensive

---

[2]Replicability is one of the tenets of the scientific method: It always has to be demonstrated that the same results can be obtained by different researchers. Yet, in cross-cultural psychology, as in anthropology, there are very few reported attempts at replication (and occasionally distressing reports of complete failure when attempting to replicate, such as the controversy on adolescence in Samoa between Freeman [1983] and Mead). This is certainly due to several reasons, among which is the fact that researchers tend to have their favorite field sites, to which it is difficult for another researcher to gain access.

[3]There are more specialized texts for this purpose, for example, Lonner and Berry (1986) and Berry et al. (in press).

funding, and this is more difficult to secure than it was during some earlier periods. For this reason, and for others linked to the ethics and politics of cross-cultural research (see Warwick, 1980; Vinsonneau, 1980), we expect to see the following trends:

1. There will be less research carried out by itinerant expatriates, and more research carried out by psychologists working in their own societies. The Western psychologists who used to travel afar will spend more time studying cultural subgroups within their own society; massive migration movements and the development of multicultural societies favor this trend. Increasingly, there are psychologists in all parts of the world able to carry out research within their own cultural framework. For some time, psychologists in Third-World universities have tended to copy the models they had learned during their studies in the West. It takes courage to slough off the leading paradigms in scientific psychology, even if they are obviously inappropriate to a culturally sensitive psychology. In recent years, however, several research programs have developed more appropriate paradigms. A few examples of research by psychologists working in their own lands on problems of local relevance and with concepts and instruments rooted in their own cultures have been included in this book. The future, we hope, will provide many more examples.

2. There is also likely to develop more truly collaborative research efforts between psychologists of different countries. These would not be limited to projects designed, funded, and directed from the West, and therefore dominated by the Western researcher, but research designed and carried out by two partners of equal status and power. In the meantime, there will still be PhD students from non-Western countries studying at Western institutions and carrying out their field work in their own society; this form of research can be very valuable, if only the supervisors are at least informed in cross-cultural psychology.

3. As a consequence of the trends outlined above, cross-cultural research is likely to become more applied. On the one hand, funding for so-called pure research is becoming tighter, and on the other hand, many researchers, and especially those working within their own societies, are becoming more aware of the importance of contributing to the solutions of major social problems that have local manifestations. Psychology, in general, and cross-cultural psychology, in particular, have not yet realized their potential in this respect and are still likely to be ignored by policy makers. This is, we think, due to two reasons: (a) The public image of psychology as a helping profession is linked to clinical psychology or psychoanalysis, or as a technique restricted to testing and (b) most of mainstream psychology ignores the social and cultural variables that impinge on individual behavior and that make scientific psychology more

relevant to social policy. The cross-cultural approach, as a scientific method, should help to improve the image and the impact of psychology.

These three trends combined should influence the future of cross-cultural psychology in the following ways: There will be a movement away from a mainly theory-testing discipline that relies either on the hologeistic method-ology alone or on the careful comparison of means across samples drawn from various societies. Research will tend to focus more on single societies, while still taking sociocultural variables seriously, by comparing subgroups or studying individual differences and correlates rather than by relying on means across samples. Research will also become more truly interdiscipli-nary, combining biological, sociological, anthropological, and psycholog-ical methods and paradigms.

There may well come a time when we will no longer speak of cross-cultural psychology as such. The basic premise of this field—that to under-stand human behavior, we must study it in its sociocultural context—may become so widely accepted that all psychology will be inherently cultural.

Under these conditions, it becomes questionable whether one will still use the term *cross-cultural psychology*. The adjective *cultural* may suffice to indicate the fundamental importance of cultural variables,[4] and *ethnic psy-chology* (Berry, 1985) may come to be used to refer to intranational research. As for general psychology, it may progressively fuse into a more general social-science research paradigm that considers both individual and group variables. In any event, cross-cultural psychology as presented in this book encompasses all of these approaches.

Cross-cultural psychology may have a way to go, but as we think this book shows, it has already come a long way. We have filled many pages with accounts of the work of cross-cultural psychologists and still could not cover in sufficient detail all the topics that today constitute our knowledge of human behavior. To tell more of the story of cross-cultural psychology in ways that emphasize its theoretical and methodological underpinnings, the authors of this book have prepared another volume (Berry et al., in press; see also Malpass, 1977, for a discussion of cross-cultural theory and method). Some topics on which we merely touched briefly in the present book are treated in more depth in that volume. Thus, language and person-ality are central issues in Berry et al., whereas they are treated briefly in the present book, the former in Chapter 1 and the latter in Chapter 10. We also do not deal very much in this book with applications of cross-cultural psychology, whereas in the Berry et al. volume there are whole chapters on

---

[4]Cole in the United States, Camillieri in France, and Eckensberger in Germany were already using the phrase *cultural psychology* in the 1980s.

cross-cultural theories and their application to health, organizational psychology, intercultural communication, and ethnic groups and minorities.

So we end this textbook on the study of human behavior in global perspective by reminding our readers that those who wish to pursue the matter further can find the means to do so. There is indeed more to cross-cultural psychology than we have been able to include here. But we hope that we have made our introduction comprehensive, accurate, and challenging. We have tried to be vigilant with respect to our own ethnocentrisms but suspect that some have crept in.

With the hope that the reader's sensitivity to the marvelous diversity of humankind has been enhanced, we bring this book to an end by reaffirming that to understand human behavior, it *must* be viewed in the sociocultural context in which it occurs.

References

Adinolfi, A., & Klein, R. (1972). The value orientations of Guatemalan subsistence farmers: Measurement and implications. *Journal of Social Psychology, 87,* 13–20.

Adorno, T. W., Frenkel-Brunswik, E., Levinson, D. J., & Sanford, N. (1950). *The authoritarian personality.* New York: Harper.

Ahmed, M. (1983). Le non-formel et les questions critiques de l'éducation. [Important questions on non-formal education.] *Perspectives, 13,* 37–47.

Akinnaso, F. (1981). The consequences of literacy in pragmatic and theoretical perspectives. *Anthropology and Education Quarterly, 12,* 163–200.

Allport, F. H. (1924). *Social psychology.* Boston: Houghton Mifflin.

Allport, F. H. (1933). *Institutional behavior.* Chapel Hill: University of North Carolina Press.

Ardrey, R. (1966). *The territorial imperative.* New York: Atheneum.

Armstrong, R. E., Rubin, E. V., Stewart, M., & Kuntner, L. (1970). *Susceptibility to the Müller-Lyer, Sander parallelogram, and Ames distorted room illusions as a function of age, sex, and retinal pigmentation among urban midwestern children.* Unpublished manuscript, Northwestern University, Department of Psychology, Evanston, IL.

Aronson, E. (1958). The need for achievement as measured in graphic expression. In J. W. Atkinson (Ed.), *Motives in fantasy, action, and society* (pp. 249–265). Princeton, NJ: Van Nostrand.

Ashton, P. T. (1975). Cross-cultural Piagetian research: An experimental perspective. *Harvard Educational Review, 45,* 475–506.

Atkinson, J. W. (Ed.). (1958). *Motives in fantasy, action, and society.* Princeton, NJ: Van Nostrand.

Bacon, M. K., Child, I. L., & Barry, H., III. (1963). A cross-cultural study of correlates of crime. *Journal of Abnormal and Social Psychology, 66,* 291–300.

Bandura, A. (1971). *Social learning theory.* New York: General Learning Press.

Bandura, A., & Walters, R. (1963). *Social learning and personality development.* New York: Holt, Rinehart & Winston.

Barel, Y. (1977). La ville avant la planification urbaine. In M. Conan & L. Scheer (Eds.), *Prendre la ville. Esquisse d'une histoire de l'urbanisme d'Etat.* [The city before town-planning. A historical sketch of state urbanism.] (pp. 13–66) Paris: Anthropos.

Barnlund, D. C., & Araki, S. (1985). Intercultural encounters: The management of compliments by Japanese and Americans. *Journal of Cross-Cultural Psychology, 16,* 9–26.

Barry, H., III, Bacon, M. K., & Child, I. L. (1957). A cross-cultural survey of some sex differences in socialization. *Journal of Abnormal and Social Psychology, 55,* 327–332.

Barry, H., III, Bacon, M. K., & Child, I. L. (1967). Definitions, ratings and bibliographic sources of child-training practices of 110 cultures. In C. S. Ford (Ed.), *Cross-cultural approaches* (pp. 293-331). New Haven, CT: HRAF Press.

Barry, H., III, Child, I. L., & Bacon, M. K. (1959). Relation of child training to subsistence economy. *American Anthropologist, 61*, 51-63.

Barry, H., III, Josephson, L., Lauer, E., & Marshall, C. (1976). Traits inculcated in childhood: Cross-cultural codes V. *Ethnology, 15*, 83-114.

Bartlett, F. C. (1932). *Remembering*. Cambridge: Cambridge University Press.

Baudet, J., & Sarazanas, R. (1982). *L'enfant, les jouets et les nouveaux jouets*. [The child, toys and toy novelties.] Brussels: Casterman.

Beach, F. (1955). The descent of instinct. *Psychological Review, 62*, 401-410.

Béart, C. (1955). *Jeux et jouets de l'Ouest africain*, [Games and toys in West Africa.] 2 volumes. Mémoires de l'IFAN (Dakar), no. 42.

Becker, E. (1973). *The denial of death*. New York: Free Press.

Bem, S. L. (1974). The measurement of psychological androgyny. *Journal of Consulting and Clinical Psychology, 42*, 155-162.

Berkeley, G. (1927). *Three dialogues between Hylas and Philonous*. Chicago: Open Court. (Original work published 1713)

Berkowitz, L. (1958). The expression and reduction of hostility. *Psychological Bulletin, 55*, 257-283.

Berlin, B., & Kay, P. (1969). *Basic color terms: their universality and evolution*. Berkeley: University of California Press.

Berman, J. J., Murphy-Berman, V., & Singh, P. (1985). Cross-cultural similarities and differences in perceptions of fairness. *Journal of Cross-Cultural Psychology, 16*, 55-67.

Bernstein, B. (1961). Social class and linguistic development: A theory of social learning. In A. H. Halsey, J. Floud, & C. A. Anderson (Eds.), *Education, economy and society* (pp. 288-314). New York: Free Press.

Berry, J. W. (1966). Temne and Eskimo perceptual skills. *International Journal of Psychology, 1*, 207-229.

Berry, J. W. (1969). On cross-cultural comparability. *International Journal of Psychology, 4*, 119-128.

Berry, J. W. (1971a). Müller-Lyer susceptibility: Culture, ecology, or race? *International Journal of Psychology, 6*, 193-197.

Berry, J. W. (1971b). Ecological and cultural factors in spatial perceptual development. *Canadian Journal of Behavioural Science, 3*, 324-336.

Berry, J. W. (1974). Radical cultural relativism and the concept of intelligence. In J. W. Berry & P. R. Dasen (Eds.), *Culture and cognition* (pp. 225-230). London: Methuen. (Original work published in 1972)

Berry, J. W. (1975). An ecological approach to cross-cultural psychology. *Nederlands Tijdschrift voor de Psychologie, 30*, 51-84.

Berry, J. W. (1976a). Sex differences in behaviour and cultural complexity. *Indian Journal of Psychology, 51*, 89-97.

Berry, J. W. (1976b). *Human ecology and cognitive style: Comparative studies in cultural and psychological adaptation*. New York: Sage/Halsted/Wiley.

Berry, J. W. (1979). Culture and cognitive style. In A. J. Marsella, R. G. Tharp, & T. J. Ciborowski (Eds.), *Perspectives on cross-cultural psychology* (pp. 117-135). New York: Academic Press.

Berry, J. W. (1981). Developmental issues in the comparative study of psychological differentiation. In R. H. Munroe, R. L. Munroe, & B. B. Whiting (Eds.), *Handbook of cross-cultural human development* (pp. 475-500). New York: Garland STPM.

Berry, J. W. (1983). The sociogenesis of social sciences: An analysis of the cultural relativity of social psychology. In B. Bain (Ed.), *The sociogenesis of language and human conduct* (pp. 449–454). New York: Plenum Press.

Berry, J. W. (1984). Towards a universal psychology of cognitive competence. *International Journal of Psychology, 19*, 335–361.

Berry, J. W. (1985). Cultural psychology and ethnic psychology, a comparative analysis. In I. Reyes Lagunes & Y. H. Poortinga (Eds.), *From a different perspective: Studies of behavior across cultures* (pp. 3–15). Lisse, Netherlands: Swets & Zeitlinger.

Berry, J. W. (1986). The comparative study of cognitive abilities: A summary. In S. E. Newstead, S. H. Irvine, & P. L. Dann (Eds.), *Human assessment: Cognition and motivation* (pp. 57–74). Dordrecht, Netherlands: Martinus Nijhoff.

Berry, J. W., & Dasen, P. R. (Eds.). (1974). *Culture and cognition: Readings in cross-cultural psychology*. London: Methuen.

Berry, J. W., Irvine, S. H., & Hunt, E. B. (1988). *Indigenous cognition: Functioning in cultural context*. Dordrecht, Netherlands: Martinus Nijhoff.

Berry, J. W., Poortinga, Y. H., Segall, M. H., & Dasen, P. R. (in press). *Cross-cultural psychology: Theory, method and applications*. Cambridge: Cambridge University Press.

Berry, J. W., van de Koppel, J. M. H., Sénéchal, C., Annis, R. C., Bahuchet, S., Cavalli-Sforza, L. L., & Witkin, H. A. (1987). *On the edge of the forest: Cultural adaptation and cognitive development in Central Africa*. Lisse, Netherlands: Swets & Zeitlinger.

Beshai, J. A. (1972). Content analysis of Egyptian stories. *Journal of Social Psychology, 87*, 197–203.

Biesheuvel, S. (1943). *African intelligence*. Johannesburg: South African Institute of Race Relations.

Biesheuvel, S. (1949). Psychological tests and their application to non-European peoples. In G. B. Jeffrey (Ed.), *The yearbook of education* (pp. 90–104). London: Evans.

Biesheuvel, S. (1974). The nature of intelligence: Some practical implications of its measurement. In J. W. Berry & P. R. Dasen (Eds.), *Culture and cognition* (pp. 221–224). London: Methuen. (Original work published in 1959)

Binet, A. (1965). La mesure des illusions visuelles chez les enfants. In R. H. Pollack & F. K. Zetland (Eds. and Trans.), *Perceptual and Motor Skills*, 1965, 20, 917–930. (Original work published in 1895)

Biri, E. W., Pendleton, B. F., & Garland, T. N. (1987). Correlates of men's attitudes toward women's roles in Libya. *International Journal of Intercultural Relations, 11*, 295–312.

Bisilliat, J., Laya, D., Pierre, E., & Pidoux, C. (1967). La notion de lakkal dans la culture Djerma-Songhai. [The concept of lakkal in Djerma-Songhai culture.] *Psychopathologie Africaine, 3*, 207–264.

Blake, R., & Dennis, W. (1943). Development of stereotypes concerning the Negro. *Journal of Abnormal and Social Psychology, 38*, 525–531.

Blau, Z. S. (1981). *Black children – White children: Competence, socialization, and social structure*. New York: Free Press.

Bloom, A. H. (1977). Two dimensions of moral reasoning: Social principledness and social humanism in cross-cultural perspective. *Journal of Social Psychology, 101*, 29–44.

Boas, F. (1911). *The mind of primitive man*. New York: Macmillan.

Bochner, S. (1986). Observational methods. In W. J. Lonner & J. W. Berry (Eds.), *Field methods in cross-cultural research* (pp. 165–201). Newbury Park, CA: Sage.

Boesch, C., & Boesch, H. (1984). Mental map in wild chimpanzees: An analysis of hammer transports for nut cracking. *Primates, 25*(2), 160–170.

Bogardus, E. S. (1925). Measuring social distance. *Journal of Applied Sociology, 9*, 299–308.

Bogardus, E. S. (1928). *Immigration and race attitudes*. Lexington, MA: Heath.

Bolton, R. (1973). Aggression and hypoglycemia among the Qolla: A study in psychobiological anthropology. *Ethnology, 12*, 227–257.

Bolton, R. (1984). The hypoglycemia-aggression hypothesis: Debate versus research. *Current Anthropology, 25*, 1–53.

Bolton, R., Michelson, C., Wilde, J., & Bolton, C. (1975). The heights of illusion: On the relationship between altitude and perception. *Ethos, 3*, 403–424.

Bond, M. H. (Ed.). (1986). *The psychology of the Chinese people*. Hong Kong: Oxford University Press.

Bond, M. H. (Ed.). (1988). *The cross-cultural challenge to social psychology*. Newbury Park, CA: Sage.

Bond, M. H., Wan, K-C., Leung, K., & Giacalone, R. A. (1985). How are responses to verbal insult related to cultural collectivism and power distance? *Journal of Cross-Cultural Psychology, 16*, 111–127.

Boring, E. G. (1929). *A history of experimental psychology*. New York: Century.

Boring, E. G. (1942). *Sensation and perception in the history of experimental psychology*. New York: Appleton-Century-Crofts.

Bornstein, M. (1973). The psychophysiological component of cultural differences in color naming and illusion susceptibility. *Behavioral Science Notes, 8*, 41–101.

Bossel-Lagos, M. (in press). Catégorisation et prototypicalité: étude interculturelle. [Categorization and prototypicality: A cross-cultural study.] *Cahiers Latinoaméricains (Revue Suisse d'Etudes Latinaméricaines)*

Botha, E. (1968). Verbally expressed values of bilinguals. *Journal of Social Psychology, 75*, 159–164.

Bovet, M. (1974). Cognitive processes among illiterate children and adults. In J. W. Berry & P. R. Dasen (Eds.), *Culture and cognition* (pp. 311–334). London: Methuen.

Boyd, R., & Richerson, P. J. (1985). *Culture and the evolutionary process*. Chicago: University of Chicago Press.

Bradburn, N. M. (1963). N achievement and father dominance in Turkey. *Journal of Abnormal and Social Psychology, 67*, 464–468.

Bradburn, N. M., & Berlew, D. E. (1961). Need for achievement and English economic growth. *Economic Development and Cultural Change, 10*, 8–20.

Brenner, M. E. (1985). The practice of arithmetic in Liberian schools. *Anthropology and Education Quarterly, 16*, 177–186.

Brewer, M. B., & Campbell, D. T. (1976). *Ethnocentrism and intergroup attitudes*. New York: John Wiley.

Bril, B. (1983). Analyse d'un geste de percussion perpendiculaire lancée: La mouture du mil dans un village bambara (Dugurakoro-Mali). [The analysis of a perpendicular throwing movement: the pounding of millet in a bambara village.] *Geste & Image, 3*, 97–118.

Bril, B. (1984). Description du geste technique: Quelles méthodes? [Describing technical movements: Which methods?] *Techniques & Culture*, no. 3, 81–96.

Bril, B., & Lehalle, H. (1988). *Le développement psychologique est-il universel?* [Is psychological development universal?] Paris: Presses Universitaires de France.

Brislin, R. W. (1974). The Ponzo illusion: Additional cues, age, orientation, and culture. *Journal of Cross-Cultural Psychology, 5*, 139–161.

Brislin, R., & Keating, C. (1976). Cultural differences in the perception of a three-dimensional Ponzo illusion. *Journal of Cross-Cultural Psychology, 7*, 397–411.

Brislin, R. W., Lonner, W. J., & Thorndike, R. M. (1973). *Cross-cultural research methods*. New York: John Wiley.

Bronfenbrenner, U. (1961). The mirror image in Soviet-American relations: A social psychological report. *Journal of Social Issues, 17*, 45–56.

Broude, G. (1980). Extramarital sex norms in cross-cultural perspective. *Behavior Science Research, 15*(3), 181–218.

Broude, G. (1983). Male-female relationships in cross-cultural perspective: A study of sex and intimacy. *Behavior Science Research, 18*(2), 154–181.

Brown, N. (1959). *Life against death: The psychoanalytical meaning of history.* New York: Viking.

Bruner, J. S. (1966). On cognitive growth. In J. S. Bruner, R. R. Olver, & P. M. Greenfield, *Studies in cognitive growth* (pp. 1–67). New York: John Wiley.

Bruner, J. S., Olver, R. R., & Greenfield, P. M. (1966). *Studies in cognitive growth.* New York: John Wiley.

Brunswik, E. (1956). *Perception and the representative design of psychological experiments.* Berkeley: University of California Press.

Burton, R. V., & Whiting, J. W. M. (1961). The absent father and cross-sex identity. *Merrill-Palmer Quarterly, 7,* 85–95.

Cador, L. (1982). *Etudiant ou apprenti.* [Student or apprentice.] Paris: Presses Universitaires de France.

Camilleri, C. (1985). La psychologie culturelle. [Cultural psychology.] *Psychologie française, 30,* 147–151.

Camilleri, C. (1986). *Cultural anthropology and education.* Paris: UNESCO. London: Kegan Page.

Camilleri, C. (1989). Réflexion d'ensemble. [Synthesis.] In C. Clanet (Ed.), Socialisations et cultures. [Socialisations and cultures.] (pp. 435–445). Toulouse: Presses Universitaires du Mirail.

Campbell, D. T. (1961). The mutual methodological relevance of anthropology and psychology. In F. L. K. Hsu (Ed.), *Psychological anthropology* (pp. 333–352). Homewood, IL: Dorsey.

Campbell, D. T. (1964). Distinguishing differences of perception from failure of communication in cross-cultural studies. In F. Northrup & H. Livingston (Eds.), *Cross-cultural understandings: Epistemology in anthropology* (pp. 308–336). New York: Harper & Row.

Campbell, D. T. (1965). Variation and selective retention in sociocultural evolution. In H. R. Barringer, G. I. Blanksten, & R. W. Mack (Eds.), *Social change in developing areas: A reinterpretation of evolutionary theory* (pp. 19–49). Cambridge, MA: Schenkman.

Campbell, D. T. (1975). On the conflicts between biological and social evolution and between psychology and moral tradition. *American Psychologist, 30,* 1103–1126.

Campbell, D. T., & Naroll, R. (1972). The mutual methodological relevance of anthropology and psychology. In F. L. K. Hsu (Ed.), *Psychological anthropology* (rev. ed.) (pp. 435–463). Cambridge, MA: Schenkman.

Caplan, N., & Paige, J. M. (1968, August). A study of ghetto rioters. *Scientific American* pp. 15–21.

Carlson, J. (1976). Cross-cultural Piagetian studies: What can they tell us? In K. Riegel & J. Meacham (Eds.), *The developing individual in a changing world: Vol. 1* (pp. 334–345). The Hague: Mouton.

Carlson, M., & Miller, N. (1988). Bad experiences and aggression. *SSR, 72,* 155–157.

Carr, E. G. (1981). Contingency management. In A. P. Goldstein, E. G. Carr, W. S. Davidson, II, & P. Wehr (Eds.), *In response to aggression: Methods of control and pro-social alternatives* (pp. 1–65). Elmsford, NY: Pergamon Press.

Carraher, T. N. (1986). From drawings to buildings: Working with mathematical scales. *International Journal of Behavioural Development, 9,* 527–544.

Carraher, T. N., Carraher, D. W., & Schliemann, A. D. (1985). Mathematics in the streets and in schools. *British Journal of Developmental Psychology, 3,* 21–29.

Carraher, T. N., Carraher, D. W., & Schliemann, A. D. (1987). Written and oral mathematics. *Journal of Research in Mathematics Education, 18,* 83–97.

Carraher, T. N., Schliemann, A. D., & Carraher, D. W. (1988). Mathematical concepts in everyday life. In G. B. Saxe & M. Gearhart (Eds.), *Children's mathematics: New directions in child development* (pp. 71–87). San Francisco: Jossey-Bass.

Case, R. (1985). *Intellectual development: Birth to adulthood*. New York: Academic Press.

Cauthen, N. R., Robinson, I. E., & Krauss, H. H. (1971). Stereotypes: A review of the literature 1926–1968. *Journal of Social Psychology, 84*, 103–125.

Chaffee, S. H., & McLeod, J. M. (1971, September). *Adolescents, parents and television violence.* Paper presented at the American Psychological Association meetings, Washington, D.C.

Chamoux, M. N. (1981). Les savoir-faire techniques et leur appropriation: Le cas des Nahuas du Mexique. [Technical know-how and its appropriation: A case study among the Nahuas of Mexico.] *L'Homme, 21*(3), 71–94.

Chamoux, M. N. (1983). La division des savoir-faire textiles entre indiens et métis dans la Sierra de Puebla (Mexique). [The sharing of textile know-how between indians and mestizos in Sierra de Puebla, Mexico.] *Techniques & Culture, 2*, 99–124.

Chamoux, M. N. (1985). Pédagogies "informelles" et transmission des savoirs et savoir-faire chez les paysans indiens du Mexique. [Informal education and the transmission of knowledge and know-how among indian farmers in Mexico.] In Ministère de l'Agriculture (Ed.), *Enseignements agricoles et formation des ruraux.* [The teaching of agriculture and the education of rural people.] (pp. 23–25). Paris: Agri Nathan International.

Chamoux, M. N. (1986). Apprendre autrement: Aspects des pédagogies dites informelles chez les Indiens du Mexique. [To learn differently: Aspects of so-called informal education among Mexican indians.] In P. Rossel (Ed.), *Demain l'artisanat?* [Arts and crafts tomorrow.] (pp. 211–335). Paris: Presses Universitaires de France.

Child, I. L. (1954). Socialization. In G. Lindzey (Ed.), *Handbook of social psychology* (Vol. 2) (pp. 655–692). Cambridge, MA: Addison-Wesley.

Child, I. L., Storm, T., & Veroff, J. (1958). Achievement themes in folk tales related to socialization practices. In J. W. Atkinson (Ed.), *Motives in fantasy, action, and society* (pp. 479–492). Princeton, NJ: Van Nostrand.

Childs, C. P., & Greenfield, P. M. (1980). Informal modes of learning and teaching: The case of Zinacanteco weaving. In N. Warren (Ed.), *Studies in cross-cultural psychology: Vol. 2* (pp. 269–316). London: Academic Press.

Ching, C. C. (1984). Psychology and the four modernizations in China. *International Journal of Psychology, 19*, 57–65.

Ciborowski, T. (1980). The role of context, skill, and transfer in cross-cultural experimentation. In H. C. Triandis & J. W. Berry (Eds.), *Handbook of cross-cultural psychology: Vol. 2. Methodology* (pp. 279–296). Boston: Allyn & Bacon.

Clanet, C. (Ed.). (1989). *Socialisations et cultures.* [Socializations and Cultures] Toulouse: Presses Universitaires du Mirail.

Cole, M. (1975). An ethnographic psychology of cognition. In R. W. Brislin, S. Bochner, & W. J. Lonner (Eds.). *Cross-cultural perspectives on learning* (pp. 157–175). Beverly Hills: Sage.

Cole, M. (1978). Literacy without schooling: Testing for intellectual effects. *Harvard Educational Review, 48*(4), 448–460.

Cole, M., & Bruner, J. S. (1971). Cultural differences and inferences about psychological processes. *American Psychologist, 26*, 867–876. (Reprinted in Berry, J. W., & Dasen, P. R., Eds., 1974, *Culture and cognition*, pp. 231–246. London: Methuen.)

Cole, M., & Cole, S. R. (1989). *The development of children.* New York: W. H. Freeman.

Cole, M., & Gay, J. (1972). Culture and memory. *American Anthropologist, 74*, 1066–1084.

Cole, M., Gay, J., Glick, J. A., & Sharp, D. W. (1971). *The cultural context of learning and thinking: An exploration in experimental anthropology.* New York: Basic Books.

Cole, M., & Scribner, S. (1974). *Culture and thought: A psychological introduction.* New York: John Wiley.

Cole, M., & Scribner, S. (1977). Developmental theories applied to cross-cultural cognitive research. *Annals of the New York Academy of Sciences, 285*, 366-373.

Cole, M., Sharp, D. W., & Lave, C. (1976). The cognitive consequences of education: Some empirical evidence and theoretical misgivings. *The Urban Review, 9*(4), 218-233.

Cordier, F. (1981). Catégorisation d'exemplaires et degré de typicalité: Etude chez des enfants. [Categorization of examples and degree of typicality: A study with children.] *Cahiers de Psychologie Cognitive, 1*, 75-83.

The Chinese Culture Connection. (1987). Chinese values and the search for culture-free dimensions of culture. *Journal of Cross-Cultural Psychology, 18*, 143-164.

Curran, V. H. (Ed.). (1984). *Nigerian children: Developmental perspectives.* London: Routledge & Kegan Paul.

Darwin, C. (1859). *On the origins of species by means of natural selection, or the preservation of favoured races in the struggle for life.* London: John Murray.

Dasen, P. R. (1972a). Cross-cultural Piagetian research: A summary. *Journal of Cross-Cultural Psychology, 7*, 75-85.

Dasen, P. R. (1972b). The development of conservation in Aboriginal children. A replication study. *International Journal of Psychology, 7*, 75-85.

Dasen, P. R. (1974). The influence of ecology, culture and European contact on cognitive development in Australian Aborigines. In J. W. Berry & P. R. Dasen (Eds.), *Culture and cognition* (pp. 381-408). London: Methuen.

Dasen, P. R. (1975). Concrete operational development in three cultures. *Journal of Cross-Cultural Psychology, 6*, 156-172.

Dasen, P. R. (1980). Psychological differentiation and operational development: A cross-cultural link. *Quarterly Newsletter of the Laboratory of Comparative Human Cognition, 2*, 81-86.

Dasen, P. R. (1982). Cross-cultural aspects of Piaget's theory: The competence/performance model. In L. L. Adler (Ed.), *Cross-cultural research at issue* (pp. 163-170). New York: Academic Press.

Dasen, P. R. (1983). Aspects fonctionnels du développement opératoire: Les recherches interculturelles. [Functional aspects of operational development: Cross-cultural studies.] *Archives de Psychologie, 51*, 57-60.

Dasen, P. R. (1984). The cross-cultural study of intelligence: Piaget and the Baoulé. *International Journal of Psychology, 19*, 407-434.

Dasen, P. R. (1988a). Développement psychologique et activités quotidiennes chez des enfants africains. [Psychological development and everyday activities among African children.] *Enfance, 41*, 3-24.

Dasen, P. R. (1988b). Cultures et développement cognitif: La recherche et ses applications. [Culture and cognitive development: Research and its applications.] In R. Bureau & D. de Saivre (Eds.), *Apprentissage et culture.* [Cultures and learning.] (pp. 123-142). Paris: Karthala.

Dasen, P. R. (1988c, September). *The contribution of a cross-cultural approach to developmental psychology.* Paper presented at the 22nd International Congress of Psychology (IUPS), Sydney, Australia.

Dasen, P. R., Berry, J. W., & Witkin, H. A. (1979). The use of developmental theories cross-culturally. In L. Eckensberger, Y. Poortinga, & W. Lonner (Eds.), *Cross-cultural contributions to psychology* (pp. 69-82). Amsterdam: Swets & Zeitlinger.

Dasen, P. R., Dembele, B., Ettien, K., Kabran, K., Kamagate, D., Koffi, D. A., & N'Guessan, A. (1985). N'glouèlê, l'intelligence chez les Baoulé. [N'glouèlê, intelligence among the Baoulé.] *Archives de Psychologie, 53*, 293-324.

Dasen, P. R., & de Ribaupierre, A. (1987). Neo-Piagetian theories: Cross-cultural and differential perspectives. *International Journal of Psychology, 22*, 793-832.

Dasen, P. R., & Heron, A. (1981). Cross-cultural tests of Piaget's theory. In H. C. Triandis & A. Heron (Eds.), *Handbook of cross-cultural psychology: Vol. 4. Developmental psychology* (pp. 295-342). Boston: Allyn & Bacon.

Dasen, P. R., Inhelder, B., Lavallée, M., & Retschitzki, J. (1978). *Naissance de l'intelligence chez l'enfant Baoulé de Côte d'Ivoire.* [The origins of intelligence in Baoulé children (d'Ivoire).] Berne: Hans Huber.

Dasen, P. R., & Jahoda, G. (Eds.). (1986). Cross-cultural human development [Special issue]. *International Journal of Behavioural Development, 9*(4).

Dasen, P. R., Lavallée, M., & Retschitzki, J. (1979). Training conservation of quantity (liquids) in West African (Baoulé) children. *International Journal of Psychology, 14*, 57-68.

Dasen, P. R., Ngini, L., & Lavallée, M. (1979). Cross-cultural training studies of concrete operations. In L. Eckensberger, Y. Poortinga, & W. Lonner (Eds.), *Cross-cultural contributions to psychology* (pp. 94-104). Amsterdam: Swets & Zeitlinger.

Davidson, G. R. (1979). An ethnographic psychology of Aboriginal cognitive ability. *Oceania, 49*, 270-294.

Davies, E. (1969, November). This is the way Crete went—Not with a bang but a simper. *Psychology Today*, pp. 43-47.

Dawson, J. L. M. (1967). Traditional vs. Western attitudes in West Africa: The construction, validation, and application of a measuring device. *British Journal of Social and Clinical Psychology, 6*, 81-96.

Dawson, J. L. M. (1969). Attitude change and conflict among Australian aborigines. *Australian Journal of Psychology, 21*, 101-116.

Dawson, J. L. M. (1972). Temne-Arunta hand-eye dominance and cognitive style. *International Journal of Psychology, 7*, 219-233.

Dawson, J. L. M. (1973). Effects of ecology and subjective culture on individual traditional-modern attitude change, achievement motivation, and potential for economic development in the Japanese and Eskimo societies. *International Journal of Psychology, 8*, 215-225.

De Certeau, M. (1980). L'invention du quotidien. Tome 1. Arts de faire. [The invention of daily life. Vol. 1. The art of doing.] Paris: Union Générale d'Editions (Collection 10/18).

de Lacey, P. R., & Poole, M. E. (Eds.). (1979). *Mosaic or melting pot: Cultural evolution in Australia.* Sydney: Harcourt Brace Jovanovich.

De la Rocha, O. (1985). The reorganization of arithmetic practice in the kitchen. *Anthropology and Education Quarterly, 16*, 193-198.

Delbos, G., & Jorion, P. (1984). *La transmission des savoirs.* [The transmission of knowledge.] Paris: Maison des Sciences de l'Homme.

de Lemos, M. M. (1966). *The development of the concept of conservation in Australian Aboriginal children.* Unpublished doctoral dissertation, Australian National University, Canberra.

Deregowski, J. B. (1968). Difficulties in pictorial depth perception in Africa. *British Journal of Psychology, 59*, 195-204.

Deregowski, J. B. (1971). Orientation and perception of pictorial depth. *International Journal of Psychology, 6*, 111-114.

Deregowski, J. B. (1972, November). Pictorial perception and culture. *Scientific American*, pp. 82-88.

Deregowski, J. B. (1980). Perception. In H. C. Triandis & W. J. Lonner (Eds.), *Handbook of cross-cultural psychology: Vol. 3. Basic processes* (pp. 21-115). Boston: Allyn & Bacon.

Deregowski, J. B. (1989). Real space and represented space: Cross-cultural perspectives. *Behavioral and Brain Sciences, 12*, 51-119.

Deregowski, J. B., Dziurawiec, S., & Annis, R. C. (Eds.). (1983). *Expiscations in cross-cultural psychology.* Lisse, The Netherlands: Swets & Zeitlinger.

Desalmand, P. (1983). *Histoire de l'éducation en Côte d'Ivoire.* [The history of education in Côte d'Ivoire.] Abidjan: Centre d'Edition et de Diffusion Africaines; Paris: Hatier/L'Harmattan.

DeVos, G. A., & Hippler, A. E. (1969). Cultural psychology: Comparative studies of human behaviors. In G. Lindzey & E. Aronson (Eds.), *Handbook of social psychology: Vol. 4. Group psychology and phenomena of interaction* (pp. 323–417). Reading, MA: Addison-Wesley.

Dewey, J. (1896). The reflex arc concept in psychology. *Psychological Review, 3,* 357–370.

Diaz-Guerrero, R. (1987). Historical sociocultural premises and ethnic socialization. In J. S. Phinney & M. J. Rotheram (Eds.), *Children's ethnic socialization* (pp. 239–250). Newbury Park, CA: Sage.

Diaz-Loving, R., Diaz-Guerrero, R., Helmreich, R. L., & Spence, J. T. (1981). Cross-cultural comparison and psychometric analysis of masculine (instrumental) and feminine (expressive) traits. *Revista Associacion Latinamericana Psicological Sociedad, 1,* 3–37.

Doise, W. (1985). Les représentations sociales: Définition d'un concept. [Social representations: Definition of a concept.] *Connexions, 45,* 243–253.

Doise, W., & Mugny, G. (1981). *Le développement social de l'intelligence.* [The social construction of intelligence.] Paris: InterEditions.

Doise, W., Mugny, G., & Perret-Clermont, A. N. (1975). Social interaction and the development of cognitive operations. *European Journal of Social Psychology, 5,* 367–383.

Dollard, J., Doob, L., Miller, N., Mowrer, O., & Sears, R. (1939). *Frustration and aggression.* New Haven, CT: Yale University Press.

Doob, L. W. (1957). An introduction to the psychology of acculturation. *Journal of Social Psychology, 45,* 143–160.

Doob, L. W. (1958). The effect of Jamaican Patois on attitude and recall. *American Anthropologist, 60,* 574–575.

Doob, L. W. (1960). *Becoming more civilized: A psychological exploration.* New Haven, CT: Yale University Press.

Doob, L. W. (1962). From tribalism to nationalism in Africa. *Journal of International Affairs, 16*(2), 144–155.

Doob, L. W. (1964). Eidetic images among the Ibo. *Ethnology, 3,* 357–363.

Doob, L. W. (1966). Eidetic imagery: A cross-cultural will-o-the-wisp? *Journal of Psychology, 63,* 13–34.

Doob, L. W. (1967). Scales for assaying psychological modernization in Africa. *Public Opinion Quarterly, 31,* 414–421.

Doob, L. W. (1970). Correlates of eidetic imagery in Africa. *Journal of Psychology, 76,* 223–230.

Doob, L. W. (1971). *Patterning of time.* New Haven, CT and London: Yale University Press.

Dougherty, J. W. D. (Ed.). (1985). *Directions in cognitive anthropology.* Urbana, IL: University of Chicago Press.

Draper, P. (1976). Social and economic constraints on child life among the !Kung. In R. B. Lee & I. DeVore (Eds.), *Kalahari hunter-gatherers: Studies of the !Kung San and their neighbors* (pp. 199–217). Cambridge: Harvard University Press.

Droz, R., & Rahmy, M. (1972). *Lire Piaget.* [Reading Piaget.] Brussels: Dessart.

DuBois, C. (1944). *The people of Alor.* Minneapolis: University of Minnesota Press.

Dumont, M. (Ed.). (1977). *Mathématique et environnement, de la maternelle au CE. Projet mathématique Nuffield.* [Mathematics and environment, from pre-school to fourth grade. The Nuffield mathematics project.] Paris: OCDL.

Durkheim, E. (1897). *Le suicide: Étude de sociologie.* [Suicide: Sociological study.] Paris: Félix Alcan.

Durojaiye, S. M. (1977). Children's traditional games and rhymes in three cultures. *Educational Research, 19,* 223–226.

Edgerton, R. B., & Langness, L. L. (1974). *Methods and styles in the study of culture.* San Francisco: Chandler & Sharp.

Ekman, P. (1971). Universals and cultural differences in facial expressions of emotion. In J. K. Cole (Ed.), *Nebraska symposium on motivation* (Vol. 19). (pp. 207–283). Lincoln, NE: University of Nebraska Press.

Ekman, P. (1973). *Darwin and facial expression.* New York: Academic Press.

Elkin, A. P. (1943). *The Australian Aborigines: How to understand them.* Sydney: Angus & Robertson.

Ember, C. R. (1973). Feminine task assignments and the social behavior of boys. *Ethos, 1,* 424–439.

Ember, C. R. (1977). Cross-cultural cognitive studies. *Annual Review of Anthropology, 6,* 33–56.

Ember, C. R. (1981). A cross-cultural perspective on sex differences. In R. H. Munroe, R. L. Munroe, & B. B. Whiting (Eds.), *Handbook of cross-cultural human development* (pp. 531–580). New York: Garland.

Ember, C. R., & Ember, M. (1985). *Anthropology.* (4th ed). Englewood Cliffs, NJ: Prentice-Hall.

Eron, L. D., & Huesman, L. R. (1982). The role of television in the development of prosocial and antisocial behavior. In J. Block, D. Olweus, & M. Radke-Yarrow (Eds.), *Development of antisocial and prosocial behavior* (pp. 285–314). New York: Academic Press.

Erny, P. (1981). *Ethnologie de l'éducation.* [Ethnology of education.] Paris: Presses Universitaires de France.

Evans, J. L. (1975). Learning to classify by color and by class: A study of concept discovery within Colombia, South America. *Journal of Social Psychology, 97,* 3–14.

Evans, J. L., & Segall, M. H. (1969). Learning to classify by color and by function: A study of concept-discovery by Ganda children. *Journal of Social Psychology, 77,* 35–55.

Evans-Pritchard, E. E. (1971). Introduction. In L. Lévy-Bruhl, *The soul of the primitive.* Chicago: Regnery.

Eysenck, H. J. (1971). *The IQ argument: Race, intelligence and education.* New York: The Library Press.

Faucheux, C. (1976). Cross-cultural research in experimental social psychology. *European Journal of Social Psychology, 6,* 269–322.

Feldman, M. (1968). Eidetic imagery in Ghana: A cross-cultural will-o'-the-wisp? *Journal of Psychology, 69,* 259–269.

Feldman, R. E. (1971). Honesty toward compatriot and foreigner: Field experiments in Paris, Athens, and Boston. In W. W. Lambert & R. Weisbrod (Eds.), *Comparative perspectives on social psychology* (pp. 321–335). Boston: Little, Brown.

Feldman, R. H. (1972). *The effect of education on traditional-modern attitudes among the Gusii of Kenya.* Unpublished doctoral dissertation, Syracuse University, Syracuse, NY.

Feuerstein, R. (1980). *Instrumental enrichment. An intervention program for cognitive modifiability.* Baltimore: University Park Press.

Finison, L. J. (1976). The application of McClelland's national development model to recent data. *Journal of Social Psychology, 98,* 55–59.

Fischer, K. W., & Bullock, D. (1984). Cognitive development in school-age children: Conclusions and new directions. In W. A. Collins (Ed.), *Development during middle childhood: The years from six to twelve* (pp. 70–146). Washington, DC: National Academy of Sciences Press.

Flavell, J. H. (1963). *The developmental psychology of Jean Piaget.* Princeton, NJ: Van Nostrand.

Fleming, J. (1975). Fear of success imagery in urban Kenya. *Kenya Education Review, 2*(2), 121–129.

Florian, V., & Kravetz, S. (1985). Children's concepts of death: A cross-cultural comparison among Muslims, Druze, Christians, and Jews in Israel. *Journal of Cross-Cultural Psychology, 16,* 174–189.

Flynn, J. R. (1980). *Race, I.Q., and Jensen.* London: Routledge & Kegan Paul.

Fortes, M. (1938). Social and psychological aspects of education in Taleland. *Africa,* Supplement to Volume XI, 1–64.

Fortes, M. (1970). *Time and social structure and other essays.* London: Athlone Press.

Foster, G. M. (1967). *Tzintzuntzan: Mexican peasants in a changing world.* Boston: Little, Brown.

Frazcek, A. (1985). Moral approval of aggressive acts: A Polish-Finnish comparative study. *Journal of Cross-Cultural Psychology, 16,* 41–54.

Frazer, J. G. (1890). *The golden bough: A study in magic and religion.* London: Macmillan (abridged edition, 1922).

Freeman, D. (1983). *Margaret Mead and Samoa: The making and unmaking of an anthropological myth.* Cambridge: Harvard University Press.

Frijda, N., & Jahoda, G. (1966). On the scope and methods of cross-cultural research. *International Journal of Psychology, 1,* 110–127.

Fuchs, I., Eisenberg, N., Hertz-Lazarowitz, R., & Sharabany, R. (1986). Kibbutz, Israeli city and American children's moral reasoning about prosocial moral conflicts. *Merrill-Palmer Quarterly, 32*(1), 37–50.

Furby, L. (1971). A theoretical analysis of cross-cultural research in cognitive development: Piaget's conservation task. *Journal of Cross-Cultural Psychology, 2,* 241–256.

Furnam, A., & Karani, R. (1985). A cross-cultural study of attitudes to women, just world, and locus of control beliefs. *Psychologia, 28*(1), 11–20.

Gabrenya, W. K., Jr., Latané, B., & Wang, Y. E. (1983). Social loafing in cross-cultural perspective: Chinese on Taiwan. *Journal of Cross-Cultural Psychology, 14,* 368–384.

Gabrenya, W. K., Jr., Wang, Y. E., & Latané, B. (1985). Social loafing on an optimizing task: Cross-cultural differences among Chinese and Americans. *Journal of Cross-Cultural Psychology, 16,* 223–242.

Gallimore, R. (1981). Affiliation, social context, industriousness, and achievement. In R. H. Munroe, R. L. Munroe, & B. B. Whiting (Eds.), *Handbook of cross-cultural human development* (pp. 689–716). New York: Garland STPM.

Gallo, P. S., & McClintock, C. G. (1965). Cooperative and competitive behavior in mixed-motive games. *Journal of Conflict Resolution, 9,* 68–78.

Gardner, B. T., & Gardner, R. A. (1975). Evidence for sentence constituents in the early utterances of child chimpanzees. *Journal of Experimental Psychology, 104,* 244–267.

Gardner, H. (1985). *The mind's new science: A history of the cognitive revolution.* New York: Basic Books.

Geiger, L. (1880). *Contributions to the history and development of the human race.* London: English and Foreign Philosophical Library.

Giard, L. (1980). Faire la cuisine. [Cooking.] In L. Giard & P. Mayol, *L'invention du quotidien: Tome 2. Habiter, cuisiner.* [The invention of daily life: Vol. 2. Housing, cooking.] Paris: Union Générale d'Editions (Collection 10/18).

Gibson, J. J. (1950). *The perception of the visual world.* Boston: Houghton Mifflin.

Gilbert, G. M. (1951). Stereotypes' persistence and change among college students. *Journal of Abnormal and Social Psychology, 46,* 245–254.

Gill, R., & Keats, D. (1980). Elements of intellectual competence: Judgements by Australian and Malay university students. *Journal of Cross-Cultural Psychology, 11,* 233–243.

Gilligan, C. (1982). *In a different voice: Psychological theory and women's development.* Cambridge: Harvard University Press.

Gillet, B. (1976). Etudes comparatives sur l'influence de la scolarité. [Comparative studies on the influence of schooling.] In M. Reuchlin (Ed.), *Cultures et conduites* [Culture and behavior] (pp. 313–332). Paris: Presses Universitaires de France.

Ginsburg, H. P. (1977). Some problems in the study of schooling and cognition. *Quarterly Newsletter of the Institute of Comparative Human Development, 1*(4), 7-10.

Ginsburg, H. P., & Allardice, B. S. (1984). Children's difficulties with school mathematics. In B. Rogoff & J. Lave (Eds.), *Everyday cognition: Its development in social context* (pp. 194-219). Cambridge: Harvard University Press.

Ginsburg, H. P., & Opper, S. (1969). *Piaget's theory of intellectual development. An introduction.* Englewood Cliffs, NJ: Prentice-Hall.

Ginsburg, H. P., Posner, J. K., & Russell, R. L. (1981). The development of knowledge concerning written arithmetic: A cross-cultural study. *International Journal of Psychology, 16*, 13-34.

Ginsburg, H. P., & Russel, R. L. (1981). Social class and racial influences on early mathematical thinking. *Monographs of the Society for Research in Child Development, 46*(6, Serial No. 193).

Gladstone, W. E. (1858). *Studies on Homer and Homeric Age: Vol. III.* Oxford: Oxford University Press.

Glassford, R. G. (1970). Organization of games and adaptive strategies of the Canadian Eskimo. In G. Lueschen (Ed.), *A cross-cultural analysis of sports and games* (pp. 70-81). Champaign, IL: Stipes.

Glueck, S., & Glueck, E. (1950). *Unraveling juvenile delinquency.* New York: Commonwealth Fund.

Godwin, R. K. (1974). Two theory theoretical triangles: The relationships between personality variables and modernization. *Journal of Developing Areas, 8*, 181-198.

Goldschmidt, W. (1966). *Comparative functionalism.* Berkeley: University of California Press.

Goldstein, A. P. (1983). U.S.: Causes, controls and alternatives to aggression. In A. P. Goldstein, & M. H. Segall (Eds.), *Aggression in global perspective* (pp. 435-474). Elmsford, NY: Pergamon Press.

Goldstein, A. P., & Segall, M. H. (Eds.). (1983). *Aggression in global perspective.* Elmsford, NY: Pergamon Press.

Goldstein, S. B., & Ibaraki, T. (1983). Japan: Aggression and aggression control in Japanese society. In A. P. Goldstein & M. H. Segall (Eds.), *Aggression in global perspective* (pp. 313-324). Elmsford, NY: Pergamon Press.

Goodall, J. Van Lawick-. (1971). *In the shadow of man.* Boston: Houghton-Mifflin.

Goodnow, J. J. (1981a). Everyday ideas about cognitive development. In J. P. Forgas (Ed.), *Social cognition: Perspectives on everyday understanding* (pp. 85-112). London: Academic Press.

Goodnow, J. J. (1981b). Parents' ideas about parenting and development: A review of issues and recent work. In M. Lamb, A. Brown, & B. Rogoff (Eds.), *Advances in developmental psychology* (pp. 193-242). Hillsdale, NJ: Lawrence Erlbaum.

Goodnow, J. J. (1985). Change and variation in ideas about childhood and parenting. In I. E. Sigel (Ed.), *Parental belief systems* (pp. 235-270). Hillsdale, NJ: Lawrence Erlbaum.

Goodnow, J. J., & Knight, R. (1983). Adult social cognition: Implications of parents' ideas for approaches to development. In M. Perlmutter (Ed.), *Minnesota symposium on child development.*

Goody, J. R. (1968). *Literacy in traditional societies.* Cambridge: Cambridge University Press.

Goody, J. R. (1977). *The domestication of the savage mind.* Cambridge: Cambridge University Press.

Goody, J. R. (1980). Thought and writing. In E. Gellner (Ed.), *Soviet and western anthropology* (pp. 119-133). New York: Columbia University Press.

Goody, J. R., Cole, M., & Scribner, S. (1977). Writing and formal operations. *Africa, 47*, 289-304.

Goody, J. R., & Watt, I. (1963). The consequences of literacy. *Comparative Studies in Society and History, 5*, 304-345.

Gordon, H. (1923). *Mental and scholastic tests among retarded children* (Educational Pamphlet No. 44.). London: Board of Education. (Reprinted in abridged form in I. Al-Issa &

W. Dennis, Eds., *Cross-cultural studies of behavior*, pp. 111-119. New York: Holt, Rinehart & Winston, 1970.)

Goslin, D. B. (Ed.). (1969). *Handbook of socialization theory and research*. Chicago: Rand McNally.

Gould, S. J. (1981). *The mismeasure of man*. New York: Norton.

Grand, P., Puhl, P., Tagini, J., Simonin, A., & Niederer, A. (1983). *Jeux de notre enfance. Jeux de nos enfants.* [Games of our childhood. Games of our children.] Sierre: Monographic.

Graves, T. D. (1967). Psychological acculturation in a tri-ethnic community. *Southwestern Journal of Anthropology, 23*, 337-350.

Greenfield, P. M. (1966). On culture and conservation. In J. S. Bruner, R. R. Olver, & P. M. Greenfield (Eds.), *Studies in cognitive growth* (pp. 225-256). New York: John Wiley.

Greenfield, P. M. (1972). Oral and written language: The consequences for cognitive development in Africa, the United States, and England. *Language and Speech, 15*, 169-178.

Greenfield, P. M. (1976). Cross-cultural research and Piagetian theory: Paradox and progress. In K. F. Riegel & J. A. Meacham (Eds.), *The developing individual in a changing world: Vol. 1* (pp. 322-333). The Hague: Mouton.

Greenfield, P. M. (1984). A theory of the teacher in the learning activities of everyday life. In B. Rogoff & J. Lave (Eds.), *Everyday cognition* (pp. 117-138). Cambridge: Harvard University Press.

Greenfield, P. M., & Bruner, J. S. (1966). Culture and cognitive growth. *International Journal of Psychology, 1*, 89-107.

Greenfield, P. M., & Bruner, J. S. (1969). Culture and cognitive growth. In D. A. Goslin (Ed.), *Handbook of socialization: Theory and research* (pp. 633-657). Chicago: Rand McNally.

Greenfield, P. M., & Childs, C. P. (1977). Weaving skill, color terms and pattern representation: Cultural influences and cognitive development among the Zinacantecos of Southern Mexico. *Interamerican Journal of Psychology, 2*, 23-48.

Greenfield, P. M., & Lauber, B. A. (1988). *Inductive discovery in the mastery and transfer of video game expertise*. Unpublished manuscript.

Greenfield, P. M., & Lave, J. (1979). Aspects cognitifs de l'éducation non scolaire. *Recherche, Pédagogie et Culture, 8*(44), 16-35. (Reprinted as Greenfield, P. M., & Lave, J. (1982). Cognitive aspects of informal education. In D. A. Wagner & H. W. Stevenson (Eds.), *Cultural perspectives on child development* (pp. 181-207). San Francisco: W. H. Freeman.

Greenfield, P. M., Reich, L. C., & Olver, R. R. (1966). On culture and equivalence II. In J. S. Bruner, R. R. Olver, & P. M. Greenfield, *Studies in cognitive growth* (pp. 270-318). New York: John Wiley.

Groebel, J. (1986). International research on television violence: Synopsis and critique. In L. R. Huesman & L. D. Eron (Eds.), *Television and the aggressive child: A cross-national comparison* (pp. 259-281). Hillsdale, NJ: Lawrence Erlbaum.

Gupta, A. (1971). *Indians abroad: Asia and Africa*. New York: Orient Longman.

Guthrie, G. M. (1970). *The psychology of modernization in the rural Philippines* (Institute of Philippines Culture Papers, No. 8). Quezon City: Ateneo de Manila University Press.

Guthrie, G. M. (1971). Unexpected correlations and the cross-cultural method. *Journal of Cross-Cultural Psychology, 2*, 315-323.

Guthrie, G. M. (1977). A social-psychological analysis of modernization in the Philippines. *Journal of Cross-cultural Psychology, 8*, 177-206.

Hagen, E. E. (1962). *On the theory of social change*. Homewood, IL: Dorsey Press.

Hallowell, A. I. (1955). *Culture and experience*. Philadelphia: University of Pennsylvania Press.

Hallpike, C. R. (1979). *The foundations of primitive thought*. Oxford: Clarendon Press.

Hamilton, A. (1981). *Nature and nurture: Aboriginal child-rearing in North-Central Arnhem Land*. Canberra, ACT: Australian Institute of Aboriginal Studies, Atlantic Highlands, NJ: Humanities Press.

Haque, A. (1973). Mirror image hypothesis in the context of Indo-Pakistan conflict. *Pakistan Journal of Psychology* (Abstract in *Newsletter of the International Association of Cross-Cultural Psychology*).

Harkness, S. (1973). Universal aspects of learning color codes: A study in two cultures. *Ethos, 1*, 175–200.

Harkness, S., & Super, C. M. (1983). The cultural construction of child development. *Ethos, 11*, 221–231.

Harrington, C. (1968). Sexual differentiation in socialization and some male genital mutilations. *American Anthropologist, 70*, 952–956.

Harrington, C., & Whiting, J. W. M. (1972). Socialization process and personality. In F. L. K. Hsu (Ed.), *Psychological anthropology* (rev. ed.) (pp. 469–508). Cambridge, MA: Shenkman.

Harris, M. (1968). *The rise of anthropological theory*. New York: T. Y. Crowell.

Harris, P., & Heelas, P. (1979). Cognitive processes and collective representations. *Archives Européennes de Sociologie, 20*, 211–241.

Hatano, G. (1982). Cognitive consequences of practice in culture specific procedural skills. *Quarterly Newsletter of the Laboratory of Comparative Human Cognition, 4*(1), 15–18.

Hatano, G., Miyake, Y., & Binks, M. G. (1977). Performance of expert abacus operators. *Cognition, 5*, 47–55.

Hebb, D. O. (1949). *The organization of behavior*. New York: John Wiley.

Hebert, J. P. (1977). *Race et intelligence*. Paris: Copernic.

Heider, E. R. (1971). "Focal" color areas and the development of color names. *Developmental Psychology, 4*, 447–455.

Heider, E. R. (1972a). Probabilities, sampling, and ethnographic method: The case of Dani color names. *Man, 7*, 448–466

Heider, E. R. (1972b). The structure of the color space in naming and memory for two languages. *Cognitive Psychology, 3*, 337–354.

Heider, E. R. (1972c). Universals in color naming and memory. *Journal of Experimental Psychology, 93*, 10–20.

Heilbroner, R. L. (1975). *An inquiry into the human prospect*. New York: Norton.

Herbart, J. F. (1897). *Lehrbuch zur psychologie*. (M. K. Smith, Trans.). New York: Appleton & Co. (Original work published 1816)

Heron, A., & Kroeger, E. (1981). Introduction to developmental psychology. In H. C. Triandis & A. Heron (Eds.), *Handbook of cross-cultural psychology: Vol. 4. Developmental psychology* (pp. 1–15). Boston: Garland STPM.

Herskovits, M. J. (1927). *The Negro and intelligence tests*. Hanover, NH: Sociological Press.

Herskovits, M. J. (1948). *Man and his works: The science of cultural anthropology*. New York: Alfred A. Knopf.

Herskovits, M. J. (1955). *Cultural anthropology*. New York: Alfred A. Knopf.

Hippler, A. E. (1980). Editorial. *IACCP Cross-Cultural Psychology Newsletter, 14*(3), 2–3.

Ho, D. Y. F. (1985). Cultural values and professional issues in clinical psychology: Implications from the Hong Kong experience. *American Psychologist, 40*, 1212–1218.

Hofstede, G. (1980). *Culture's consequences: International differences in work-related values*. Beverly Hills, CA: Sage.

Hofstede, G. (1983). Dimensions of national cultures in fifty countries and three regions. In J. B. Deregowski, S. Dziurawiec, & R. C. Annis (Eds.), *Expiscations in cross-cultural psychology* (pp. 335–355). Lisse, Netherlands: Swets & Zeitlinger.

Horner, M. S. (1969). Fail: Bright women. *Psychology Today, 3*, 36–38, 62.

Horner, M. S. (1972). Toward an understanding of achievement-related conflicts in women. *Journal of Social Issues, 28*, 157–176.

Horton, R. (1967a). African traditional thought and Western science. Part I. From tradition to science. *Africa, 37*(1), 50–71.

Horton, R. (1967b). African traditional thought and Western science. Part II. The "closed" and "open" predicaments. *Africa, 37*(2), 155–187.

Horton, R. (1973). Lévy-Bruhl, Durkheim and the scientific revolution. In R. Horton & R. Finnegan (Eds.), *Modes of thought: Essays on thinking in Western and Non-Western societies* (pp. 249–305). London: Faber & Faber.

Howard, A., & Scott, R. A. (1981). The study of minority groups in complex societies. In R. H. Munroe, R. L. Munroe, & B. B. Whiting (Eds.), *Handbook of cross-cultural human development* (pp. 113–152). New York: Garland STPM.

Hsu, F. L. K. (Ed.). (1961). *Psychological anthropology*. Homewood, IL: Dorsey.

Hsu, F. L. K. (Ed.). (1972). *Psychological anthropology* (rev. ed.). Cambridge, MA: Schenkman.

Hsu, F. L. K. (1981). *Americans and Chinese: Two ways of life*. Honolulu: University of Hawaii Press.

Hui, C. H. (1984). *Individualism-collectivism: Theory, measurement, and its relation to reward allocation*. Unpublished doctoral dissertation, University of Illinois, Urbana.

Hui, C. H., & Triandis, H. C. (1984). *What does individualism-collectivism mean: A study of social scientists*. Unpublished manuscript, University of Illinois Department of Psychology, Urbana.

Hui, C. H., & Triandis, H. C. (1985). Measurement in cross-cultural psychology: A review and comparison of strategies. *Journal of Cross-Cultural Psychology, 16*, 131–152.

Hull, C. L. (1943). *Principles of behavior*. New York: Appleton-Century-Crofts.

Husén, T. (1967). *International study of achievement in mathematics: A comparison of twelve countries: Vol. 1*. New York: John Wiley.

Huteau, M. (1987). *Style cognitif et personnalité. La dépendance-indépendance à l'égard du champ*. [Cognitive style and personality. Field-dependence and -independance.] Lille, France: Presses Universitaires de Lille.

Hutt, C. (1972). Neuroendocrinological, behavioral, and intellectual aspects of sexual differentiation in human development. In C. Ounsted & D. C. Taylor (Eds.), *Gender differences: Their ontogeny and significance* (pp. 73–121). Edinburgh: Churchill Livingston.

Ifrah, G. (1985). *Les chiffres ou l'histoire d'une grande invention*. [Numbers or the history of a great invention.] Paris: Laffont.

Inhelder, B., Sinclair, H., & Bovet, M. (1974). *Apprentissage et structures de la connaissance*. Paris: Presses Universitaires de France. [Transl. S. Wedgewood. (1974). Learning and the development of cognition. London: Routledge and Kegan Paul.]

Inkeles, A. (1966). The modernization of men. In M. Weiner (Ed.), *Modernization: The dynamics of growth* (pp. 138–150). New York: Basic Books.

Inkeles, A. (1969). Making men modern: On the causes and consequences of individual change in six developing countries. *American Journal of Sociology, 75*, 208–225.

Inkeles, A. (1975, October). *Individual modernity in different ethnic and religious groups: Data from a six-nation study*. Paper presented at the Conference on Issues in Cross-Cultural Research, New York Academy of Sciences, New York.

Inkeles, A., & Smith, D. H. (1974). *Becoming modern*. Cambridge: Harvard University Press.

Irvine, S. H. (1983a). Cross-cultural conservation studies at the asymptote: Striking out against the curve. In S. Modgil (Ed.), *Jean Piaget: An interdisciplinary critique* (pp. 42–57). London: Routledge and Kegan Paul.

Irvine, S. H. (1983b). Testing in Africa and America: The search for routes. In S. H. Irvine & J. W. Berry (Eds.), *Human assessment and cultural factors* (pp. 45–58). New York: Plenum Press.

Irvine, S. H., & Berry, J. W. (Eds.). (1988). *Human abilities in cultural context*. Cambridge: Cambridge University Press.

Irwin, M., Klein, R. E., Engle, P. L., Yarbrough, C., & Nerlove, S. B. (1977). The problem of establishing validity in cross-cultural measurements. *Annals of the New York Academy of Sciences, 285*, 308–325.

Ivic, I., & Marjanovic, A. (Eds.). (1986). *Traditional games and children of today.* Belgrade: OMEP & Institute of Psychology, University Belgrade.

Jacquard, A. (Ed.). (1978). *Eloge de la différence, la génétique et les hommes.* [In praise of differences, human genetics.] Paris: Seuil.

Jahoda, G. (1970). Supernatural beliefs and changing cognitive structures among Ghanaian university students. *Journal of Cross-Cultural Psychology, 1*, 115–130.

Jahoda, G. (1971). Retinal pigmentation, illusion susceptibility and space perception. *International Journal of Psychology, 6*, 199–208.

Jahoda, G. (1975). Retinal pigmentation and space perception: A failure to replicate. *International Journal of Psychology, 97*, 133–134.

Jahoda, G. (1977). In pursuit of the emic-etic distinction: Can we ever capture it? In Y. H. Poortinga (Ed.), *Basic problems in cross-cultural psychology* (pp. 55–63). Lisse, Netherlands: Swets & Zeitlinger.

Jahoda, G. (1982). *Psychology and anthropology: A psychological perspective.* London: Academic Press.

Jahoda, G. (1983). The cross-cultural emperor's new clothes: The emic-etic issue revisited. In J. B. Deregowski, S. Dziurawiec, R. C. Annis, (Eds.), *Expiscations in cross-cultural psychology* (pp. 19–37). Amsterdam: Swets & Zeitlinger.

Jensen, A. R. (1969). How much can we boost IQ and scholastic achievement? *Harvard Educational Review, 39*, 1–123.

Jensen, A. R. (1978). The current status of the IQ controversy. *Australian Psychologist, 13*, 7–28.

Jensen, A. R. (1980). *Bias in mental testing.* New York: Free Press.

Jensen, A. R. (1981). *Straight talk about mental tests.* London: Methuen.

Kagitcibasi, C. (1984). Socialization in traditional society: A challenge to psychology. *International Journal of Psychology, 19*, 145–157.

Kagitcibasi, C. (1988). Diversity of socialization and social change. In P. Dasen, J. Berry, & N. Sartorius (Eds.), *Health and cross-cultural psychology: Towards applications* (pp. 25–47). Newbury Park, CA: Sage.

Kahl, J. (1968). *The measurement of modernism: A study of values in Brazil and Mexico.* Austin: The University of Texas Press.

Kahn, R. L. (1972). The justification of violence: Social problems and social solutions. *Journal of Social Issues, 28*, 155–175.

Kalin, R., Heusser, C., & Edmonds, J. (1982). Cross-national equivalence of a sex-role ideology scale. *Journal of Social Psychology, 116*, 141–142.

Kamara, A. I., & Easley, J. A., Jr. (1977). Is the rate of cognitive development uniform across cultures? A methodological critique with new evidence from Themne children. In P. R. Dasen (Ed.), *Piagetian psychology: Cross-cultural contributions* (pp. 26–63). New York: Gardner/Wiley.

Kardiner, A. (1945). *The psychological frontiers of society.* New York: Columbia University Press.

Kariuki, P. W. (1983). Attitudes and action: The problem of child abuse in Kenya. In S. H. Irvine & J. W. Berry (Eds.), *Human assessment and cultural factors* (pp. 513–520). New York: Plenum Press.

Kaschak, E., & Sharratt, S. (1983). A Latin American sex role inventory. *Cross-Cultural Psychology Bulletin, 18*(1), 3–6.

Katz, D., & Braly, K. W. (1933). Racial stereotypes of 100 college students. *Journal of Abnormal and Social Psychology, 28*, 280–290.

Katz, P. A., & Taylor, D. A. (1988). *Eliminating racism: Profiles in controversy.* New York: Plenum Press.

Kaye, B. (1962). *Bringing up children in Ghana*. London: George Allen and Unwin.

Keats, D. M. (1982). Cultural bases of concepts of intelligence: A Chinese versus Australian comparison. In P. Sukontasarp, N. Yongsiri, P. Intasuwan, N. Jotiban & C. Suvannathat (Eds.), *Proceedings of the Second Asian Workshop on Child and Adolescent Development* (pp. 67–75). Bangkok: Burapasilpa Press.

Keats, D. M. (1985). Strategies in formal operational thinking: Malaysia and Australia. In I. Reyes Lagunes & Y. H. Poortinga (Eds.), *From a different perspective. Studies of behavior across cultures* (pp. 304–318). Lisse, Netherlands: Swets & Zeitlinger.

Keller, F., & Schoenfeld, W. N. (1950). *Principles of behavior*. New York: Appleton-Century-Crofts.

Kelly, M., & Philp, H. (1975). Vernacular test instructions in relation to cognitive task behavior among highland children of Papua New Guinea. *British Journal of Educational Psychology, 45*, 189–197.

Kelman, H. D. (1968). Social psychology and national development: Background of the Ibadan Conference. *Journal of Social Issues, 24*(2), 9–20.

Kelman, H. D. (1976, October). *Sources of attachment to the nation-state: An analysis of the social psychological dimensions of nationalism*. Third Annual Floyd Allport Lecture, The Maxwell School, Syracuse University, Syracuse, New York.

Kendler, T. S., Kendler, H. H., & Carrick, M. (1966). The effect of verbal labels on inferential problem solution. *Child Development, 37*, 749–763.

Kenyatta, J. (1965). *Facing Mount Kenya: The tribal life of the Gikuyu*. New York: Random House. (Original work published 1938)

Kierkegaard, S. (1954). *The sickness unto death*. (W. Lowie, Trans.). New York: Anchor. (Original work published 1849)

Kierkegaard, S. (1957). *The concept of dread*. (W. Lowie, Trans.). Princeton, NJ: Princeton University Press. (Original work published 1849)

Kilbride, P., & Leibowitz, H. W. (1975). Factors affecting the magnitude of the Ponzo perspective illusion among the Baganda. *Perception and Psychophysics, 17*, 543–548.

Kim, J. K. (1984). Use of cultural criterion groups and discriminant analysis in acculturation studies. *International Journal of Intercultural Relations, 8*, 29–43.

Kiray, M. B. (1968). Values, social stratification and development. *Journal of Social Issues, 24*(2), 87–100.

Klein, R. E., Freeman, H. P., & Millett, R. (1973). Psychological test performance and indigenous conceptions of intelligence. *Journal of Psychology, 84*, 219–222.

Kline (1977). Cross-cultural studies and Freudian theory. In N. Warren (Ed.), *Studies in cross-cultural psychology. Vol. 1*. (pp. 51–90). London: Academic Press.

Klineberg, O. (1954). *Social psychology* (rev. ed.). New York: Holt.

Kluckhohn, C. K. M. (1953). Universal categories of culture. In A. L. Kroeber (Ed.), *Anthropology today: An encyclopedic inventory* (pp. 507–523). Chicago: University of Chicago Press.

Kluckhohn, C. K. M., & Murray, H. A. (Eds.). (1953). *Personality in nature, society, and culture*. New York: Alfred A. Knopf.

Kluckhohn, F. R. (1949–1950). Dominant and substitute profiles of culture and orientation: Their significance for the analysis of social stratification. *Social Forces, 28*, 376–393.

Knapen, M.-T. (1970). *L'enfant Mukongo. Orientation de base du système éducatif et développement de la personnalité*. [The Mukongo child, Basic orientations of the educational system and the development of personality.] Louvain, Belgium: Ed. Nauwelaerts.

Kohlberg, L. (1969a). Stage and sequence: The cognitive-development approach to socialization. In D. A. Goslin (Ed.), *Handbook of socialization theory and research* (pp. 347–480). Chicago: Rand McNally.

Kohlberg, L. (1969b). *Stages in the development of moral thought and action*. New York: Holt, Rinehart & Winston.

Kohlberg, L. (1970). The child as a moral philosopher. In P. Cramer (Ed.), *Readings in develop-mental psychology today* (pp. 109–115). Del Mar, CA: CRM Books.

Konner, M. (1988, August 14). The aggressors. *The New York Times Magazine*, pp. 33–34.

Koocher, G. P. (1974). Talking with children about death. *American Journal of Orthopsy-chiatry, 44*, 104–111.

Kranau, E. J., Green, V., & Valencia-Weber, G. (1982). Acculturation and the Hispanic woman: Attitudes toward women, sex-role attribution, sex-role behavior, and demographics. *Hispanic Journal of Behavioral Science, 4*, 21–40.

Kroeber, A. L. (1948). *Anthropology*. New York: Harcourt, Brace & World.

Kurokawa, M. (1971). Mutual perceptions of racial images: White, black, and Japanese Americans. *Journal of Social Issues, 27*(4), 213–235.

Laboratory of Comparative Human Cognition. LHCH (1979). What's cultural about cross-cultural psychology? *Annual Review of Psychology, 30*, 145–172.

Laboratory of Comparative Human Cognition. LHCH (1983). Culture and cognitive development. In W. Kessen (Ed.), *Handbook of child psychology: Vol. 1. History, theory and methods* (pp. 295–356). New York: John Wiley.

Labov, W. (1970). The logical non-standard English. In F. Williams (Ed.), *Language and poverty* (pp. 153–189). Chicago: Markham Press.

Lagerspetz, K., & Westman, M. (1980). Moral approval of aggressive acts: A preliminary investigation. *Aggressive Behavior, 6*, 119–130.

Lagerspetz, K., & Viemero, V. (1986). Television and aggressive behavior among Finnish children. In R. Huesmann & L. D. Eron (Eds.), *Television and the aggressive child: A cross-national comparison* (pp. 81–117). Hillsdale, NJ: Lawrence Erlbaum.

Lagmay, A. V. (1984). Western psychology in the Philippines: Impact and response. *International Journal of Psychology, 19*, 31–44.

Lambert, W. W. (1971). Cross-cultural backgrounds to personality development and the social-ization of aggression: Findings from the Six Culture study. In W. W. Lambert & R. Weisbrod (Eds.), *Comparative perspectives on social psychology* (pp. 49–61). Boston: Little, Brown.

Lambert, W. W. (1981). Toward an integrative theory of children's aggression. *The Italian Journal of Psychology, 7*, 153–164.

Lambert, W. W., & Tan, A. L. (1979). Expressive styles and strategies in the aggressive actions of children of six cultures. *Ethos, 7*, 19–36.

Lambley, P. (1973). Authoritarianism and prejudice in South African student samples. *Journal of Social Psychology, 91*, 341–342.

Landau, S. F. (1984). Trends in violence and aggression: A cross-cultural analysis. *International Journal of Comparative Sociology, 24*, 133–158.

Larose, F. (1988). Le jeu traditionnel algonquin au sein du processus d'intégration socio-économique dans une société semi-nomade et son utilité pédagogique. [Traditional Algon-quin games as part of the process of socio-economic integration in a semi-nomadic society and their educational value.] *Enfance, 41*, 25–43.

Latané, B. (1981). *Social loafing in Tailand in the sound production procedure*. Unpublished manuscript.

Latané, B., & Nida, S. (1981). Ten years of research on group size and helping. *Psychological Bulletin, 89*, 308–324.

Latané, B., Williams, K., & Harkins, S. (1979). Many hands make light the work: Causes and consequences of social loafing. *Journal of Personality and Social Psychology, 37*, 822–832.

Laurendau-Bendavid, M., & Pinard, A. (1968). *Les premières notions spatiales de l'enfant.* [The development of the concept of space in the child.] Neuchâtel: Delachaux & Niestlé. *The development of the concept of space in the child.* (1970). New York: International Universi-ties Press.

Laurendeau-Bendavid, M. (1977). Culture, schooling, and cognitive development: A comparative study of children in French Canada and Rwanda. In P. R. Dasen (Ed.), *Piagetian psychology: Cross-cultural contributions* (pp. 123–168). New York: Gardner/Wiley.

Lautrey, J., de Ribaupierre, A., & Rieben, L. (1986). Les différences dans la forme du développement cognitif évalué avec des épreuves piagétiennes: une application de l'analyse des correspondances. [Differences in the types of cognitive development as assessed with Piagetian tasks: an application of multivariate analysis.] *Cahiers de Psychologie Cognitive, 6,* 575–613.

Lautrey, J., de Ribaupierre, A., & Rieben, L. (in press). L'intégration des aspects génétiques et différentiels du développement cognitif. [The integration of individual differences and developmental aspects of cognitive development.] In M. Reuchlin (Ed.). *Les différences individuelles dans le développement cognitif.* [Individual differences in cognitive development.] Nancy: Presses Universitaires de Nancy.

Lautrey, J., & Rodriguez Tome, H. (1976). Etudes interculturelles de la notion de conservation. [Cross-cultural studies of conservation.] In M. Reuchlin (Ed.), *Cultures et conduites* [Cultures and behavior] (pp. 247–282). Paris: Presses Universitaires de France.

Lave, J. (1977). Cognitive consequences of traditional apprenticeship in West Africa. *Anthropology and Education Quarterly, 8*(3), 177–180.

Lave, J. (1985). The social organization of knowledge and practice: A symposium [Special issue]. *Anthropology & Education Quarterly, 16,* 171–213.

Lave, J. (1988). *Cognition in practice: Mind, mathematics and culture in everyday life.* Cambridge: Cambridge University Press.

Lave, J., Murtaugh, M., & de la Rocha, O. (1984). The dialectic of arithmetic in grocery shopping. In B. Rogoff & J. Lave (Eds.), *Everyday cognition: Its development in social context* (pp. 67–94). Cambridge: Harvard University Press.

Laye, C. (1963). *The African child.* London: Collins Press, Fontana Books.

Le Bon, G. (1896). *The crowd.* London: E. Benn.

LeCompte, W., & LeCompte, G. (1970). Effects of education and intercultural contact on traditional attitudes in Turkey. *Journal of Social Psychology, 80,* 11–21.

Lefkowitz, M., Eron, L. D., Walder, L. W., & Huesman, L. R. (1977). *Growing up to be violent: A longitudinal study of the development of aggression.* Elmsford, New York: Pergamon Press.

Leibowitz, H. W., & Pick, H. A. (1972). Cross-cultural and educational aspects of the Ponzo perspective illusion. *Perception and Psychophysics, 12,* 430–432.

Leibowitz, H. W., Brislin, R., Perlmutter, L., & Hennessey, R. (1969). Ponzo perspective illusion as a manifestation of space perception. *Science, 166,* 1174–1176.

Leis, P. E. (1972). *Enculturation and socialization in an Ijaw village.* New York: Holt, Rinehart and Winston.

Lerner, D. (1958). *The passing of traditional society: Modernizing the Middle East.* Glencoe, IL: Free Press.

Leung, K., & Bond, M. H. (1984). The impact of cultural collectivism on reward allocation. *Journal of Personality and Social Psychology, 47,* 793–804.

Levak, M. D. (1969). Eidetic images among the Bororo of Brazil. *Journal of Social Psychology, 79,* 135–137.

LeVine, R. A. (1966). *Dreams and deeds.* Chicago: University of Chicago Press.

LeVine, R. A. (1970). Cross-cultural study in child psychology. In P. Mussen (Ed.), *Carmichael's manual of child psychology: Vol. 2* (3rd ed.) (pp. 559–612). New York: John Wiley.

LeVine, R. A. (1973). Patterns of personality in Africa. *Ethos, 1,* 123–152.

LeVine, R. A., & Campbell, D. T. (1972). *Ethnocentrism: Theories of conflict, ethnic attitudes and group behavior.* New York: John Wiley.

Lévi-Strauss, C. (1962). *La pensée sauvage.* Paris: Plon. (G. Weidenfeld and Nicholson, Ltd., Trans., 1966, *The savage mind.* Chicago: University of Chicago Press.)

Lévy-Bruhl, L. (1910). *Les fonctions mentales dans les sociétés inférieures*. Paris: Alcan. (Trans., 1928, *How natives think*. London: Allen & Unwin).

Lévy-Bruhl, L. (1922). *Mentalité primitive*. Paris: Alcan. (L. A. Clare, Trans., 1923, *Primitive mentality*. London: Allen & Unwin).

Lévy-Bruhl, L. (1949). *Les carnets de Lucien Lévy-Bruhl*. [The notebooks of Lucien Lévy-Bruhl.] Paris: Presses Universitaires de France.

Lewis, O. (1951). *Life in a Mexican village: Tepoztlan restudied*. Urbana: University of Illinois Press.

Lewis, O. (1966). The culture of poverty. *Scientific American*, pp. 19–25.

Lewis, O. (1969). By Oscar Lewis. [Review of *Culture and poverty: A critique and counterproposals*]. *Current Anthropology, 10*, 189–192.

Liebert, R. M., Neale, J. M., & Davidson, E. S. (1973). *The early window: Effects of television on children and youth*. Elmsford, New York: Pergamon Press.

Lindgren, H. C., & Tebcherani, A. (1971). Arab and American auto- and heterostereotypes: A cross-cultural study of empathy. *Journal of Cross-Cultural Psychology, 2*, 173–180.

Lindzey, G. (1961). *Projective techniques and cross-cultural research*. New York: Appleton-Century-Crofts.

Linton, R. (1945a). *The cultural background of personality*. New York: Appleton-Century-Crofts.

Linton, R. (1945b). Foreword to *The psychological frontiers of society*, by A. Kardiner. New York: Columbia University Press.

Locke, J. (1975). *An essay concerning human understanding*. Oxford: Clarendon Press. (Original work published 1690)

Lombard, C. (1978). *Les jouets des enfants baoulés*. [Baoulé children's toys.] Paris: Editions Quatre Vents.

Longabaugh, R. (1980). The systematic observation of behavior in naturalistic settings. In H. C. Triandis & J. W. Berry (Eds.), *Handbook of cross-cultural psychology: Vol. 2. Methodology* (pp. 57–126). Boston: Allyn & Bacon.

Longeot, F. (1974). *L'échelle de développement de la pensée logique (EPL)*. [The logical reasoning development scale (EPL).] Issy-les-Moulineaux: Éd. Scientifiques et Psychotechniques.

Longeot, F. (1978). *Les stades opératoires de Piaget et les facteurs de l'intelligence*. [Piaget's stages of operational reasoning and factors of intelligence.] Grenoble: Presses Universitaires de Grenoble.

Lonner, W. J. (1980). The search for psychological universals. In H. C. Triandis & W. W. Lambert (Eds.), *Handbook of cross-cultural psychology: Vol. 1. Perspectives* (pp. 143–204). Boston: Allyn & Bacon.

Lonner, W. J. (1988, August). *The introductory psychology text and cross-cultural psychology: Beyond Ekman, Whorf and biased IQ tests*. Paper presented at the 9th International Congress of the IACCP (International Association for Cross-cultural Psychology), Newcastle, New South Wales.

Lonner, W. J., & Berry, J. W. (Eds.). (1986). *Field methods in cross-cultural research*. London: Sage.

Lorenz, K. (1963). *On aggression*. New York: Harcourt Brace Jovanovich.

Luce, R. D., & Raiffa, H. (1957). *Games and decisions*. New York: John Wiley.

Luria, A. R. (1976). *Cognitive development: Its cultural and social foundations*. M. Lopez Morillas and L. Solotaroff, transl. Cambridge: Harvard University Press. (Original work published 1974)

MacArthur, R. S. (1973). Some ability patterns: Central Eskimos and Nsenga Africans. *International Journal of Psychology, 8*, 239–248.

Maccoby, E. E. (Ed.). (1966). *The development of sex differences*. Stanford: Stanford University Press.

Maccoby, E. E., & Jacklin, C. N. (1974). *The psychology of sex differences*. Stanford: Stanford University Press.

Madsen, M. C. (1967). Cooperative and competitive motivation of children in three Mexican subcultures. *Psychological Reports, 20*, 1307–1320.

Madsen, M. C. (1971). Developmental and cross-cultural differences in the cooperative and competitive behavior of young children. *Journal of Cross-Cultural Psychology, 2*, 365–371.

Mahler, I., Greenberg, L., & Hayashi, H. (1981). A comparative study of rules of justice: Japanese vs. American. *Psychologia, 24*(1), 1–8.

Maistriaux, R. (1955, 1956). La sous-évolution des Noirs d'Afrique. [The underdevelopment of black Africans.] *Revue de Psychologie des Peuples, 10*, 167–191, 397–456; *11*, 80–90, 134–173.

Malinowski, B. (1927). *Sex and repression in savage society*. London: Humanities Press.

Maloney, P., Wilkof, J., & Dambrot, F. (1981). Androgeny across two cultures: United States and Israel. *Journal of Cross-Cultural Psychology, 12*, 95–102.

Malpass, R. S. (1977). Theory and method in cross-cultural psychology. *American Psychologist, 32*, 1069–1079.

Mangan, J. (1978). Piaget's theory and cultural differences: The case for value-based modes of cognition. *Human Development, 21*, 170–189.

Mauviel, M. (1984). *L'idée de culture et de pluralisme culturel (aspects historiques, conceptuels et comparatifs)*. [The concept of culture and cultural pluralism. Historical, conceptual and comparative aspects.] Unpublished doctoral dissertation (3ème cycle), Université de Paris V.

Mazur, A. (1976). Effects of testosterone on status in primary groups. *Folia Primatologica, 26*, 214–226.

Mazur, A. (1985). A biosocial model of status in face-to-face primate groups. *Social Forces, 64*, 377–402.

McClelland, D. C. (1958). The use of measures of human motivation in the study of society. In J. W. Atkinson (Ed.), *Motives in fantasy, action, and society* (pp. 518–554). Princeton, NJ: Van Nostrand.

McClelland, D. C. (1961). *The achieving society*. Princeton, NJ: Van Nostrand.

McClelland, D. C. (1965). *N* achievement and entrepreneurship: A longitudinal study. *Journal of Personality and Social Psychology, 1*, 389–392.

McClelland, D. C. (1971). *Motivational trends in society*. New York: General Learning Press.

McClelland, D. C., & Winter, D. G. (1969). *Motivating economic achievement*. Glencoe, IL: Free Press.

McDougall, W. (1908). *Introduction to social psychology*. London: Methuen.

McElwain, D. W., & Kearney, G. E. (1970). *Queensland test handbook*. Hawthorne, Victoria: Australian Council for Educational Research.

McFie, J. (1961). The effect of education on African performance on a group of intellectual tests. *British Journal of Educational Psychology, 31*, 232–240.

McLuhan, M. (1962). *The Gutenberg galaxy*. Toronto: University of Toronto Press.

McShane, D. A. (1983). Cognition, affect, and behavior in American Indian children: A developmental perspective of a transcultural situation. *Peabody Journal of Education, 61*, 34–48.

McShane, D., & Berry, J. W. (1988). Native North Americans: Indian and Inuit abilities. In S. H. Irvine & J. W. Berry (Eds.), *Human abilities in cultural context* (pp. 385–426). Cambridge: Cambridge University Press.

McWhirter, L., Young, V., & Majury, Y. (1983). Belfast children's awareness of violent death. *British Journal of Psychology, 22*, 81–92.

Mead, G. H. (1934). *Mind, self and society* (C. M. Morris, Ed.). Chicago: University of Chicago Press.

Mead, M. (1928). *Coming of age in Samoa*. New York: Morrow.

Melikian, L. H. (1984). The transfer of psychological knowledge to the Third World countries and its impact on development: The case of the five Arab oil-producing states. *International Journal of Psychology, 19*, 65–77.

Meljac, C. (1979). *Décrire, agir et compter—l'enfant et le dénombrement spontané.* [To describe, to act and to count—the child and spontaneous counting.] Paris: Presses Universitaires de France.

Mellah, F. (1979). L'école coranique, une institution en voie de disparition? [Qu'ranic schooling, a disappearing institution?] *Entwicklung/Développement,* no. 2, 2–3.

Mervis, C. B., & Rosch, E. (1981). Categorization of natural objects. *Annual Review of Psychology, 32*, 89–115.

Milgram, S., & Shotland, R. L. (1973). *Television and anti-social behavior.* New York: Academic Press.

Miller, A. G., & Thomas, R. (1972). Cooperation and competition among Blackfoot Indian and urban Canadian children. *Child Development, 43*, 1104–1110.

Miller, S. A. (1988). Parents' beliefs about children's cognitive development. *Child Development, 59*, 259–285.

Miller, N. E. (1941). The frustration-aggression hypothesis. *Psychological Review, 48*, 337–342.

Miller, N. E., & Bugelski, R. (1948). Minor studies in aggression: The influence of frustrations imposed by the in-group on attitudes expressed toward out-groups. *Journal of Psychology, 25*, 437–442.

Minge-Klevana, W. (1980). Does labor time decrease with industrialization? A survey of time-allocation studies. *Current Anthropology, 21*, 279–298.

Mischel, W. (1958). Preference for delayed reinforcement: An experimental study of a cultural observation. *Journal of Abnormal and Social Psychology, 56*, 57–61.

Mischel, W. (1961a). Delay of gratification, need for achievement, and acquiescence in another culture. *Journal of Abnormal and Social Psychology, 62*, 543–552.

Mischel, W. (1961b). Father absence and delay of gratification. *Journal of Abnormal and Social Psychology, 63*, 116–124.

Monahan, L., Kuhn, D., & Shaver, P. (1974). Intrapsychic versus cultural explanations of the "fear of success" motive. *Journal of Personality and Social Psychology, 29*(1), 60–64.

Moore, O. K., & Lewis, D. J. (1952). Learning theory and culture. *Psychological Review, 59*, 380–388.

Morgan, L. H. (1877). *Ancient society.* New York: Henry Holt.

Morris, D. (1967). *The naked ape.* New York: McGraw-Hill.

Moscovici, S. (1972). Society and theory in social psychology. In J. Israel & H. Tajfel (Eds.), *The context of social psychology: A critical assessment,* (pp. 17–68). London: Academic Press.

Moscovici, S. (1984). The phenomenon of social representations. In R. M. Farr & S. Moscovici (Eds.), *Social representations.* Cambridge: Cambridge University Press.

Moyer, K. E. (1974). Sex differences in aggression. In R. C. Friedman, R. M. Richart, & R. L. Vande Wiele (Eds.), *Sex differences in behavior* (pp. 335–372). New York: John Wiley & Sons.

Mugny, G., & Carugati, F. (1985). *L'intelligence au pluriel. Les représentations sociales de l'intelligence et de son développement.* [Intelligence in the plural. The social representations of intelligence and of its development.] Cousset, Fribourg, Switzerland: DelVal.

Mukene, P. (1988). *L'ouverture entre l'école et le milieu en Afrique noire: Pour une gestion pertinente des connaissances.* [The interchange between the school and its context in black Africa.] Fribourg, Switzerland: Editions Universitaires.

Mundy-Castle, A. C. (1974). Social and technological intelligence in Western and non-Western cultures. *Universitas* (University of Ghana, Legon), *4*, 46–52. (Also in S. Pilowsky (Ed.), (1975), *Cultures in collision.* Adelaide: Australian Nat. Association for Mental Health.)

Mundy-Castle, A. C., & Bundy, R. (1988). Moral values in Nigeria. *Journal of African Psychology, 1*, 25–40.

Mundy-Castle, A. C., & Okonji, M. O. (1976). *Mother-infant interactions in Nigeria*. Unpublished manuscript, University of Lagos, Nigeria.

Munroe, R. H., & Munroe, R. L. (1971). Household density and infant care in an East African society. *Journal of Social Psychology, 83*, 3–13.

Munroe, R. H., & Munroe, R. L. (1980). Perspectives suggested by anthropological data. In H. C. Triandis (Ed.), *Handbook of cross-cultural psychology: Vol. 1. Perspectives* (pp. 253–318). Boston: Allyn & Bacon.

Munroe, R. H., Munroe, R. L., & Michelson, C. (1983). Time allocation in four societies. *Ethnology, 22*, 355–370.

Munroe, R. H., Munroe, R. L., & Shimmin, H. S. (1984). Children's work in four cultures: Determinants and consequences. *American Anthropologist, 86*, 369–379.

Munroe, R. H., Munroe, R. L., & Whiting, B. B. (Eds.). (1981). *Handbook of cross-cultural human development*. New York: Garland STPM.

Munroe, R. H., Shimmin, H. S., & Munroe, R. L. (1984). Gender understanding and sex role preference in four cultures. *Developmental Psychology, 20*, 673–682.

Munroe, R. L., & Munroe, R. H. (1975). *Cross-cultural human development*. Monterey, CA: Brooks/Cole.

Munroe, R. L., & Munroe, R. H. (1977). Cooperation and competition among East African and American children. *Journal of Social Psychology, 101*, 145–146.

Munroe, R. L., & Munroe, R. H. (1988, February). *Further thoughts — and more evidence — on the couvade*. Paper presented at the meeting of the Society for Cross-Cultural Research, El Paso, Texas.

Munroe, R. L., Munroe, R. H., & Whiting, J. W. M. (1981). Male sex-role resolutions. In R. H. Munroe, R. L. Munroe, & B. B. Whiting (Eds.), *Handbook of cross-cultural human development* (pp. 611–632). New York: Garland STPM.

Muralidharan, R., Khosla, R., Mian, G. M., & Kaur, B. (1981). *Children's games*. New Delhi: [National Council of Educational Research and Training.].

Murdock, G. P. (1937). Comparative data on the division of labor by sex. *Social Forces, 15*, 551–553.

Murdock, G. P. (1967). *Ethnographic atlas*. Pittsburgh, PA: University of Pittsburgh Press.

Murdock, G. P., & White, R. R. (1969). Standard cross-cultural sample. *Ethnology, 8*, 329–369.

Murray, D. J. (1983). *A history of Western psychology*. Englewood Cliffs, NJ: Prentice-Hall.

Murtaugh, M. (1985). The practice of arithmetic by American grocery shoppers. *Anthropology and Education Quarterly, 16*, 186–192.

Muschinske, D. (1977). The non-white as a child: G. Stanley Hall on the education of non-white peoples. *Journal of the History of the Behavioral Sciences, 13*, 328–336.

N'guessan, A. G. (1989). Contribution du jeu dans l'insertion sociale de l'enfant ivoirien en milieu rural. [The contribution of play to the socialization of the child in rural Côte d'Ivoire.] In C. Clanet (Ed.) *Socialisations et cultures*. [Cultures and socializations.] (pp. 143–152). Toulouse: Presses Universitaires du Mirail.

Naroll, R. (1970a). What have we learned from cross-cultural surveys? *American Anthropologist, 72*, 1227–1288.

Naroll, R. (1970b). Cross-cultural sampling. In R. Naroll & R. Cohen (Eds.), *A Handbook of method in cultural anthropology* (pp. 889–926). New York: American Museum of Natural History.

Naroll, R. (1983). *The moral order: An introduction to the human situation*. Beverley Hills, CA: Sage.

Nerlove, S. B., Roberts, J. R., Klein, R. F., Yarbrough, C., & Habicht, J. P. (1974). Natural indicators of cognitive development: An observational study of rural Guatemalan children. *Ethos, 2*, 265–295.

Nerlove, S. B., & Snipper, A. S. (1981). Cognitive consequences of cultural opportunity. In R. H. Munroe, R. L. Munroe, & B. B. Whiting (Eds.), *Handbook of cross-cultural human development* (pp. 423–474). New York: Garland STPM.

Newman, G. (1979). *Understanding violence.* New York: Lippincott.

Newman, D., Griffin, P., & Cole, M. (1984). Social constraints in laboratory and classroom tasks. In B. Rogoff & J. Lave (Eds.), *Everyday cognition* (pp. 172–193). Cambridge: Harvard University Press.

Nichols, K. R., & McAndrew, F. T. (1984). Stereotyping and autostereotyping in Spanish, Malaysian, and American college students. *Journal of Social Psychology, 124*(2), 179–189.

Nijhuis, T. (1981). *Afrikanische Kinderspiele.* [Children's games in Africa.] Wuppertal, W. Germany: Jugenddienst-Verlag.

Nimkoff, M. F., & Middleton, R. (1960). Types of family and types of economy. *American Journal of Sociology, 66*, 215–225.

Nuffield Foundation. (1970). *Shape and size.* Edinburgh: Chambers.

Nuffield Foundation. (1972). *Beginnings.* Edinburgh: Chambers.

Nyiti, R. M. (1982). The validity of "cultural differences explanations" for cross-cultural variation in the rate of Piagetian cognitive development. In D. A. Wagner & H. W. Stevenson (Eds.), *Cultural perspectives on child development* (pp. 146–165). San Francisco: W. H. Freeman.

Ogbu, J. U. (1978). *Minority education and caste.* New York: Academic Press.

Ohuche, R. O., & Otaala, B. (Eds.). (1981). *The African child and his environment.* Oxford: Pergamon Press.

Okonji, O. M. (1971). The effects of familiarity on classification. *Journal of Cross-Cultural Psychology, 2*, 39–49.

Okonji, M. O. (1980). Cognitive styles across cultures. In N. Warren (Ed.), *Studies in cross-cultural psychology: Vol. 2* (pp. 1–50). London: Academic Press.

Olson, D. R. (1977). From utterance to text: The bias of language in speech and writing. *Harvard Educational Review, 47*, 257–281.

Omari, T. P. (1960). Changing attitudes of students in West African society toward marriage and family relationships. *British Journal of Sociology, 11*, 197–210.

Ogunlade, J. A. (1971). National stereotypes of university students in Western Nigeria. *Journal of Cross-Cultural Psychology, 2*, 173–180.

Oppong, C. (Ed.). (1980). *Child development in African contexts: A collection of readings.* London: Allen & Unwin.

Orpen, C. (1971). Authoritarianism and racial attitudes among English-speaking South Africans. *Journal of Social Psychology, 84*, 301–302.

Orpen, C. (1972). The effect of race and similar attitudes on interpersonal attraction among white Rhodesians. *Journal of Social Psychology, 86*, 143–145.

Orpen, C., & Pors, H. (1972). Race and belief: A test of Rokeach's theory in an authoritarian culture. *International Journal of Psychology, 7*, 53–56.

Orpen, C., & Rookledge, Q. (1972). Dogmatism and prejudice in white South Africa. *Journal of Social Psychology, 86*, 151–153.

Ortigues, M. C., & Ortigues, E. (1966). *Oedipe africain.* [African Oedipus.] Paris: Plon.

Oskamp, S., & Perlman, D. (1966). Effects of friendship and disliking on cooperation in a mixed-motive game. *Journal of Conflict Resolution, 10*, 221–226.

Pareek, U. (1968). A motivational paradigm of development. *Journal of Social Issues, 24*(2), 115–122.

Parsons, T. (1951). *The social system.* New York: Free Press.

Pearson, R. E. (1980). Piagetian tasks in a small group format. In W. F. Archenhold, R. H. Driver, A. Orton, & D. Wood-Robinson (Eds.), *Cognitive development research in science and mathematics* (pp. 104–113). Leeds: University of Leeds Press.

Peck, R. F. (1967). A comparison of the value system of Mexican and American youth. *Interamerican Journal of Psychology, 1*, 41–51.

Pepitone, A., Faucheux, C., Moscovici, S., Cesa-Bianchi, M., Magistretti, G., Iacono, G., Asprea, A. M., & Villone, G. (1967). The role of self-esteem in competitive choice behavior. *International Journal of Psychology, 2*, 147–159.

Perret-Clermont, A. N. (1979). *La construction de l'intelligence dans l'interaction sociale.* [The construction of intelligence in social interaction.] Bern: Peter Lang.

Petitto, A. L. (1982). Practical arithmetic and transfer: A study among West African tribesmen. *Journal of Cross-Cultural Psychology, 13*, 15–28.

Petitto, A. L., & Ginsburg, H. P. (1982). Mental arithmetic in Africa and America: Strategies, principles and explanations. *International Journal of Psychology, 17*, 81–102.

Pettigrew, T. F. (1959). Regional differences in anti-Negro prejudice. *Journal of Abnormal and Social Psychology, 59*, 28–36.

Pettigrew, T. F. (1960). Social distance attitudes of South African students. *Social Forces, 38*, 246–253.

Piaget, J. (1926). *La représentation du monde chez l'enfant.* Paris: Alcan. *The child's conception of the world* (J. Tomlinson & A. Tomlinson, Trans.). (1929). New York: Harcourt & Brace).

Piaget, J. (1932). *Le jugement moral chez l'enfant.* Paris: Alcan. *The moral judgment of the child* (M. Gabain, Trans.). London: Routledge & Kegan Paul.

Piaget, J. (1937). *La construction du réel chez l'enfant.* Neuchâtel: Delachaux & Niestlé. *The child's construction of reality.* (Margaret Cook, Trans.). (1954). New York: Basic Books.

Piaget, J. (1961). *Les mécanismes perceptifs.* Paris: P.U.F. *Mechanisms of perception* (G. N. Seagrim, Trans.). (1969). London: Routledge.

Piaget, J. (1966). Nécessité et signification des recherches comparatives en psychologie génétique. *Journal International de Psychologie, 1*, 3–13. Need and significance of cross-cultural studies in genetic psychology (C. Dasen, Trans.). In J. W. Berry & P. R. Dasen (Eds.). (1974), *Culture and cognition* (pp. 299–309). London: Methuen.

Piaget, J. (1970). Piaget's theory. In P. H. Mussen (Ed.), *Carmichael's manual of child psychology: Vol. 1 (3rd ed.)* (pp. 703–732). New York: John Wiley.

Piaget, J. (1972). Intellectual evolution from adolescence to adulthood. *Human Development, 15*, 1–12.

Piaget, J., & Garcia, R. (1983). *Psychogenèse et histoire des sciences.* [Developmental psychology and the history of sciences.] Paris: Flammarion.

Piaget, J., & Inhelder, B. (1966). *La psychologie de l'enfant.* Paris: Presses Universitaires de France. (*The psychology of the child* (H. Weaver, Trans.). (1969). London: Routledge & Kegan Paul).

Piéron, H. (1957). *Vocabulaire de la psychologie.* [The vocabulary of psychology.] Paris: Presses Universitaires de France.

Pike, K. L. (1954). Emic and etic standpoints for the description of behavior. In K. L. Pike *Language in relation to a unified theory of the structure of human behavior*, Pt. 1 (Preliminary ed.). (pp. 8–28). Glendale, CA: Summer Institute of Linguistics.

Pike, K. L. (1967). *Language in relation to a unified theory of the structure of human behavior.* The Hague: Mouton.

Plato. (1956). *Republic.* In W. H. F. Rouse (Trans.), *The great dialogues of Plato.* New York: Mentor.

Pollack, R. H. (1963). Contour detectability thresholds as a function of chronological age. *Perceptual and Motor Skills, 17*, 411–417.

Pollack, R. H. (1970). Müller-Lyer illusion: Effect of age, lightness contrast and hue. *Science, 170*, 93–94.

Pollack, R. H., & Silvar, S. D. (1967). Magnitude of the Müller-Lyer illusion in children as a function of pigmentation of the Fundus oculi. *Psychonomic Science, 8*, 83–84.

Pollnac, R. B. (1977). Illusion susceptibility and adaptation to the marine environment: Is the carpentered world hypothesis seaworthy? *Journal of Cross-Cultural Psychology, 8*, 425–433.

Pomerantz, A. (1978). Compliment response. In J. S. Schenkein (Ed.), *Studies in the organization of conversational interaction* (pp. 79–112). New York: Academic Press.

Poortinga, Y. H. (1975). Some implications of three different approaches to intercultural comparison. In J. W. Berry & W. J. Lonner (Eds.), *Applied cross-cultural psychology* (pp. 327–332). Amsterdam: Swets & Zeitlinger.

Poortinga, Y. (Ed.). (1977). *Basic problems in cross-cultural psychology.* Amsterdam: Swets & Zeitlinger.

Porteus, S. D. (1917). Mental tests with delinquents and Australian Aboriginal children. *Psychological Review, 14*, 32–41.

Porteus, S. D. (1937). *Intelligence and environment.* New York: Macmillan.

Posner, J. K., & Baroody, A. J. (1979). Number conservation in two West African societies. *Journal of Cross-Cultural Psychology, 10*, 479–496.

Postic, M., & de Ketele, J. M. (1988). *Observer les situations éducatives.* [Observing educational situations.] Paris: Presses Universitaires de France.

Postman, L. (1971). Transfer, interference and forgetting. In J. W. Kling & L. A. Riggs (Eds.), *Woodworth & Schlosberg's Experimental Psychology* (3rd ed.) (pp. 1019–1132). New York: Holt, Rinehart and Winston.

Preiswerk, R. (1976). Jean Piaget et l'étude des relations interculturelles. [Jean Piaget and the study of cross-cultural relations.] In G. Busino (Ed.), Les sciences sociales avec et après Jean Piaget. [The social sciences with and after Jean Piaget.] *Revue Européenne des Sciences Sociales, 14*, 495–511.

Preiswerk, R., & Perrot, D. (1975). *Ethnocentrisme et histoire. L'Afrique, l'Amérique indienne et l'Asie dans les manuels occidentaux.* [Ethnocentrism and history. Africa, American indians and Asia in Western textbooks.] Paris: Anthropos.

Premack, D. (1976). *Intelligence in ape and man.* Hillsdale, NJ: Lawrence Erlbaum.

Price-Williams, D. R. (1961). A study concerning concepts of conservation of quantities among primitive children. *Acta Psychologica, 18*, 297–305.

Price-Williams, D. R. (1962). Abstract and concrete modes of classification in a primitive society. *British Journal of Educational Psychology, 32*, 50–61.

Price-Williams, D. R. (1975). *Explorations in cross-cultural psychology.* San Francisco: Chandler & Sharp.

Price-Williams, D. (1981). Concrete and formal operations. In R. H. Munroe, R. L. Munroe, & B. B. Whiting (Eds.), *Handbook of cross-cultural human development* (pp. 403–422). New York: Garland.

Price-Williams, D. R., & Ramirez, M., III. (1974). Ethnic differences in delay of gratification. *Journal of Social Psychology, 93*, 23–30.

Putnam, D. B., & Kilbride, P. L. (1980, February). *A relativistic understanding of intelligence: social intelligence among the Songhay of Mali and the Samia of Kenya.* Paper presented at Society for Cross-Cultural Research (SCCR) conference, Philadelphia.

Rank, O. (1958). *Beyond psychology.* New York: Dover Books. (Original work published 1941)

Rank, O. (1961). *Psychology and the soul.* New York: Perpetua Books. (Original work published 1931)

Reed, H. J., & Lave, J. (1979). Arithmetic as a tool for investigating relations between culture and cognition. *American Ethnologist, 6*(3), 568–582.

Reigrotski, E., & Anderson, N. (1959). National stereotypes and foreign contacts. *Public Opinion Quarterly, 23*, 515–528.

Reiss, I. L. (1986). *Journey into sexuality: An exploratory voyage.* Englewood Cliffs, NJ: Prentice-Hall.

Ribaupierre de, A., Rieben, L., & Lautrey, J. (1985). Horizontal decalages and individual differences in the development of concrete operations. In V. Shulman, L. Restaino-Baumann, & L. Butler (Eds.), *The future of Piagetian theory: The neo-Piagetians* (pp. 175–197). New York: Plenum Press.

Rist, G., & Sabelli, F. (Eds.). (1986). *Il était une fois le développement [Once Upon a Time . . . Development].* Lausanne: Editions d'en bas.

Ristau, C. A., & Robbins, D. (1982). Language in the great apes: A critical review. *Advances in the Study of Behavior, 12*, 141–255.

Rivers, W. H. R. (1901). Introduction and vision. In A. C. Haddon (Ed.), *Reports of the Cambridge anthropological expedition to the Torres Straits: Vol. 2, Pt. 1.* Cambridge: Cambridge University Press.

Rivers, W. H. R. (1905). Observations on the senses of the Todas. *British Journal of Psychology, 1*, 321–396.

Roberts, J. M., & Barry, H., III. (1976). Inculcated traits and games type combinations: A cross-cultural view. In T. T. Craig (Ed.), *The humanistic and mental health aspects of sports, exercise and recreation* (pp. 5–11). Chicago: American Medical Association.

Rogoff, B. (1978). Spot observation: An introduction and examination. *The Quarterly Newsletter of the Institute of Comparative Human Development, 2*, 21–26.

Rogoff, B. (1981). Schooling and the development of cognitive skills. In H. C. Triandis & A. Heron (Eds.), *Handbook of cross-cultural psychology: Vol. 4. Developmental psychology* (pp. 233–294). Boston: Allyn & Bacon.

Rogoff, B. (1982). Literacy, schooling, and cognitive skills. [Review of S. Scribner & M. Cole, *The psychology of literacy*]. *Science, 215*, 1494–1495.

Rogoff, B., & Gardner, W. (1984). Adult guidance of cognitive development. In B. Rogoff & J. Lave (Eds.), *Everyday cognition* (pp. 95–116). Cambridge: Harvard University Press.

Rogoff, B., & Lave, J. (1984). (Eds.). *Everyday cognition: Its development in social context.* Cambridge: Harvard University Press.

Rohner, R. P. (1976). Sex differences in aggression: Phylogenetic and enculturation perspectives. *Ethos, 4*, 57–72.

Rohner, R. (1984). Toward a conception of culture for cross-cultural psychology. *Journal of Cross-Cultural Psychology, 15*, 111–138.

Rohrer, J. H., & Edmonson, M. E. (Eds.). (1960). *The eighth generation: Cultures and personalities of New Orleans Negroes.* New York: Harper and Row.

Rokeach, M. (Ed.). (1960). *The open and closed mind.* New York: Basic Books.

Rokeach, M., Smith, P. W., & Evans, R. I. (1960). Two kinds of prejudice or one? In M. Rokeach (Ed.), *The open and closed mind* (pp. 132–168). New York: Basic Books.

Rosch, E. (1977). Human categorization. In N. Warren (Ed.), *Studies in cross-cultural psychology: Vol. 1* (pp. 1–49). London: Academic Press.

Rosen, B. C. (1962). Socialization and achievement motivation in Brazil. *American Sociological Review, 27*, 612–624.

Rosen, B. C., & D'Andrade, R. (1959). The psychological origins of achievement motivation. *Sociometry, 22*, 185–218.

Rosenblatt, P. C. (1966). A cross-cultural study of child-rearing and romantic love. *Journal of Personality and Social Psychology, 4*, 336–338.

Rosin, R. T. (1973). Gold medallions: The arithmetic calculations of an illiterate. *Council on Anthropology and Education Newsletter, 4*(2), 1–9.

Roskies, D. (1979). Alphabet instruction in the East European heder: Some comparative and historical notes. *YIVO Annual of Jewish Social Studies, 17*.

Ross, E. A. (1908). *Social psychology*. New York: Macmillan.

Ross, B. M., & Millsom, C. (1970). Repeated memory of oral prose in Ghana and New York. *International Journal of Psychology, 5*, 173–181.

Rule, B. G., & Nesdale, A. R. (1976). Moral judgment of aggressive behavior. In R. G. Green & E. C. O'Neal (Eds.), *Perspectives on aggression* (pp. 37–60). New York: Academic Press.

Sahlins, M. (1972). *Stone age economics*. Chicago: Aldine.

Salazar, J. M. (1984). The use and impact of psychology in Venezuela: Two examples. *International Journal of Psychology, 19*, 113–122.

Santerre, R. (1973). *Pédagogie musulmane d'Afrique noire*. [Muslim schooling in black Africa.] Montréal: Les Presses de l'Université de Montréal.

Santerre, R., & Mercier-Tremblay, C. (1982). *La quête du savoir: Essais pour une anthropologie de l'éducation camérounaise* [The quest for knowledge: Essays for and anthropology of education in Cameroon]. Montréal: Presses de l'Université de Montréal.

Saraswathi, T. S., & Dutta, R. (1987). *Developmental psychology in India, 1975-1986: An annotated bibliography*. New Delhi: Sage.

Sargent, E. D. (1986, March 2). The black "fratricide" epidemic. *The Washington Post*, Section C, p. 1. 3. (Reprinted in *The Syracuse Post-Standard*, March 15, p. A-4)

Savage-Rumbaugh, E. S., Sevcik, R. A., Rumbaugh, D. M., & Rupert, E. (1985). The capacity of animals to acquire language: Do species differences have anything to say to us? *Philosophical Transactions. Royal Society of London, B308*, 177–185.

Saxe, G. B. (1981a). Body parts as numerals: A developmental analysis of numeration among remote Oksapmin village populations in Papua New Guinea. *Child Development, 52*, 306–316.

Saxe, G. B. (1981b). When fourth can precede second. A developmental analysis of an indigenous numeration system among Ponam islanders in Papua New Guinea. *Journal of Cross-Cultural Psychology, 12*, 37–50.

Saxe, G. B. (1982). Culture and the development of numerical cognition: Studies among the Oksapmin of Papua New Guinea. In C. J. Brainerd (Ed.), *Children's logical and mathematical cognition* (pp. 157–176). New York: Springer.

Scarr, S. (1981). *Race, social class, and individual differences in I.Q.* Hillsdale, NJ: Lawrence Erlbaum.

Scarr-Salapatek, S. (1971). Unknowns in the I.Q. equation. *Science, 174*(4015), 1283–1288.

Scher, D., Nevo, B., & Beit-Hallahmi, B. (1979). Beliefs about equal rights for men and women among Israeli and American students. *Journal of Social Psychology, 109*, 11–15.

Schlegel, A., & Barry, H., III. (1986). The cultural consequences of female contribution to subsistence. *American Anthropologist, 88*, 142–150.

Schliemann, A. D. (1988). Understanding the combinatorial system: Development, school learning, and everyday experience. *Quarterly Newsletter of the Laboratory of Comparative Human Cognition, 10*, 3–7.

Schliemann, A. D., & Carraher, T. N. (1988). *Everyday experience as a source of mathematical learning: Knowledge complexity and transfer*. Paper presented at the 1988 Annual meeting of the American Educational Research Association (AEREA).

Schnaiberg, A. (1970). Measuring modernism: Theoretical and empirical explanations. *American Journal of Sociology, 76*, 399–425.

Schneuwly, B., & Bronckart, J. P. (1985). *Vygotsky*. Lausanne: Delachaux & Niestlé.

Schoenfeld, N. (1942). An experimental study of some problems relating to stereotypes. *Archives of Psychology, 38* (Whole No. 270).

Schulte-Tenckhoff, I. (1985). *La vue portée au loin: Une histoire de la pensée anthropologique*. [To see afar. A history of anthropological thinking.] Lausanne: Editions d'en bas.

Scribner, S. (1974). Developmental aspects of categorized recall in a West African society. *Cognitive Psychology, 6*, 475–494.

Scribner, S. (1979). Modes of thinking and ways of speaking: Culture and logic reconsidered. In

R. O. Freedle (Ed.), *New directions in discourse processing* (pp. 223–243). Norwood, NJ: Ablex.

Scribner, S. (1984). Studying working intelligence. In B. Rogoff & J. Lave (Eds.), *Everyday cognition: Its development in social context* (pp. 9–40). Cambridge: Harvard University Press.

Scribner, S., & Cole, M. (1973). The cognitive consequences of formal and informal education. *Science, 182*, 553–559.

Scribner, S., & Cole, M. (1978). Unpacking literacy. *Social Science Information, 17*, 19–40.

Scribner, S., & Cole, M. (1981). *The psychology of literacy*. Cambridge: Harvard University Press.

Segall, M. H. (1976). *Human behavior and public policy: A political psychology*. Elmsford, NY: Pergamon Press.

Segall, M. H. (1983). Aggression in global perspective: A research strategy. In A. P. Goldstein & M. H. Segall (Eds.), *Aggression in global perspective* (pp. 1–43). Elmsford, NY: Pergamon Press.

Segall, M. H. (1984). More than we need to know about culture but are afraid not to ask. *Journal of Cross-Cultural Psychology, 15*, 153–162.

Segall, M. H. (1986). Culture and behavior: Psychology in global perspective. *Annual Review of Psychology, 37*, 523–564.

Segall, M. H. (1988). Psychocultural antecedents of male aggression: Some implications involving gender, parenting, and adolescence. In P. R. Dasen, J. W. Berry, & N. Sartorius (Eds.), *Health and cross-cultural psychology: Towards applications* (pp. 71–92). Newbury Park, CA: Sage.

Segall, M. H., Campbell, D. T., & Herskovits, M. J. (1963). Cultural differences in the perception of geometric illusions. *Science, 193*, 769–771.

Segall, M. H., Campbell, D. T., & Herskovits, M. J. (1966). *The influence of culture on visual perception*. Indianapolis: Bobbs-Merrill.

Segall, M. H., Doornbos, M., & Davis, C. (1976). *Political identity: A case study from Uganda*. Syracuse, NY: Maxwell Foreign and Comparative Studies/East Africa XXIV.

Serpell, R. (1976). *Culture's influence on behaviour*. London: Methuen.

Serpell, R. (1977a). Strategies for investigating intelligence in its cultural context. *Quarterly Newsletter of the Institute for Comparative Human Development, 1*(3), 11–15.

Serpell, R. (1977b). Estimates of intelligence in a rural community of Eastern Zambia. In F. M. Okatcha (Ed.), *Modern psychology and cultural adaptation* (pp. 179–216). Nairobi: Swahili Language Consultants and Publishers.

Serpell, R. (1979). How specific are perceptual skills? A cross-cultural study of pattern reproduction. *British Journal of Psychology, 70*, 365–380.

Serpell, R. (1984). Commentary: The impact of psychology on Third World development. *International Journal of Psychology, 19*, 179–192.

Serpell, R. (1989). Dimensions endogènes de l'intelligence chez les A-Chewa et autres peuples africains. [Indigenous dimensions of intelligence among the A-Chewa and other African people.] In J. Retschitzki, M. Bossel-Lagos, & P. R. Dasen (Eds.), *La recherche interculturelle. Tome 2.* [Cross-cultural research. Vol. 2.] (pp. 164–179) Paris: L'Harmattan.

Shapira, A., & Madsen, M. C. (1969). Cooperative and competitive behavior of kibbutz and urban children in Israel. *Child Development, 40*, 609–617.

Sharp, D., Cole, M., & Lave, C. (1978). Education and cognitive development: The evidence from experimental research. *Monographs of the Society for Research in Child Development, 44*(1–2), 1–112.

Shayer, M., Demetriou, A., & Pervez, M. (1988). The structure and scaling of concrete operational thought: Three studies in four countries and only one story. *Genetic Psychology Monographs, 114*, 307–376.

Shea, J. D. (1985). Studies of cognitive development in Papua New Guinea. *International Journal of Psychology, 20*, 33–61.

Sheehan, P. W. (1973). The variability of eidetic imagery among Australian Aboriginal children. *Journal of Social Psychology, 91*, 29–36.

Sheehan, P. W. (1976). The methodology of cross-cultural psychology. In G. E. Kearney & D. W. McElwain (Eds.), *Aboriginal cognition* (pp. 185–198). Canberra: Australian Institute of Aboriginal Studies; Atlantic Highlands, NJ: Humanities Press.

Sheehan, P. W., & Stewart, S. J. (1972). A cross-cultural study of eidetic imagery among Australian Aboriginal children. *Journal of Social Psychology, 87*, 179–188.

Shipley, T. (Ed.). (1961). *Classics in psychology*. New York: Philosophical Library.

Siann, G. (1985). *Accounting for aggression: Perspectives on aggression and violence*. Boston: Allen & Unwin.

Silvar, S. D., & Pollack, R. H. (1967). Racial differences in pigmentation of the Fundus oculi. *Psychonomic Science, 7*, 159–160.

Sinha, D. (1986). *Psychology in a third world country: The Indian experience*. New Delhi and London: Sage.

Sinha, D. (1988). The family scenario in a developing country and its implications for mental health: The case of India. In P. R. Dasen, J. W. Berry, & N. Sartorius (Eds.), *Health and cross-cultural psychology: Toward applications* (pp. 48–70). Newbury Park, CA: Sage.

Sinha, D., & Holtzman, W. H. (Eds.). (1984). The impact of psychology on third world development [Special issue]. *International Journal of Psychology, 19*, 3–192.

Skinner, B. F. (1974). *About behaviorism*. New York: Alfred A. Knopf.

Slovic, P. (1966). Risk-taking in children: Age and sex differences. *Child Development, 37*, 169–176.

Smilansky, S. N. (1980). The concept of death among Israeli children. In A. Raviv, A. Klingman, & M. Horowitz (Eds.), *Children in situations of death and crisis*. Tel-Aviv: Atzer Hamoreh (Hebrew). (See Florian & Kravetz, 1985).

Smilansky, S. N. (1981). *Manual for questionnaire of the development of death conceptualization*. Unpublished manuscript, Tel-Aviv University, Department of Psychology (Hebrew). (See Florian & Kravetz, 1985).

Smith, A. (1759). *The theory of moral sentiments*. London: A. Miller.

Smith, D. H., & Inkeles, A. (1966). The OM Scale: A comparative socio-psychological measure of individual modernity. *Sociometry, 29*, 353–377.

Snarey, J. R., Reimer, J., & Kohlberg, L. (1985). Development of social-moral reasoning among kibbutz adolescents: A longitudinal cross-cultural study. *Developmental Psychology, 21*, 3–11.

Soto, E., & Shaver, P. (1982). Sex-role traditionalism, assertiveness, and symptoms of Puerto Rican women living in the United States. *Hispanic Journal of Behavioral Sciences, 4*, 1–19.

Sow, I. (1977). *Psychiatrie dynamique africaine*. [African dynamic psychiatry.] Paris: Payot.

Sow, I. (1978). *Les structures anthropologiques de la folie en Afrique noire*. [Anthropological structures of mental illness in black Africa.] Paris: Payot.

Spencer, H. (1876). *Principles of sociology*. New York: D. Appleton.

Spiro, M. E. (1961). Social systems, personality, and functional analysis. In B. Kaplan (Ed.), *Studying personality cross-culturally* (pp. 93–127). Evanston, IL: Row, Peterson.

Spiro, M. E. (1982). *Oedipus in the Trobriands*. Chicago: University of Chicago Press.

Stein, D. D., Hardyck, J. A., & Smith, M. B. (1965). Race and belief: An open and shut case. *Journal of Personality and Social Psychology, 1*, 281–289.

Stewart, V. M. (1973). Tests of the "carpentered world" hypothesis by race and environment in America and Zambia. *International Journal of Psychology, 8*, 83–94.

Stigler, J. W. (1984). "Mental abacus": The effect of abacus training on Chinese children's mental calculation. *Cognitive Psychology, 16*, 145–176.

Stigler, J. W., Barclay, C., & Aiello, P. (1982). Motor and mental abacus skill: A preliminary look at an expert. *Quarterly Newsletter of the Laboratory of Comparative Human Cognition, 4*(1), 12-14.

Storr, A. (1968). *Human aggression.* New York: Atheneum.

Strauss, C. (1984). Beyond "formal" versus "informal" education: Uses of psychological theory in anthropological research. *Ethos, 12*, 195-222.

Suchman, R. G. (1966). Cultural differences in children's color and form perception. *Journal of Social Psychology, 70*, 3-10.

Sumner, W. G. (1906). *Folkways.* Boston: Ginn.

Super, C. M. (1983). Cultural variations in the meaning and uses of children's "intelligence." In J. B. Deregowski, S. Dziurawiec, & R. C. Annis (Eds.), *Expiscations in cross-cultural psychology* (pp. 199-212). Lisse, Netherlands: Swets & Zeitlinger.

Super, C., & Harkness, S. (1986). The developmental niche: A conceptualization at the interface of society and the individual. *International Journal of Behavioral Development, 9*(4), 545-570.

Sutton-Smith, B., & Roberts, J. M. (1981). Play, toys, games, and sports. In H. C. Triandis & A. Heron (Eds.), *Handbook of cross-cultural psychology: Vol. 4. Developmental psychology* (pp. 425-471). Boston: Allyn & Bacon.

Suvannathat, C., Bhanthumnavin, D., Bhuapirom, L., & Keats, D. M. (1985). *Handbook of Asian child development and child rearing practices.* Bangkok: Behavioral Science Research Institute.

Tambiah, S. J. (1968). Literacy in a Buddhist village in North-East Thailand. In J. Goody (Ed.), *Literacy in traditional societies* (pp. 85-131). Cambridge: Cambridge University Press.

Tapé, G. (1987). *Milieu africain et développement cognitif: Une étude du raisonnement expérimental chez l'adolescent ivoirien.* [The African environment and cognitive development. A study of experimental reasoning in adolescents from Côte d'Ivoire.]. Unpublished doctoral dissertation, Université de Caen, France.

Tarde, G. (1903). *The laws of imitation.* New York: Holt.

Tajfel, H. C. (1982). Social psychology of intergroup relations. *Annual Review of Psychology, 33*, 1-39.

Taylor, H. F. (1980). *The IQ game: A methodological study into the heredity-environment controversy.* London: Harvester.

Taylor, D. M., & Moghaddam, F. M. (1987). *Theories of intergroup relations: Social psychological perspectives.* New York: Praeger.

Tedeschi, J. T., Gaes, G. G., & Rivera, A. N. (1977). Aggression and the use of coercive power. *Journal of Social Issues, 33*, 101-125.

Tedeschi, J. T., & Melburg, V. (1983). Aggression and the illegitimate use of coercive power. In H. H. Blumberg, A. P. Hare, V. Kent, & M. Davies (Eds.), *Small groups and social interaction* (pp. 255-266). New York: John Wiley.

Tedeschi, J. T., Smith, R. B., & Brown, R. C. (1974). A reinterpretation of research on aggression. *Psychological Bulletin, 81*, 540-563.

Terrace, H. S. (1979). *Nim.* New York: Alfred A. Knopf.

Terrace, H. S. (1985). In the beginning was the "name". *American Psychologist, 40*, 1011-1028.

Terrace, H. S., Petitto, L. A., Sanders, R. J., & Bever, T. G. (1979). Can an ape create a sentence? *Science, 206*, 891-902.

Tornblom, K., & Foa, U. (1983). Choice of a distribution principle: Cross-cultural evidence on the effects of resources. *Acta Sociologica, 2*, 161-173.

Traoré, A. (1979). Apprendre en jouant: Les jeux africains, une initiation aux mathématiques. [Learning while playing: African games as an initiation into mathematics.] *Recherche, Pédagogie et Culture, 40*, 38-42.

Triandis, H. C. (1961). A note on Rokeach's theory of prejudice. *Journal of Abnormal and Social Psychology, 62,* 184–186.

Triandis, H. C. (1972). *The analysis of subjective culture.* New York: John Wiley.

Triandis, H. C. (1973). Subjective culture and economic development. *International Journal of Psychology, 8,* 163–180.

Triandis, H. C. (1975). Social psychology and cultural analysis. *Journal for the Theory of Social Behavior, 5,* 81–106.

Triandis, H. C. (1978). Some universals of social behavior. *Personality and Social Psychology Bulletin, 4,* 1–16.

Triandis, H. C. (1983). *Allocentric vs. idiocentric social behavior: A major cultural difference between Hispanics and the Mainstream* (ONR Technical Report 16). Champaign: University of Illinois, Department of Psychology.

Triandis, H. C. (1988). Collectivism vs. individualism: A reconceptualization of a basic concept in cross-cultural psychology. In C. Bagley & G. K. Verma (Eds.), *Personality, cognition and values: Cross-cultural perspectives of childhood and adolescence.* (pp. 60–95). London: Macmillan.

Triandis, H. C., & Draguns, J. (1980). *Handbook of cross-cultural psychology: Vol. 6. Psychopathology.* Boston: Allyn & Bacon.

Triandis, H. C., & Heron, A. (Eds.). (1981). *Handbook of cross-cultural psychology: Vol. 4. Developmental psychology.* Boston: Allyn & Bacon.

Triandis, H. C., Lambert, W. W., Berry, J. W., Brislin, R. W., Draguns, J., Lonner, W., & Heron, A. (Eds.). (1980). *Handbook of cross-cultural psychology* (6 vols.). Boston: Allyn & Bacon.

Triandis, H. C., & Triandis, L. M. (1962). A cross-cultural study of social distance. *Psychological Monographs, 76* (21, Whole No. 540).

Triandis, H. C., & Vassiliou, V. (1967). Frequency of contact and stereotyping. *Journal of Personality and Social Psychology, 7,* 316–328.

Triandis, H. C., Vassiliou, V., & Nassiakou, M. (1968). Three cross-cultural studies of subjective culture. *Journal of Personality and Social Psychology Monographs, 8* (4, Pt. 2)

Trommsdorff, G. (1987). German cross-cultural psychology. *German Journal of Psychology, 10,* 240–266.

Tulviste, P. (1978). On the origins of theoretic syllogistic reasoning in culture and in the child. *Acta et Commentationes Universitatis Tartuensis,* no. 474, 3–22.

Tylor, E. B. (1865). *Researches into the early history of mankind and development of civilization.* London: John Murray.

Tylor, E. B. (1871). *Primitive culture. Researches into the development of mythology, philosophy, religion, art and customs* (2 vols.). London: John Murray.

Tyler, S. A. (Ed.). (1969). *Cognitive anthropology.* New York: Holt, Rinehart & Winston.

Van Leeuwen, M. S. (1978). A cross-cultural examination of psychological differentiation in males and females. *International Journal of Psychology, 13,* 87–122.

Vergnaud, D. (1983). *L'enfant, la mathématique et la réalité.* [Mathematics and reality in childhood.] Berne: Peter Lang.

Vernon, P. E. (1955). The assessment of children. *Studies in Education, 7,* 189–215.

Vernon, P. E. (1965). Ability factors and environmental influences. *American Psychologist, 20,* 723–733.

Vernon, P. E. (1967). Abilities and educational attainments in an East African environment. *Journal of Special Education, 1,* 335–345.

Viljoen, H. G. (1974). Relationship between stereotypes and social distance. *Journal of Social Psychology, 92,* 313–314.

Vinacke, W. E. (1956). Explorations in the dynamics of stereotyping. *Journal of Social Psychology, 43,* 105–132.

Vinsonneau, G. (1980). Problèmes méthodologiques liés à une recherche en psychologie inter-culturelle. [Methodological problems linked to research in cross-cultural psychology.] *Psychologie Française, 25*, 39–50.

Vygotsky, L. S. (1962). *Thought and language.* Cambridge: MIT Press. (Originally published 1934).

Vygotsky, L. S. (1978). *Mind in society: The development of higher psychological processes.* (E. Hanfmann & G. Vakar, Trans.). Cambridge: Harvard University Press.

Wagner, D. A. (1974). The development of short-term memory and incidental memory: A cross-cultural study. *Child Development, 45*, 389–396.

Wagner, D. A. (1975). The effects of verbal labeling on short-term and incidental memory: A cross-cultural and developmental study. *Memory and Cognition, 3*, 595–598.

Wagner, D. A. (1977). Ontogeny of the Ponzo illusion: Effects of age, schooling, and environment. *International Journal of Psychology, 12*, 161–176.

Wagner, D. A. (1978a). Culture and mnemonics. In M. M. Gruneberg, P. Morris, & R. N. Sykes (Eds.), *Practical aspects of memory* (pp. 180–188). New York: Academic Press.

Wagner, D. A. (1978b). Memories of Morocco: The influence of age, schooling and environment on memory. *Cognitive Psychology, 10*, 1–28.

Wagner, D. A. (1981). Culture and memory development. In H. C. Triandis & A. Heron (Eds.), *Handbook of cross-cultural psychology: Vol. 4. Developmental psychology* (pp. 187–232). Boston: Allyn & Bacon.

Wagner, D. A. (1982). Traditional pedagogies: Past and present. *Cross-Cultural Psychology Bulletin, 16*(1), 9–10.

Wagner, D. A. (1983). Indigenous education and literacy in the third world. In D. A. Wagner (Ed.), *Child development and international development: Research-policy interfaces* (pp. 77–85). San Francisco: Jossey-Bass.

Wagner, D. A. (1985). Islamic education: Traditional pedagogy and contemporary change. In T. Husen & T. N. Postlethwaite (Eds.), *International encyclopedia of education: Vol. 5. Research and studies* (pp. 2714–2716). NY: Pergamon Press.

Wagner, D. A. (1987). Le développement précoce de la mémoire spécialisée. [The early development of specialized memory.] *Cahiers de Psychologie Cognitive, 7*, 56–67.

Wagner, D. A. (1988a). "Appropriate education" and literacy in the third world. In P. R. Dasen, J. W. Berry, & N. Sartorius (Eds.), *Health and cross-cultural psychology: Toward applications* (pp. 93–111). Newbury Park, CA: Sage.

Wagner, D. A. (1988b). L'acquisition du savoir et le "par coeur": Passé et présent. [The acquisition of knowledge and rote learning: Past and present.] In R. Bureau & D. de Saivre (Eds.), *Apprentissage et cultures.* [Cultures and learning.] (pp. 169–175). Paris: Karthala.

Wagner, D. A., & Lofti, A. (1980). Traditional Islamic education in Morocco: Socio-historical and psychological perspectives. *Comparative Education Review, 24*, 238–251.

Wagner, D. A., & Spratt, J. E. (1987). Cognitive consequences of contrasting pedagogies: The effects of Quranic preschooling in Morocco. *Child Development, 58*, 1207–1219.

Wagner, D. A., & Stevenson, H. W. (Eds.). (1982). *Cultural perspectives on child development.* San Francisco: W. H. Freeman.

Wallace, A. F. C. (1961). *Culture and Personality.* New York: Random House.

Ward, C. (1982). *Social loafing in Malaysia in the sound production procedure.* Unpublished manuscript.

Warwich, D. P. (1980). The politics and ethics of cross-cultural research. In H. C. Triandis & W. W. Lambert (Eds.), *Handbook of cross-cultural psychology: Vol. 1. Perspectives* (pp. 319–372). Boston: Garland STPM.

Washburn, S. L. (1978). What we can't learn about people from apes. *Human Nature, 1*(11), 70–75.

Wassmann, J., & Dasen, P. R. (1989, June). *Yupno number system and counting.* Paper presented at the Second Regional European Conference of the International Association for Cross-Cultural Psychology (IACCP), Amsterdam.

Watson, J. B. (1925). *Behaviorism*. New York: Norton.

Weaver, D. B. (1974). *An intra-cultural test of empiricistic vs. physiological explanations for cross-cultural differences in geometric illusion susceptibility using two illusions in Ghana.* Unpublished doctoral dissertation, Northwestern University, Evanston, IL.

Weber, M. (1904). *The Protestant ethic and the spirit of capitalism.* New York: Scribner's.

Weiner, N., Pandey, J., & Latané, B. (1981, September). *Individual and group productivity in the United States and India.* Paper presented at the annual meeting of the American Psychological Association, Los Angeles, CA.

Werner, H. (1948). *Comparative psychology of mental development.* New York: Science Editions. (Rev. ed. 1957. New York: International Universities Press)

Werner, H., & Kaplan, B. (1956). *Symbol formation.* New York: John Wiley. (Revised 1963)

Wertsch, J. V., Minick, N., & Arns, J. (1984). The creation of context in joint problem-solving. In B. Rogoff & J. Lave (Eds.), *Everyday cognition* (pp. 151–171). Cambridge: Harvard University Press.

White, L. A. (1947). Culturological vs. psychological interpretations of human behavior. *American Sociological Review, 12*, 686–698.

Whiting, B. B. (Ed.). (1963). *Six cultures: Studies of child rearing.* Cambridge: Harvard University Press.

Whiting, B. B. (1965). Sex identity conflict and physical violence: A comparative study. *American Anthropologist, 67*, 123–140.

Whiting, B. B. (1973). The Kenyan career woman: Traditional and modern. *Annals of the New York Academy of Sciences, 208*, 71–75.

Whiting, B. B. (1980). Culture and social behavior: A model for the development of social behavior. *Ethos, 8*, 95–116.

Whiting, B. B., & Edwards, C. P. (1973). A cross-cultural analysis of sex differences in the behavior of children aged three through eleven. *Journal of Social Psychology, 91*, 171–188.

Whiting, B. B., & Whiting, J. W. M. (1971). Task assignment and personality: A consideration of the effects of herding on boys. In W. W. Lambert & R. Weisbrod (Eds.), *Comparative perspectives on social psychology* (pp. 33–45). Boston: Little, Brown.

Whiting, B. B., & Whiting, J. W. M. (1975). *Children of six cultures: A psycho-cultural analysis.* Cambridge: Harvard University Press.

Whiting, J. W. M. (1962). Comment. *American Journal of Sociology, 67*, 391–393.

Whiting, J. W. M. (1981). Environmental constraints on infant care practices. In R. H. Munroe, R. L. Munroe, & B. B. Whiting (Eds.), *Handbook of cross-cultural human development* (pp. 155–180). New York: Garland STPM.

Whiting, J. W. M., & Child, I. L. (1953). *Child training and personality.* New Haven, CT: Yale University Press.

Whiting, J. W. M., Kluckhohn, R., & Anthony, A. (1958). The function of male initiation ceremonies at puberty. In E. E. Maccoby, T. Newcomb, & E. L. Hartley (Eds.), *Readings in social psychology* (3rd ed.) (pp. 359–370). New York: Holt.

Williams, J. E., & Best, D. L. (1982). *Measuring sex stereotypes: A thirty nation study.* Beverly Hills, CA: Sage.

Williams, J. E., & Best, D. L. (1989). *Sex and psyche: Self concept viewed cross-culturally.* Newbury Park, CA: Sage.

Williams, K., Williams, K., Kawana, Y., & Latané, B. (1984, May). *Social loafing in Japan: A developmental cross-cultural study.* Paper presented at the annual meeting of the Midwestern Psychological Association, Chicago, IL.

Wilson, E. O. (1975). *Sociobiology.* Cambridge: Harvard University Press.

Wilson, E. O., & Herrnstein, R. J. (1985). *Crime and human nature*. New York: Simon and Schuster.

Witkin, H. A. (1978). *Cognitive style in personal and cultural adaptation*. Worcester, MA: Clark University Press.

Witkin, H. A., & Berry, J. W. (1975). Psychological differentiation in cross-cultural perspective. *Journal of Cross-Cultural Psychology, 6*, 4–87.

Witkin, H. A., Dyk, R. B., Faterson, H. F., Goodenough, D. R., & Karp, S. A. (1962). *Psychological differentiation*. New York: John Wiley.

Witkin, H. A., & Goodenough, D. R. (1981). *Cognitive styles: Essence and origins*. New York: International Universities Press.

Wober, M. (1966). Sensotypes. *Journal of Social Psychology, 70*, 181–189.

Wober, M. (1967). Adapting Witkin's field independence theory to accommodate new information from Africa. *British Journal of Psychology, 58*, 29–38.

Wober, M. (1969). Distinguishing centri-cultural from cross cultural tests and research. *Perceptual and Motor Skills, 28*, 488.

Wober, M. (1974). Towards an understanding of the Kiganda concept of intelligence. In J. W. Berry & P. R. Dasen (Eds.), *Culture and cognition* (pp. 261–280). London: Methuen.

Wober, M., & Musoke-Mutanda, F. (1972). Patience and gratification preferences among Ugandan school children. *Journal of Social Psychology, 87*, 141–142.

Wohlwill, J. F. (1962). The perspective illusion: Perceived size and distance in fields varying in suggested depth, in children and adults. *Journal of Experimental Psychology, 64*, 300–310.

Wolfson, N. (1981). Compliment in cross-cultural perspective. *TESLE Quarterly, 15*, 117–124.

Woodworth, R. S. (1938). *Experimental psychology*. New York: Holt.

Wormley, S. L. Jr., (1985, March 10). Fighting back. *The New York Times Magazine*, p. 80.

Wundt, W. (1900–1920). *Völkerpsychologie*. [Psychology of societies.] (10 vols.). Leipzig: Englemann.

Za'rour, G. I. (1972). Superstitions among certain groups of Lebanese Arab students in Beirut. *Journal of Cross-Cultural Psychology, 3*, 273–282.

Zack, M., & Bril, B. (1989). Comment les mères françaises et bambara du Mali se représentent-elles le développement de leur enfants? [What are the social representations of French mothers and Bambara mothers in Mali about the development of their children?] In J. Retschitzki, M. Bossel-Lagos & P. Dasen (Eds.), *La recherche interculturelle, Tome 2*. [Cross-cultural research, vol. 2.] (pp. 7–17). Paris: L'Harmattan.

Zimet, S. G., Wiberg, J. L., & Blom, G. E. (1971). Attitudes and values in primers from the U.S. and twelve other countries. *Journal of Social Psychology, 84*, 167–174.

Author Index

389

Subject Index

About the Authors

Marshall H. Segall, Professor of Social and Political Psychology in the Maxwell School and Associate Dean of the College of Arts and Sciences at Syracuse University in the United States, first considered the possibility of a cross-cultural approach to psychology when he rounded out his undergraduate education by spending a year as an international student at the University of Geneva in Switzerland from 1952 to 1953. Returning to the United States for post-graduate training, first at Yale, then at Northwestern, his commitment to cross-cultural psychology was reinforced by contacts with Leonard Doob in New Haven and Donald Campbell in Evanston. With the latter and with the Africanist anthropologist Melville Herskovits, Segall did a multi-cultural study of visual perception in the early 1960s. Several fieldwork projects in Uganda, Kenya, and Tanzania followed, during one of which he helped launch a teaching program in psychology at Makerere University in Uganda. Over the past two decades, Segall published several books, chapters, and articles in the field of cross-cultural psychology. His books include *Human Behavior and Public Policy* (Pergamon Press) and *Cross-Cultural Psychology* (Brooks/Cole). He has served as the North American representative of l'Association pour la Recherche Interculturelle (ARIC) and President of the Society for Cross-Cultural Research (SCCR).

Pierre R. Dasen studied developmental psychology in Geneva with Jean Piaget and received his Ph.D. from the Australian National University in 1971. His research has concentrated on the cross-cultural use of Piagetian theory; in particular, he has studied ecocultural, nutritional and other environmental and cultural factors influencing the cognitive development of children in Australia (Aborigines), Canada (Inuit), Côte d'Ivoire (Baoulé), and Kenya (Kikuyu). He was the founder and first President of the l'Association pour la Recherche Interculturelle (ARIC), is senior editor of the series

"Espaces interculturels" with *L'Harmattan* (Paris), and associate editor of the *Journal of Cross-Cultural Psychology, International Journal of Psychology* and *International Journal of Behavioral Development*. He has held appointments at the Universities of Nairobi, Fribourg, Nice, and the Ecole des Hautes Etudes en Sciences Sociales (EHESS) in Paris, and is now Professor of Cross-Cultural Education at the Université de Genève. His present research interests include everyday cognition and informal education.

John Berry is a Professor of Psychology at Queen's University, Kingston. After working for a few years as a merchant seaman, he received his B.A. from Sir George Williams University (Montréal) in 1963, and his Ph.D. from the University of Edinburgh in 1966. He has been a lecturer at the University of Sydney for three years, a Fellow of the Netherlands Institute for Advanced Study and a visiting Professor at the Université de Nice and the Université de Genève. His field research has taken him to the Canadian Arctic, West and Central Africa, India, Central Australia, New Guinea and Highland Scotland. He is a past president of the International Association for Cross-Cultural Psychology, and an Associate Editor of the *Journal of Cross-Cultural Psychology*. He is author or editor of a number of books in the areas of cross-cultural, social and cognitive psychology, and is particularly interested in the application of cross-cultural psychology to public policy and programs in the areas of acculturation, immigration, health and education.

Ype H. Poortinga studied experimental psychology at the Free University in Amsterdam where he obtained his Ph.D. (in 1972) on work carried out at the National Institute for Personnel Research, a center for cross-cultural psychology in Johannesburg. He has been on the staff of Tilburg University in the Netherlands since 1973. Poortinga's most consistent interest has been with the conditions under which psychological data obtained in different cultures can be meaningfully compared. His empirical studies, mainly based on data from Holland, India, and Southern Africa reflect his experimental background; they tend to focus on perception and basic personality variables. His recent publications include two chapters with Roy Malpass in "Field Methods in Cross-Cultural Psychology." Poortinga has been Secretary-General and President of the International Association for Cross-Cultural Psychology (IACCP); he has also been President of the Netherlands Psychological Association.

General Psychology Series

Editors: **Arnold P. Goldstein,** Syracuse University
Leonard Krasner, Stanford University &
SUNY at Stony Brook

*Out of print in original format. Available in custom reprint edition.